EDITED BY JOH

CONTRIBUTORS: JOHN G.FAHY,
CAROLE SCULLY, MARIE DUN
AND MARTIN WAL

NEW

EXPLORATIONS

COMPLETE **LEAVING CERTIFICATE POETRY**

FOR EXAMINATION IN 2019

AND ONWARDS

g GILL EDUCATION

Gill Education
Hume Avenue
Park West
Dublin 12
www.gilleducation.ie

Gill Education is an imprint of M.H. Gill & Co.

© John G. Fahy, Louise O'Reilly, Carole Scully and Martin Wallace 2017

ISBN: 978-0-7171-72863

Design: Tanya M. Ross, Elementinc.ie

At the time of going to press, all web addresses were active and contained information relevant to the topics in this book. Gill Education does not, however, accept responsibility for the content or views contained on these websites. Content, views and addresses may change beyond the publisher or author's control. Students should always be supervised when reviewing websites.

The paper used in this book is made from the wood pulp of managed forests. For every tree felled, at least one tree is planted, thereby renewing natural resources.

Course Overview

Poems Prescribed for Ordinary Level

JUNE 2019 EXAMINATION

JUNE 2020 EXAMINATION

JUNE 2021 EXAMINATION

JUNE 2022 EXAMINATION

New Explorations Digital Resources

✓ **Detailed Critical Notes** on all the prescribed poems for Higher and Ordinary Level English for students sitting the Leaving Certificate examination in 2019 and onwards are available on:

- the **CD included with this book**
- **www.gillexplore.ie**, our digital resources website for teachers and students

✓ **Audio feature** with Brendan Kennelly, Seamus Heaney, Eiléan Ní Chuilleanáin, Eavan Boland, Paul Durcan and Julie O'Callaghan reading a selection of their poems from your course is available:

- via your **free eBook**
- via **www.gillexplore.ie**, our digital resources website for teachers and students

To access your free eBook and digital resources, follow the easy-access instructions on the inside front cover of this book.

Contents

Gerard Manley Hopkins (1844–89)

William Butler Yeats (1865–1939)

Robert Frost (1874–1963)

Ordinary Level

WILLIAM
WORDSWORTH
(1770–1850)

Prescribed for Higher Level exams in 2020 and 2022

William Wordsworth was born on 7 April 1770 in Cockermouth, Cumberland. The family was well-to-do and had a good social standing. Dorothy, his sister, was born in December 1771 and the two children developed a close relationship that was to continue into adulthood. Sadly, when he was eight years old his mother died, and five years later his father also died. Wordsworth attended Hawkshead Grammar School and at the age of seventeen entered St John's College, Cambridge.

In 1790, during his summer holidays, he went on a walking tour through France and the Alps. After receiving his BA, Wordsworth returned to France and became interested in the revolutionary movement. He had an affair with Annette Vallon, who bore him a daughter. Under pressure from his friends, who were anxious about the political instability in France, Wordsworth returned to England and published some of his writing. The books received little attention, but they did lead to his friendship with Samuel Taylor Coleridge. Together they worked on a book of poems entitled *The Lyrical Ballads*, generally recognised as marking the beginning of the Romantic Movement in English poetry. For much of his life Wordsworth lived with Dorothy, his wife Mary, and his children in the beautiful Lake District. However, he enjoyed travelling on the Continent as well as around Britain and Ireland.

Although Wordsworth's work was not generally popular, among the literary set he was recognised as the initiator of a new form of poetic writing. Towards the end of his life he became more generally appreciated. In 1843, he was appointed Poet Laureate and received a state pension. He died in 1850 at the age of eighty and is buried in Grasmere churchyard.

TO MY SISTER

It is the first mild day of March:
Each minute sweeter than before,
The redbreast sings from the tall larch
That stands beside our door.

There is a blessing in the air,   5
Which seems a sense of joy to yield
To the bare trees, and mountains bare,
And grass in the green field.

My sister! ('tis a wish of mine)
Now that our morning meal is done,   10
Make haste, your morning task resign;
Come forth and feel the sun.

Edward will come with you; — and, pray,
Put on with speed your woodland dress;
And bring no book: for this one day   15
We'll give to idleness.

No joyless forms shall regulate
Our living calendar:
We from today, my Friend, will date
The opening of the year.   20

Love, now a universal birth,
From heart to heart is stealing,
From earth to man, from man to earth:
— It is the hour of feeling.

One moment now may give us more   25
Than years of toiling reason:
Our minds shall drink at every pore
The spirit of the season.

Some silent laws our hearts will make,
Which they shall long obey: 30
We for the year to come may take
Our temper from to-day.

And from the blessed power that rolls
About, below, above,
We'll frame the measure of our souls: 35
They shall be tuned to love.

Then come, my Sister! come, I pray,
With speed put on your woodland dress;
And bring no book: for this one day
We'll give to idleness.   40

NOTES

11	make haste:	hurry
11	task:	piece of work to be done
26	toiling:	hard work
32	temper:	mood or mental attitude

EXPLORATIONS

First reading

1. What do you notice about the way Wordsworth uses language in this poem? Is it what you would expect in a piece of poetic writing? Do you like it or not?

2. Can you work out the time of year and the type of weather that has inspired Wordsworth? Support your view by close reference to the poem. Do you think that he would have been equally inspired had the day been wet and windy? Perhaps he might have written a different type of poem — discuss what it might have been like.

3. Why does Wordsworth want his sister to come outside? If you were Dorothy, would this poem persuade you to do as he asks?

4. How, in Wordsworth's view, will a day outside affect the group? Do you agree or disagree with his opinion? Have you ever been positively influenced by a day in the open air?

Second reading

5. Wordsworth twice asks his sister to put on her 'woodland dress'. Can you suggest why he repeated this request? Do you think that there is more to it than simply asking her to change her clothes?

6. In the sixth stanza Wordsworth introduces the idea of 'Love'. Discuss how this connects with the time of year described in the poem. Examine in detail what Wordsworth actually means by his use of the word 'Love'. Would you agree with his interpretation of the word? Why?

7. Wordsworth refers to Time throughout this poem. Consider the different aspects of Time that occur. Does he suggest that there is a fundamental difference in the way that they affect Man?

8. 'We'll give the day to idleness.' Did Wordsworth really believe that the day would be spent in 'idleness'?

Third reading

9. Now read 'It is a Beauteous Evening, Calm and Free'. Are there any similarities between these two poems? Consider in particular the use of language, the senses and the underlying philosophy.

A SLUMBER DID MY SPIRIT SEAL

A slumber did my spirit seal;
I had no human fears:
She seemed a thing that could not feel
The touch of earthly years.

No motion has she now, no force;   5
She neither hears nor sees;
Rolled round in earth's diurnal course,
With rocks, and stones, and trees.

NOTES

1	seal:	close securely, put barriers around
7	diurnal:	daily

EXPLORATIONS

First reading

1. What mood do you think Wordsworth is trying to create in this poem? Do the actual sounds of the words help to reinforce the effect? Is there any particular phrase that you feel encapsulates this mood?

2. Wordsworth tries to communicate a particular state in lines 3–6. Try to visualise yourself in this state. Write down any words that occur to you as descriptions of what you feel. Discuss your ideas with a view to choosing the five most successful descriptive words suggested.

3. In the final two lines, Wordsworth uses an image that we will meet in 'Skating'. What is he describing? Do you find it an effective description? How does it relate to the mood of the piece?

Second reading

4. Discuss the language used by Wordsworth in this poem. What are your initial impressions of it? Are you more aware of a degree of ambiguity after a second reading? Can you locate the cause of this ambiguity?

5. Examine the opening line of the poem. Explain how you interpret it. Does the fact that it is written in the past tense influence how it is interpreted?

6. In the second line Wordsworth appears to make a simple statement. Discuss how his use of the past tense could affect the meaning it conveys. Is there a further alteration in the meaning of this line when you join it with lines 3–4?

7. Wordsworth changes to the present tense in the second stanza. Discuss the ways in which this adjustment influences your reaction to his description.

Third reading

8. Consider this poem as a whole, interpreting 'she' as referring to 'my spirit'. Can you express, in your own words, what Wordsworth is trying to communicate?

9. Some critics suggest that there are indications that this poem might have been written about Lucy from the next poem, 'She Dwelt among the Untrodden Ways'. Does this change your view of the poem?

10. Look at Question 1 again. In the light of your subsequent readings and consideration of the poem, would you alter your answer?

SHE DWELT AMONG THE UNTRODDEN WAYS

OL 2020

OL 2022

She dwelt among the untrodden ways
    Beside the springs of Dove,
A Maid whom there were none to praise
    And very few to love:

A violet by a mossy stone   5
    Half hidden from the eye!
— Fair as a star, when only one
    Is shining in the sky.

She lived unknown, and few could know
    When Lucy ceased to be;   10
But she is in her grave, and, oh,
    The difference to me!

'Chamonix in the days of the conquest of Mont Blanc'
by Johann L. Bleuler (eighteenth century)

NOTES

I	dwelt:	lived
I	untrodden:	not stepped on
2	springs:	a place where water wells up from the earth
3	Maid:	a girl

EXPLORATIONS

First reading

1. Describe in your own words the type of life that Lucy led. What sort of environment did she live in? Do you think she was happy with her life? Why? Would you be happy to live like this?

2. Wordsworth does not tell us directly what Lucy looked like. In the second stanza he uses two images to suggest some of her qualities. Discuss what you consider these qualities to be. How would you react if someone compared you to a 'violet' or a 'star'?

3. What is Wordsworth's mood in this poem? Choose one phrase from the poem that you feel clearly signals this mood. What tone of voice should be used to read this poem?

Second reading

4. Do you think the first stanza is an effective way to open a piece of poetry? Why/why not?

5. What do you learn about Wordsworth himself from reading the poem? Can you suggest what sort of relationship he had with Lucy?

6. Examine Wordsworth's use of rhyme. Were you aware of it as you read the poem? How does the rhyme contribute to the overall effect of the piece?

Third reading

7. Wordsworth claims that Lucy's death made a 'difference' to him. Do you feel that the poem communicates death as distressing? Can you think of a reason why he might not be too upset?

8. Do you think that this poem conveys the flesh-and-blood Lucy, or was Wordsworth more interested in describing something else?

9. Wordsworth wanted to write poetry using 'the language really spoken by men'. Does he succeed in doing this here? How did his choice of words affect your reaction to the piece?

10. Is this poem too simple to be really interesting? Does simplicity in writing necessarily mean that it is easy to understand?

COMPOSED UPON WESTMINSTER BRIDGE, SEPTEMBER 3, 1802

Earth has not anything to show more fair:
Dull would he be of soul who could pass by
A sight so touching in its majesty:
This City now doth, like a garment, wear
The beauty of the morning; silent, bare,   5
Ships, towers, domes, theatres, and temples lie
Open unto the fields, and to the sky;
All bright and glittering in the smokeless air.
Never did sun more beautifully steep
In his first splendour, valley, rock, or hill;   10
Ne'er saw I, never felt, a calm so deep!
The river glideth at his own sweet will:
Dear God! the very houses seem asleep;
And all that mighty heart is lying still!

'Westminster Bridge under construction' by Giovanni
Antonio Canal (Canaletto) (1747)

NOTES

4	doth:	does
11	Ne'er:	never

EXPLORATIONS

First reading

1. Do you find the subject of this poem a surprising choice for Wordsworth? Why?

2. Consider Wordsworth's description of the City. Does he successfully convey 'its majesty'? Choose two images that you find especially vivid and explain why they appeal to you.

3. What effect does this scene have on Wordsworth? Why do you think he reacted in this way? Would you have felt the same emotions?

Second reading

4. Do you think that Wordsworth was restricted in any way by choosing to write this poem as a fourteen-line sonnet? Was he able to communicate his theme successfully? Would the impact of the piece have been increased or reduced had the poem been longer?

5. Do you feel that Wordsworth is suggesting a spiritual element to the appreciation of beauty? Is this a valid view? Does the spiritual quality come from the one who appreciates or the object that is being appreciated?

6. Why do you think Wordsworth wrote this poem in the present tense? Would the overall impact of the piece be altered if it had been written in the past tense? Try changing the tenses.

7. To which of the senses does this poem appeal? Why do you think Wordsworth chose to write it in this way? Would the effect of the description be altered had sounds been added?

Third reading

8. The Victorian poet Matthew Arnold believed that Wordsworth had a 'healing power'. Can words heal? Do you find any of Wordsworth's poems healing?

9. Wordsworth frequently used exclamation marks in his writing. Why do you think he does this? Did you notice them, or are they not very important to the overall effect of his poetry?

IT IS A BEAUTEOUS EVENING, CALM AND FREE

OL 2020

OL 2022

It is a beauteous evening, calm and free,
The holy time is quiet as a Nun
Breathless with adoration; the broad sun
Is sinking down in its tranquillity;
The gentleness of heaven broods o'er the Sea: 5
Listen! the mighty Being is awake,
And doth with his eternal motion make
A sound like thunder — everlastingly.
Dear Child! dear Girl! that walkest with me here,
If thou appear untouched by solemn thought,   10
Thy nature is not therefore less divine:
Thou liest in Abraham's bosom all the year;
And worshipp'st at the Temple's inner shrine,
God being with thee when we know it not.

Grasmere in the Lake District: a nineteenth-century lithograph

NOTES

12	Abraham:	in the Old Testament, Abraham was willing to sacrifice his son Isaac on God's orders. Abraham stands for unswerving faith.
13	Temple's inner shrine:	the Temple in the Old Testament, where God was worshipped, was divided into two areas: one part where the congregation gathered; and the more sacred inner shrine which could only be entered by the priests.

EXPLORATIONS

First reading

1. What time of day does Wordsworth describe in the first five lines of the poem? Choose one phrase that you find particularly effective. Have you ever been moved by a scene in nature? Write about your own experience.

2. Discuss who or what is 'the mighty Being' in line 6. (You should find lines 7–8 helpful.) What do you feel about this description — is it vivid, surprising, confusing, or do you have a different reaction?

3. Does the way in which Wordsworth describe the scene in lines 1–8 tell you anything about what he felt at the time? Suggest two words to summarise his reaction.

4. In lines 9–14 Wordsworth tells us about his companion's reaction. How is it different from his own? Do you think that the fact she is a child affects the way she reacts? Does Wordsworth consider one reaction better than the other?

Second reading

5. Wordsworth uses an image of a nun in the opening four lines of the poem. How does he connect it with the sunset? Do you find this a successful connection of ideas? Why?

6. Why do you think Wordsworth referred to the sunset as 'The holy time'? Does the phrase tell you anything about his attitude to nature?

7. What senses does Wordsworth appeal to in this poem? What effect does this have on the overall impact of his description?

Third reading

8. Wordsworth famously wrote that, for him, poetry was stimulated by 'emotions recollected in tranquility'. Consider how the poem shows evidence of this approach.

9. Look again at 'She Dwelt among the Untrodden Ways'. Do you find any similarities in Wordsworth's attitude to nature in the two poems?

10. Find a picture, or paint one yourself, to illustrate this poem.

THE SOLITARY REAPER

Behold her, single in the field,
Yon solitary Highland Lass!
Reaping and singing by herself;
Stop here, or gently pass!
Alone she cuts and binds the grain,   5
And sings a melancholy strain;
O listen! for the Vale profound
Is overflowing with the sound.

No Nightingale did ever chaunt
More welcome notes to weary bands   10
Of travellers in some shady haunt,
Among Arabian sands:
A voice so thrilling ne'er was heard
In springtime from the Cuckoo-bird,
Breaking the silence of the seas   15
Among the farthest Hebrides.

Will no one tell me what she sings? —
Perhaps the plaintive numbers flow
For old, unhappy, far-off things,
And battles long ago: 20
Or is it some more humble lay,
Familiar matter of today?
Some natural sorrow, loss, or pain,
That has been, and may be again?

Whate'er the theme, the Maiden sang   25
As if her song could have no ending;
I saw her singing at her work,
And o'er the sickle bending; —
I listened, motionless and still;
And, as I mounted up the hill,   30
The music in my heart I bore,
Long after it was heard no more.

'Grasmere by the Rydal Road' by Francis Towne (c.1787)

NOTES

1	Behold:	see, observe
2	Yon:	yonder, over there
7	profound:	deep
9	chaunt:	chant, sing
18	plaintive:	mournful
21	lay:	song

EXPLORATIONS

First reading

1. Discuss the way in which Wordsworth opens this poem with the first stanza. Does it draw you into the poem by the vividness of the descriptions? Or perhaps you find it overdramatic in its language and use of exclamation marks?

2. In the second stanza, Wordsworth describes the quality of the reaper's singing. Do you feel that he was justified in devoting eight lines to this? Was it simply an opportunity for him to show off his descriptive powers?

3. 'Will no one tell me what she sings?' Can you explain why Wordsworth asks this question? Does he need to know what the girl was singing about? Would this affect his reaction to the singing? Do you think that it should? Do you need to know what a song is about to enjoy it?

4. In the fourth stanza Wordsworth communicates his reaction to the singing. Do you find it a believable reaction? Have you ever been stopped by a piece of music? Did it stay with you in the way that this song did with Wordsworth?

Second reading

5. There is a sense of immediacy about the first two lines of this poem. Can you explain how Wordsworth achieves this effect? Does it continue through the rest of the piece?

6. Both Wordsworth and the reaper are depicted as being on their own in nature. Does the way in which each is depicted suggest a difference in their attitude to and relationship with nature?

Third reading

7. This poem describes a scene that comes from a world very different from the one we live in. Does this reduce the relevance of the poem? Is there a time limit on artistic creation?

8. Does the title, 'The Solitary Reaper', suggest the central theme of this poem? Could you suggest a more suitable title?

9. Examine the way in which Wordsworth uses imagery from nature in this poem and two of his other poems. Do you find it a successful technique or simply an overused piece of elaboration?

10. The critic F. R. Leavis commented: 'For Wordsworth solitude is the condition of a contemplative serenity.' Discuss this statement with reference to three of Wordsworth's poems.

THE STOLEN BOAT (EXTRACT FROM *THE PRELUDE*)

One summer evening (led by her) I found
A little boat tied to a willow tree
Within a rocky cave, its usual home.
Straight I unloosed her chain, and stepping in
Pushed from the shore. It was an act of stealth   5
And troubled pleasure, nor without the voice
Of mountain-echoes did my boat move on;
Leaving behind her still, on either side,
Small circles glittering idly in the moon,
Until they melted all into one track   10
Of sparkling light. But now, like one who rows,
Proud of his skill, to reach a chosen point
With an unswerving line, I fixed my view
Upon the summit of a craggy ridge,
The horizon's utmost boundary; for above   15
Was nothing but the stars and the grey sky.
She was an elfin pinnace; lustily
I dipped my oars into the silent lake,
And, as I rose upon the stroke, my boat
Went heaving through the water like a swan;   20
When, from behind that craggy steep till then
The horizon's bound, a huge peak, black and huge,
As if with voluntary power instinct
Upreared its head. I struck and struck again,
And growing still in stature the grim shape   25
Towered up between me and the stars, and still,
For so it seemed, with purpose of its own
And measured motion like a living thing,
Strode after me. With trembling oars I turned,
And through the silent water stole my way   30
Back to the covert of the willow tree;
There in her mooring-place I left my bark, —
And through the meadows homeward went, in grave
And serious mood; but after I had seen
That spectacle, for many days, my brain   35
Worked with a dim and undetermined sense
Of unknown modes of being; o'er my thoughts
There hung a darkness, call it solitude
Or blank desertion. No familiar shapes
Remained, no pleasant images of trees,   40
Of sea or sky, no colours of green fields;
But huge and mighty forms, that do not live
Like living men, moved slowly through the mind
By day, and were a trouble to my dreams.

'Rydal Waterfall' by Joseph Wright (1795)

NOTES

4	Straight:	without delay
14	craggy:	rugged
17	pinnace:	a ship's small boat
17	lustily:	with passionate enjoyment
22	bound:	boundary
31	covert:	shelter
37	modes:	ways

EXPLORATIONS

First reading

1. What emotions does the young Wordsworth feel as he takes the boat? How does Wordsworth communicate these feelings in the first seven lines of the piece?

2. Consider Wordsworth's emotions in lines 11–20. Describe, in your own words, what you think he feels.

3. How does the appearance of the peak affect Wordsworth's actions? Can you locate the words or phrases that suggest his emotional alteration?

4. Can you explain how Wordsworth felt in the days after this incident? What particular aspect of this experience provoked these feelings? Do you feel that his reaction is understandable or rather overdramatic?

Second reading

5. Time plays an important part in this piece. Discuss how it is conveyed during and after the incident. Does Wordsworth's emotional state affect his perception of time? Has this ever happened to you?

6. Discuss how Wordsworth uses the concept of space to suggest his feelings. Can our emotions affect our awareness of space? Can space affect our emotions?

7. What do you think Wordsworth learned as a result of this experience? Have you ever found yourself in a similar situation? Consider whether such learning experiences are exclusive to the young.

Third reading

8. Compare this extract with 'Skating', which also comes from *The Prelude*. Are there any similarities between the two? Are they different in any way? This piece comes before 'Skating' in the full work. Is there any sense of this in the extracts themselves?

9. In many ways the physical activities described in 'The Stolen Boat' and 'Skating' are less important than the emotional changes stimulated by them. Discuss, supporting your view with references from both extracts.

10. Wordsworth described *The Prelude* as 'a poem on my own poetical education'. Consider what lessons he learned, as suggested in 'The Stolen Boat' and 'Skating'. Do you feel that they serve to underpin his later works?

SKATING (EXTRACT FROM *THE PRELUDE*)

OL 2020

OL 2022

And in the frosty season, when the sun
Was set, and visible for many a mile
The cottage windows blazed through twilight gloom,
I heeded not their summons: happy time
It was indeed for all of us — for me   5
It was a time of rapture! Clear and loud
The village clock tolled six, — I wheeled about,
Proud and exulting like an untired horse
That cares not for his home. All shod with steel,
We hissed along the polished ice in games   10
Confederate, imitative of the chase
And woodland pleasures, — the resounding horn,
The pack loud chiming, and the hunted hare.
So through the darkness and the cold we flew,
And not a voice was idle; with the din   15
Smitten, the precipices rang aloud;
The leafless trees and every icy crag
Tinkled like iron; while far distant hills
Into the tumult sent an alien sound
Of melancholy not unnoticed, while the stars   20
Eastward were sparkling clear, and in the west
The orange sky of evening died away.
Not seldom from the uproar I retired
Into a silent bay, or sportively
Glanced sideway, leaving the tumultuous throng,   25
To cut across the reflex of a star
That fled, and, flying still before me, gleamed
Upon the glassy plain; and oftentimes,
When we had given our bodies to the wind,
And all the shadowy banks on either side   30
Came sweeping through the darkness, spinning still
The rapid line of motion, then at once
Have I, reclining back upon my heels,
Stopped short; yet still the solitary cliffs
Wheeled by me — even as if the earth had rolled   35
With visible motion her diurnal round!
Behind me did they stretch in solemn train,
Feebler and feebler, and I stood and watched
Till all was tranquil as a dreamless sleep.

NOTES

4	heeded not:	paid no attention to
8	exulting:	triumphantly joyful
11	Confederate:	allied together
15	din:	prolonged loud noise
16	Smitten:	struck
16	precipices:	sheer cliffs
19	tumult:	uproar
19	alien:	different
20	melancholy:	sadness, depression
25	throng:	crowd
26	reflex:	reflection
33	reclining:	bending back
36	diurnal:	daily

EXPLORATIONS

First reading

1. Do you find this piece immediately understandable or rather confusing? Were you carried along by the speed of the language, or did you feel a little overwhelmed? Why do you think Wordsworth chose to write at such a rate?

2. Choose two phrases and two words that you find particularly effective in suggesting a frozen world. Explain why you chose them.

3. Have you ever been skating? Do you feel that Wordsworth successfully conveys a sense of what it is actually like to go skating? Examine the ways he suggests the freedom and speed of movement. Pay particular attention to his choice of words and to the sounds of the words.

4. Discuss the senses that Wordsworth appeals to in the piece. Consider how they contribute to the vividness of the scene.

Second reading

5. In lines 7–9 Wordsworth compares himself to a horse. Discuss the qualities he is trying to suggest by using this image. Do you think that the linking of these two ideas works? Does he use animal imagery elsewhere in the extract? Is it effective?

6. Sounds play a very important part in this poem. Can you suggest a reason for this? Try to remember being outside when there is snow and ice. Is there a particular sound word in the poem that you find especially effective?

7. Can you describe Wordsworth's mood in the poem? Does it remain the same throughout the piece, or can you detect a change? Discuss why his mood is affected.

Third reading

8. Wordsworth seems to feel that children have an instinctive ability to connect with nature. Examine this

view in relation to this extract and one of his other poems that you have read.

9. We often tend to idealise memories of our childhood. Has Wordsworth done that here or is this a realistic portrayal of being a child?

10. Wordsworth wrote 'The end of Poetry is to produce excitement in co-existence with an overbalance of pleasure.' Did you feel excitement and pleasure when you read this extract?

TINTERN ABBEY

Five years have past; five summers, with the length
Of five long winters! and again I hear
These waters, rolling from their mountain-springs
With a soft Inland murmur. — Once again
Do I behold these steep and lofty cliffs,   5
That on a wild secluded scene impress
Thoughts of more deep seclusion; and connect
The landscape with the quiet of the sky.
The day is come when I again repose
Here, under this dark sycamore, and view   10
These plots of cottage-ground, these orchard-tufts,
Which at this season, with their unripe fruits,
Are clad in one green hue, and lose themselves
'Mid groves and copses. Once again I see
These hedge-rows, hardly hedge-rows, little lines   15
Of sportive wood run wild: these pastoral farms,
Green to the very door; and wreaths of smoke
Sent up, in silence, from among the trees!
With some uncertain notice, as might seem
Of vagrant dwellers in the houseless woods,   20
Or of some Hermit's cave, where by his fire
The Hermit sits alone.
                        These beauteous forms,
Through a long absence, have not been to me
As is a landscape to a blind man's eye: 25
But oft, in lonely rooms, and 'mid the din
Of towns and cities, I have owed to them,
In hours of weariness, sensations sweet,
Felt in the blood, and felt along the heart;
And passing even into my purer mind,   30
With tranquil restoration: — feelings too
Of unremembered pleasure: such, perhaps,
As have no slight or trivial influence
On that best portion of a good man's life,
His little, nameless, unremembered, acts   35
Of kindness and of love. Nor less, I trust,
To them I may have owed another gift,
Of aspect more sublime; that blessed mood,
In which the burthen of the mystery,
In which the heavy and the weary weight   40
Of all this unintelligible world,
Is lightened: — that serene and blessed mood,

In which the affections gently lead us on, —
Until, the breath of this corporeal frame
And even the motion of our human blood   45
Almost suspended, we are laid asleep
In body, and become a living soul:
While with an eye made quiet by the power
Of harmony, and the deep power of joy,
We see into the life of things.   50
If this
Be but a vain belief, yet oh! how oft —
In darkness and amid the many shapes
Of joyless daylight; when the fretful stir
Unprofitable, and the fever of the world,   55
Have hung upon the beatings of my heart —
How oft, in spirit, have I turned to thee,
O sylvan Wye! thou wanderer thro' the woods,
How often has my spirit turned to thee!
       And now, with gleams of half-extinguished thought,   60
With many recognitions dim and faint,
And somewhat of a sad perplexity,
The picture of the mind revives again:
While here I stand, not only with the sense
Of present pleasure, but with pleasing thoughts   65
That in this moment there is life and food
For future years. And so I dare to hope,
Though changed, no doubt, from what I was when first
I came among these hills; when like a roe
I bounded o'er the mountains, by the sides   70
Of the deep rivers, and the lonely streams,
Wherever nature led: more like a man
Flying from something that he dreads than one
Who sought the thing he loved. For nature then
(The coarser pleasures of my boyish days,   75
And their glad animal movements all gone by)
To me was all in all. — I cannot paint
What then I was. The sounding cataract
Haunted me like a passion: the tall rock,
The mountain, and the deep and gloomy wood,   80
Their colours and their forms, were then to me
An appetite; a feeling and a love,
That had no need of a remoter charm,
By thought supplied, nor any interest
Unborrowed from the eye. — That time is past,   85
And all its aching joys are now no more,

And all its dizzy raptures. Not for this
Faint I, nor mourn nor murmur; other gifts
Have followed; for such loss, I would believe,
Abundant recompense. For I have learned   90
To look on nature, not as in the hour
Of thoughtless youth; but hearing often-times
The still, sad music of humanity,
Nor harsh nor grating, though of ample power
To chasten and subdue. And I have felt   95
A presence that disturbs me with the joy
Of elevated thoughts; a sense sublime
Of something far more deeply interfused,
Whose dwelling is the light of setting suns,
And the round ocean and the living air,   100
And the blue sky, and in the mind of man:
A motion and a spirit, that impels
All thinking things, all object of all thought,
And rolls through all things. Therefore am I still
A lover of the meadows and the woods,   105
And mountains; and of all that we behold
From this green earth; of all the mighty world
Of eye, and ear, — both what they half create,
And what perceive; well pleased to recognise
In nature and the language of the sense   110
The anchor of my purest thoughts, the nurse,
The guide, the guardian of my heart, and soul
Of all my moral being.
                          Nor perchance,
If I were not thus taught, should I the more   115
Suffer my genial spirits to decay:
For thou art with me here upon the banks
Of this fair river; thou my dearest Friend,
My dear, dear Friend; and in thy voice I catch
The language of my former heart, and read   120
My former pleasures in the shooting lights
Of thy wild eyes. Oh! yet a little while
May I behold in thee what I was once,
My dear, dear Sister! and this prayer I make,
Knowing that Nature never did betray   125
The heart that loved her; 'tis her privilege,
Through all the years of this our life, to lead
From joy to joy: for she can so inform
The mind that is within us, so impress
With quietness and beauty, and so feed   130

With lofty thoughts, that neither evil tongues,
Rash judgments, nor the sneers of selfish men,
Nor greetings where no kindness is, nor all
The dreary intercourse of daily life,
Shall e'er prevail against us, or disturb   135
Our cheerful faith, that all which we behold
Is full of blessings. Therefore let the moon
Shine on thee in thy solitary walk;
And let the misty mountain-winds be free
To blow against thee: and, in after years,   140
When these wild ecstasies shall be matured
Into a sober pleasure; when thy mind
Shall be a mansion for all lovely forms,
Thy memory be as a dwelling-place
For all sweet sounds and harmonies; oh! then,   145
If solitude, or fear, or pain, or grief,
Should be thy portion, with what healing thoughts
Of tender joy wilt thou remember me,
And these my exhortations! Nor, perchance —
If I should be where I no more can hear   150
Thy voice, nor catch from thy wild eyes these gleams
Of past existence — wilt thou then forget
That on the banks of this delightful stream
We stood together; and that I, so long
A worshipper of Nature, hither came   155
Unwearied in that service: rather say
With warmer love — oh! with far deeper zeal
Of holier love. Nor wilt thou then forget
That after many wanderings, many years
Of absence, these steep woods and lofty cliffs,   160
And this green pastoral landscape, were to me
More dear, both for themselves and for thy sake!

NOTES

9	repose:	rest, lie
20	vagrant:	wandering
39	burthen:	burden
44	corporeal:	physical, bodily
58	sylvan:	wooded, rural
62	perplexity:	puzzlement, confusion
69	roe:	small deer
78	cataract:	large waterfall
90	recompense:	amends
95	chasten:	restrain
98	interfused:	mixed with
116	genial:	cheerful
135	prevail:	be victorious
149	exhortations:	urgings
157	zeal:	fervour

EXPLORATIONS

First reading

1. What was your initial reaction when you saw the length of this poem? Did you find the poem difficult to read once you started, or did Wordsworth draw you along with his language and images? Was your interest sustained throughout the poem? Should a poem be limited in its length? Why?

2. Examine Wordsworth's description of the sweep of the view that is before him. Do you find it effective? Would you find such a scene appealing?

3. How does the view affect Wordsworth? What does the way in which he uses this scene suggest about Wordsworth's attitude to the different worlds he lives in? Do you think that most people have favourite scenes which they evoke as an escape from situations they find difficult? Do you?

Second reading

4. Discuss the changes that take place in Wordsworth's relationship with Nature as he matures. Do you feel that altered relationships are part of the human maturing process? Why?

5. 'A motion and a spirit, that impels/ All thinking things, all object of all thought,/And rolls through all things.'
What do you think Wordsworth is referring to in these lines? Do you think that he is deluding himself into believing that there is a way to understand this 'unintelligible world'?

6. What does Wordsworth's address to his sister, in the final section of the poem, suggest about their relationship? Do you find it surprising that he has someone else with him in this poem? If so, why?

Third reading

7. 'Thy memory be as a dwelling-place/ For all sweet sounds and harmonies'. What role does memory play in Wordsworth's poetry? Does he use the past to go forward? How?

8. Discuss how Wordsworth moves out from himself towards a wider perception. Is this process common to us all? What makes his experience worthy of being studied?

9. With Wordsworth 'an intense intellectual egotism swallows up everything' (William Hazlitt). Wordsworth 'continues to bring joy, peace, strength, exaltation' (A. C. Bradley). Wordsworth shows 'a capricious predilection for incidents that contrast with the depth and novelty of the truths that they are to exemplify' (Samuel Taylor Coleridge).
Discuss these opinions on Wordsworth's writing. Do you agree with any of them? Try to summarise your view of Wordsworth in one sentence.

10. Wordsworth commented: 'I have wished to keep the Reader in the company of flesh and blood, persuaded that by so doing I shall interest him.'
Did Wordsworth interest you? Why/ why not?

JOHN
KEATS

(1795–1821)

Prescribed for Higher Level exams in 2021 and 2022

John Keats was born at Finsbury, near London, on 31 October 1795, the eldest child of Frances Jennings Keats and Thomas Keats, a livery-stable keeper. From 1803 to 1811 he attended Rev. John Clarke's school in an old Georgian country house at Enfield, north London. John Keats was a small boy (fully grown, he was only five feet tall), but he was athletic and liked sports, and though he had a quick temper, he was generally popular.

Clarke's was a liberal, progressive boarding school, which did not allow flogging although it was a common practice at the time. The pupils, who were mostly of middle-class background and destined for the professions, received a well-rounded education. They had their own garden plots to cultivate and interest in music and the visual arts was also encouraged, as well as the usual study of history, geography, arithmetic, grammar, French and Latin. Keats received a particularly good classical Latin education.

Keats left school in 1811 to begin an apprenticeship as a surgeon. This was then the manual side of the medical profession, involving bone-setting, tooth-pulling and amputation, and was considered socially inferior to becoming a physician, which would have entailed expensive university education. After some years as an apprentice, in 1815 Keats registered as a student at Guy's Hospital, London, and attended lectures in anatomy, physiology and chemistry.

In May 1816 the sonnet 'O Solitude' was the first of Keats's poems to be published. In June, Keats wrote 'To One Who Has Been Long in City Pent'. Later that year he composed 'On First Looking into Chapman's Homer'.

He qualified in July 1816 and was licensed to practise as a surgeon and apothecary, but by then he had developed an aversion to surgery (then performed without anaesthetic, in primitive conditions) and he devoted more of his time to writing poetry. His early poems reflect liberal attitudes and a rebellious outlook on life.

Keats began to express his ideas on poetry. He placed great value on the imagination, the importance of feelings and the central place of beauty in poetry.

Sometime in January or February 1818 Keats wrote 'When I have fears that I may cease to be', a sonnet dealing with three major concerns in his life – love, death and his poetry.

In September 1818 Keats met Fanny Brawne. She became the great love of his life and they were engaged in the autumn of 1819, which was an extraordinary year, the most productive of Keats's career. He was writing mature poems, sometimes dashing them off at great speed. In April 'La Belle Dame Sans Merci' was written. Between April and May the five great odes were written, also known as the Spring Odes: 'Ode to Psyche', 'Ode to a Nightingale', 'Ode on a Grecian Urn', 'Ode on Melancholy' and 'Ode on Indolence'. Keats's poetic reputation today chiefly rests on these.

In February 1820 Keats suffered a severe lung haemorrhage, the significance of which was apparent to him, as he wrote, 'I know the colour of blood; – it is arterial blood; – I cannot be deceived in that colour; – that drop of blood is my death-warrant.' Indeed, it was the beginning of the end. He spent that summer being cared for by, and falling out with, various friends, and eventually he ended up in the care of Fanny and her mother, who nursed him in their home.

He was advised to avoid the English winter and arrived in Rome in November to stay with friends. Though ably nursed, Keats deteriorated throughout the winter and he died on 23 February 1821, aged 25. He is buried in the Protestant cemetery in Rome, having requested as an inscription for his tombstone: HERE LIES ONE WHOSE NAME WAS WRIT IN WATER.

TO ONE WHO HAS BEEN LONG IN CITY PENT

To one who has been long in city pent,
      'Tis very sweet to look into the fair
      And open face of heaven, – to breathe a prayer
Full in the smile of the blue firmament.
Who is more happy, when, with heart's content,   5
      Fatigued he sinks into some pleasant lair
      Of wavy grass, and reads a debonair
And gentle tale of love and languishment?
Returning home at evening, with an ear
      Catching the notes of Philomel, – an eye   10
Watching the sailing cloudlet's bright career,
      He mourns that day so soon has glided by:
E'en like the passage of an angel's tear
      That falls through the clear ether silently.

NOTES

1	To one …:	the opening line echoes a line of Milton's: 'As one who long in populous city pent' (*Paradise Lost*, Book IX, line 445)
1	pent:	confined, shut up in a small space
8	gentle tale:	presumed to be Leigh Hunt's *The Story of Rimini*, a retelling of a tragic love story from Dante's *Inferno*, which Keats was reading at that time
10	Philomel:	the nightingale from the classical myth of Philomela, who was turned into a nightingale

EXPLORATIONS

First reading

Examine the poem in two sections.

1. What do you see in the first section (the octave)? What words create this picture for you?

2. How does the speaker feel? What words or phrases suggest these feelings? Examine the connotations of these words. Is there any alteration in the mood?

3. Examine the speaker's mood in the sestet. What words, phrases or images suggest this mood?

Second reading

4. What ideas about nature and the lifestyle of human beings are implicit in this poem?

5. What is your reaction to the philosophy of this sonnet? Do you find it convincing? Do you think it should be read by students today?

Third reading

6. Examine this poem as an example of the sonnet form. Do you think it is a good sonnet?

ODE TO A NIGHTINGALE

I

My heart aches, and a drowsy numbness pains
    My sense, as though of hemlock I had drunk,
Or emptied some dull opiate to the drains
    One minute past, and Lethe-wards had sunk:
'Tis not through envy of thy happy lot,   5
    But being too happy in thine happiness, –
        That thou, light-winged Dryad of the trees,
           In some melodious plot
    Of beechen green, and shadows numberless,
        Singest of summer in full-throated ease.   10

II

O, for a draught of vintage! that hath been
    Cool'd a long age in the deep-delved earth,
Tasting of Flora and the country green,
    Dance, and Provençal song, and sunburnt mirth!
O for a beaker full of the warm South,   15
    Full of the true, the blushful Hippocrene,
        With beaded bubbles winking at the brim,
           And purple-stained mouth;
    That I might drink, and leave the world unseen,
        And with thee fade away into the forest dim: 20

III

Fade far away, dissolve, and quite forget
    What thou among the leaves hast never known,
The weariness, the fever, and the fret
    Here, where men sit and hear each other groan;
Where palsy shakes a few, sad, last gray hairs,   25
    Where youth grows pale, and spectre-thin, and dies;
        Where but to think is to be full of sorrow
           And leaden-eyed despairs,
    Where Beauty cannot keep her lustrous eyes,
        Or new Love pine at them beyond tomorrow.   30

IV

Away! away! for I will fly to thee,
    Not charioted by Bacchus and his pards,
But on the viewless wings of Poesy,
    Though the dull brain perplexes and retards:
Already with thee! tender is the night,   35

And haply the Queen-Moon is on her throne,
    Cluster'd around by all her starry Fays;
        But here there is no light,
Save what from heaven is with the breezes blown
    Through verdurous glooms and winding mossy ways.   40

V

I cannot see what flowers are at my feet,
    Nor what soft incense hangs upon the boughs,
But, in embalmed darkness, guess each sweet
    Wherewith the seasonable month endows
The grass, the thicket, and the fruittree wild;   45
    White hawthorn, and the pastoral eglantine;
    Fast fading violets cover'd up in leaves;
        And mid-May's eldest child,
The coming musk-rose, full of dewy wine,
    The murmurous haunt of flies on summer eves.   50

VI

Darkling I listen; and, for many a time
    I have been half in love with easeful Death,
Call'd him soft names in many a mused rhyme,
    To take into the air my quiet breath;
Now more than ever seems it rich to die,   55
    To cease upon the midnight with no pain,
    While thou art pouring forth thy soul abroad
        In such an ecstasy!
Still wouldst thou sing, and I have ears in vain –
    To thy high requiem become a sod.   60

VII

Thou wast not born for death, immortal Bird!
    No hungry generations tread thee down;
The voice I hear this passing night was heard
    In ancient days by emperor and clown:
Perhaps the selfsame song that found a path   65
    Through the sad heart of Ruth, when, sick for home,
    She stood in tears amid the alien corn;
        The same that oft-times hath
Charm'd magic casements, opening on the foam
    Of perilous seas, in faery lands forlorn.   70

VIII

Forlorn! the very word is like a bell
 To toll me back from thee to my sole self!
Adieu! the fancy cannot cheat so well
 As she is fam'd to do, deceiving elf.
Adieu! adieu! thy plaintive anthem fades   75
 Past the near meadows, over the still stream,
  Up the hill-side; and now 'tis buried deep
   In the next valley glades:
 Was it a vision, or a waking dream?
  Fled is that music: – Do I wake or sleep?   80

NOTES

2	hemlock:	a poison or sedative
3	opiate:	a sedative drug
4	Lethe-wards had sunk:	sunk into forgetfulness. In Greek mythology, Lethe was one of the rivers that flowed through Hades and whose waters had the power of making the souls of the dead forget their life on earth.
7	That:	read as 'because'
7	Dryad:	wood nymph or spirit of the tree, a poetic reference to the nightingale
13	Flora:	in Latin mythology, the goddess of flowers
14	Provençal song:	in the Middle Ages, travelling singers from Provence, a region in southern France, were famous for their music

15	warm South:	southern wine
16	Hippocrene:	a fountain on Mount Helicon, sacred to the Muses, usually referred to in connection with poetic inspiration; here Keats uses the term to describe wine, but it also carries connotations of poetic inspiration
26	Where youth…:	carries echoes of his brother Tom's death the previous December, at the age of 19, from tuberculosis
32	Bacchus:	Roman god of wine
32	pards:	leopards
33	viewless:	invisible
36	Queen-Moon:	Diana, the moon-goddess
37	Fays:	fairies
43	embalmed:	fragrant
43	sweet:	sweetness of taste and smell
46	eglantine:	the sweetbriar, a wild rose
51	Darkling:	in darkness
60	become a sod:	the poet, when dead and buried, will no longer be able to hear the nightingale's music
66	Ruth:	after the death of her husband, Ruth was driven from her native Moab by famine and went to her mother-in-law, a Jew, to Bethlehem, where she worked in the fields (Ruth 2:1-3); see also Wordsworth's poem 'The Solitary Reaper' (1807)
69	casements:	a type of window
73	fancy:	imagination

EXPLORATIONS

First reading

Read the poem aloud or close your eyes and listen to a reading of it.

1. What is your first impression of the general atmosphere in this poem? Think of the poet's repeated wishes, the predominant colours and the general sounds of the words.

2. What stanza or image made the greatest impression on you? Why?

3. What aspect of the nightingale is chiefly celebrated here?

Second reading

Stanzas 1–2

4. Do any words or phrases used here surprise or perplex you?

5. a What is the poet's mood in the first four lines? Examine it in detail.
   b Why does his heart ache?

6. How do you picture the nightingale and its environment from the detail of stanza 1?

7. What does the poet yearn for in stanza 2? Why?

8. What atmosphere is conjured up by stanza 2? Explain how the effect is created by an appeal to the senses.

9. Do you notice any similarities and contrasts between stanzas 1 and 2? Discuss.

Third reading

Stanzas 3–5

10. a Explain in detail the poet's view of life that emerges from stanza 3. What is your reaction to this view?

   b What do you think prompts this meditation at this particular point in the poem?

11. What exactly is the poet rejecting and proposing in the first three lines of stanza 4?

12. From midway in stanza 4 ('Already with thee …') to the end of stanza 5, Keats is describing the environment of the nightingale, which he is now sharing. What is your general impression of this world? How did the poet get there? How does he convey its appeal to us?

Fourth reading

Stanzas 1–5

13. What do we learn about the nightingale? Try to picture it. What do we *not* learn?

14. What do you think the nightingale means to the poet? Can you explain its attraction?

15. a In this encounter with a nightingale, what is the poet attempting to achieve?

   b Why does he turn to a 'draught of vintage' (stanza 2) and to the 'viewless wings of Poesy' (stanza 4)? Explain his motivation.

Fifth reading

Stanzas 6–8

16. Why does the poet find death attractive in stanza 6? Does he really have a death wish or is his motivation more complex? Explain.

17. In what ways does stanza 6 follow an established pattern?

18. Is the introduction of death completely surprising or has it been prepared for earlier in the poem?

19. What is the poet suggesting about art, as represented by the song of the nightingale, in stanza 7?

20. Why do you think the poet is forlorn in the final stanza? Comment on his philosophical conclusions about art and life and the general mood in that stanza.

Sixth reading

21. What is the poet writing about in this poem? Consider:

- His attitude to everyday life
- The place of art in life
- The value of imagination
- Immortality
- Death

   Read 'Sailing to Byzantium' by W. B. Yeats for similarity of theme.

22. Rereading the poem as an imaginative attempt to share in the artistic life of the nightingale, where do you consider the highs and lows of the experience to be? Examine the changing moods.

23. Trace the argument of the poem.

24. What is your reaction to Keats's claims for the significance of the imagination?

25. This is a very intimate poem in which the reader is allowed to share in the poet's suffering and joy. Examine how this is achieved in the ode.

26. What is the effect of the sensuous imagery?

27. Explore the part played by contrasts and contradictions in this poem.

28. 'In this ode, song is the predominant sound and journey the predominant metaphor.'
Discuss.

29. '"Ode to a Nightingale" is a work of pervasive darkness and mystery' (Brian Stone).
Discuss this statement.

ON FIRST LOOKING INTO CHAPMAN'S HOMER

Much have I travell'd in the realms of gold,
    And many goodly states and kingdoms seen;
    Round many western islands have I been
Which bards in fealty to Apollo hold.
Oft of one wide expanse had I been told   5
    That deep-brow'd Homer ruled as his demesne;
    Yet did I never breathe its pure serene
Till I heard Chapman speak out loud and bold:
Then felt I like some watcher of the skies
    When a new planet swims into his ken;   10
Or like stout Cortez when with eagle eyes
    He star'd at the Pacific – and all his men
Look'd at each other with a wild surmise –
    Silent, upon a peak in Darien.

NOTES

	Chapman:	George Chapman (1559–1634), a contemporary of Shakespeare, who wrote successful plays and translated Homer
	Homer:	Greek epic poet, author of The Iliad and The Odyssey
1	realms of gold:	presumably realms of the poetic imagination; possibly a reference to embossed gold leaf on book covers
3	western islands:	Britain and Ireland
4	Apollo:	the sun god, also the god of music and poetry, who could foretell the future
6	demesne:	dominion
7	serene:	air (from the Latin serenum, meaning 'clear sky')
9	watcher of the skies:	probably a reference to Herschel's discovery in 1781 of the planet Uranus
10	ken:	knowledge, range of vision, sight
11-12	Cortez; Pacific:	Keats had read about the conquest of America in J. M. Robertson's History of America. Balboa was in fact the first European to reach the Pacific; in recollection, Keats has confused Balboa's first sight of the Pacific with the amazement of Cortés's soldiers on seeing Mexico City.
14	Darien:	an older name for the Panama isthmus

EXPLORATIONS

First reading

1. Do you think the poet views his own life as an exploration, a journey? Where? How?

2. a Do you think the poet is referring to a purely geographical exploration or has he something else in mind? Discuss this.

   b What might 'realms of gold' refer to?

Second reading

3. a The high point of Keats's experience was reading Chapman's translation of Homer. How does he feel?

   b Examine the metaphorical comparisons he makes in order to convey his feelings. What is suggested by these?

4. a How does Keats feel about the reading of poetry in general? Examine in particular the connotations of 'realms of gold', 'goodly states', 'wide expanse', 'deep-brow'd Homer', 'pure serene', 'watcher of the skies', 'wild surmise'.

   b How does he communicate the sense of wonder experienced by readers?

5. Briefly explain the theme of this poem.

6. Read the poem aloud to experience its sonorous quality. What phrases or words make the greatest impression on your ear? Discuss the effects of these.

Third reading

7. The critic Brian Stone said that this poem demonstrates Keats's 'initial mastery of sonnet form'. Would you agree? Consider the poem as a sonnet and examine the following:

   a The sense of unity – trace the development of thought in the poem.

   b The volta, or change of tone or thought, in the sestet.

   c The rhyming scheme of the Petrarchan sonnet – do you think this is effective or does it limit the choice of vocabulary and so produce a strain on the language? (Consider the bookish literary terms, such as 'demesne', 'serene', 'ken'.) Is this a fault?

   d The factual error and the extra syllable in line 12 – would you consider these to be serious blemishes detracting from the perfection of the poem?

8. Do you find that this poem appeals equally to head and heart – in other words, that it has a good balance of thought and feeling, which gives it a sense of completeness? Discuss.

9. The poem celebrates 'not just the private enlightening encounter with Chapman's volume, but rather the human sense of awakening to awe-inspiring beauties and opportunities' (Cedric Watts).
   Discuss this statement with reference to the text.

ODE ON A GRECIAN URN

I

Thou still unravish'd bride of quietness,
    Thou foster-child of silence and slow time,
Sylvan historian, who canst thus express
    A flowery tale more sweetly than our rhyme:
What leaf-fring'd legend haunts about thy shape   5
    Of deities or mortals, or of both,
     In Tempe or the dales of Arcady?
    What men or gods are these? What maidens loth?
What mad pursuit? What struggle to escape?
    What pipes and timbrels? What wild ecstasy?   10

II

Heard melodies are sweet, but those unheard
    Are sweeter; therefore, ye soft pipes, play on;
Not to the sensual ear, but, more endear'd,
    Pipe to the spirit ditties of no tone:
Fair youth, beneath the trees, thou canst not leave   15
    Thy song, nor ever can those trees be bare;
     Bold lover, never, never canst thou kiss,
Though winning near the goal – yet, do not grieve;
    She cannot fade, though thou hast not thy bliss,
     For ever wilt thou love, and she be fair!   20

III

Ah, happy, happy boughs! that cannot shed
    Your leaves, nor ever bid the Spring adieu;
And, happy melodist, unwearied,
    For ever piping songs for ever new;
More happy love! more happy, happy love!   25
    For ever warm and still to be enjoy'd,
     For ever panting, and for ever young;
All breathing human passion far above,
    That leaves a heart high-sorrowful and cloy'd,
     A burning forehead, and a parching tongue.   30

IV

Who are these coming to the sacrifice?
    To what green altar, O mysterious priest,
Lead'st thou that heifer lowing at the skies,
    And all her silken flanks with garlands drest?
What little town by river or sea shore,   35

Or mountain-built with peaceful citadel,
   Is emptied of this folk, this pious morn?
And, little town, thy streets for evermore
   Will silent be; and not a soul to tell
     Why thou art desolate, can e'er return.   40

V

O Attic shape! Fair attitude! with brede
   Of marble men and maidens overwrought,
With forest branches and the trodden weed;
   Thou, silent form, dost tease us out of thought
As doth eternity: Cold Pastoral!   45
   When old age shall this generation waste,
     Thou shalt remain, in midst of other woe
Than ours, a friend to man, to whom thou say'st,
   'Beauty is truth, truth beauty,' – that is all
     Ye know on earth, and all ye need to know.   50

BACKGROUND NOTE

This ode was composed in May 1819 and published in *Annals of the Fine Arts* in January 1820 and in the collection *Poems*, 1820. It was probably inspired by more than a single Greek artefact, but there is in existence, in the Keats-Shelley Memorial House in Rome, a drawing made by Keats of the Sosibios Vase (pictured), taken from the Musée Napoléon, which may have partly been an inspiration for the poem. The 'heifer lowing at the skies' was probably inspired by the heifer being led to sacrifice in the south frieze of the Parthenon Marbles.

EXPLORATIONS

First reading

1. What do you see on the urn in the picture? How many scenes are depicted? What is your first impression of the mood or moods?

Second reading

2. What qualities of the urn appeal to the poet in the first quatrain? Examine the metaphors used to describe it and discuss the meaning and connotations of each.

3. What do you understand of the first scene from the urn that is described by the poet? Is this unexpected after Keats's initial description of the urn? Comment.

4. a In the second stanza the poet suggests that art is superior to reality ('Heard melodies are sweet, but those unheard/ Are sweeter'). How does he develop this idea in stanzas 2–3?

   b What reservations does he have about the superiority of art in these stanzas?

Third reading

5. a In the fourth stanza the poet describes a very different scene. What is the atmosphere here?

   b Why do you think he considers this scene at this particular point and what is the effect on the direction of the poem?

6. Do you think stanza 5 restates some of the misgivings of stanzas 2–3? Explain.

7. In what sense is the urn a 'Cold Pastoral'?

8. Discuss a number of possible interpretations of the aphorism 'beauty is truth, truth beauty'.

Fourth reading

9. What do you think the poem is about?

10. What values or philosophical attitudes do you think underlie this poem?

11. What conclusion does the poet reach about the value of art?

12. Examine the section 'A reading of the poem' in the critical notes. Which elements are in accordance with your reading? Which elements differ?

13. Re-examine the critical image of the urn. Consider:
    • How it is described
    • The contradictory qualities
    • Its symbolic value
    • Its particular character

14. Would you consider this ode to be a significant and coherent statement on the value of the arts to society or a mess of confused thinking?

15. Where do you find the beauty in this poem?

Fifth reading

16. 'Both "Ode to a Nightingale" and "Ode on a Grecian Urn" deal with the problems of the artist.' Discuss this statement, with appropriate references to the text.

WHEN I HAVE FEARS THAT I MAY CEASE TO BE

When I have fears that I may cease to be
    Before my pen has glean'd my teeming brain,
Before high-piled books, in charactery,
    Hold like rich garners the full ripen'd grain;
When I behold, upon the night's starr'd face,   5
    Huge cloudy symbols of a high romance,
And think that I may never live to trace
    Their shadows, with the magic hand of chance;
And when I feel, fair creature of an hour,
    That I shall never look upon thee more,   10
Never have relish in the fairy power
    Of unreflecting love; – then on the shore
Of the wide world I stand alone and think
Till love and fame to nothingness do sink.

NOTES

2	teeming:	stocked to overflowing, abundant, prolific
3	charactry:	print
4	garners:	storehouses for corn, granaries
9	fair creature of an hour:	the person referred to has not been identified

EXPLORATIONS

Before reading

1.   Read only the title. What might you
     expect the poem to feature?

First reading

2.   What are the poet's main worries?
     How do they differ from your own
     projected fears?

3.   What is his greatest fear?

4.   What is your first impression of the
     poet's overall mood? What phrases
     or images seem to be important in
     this respect?

Second reading

5.   Trace the poet's line of thought
     through each of the quatrains. What
     exactly is he saying?

6.   Examine the images and metaphors
     that convey these ideas. Do you find
     them effective? Discuss.

7.   What is your considered opinion of
     the critic Brian Stone's comment that
     'its three quatrains are organically
     separate but logically successive'?

Third reading

8.   What can we discern of Keats's
     views on the poetic process and the
     poet from this sonnet? Examine
     in particular lines 4, 6, 7–8, 10 and
     12–13.

9.   Comment on the notion of love
     featured here.

10. What aspects of this poem, either
     of theme or presentation, appeal to
     you? Explain.

LA BELLE DAME SANS MERCI

OL 2021

OL 2022

O what can ail thee, knight at arms
    Alone and palely loitering?
The sedge has withered from the Lake
    And no birds sing!

O what can ail thee knight at arms   5
    So haggard and so woe begone?
The squirrel's granary is full
    And the harvest's done.

I see a lily on thy brow
    With anguish moist and fever dew,   10
And on thy cheeks a fading rose
    Fast withereth too –

I met a Lady in the Meads
    Full beautiful, a faery's child
Her hair was long, her foot was light   15
    And her eyes were wild –

I made a Garland for her head,
    And bracelets too, and fragrant Zone:
She look'd at me as she did love
    And made sweet moan –   20

I set her on my pacing steed
    And nothing else saw all day long
For sidelong would she bend and sing
    A faery's song –

She found me roots of relish sweet   25
    And honey wild and manna dew
And sure in language strange she said
    'I love thee true' –

She took me to her elfin grot
    And there she wept and sigh'd full sore   30
And there I shut her wild wild eyes
    With kisses four.

And there she lulled me asleep
    And there I dream'd – Ah Woe betide!

The latest dream I ever dreamt   35
    On the cold hill side.

I saw pale kings and Princes too
    Pale warriors, death pale were they all;
They cried 'La belle dame sans merci
    Thee hath in thrall.'   40

I saw their starv'd lips in the gloam
    With horrid warning gaped wide
And I awoke and found me here
    On the cold hill's side

And this is why I sojourn here   45
    Alone and palely loitering;
Though the sedge is wither'd from the Lake
    And no birds sing –

'La Belle Dame Sans Merci' by Frank Dicksee (c.1901)

BACKGROUND NOTE

This poem was composed on 21 April 1819, in Keats's journal letter to George and Georgina. It was published in Hunt's new journal, the *Indicator*, on 10 May 1820. The text used here is the draft in that letter rather than the slightly altered (edited) published version.

NOTES

	La Belle Dame Sans Merci:	the beautiful lady without mercy. The title is taken from a medieval ballad composed by Aloin Chartier in 1424 and comes from the terminology of courtly love in medieval literature. This 'mercy' has been described as 'the sort of gracious kindness which prompts a woman to accept a lover's pleas' (Brian Stone).
3	sedge:	coarse grass
9	lily:	of a white or pale colour
13	Meads:	meadows
18	Zone:	girdle or ornate belt
29	elfin:	fairy (originally referred to diminutive supernatural beings in Arthurian legend)
29	grot:	grotto, cave
40	in thrall:	enslaved, in her power

EXPLORATIONS

First reading

1. What is your first impression of the atmosphere in this poem? What do you see, hear and feel? Reread and jot down significant phrases and images.

Second reading

2. Is there a change of speaker in the fourth stanza? Who is speaking from then onwards? Who asked the questions in the first three stanzas?

3. a Describe the knight's present condition.
   b What happened to him?

4. What are the indications, as the tale progresses, that the woman is an enchantress?

5. How is the otherworldly atmosphere created in this tale of enchantment? Consider:
   • The lady
   • The landscape details and imagery
   • The dream
   • The archaic language
   • The metre

Third reading

6. What view of love is behind this poem? Read the critical notes and discuss it.

7. a How do you understand the theme of this poem?
   b Do you think the ballad is an appropriate form of poem for this theme?

8. Do you think the poem is meant to instruct us? If so, comment on the moral.

9. 'The poem has a very simple view of good and evil.'
   Would you agree with this statement? Explain your views.

10. Which elements of the poem did you consider most effective? Explain.

Fourth reading

11. Consider the following statement: 'If the essence of romantic poetry is to rely on sources of inspiration other than the rational intellect can supply, this poem may be justly considered its quintessence' (Graham Hough).

TO AUTUMN

I

Season of mists and mellow fruitfulness,
    Close bosom-friend of the maturing sun;
Conspiring with him how to load and bless
    With fruit the vines that round the thatch-eves run;
To bend with apples the moss'd cottage-trees,   5
    And fill all fruit with ripeness to the core;
      To swell the gourd, and plump the hazel shells
    With a sweet kernel; to set budding more,
And still more, later flowers for the bees,
Until they think warm days will never cease,   10
    For Summer has o'er-brimm'd their clammy cells.

2

Who hath not seen thee oft amid thy store?
    Sometimes whoever seeks abroad may find
Thee sitting careless on a granary floor
    Thy hair soft-lifted by the winnowing wind;   15
Or on a half-reap'd furrow sound asleep,
    Drows'd with the fume of poppies, while thy hook
      Spares the next swath and all its twined flowers:
And sometimes like a gleaner thou dost keep
    Steady thy laden head across a brook;   20
    Or by a cider-press, with patient look,
      Thou watchest the last oozings hours by hours.

3

Where are the songs of Spring? Ay, where are they?
    Think not of them, thou hast thy music too, –
While barred clouds bloom the soft-dying day,   25
    And touch the stubble-plains with rosy hue;
Then in a wailful choir the small gnats mourn
    Among the river sallows, borne aloft
      Or sinking as the light wind lives or dies;
And full-grown lambs loud bleat from hilly bourn;   30
    Hedge-crickets sing; and now with treble soft
    The red-breast whistles from a garden-croft;
      And gathering swallows twitter in the skies.

'The Cornfield' by John Constable (1826)

BACKGROUND NOTE

The ode was written on 19 September 1819. The circumstances of its composition were alluded to briefly in a letter Keats wrote to John Reynolds on 21 September:

'How beautiful the season is now – How fine the air. A temperate sharpness about it. Really, without joking, chaste weather – Dian skies – I never lik'd stubble fields so much as now – Aye better than the chilly green of the spring. Somehow a stubble plain looks warm – in the same way that some pictures look warm – this struck me so much in my Sunday's walk that I composed verses upon it ...'

NOTES

7	gourd:	large fleshy fruit
15	winnowing:	the process of separating the grain from the chaff (or covering) at harvest time; the beaten corn was thrown in the air and the wind blew off the lighter chaff
18	swath:	a row of corn as it falls when reaped
19	gleaner:	person gathering ears of corn left by the reapers
25	barred clouds:	clouds patterned in bars
25	bloom:	used as a transitive verb and meaning 'to give a glow to'
28	sallows:	low-growing willow trees
30	bourn:	small stream
32	croft:	small agricultural holding

EXPLORATIONS

First reading

1. Decide to concentrate either on what you see or on what you hear as you listen to this poem or read it aloud yourself. What elements of either sights or sounds make an impression on you?

2. On a first reading, what particular qualities of the season are being celebrated?

Second reading

3. What do you think is a key statement in the first stanza? Why?

4. What particular aspect of autumn is depicted in the first stanza?

5. Which of our senses is engaged primarily when we read this first stanza?

Third reading

6. Comment on the mood of the second stanza.

7. What are your impressions of the personifications of autumn in the second stanza? What is suggested about the season and about humankind's relationship with nature?

8. Why do you think the poet enquires about the songs of spring in the third stanza?

9. Would you describe the mood of this final stanza as nostalgic, depressed, perfect contentment or something else? Examine the mood in detail.

Fourth reading

10. Overall, what aspects of the season appeal to the poet?

11. Comment on the sensuousness of the language used by Keats in this ode.

12. Keats's poetry is preoccupied with the quest for beauty. Explain how this poem can be seen as part of that search. Refer to specific examples.

13. Keats's other great poetic battle was with change and decay. Is there any evidence of that here?

14. Do you find the poet's attitude to life any different here from that displayed in the other odes?

15. Would you consider this a successful nature poem? Comment.

BRIGHT STAR, WOULD I WERE STEDFAST AS THOU ART

Bright star, would I were stedfast as thou art –
    Not in lone splendor hung aloft the night,
And watching, with eternal lids apart,
    Like nature's patient, sleepless Eremite,
The moving waters at their priestlike task   5
    Of pure ablution round earth's human shores,
Or gazing on the new soft-fallen mask
    Of snow upon the mountains and the moors –
No – yet still stedfast, still unchangeable,
    Pillow'd upon my fair love's ripening breast,   10
To feel for ever its soft fall and swell,
    Awake for ever in a sweet unrest,
Still, still to hear her tender-taken breath,
    And so live ever – or else swoon to death.

NOTES

1	stedfast:	steadfast, constant
4	Eremite:	a hermit, recluse
7	mask:	as in cover, lace mask, or perhaps death mask
10	ripening:	maturing

EXPLORATIONS

First reading

1. What qualities of the star does the poet particularly admire? What quality or characteristic is he less comfortable with?

2. **a**   How is the star presented in the octave? What do you think of this presentation?

    b   What do you think the star might symbolise for the poet?

Second reading

3. How would you describe the particular atmosphere of the octave? Does this change in the sestet? Explain.

4. What is the central problem the poet is trying to resolve? Discuss this.

5. How do you understand the last line? Do you think it is an effective solution?

6. What impression of the author do we get from this poem? Consider:
    *   The poet's personality
    *   His view of life
    *   His ideal of happiness

Third reading

7. The octave deals with the process of watching, contemplating. If this is a metaphor for poetic vision, what is the poet saying about the mode of poetic contemplation?

8. What particularly attracts the watcher? What is Keats thinking about the subject viewed (the world of nature)? Examine the relationship between nature and mankind as suggested in the poem.

9. One of the characteristics of a Petrarchan sonnet is the contrast between the octave and the sestet. Examine and discuss any contrasts you notice.

10. Do you think the imagery is effective? Discuss.

Fourth reading

11. Outline your personal reaction to the poem.

EMILY
DICKINSON

(1830–86)

Prescribed for Higher Level exams in 2020 and 2022

Emily Dickinson was born and lived all her life in Amherst, Massachusetts, in the US. Her family members were prominent in the community as lawyers and public representatives. Emily's early years seemed ordinary enough: education at Amherst Academy and Mount Holyoke Female Seminary; trips to Boston, Washington and Philadelphia; and running the family household when her mother became seriously ill. But she seems to have suffered some kind of psychological crisis in her early thirties, which resulted in her withdrawal from society.

She became somewhat eccentric, the 'myth' of Amherst, who didn't meet strangers or visitors and who spoke to friends from behind a half-closed door or shrouded in shadow at the head of the stairs. She produced a great number of rather cryptic poems of a most unusual form. When she died she was found to have left almost two thousand poems and fragments, in which she explored a number of themes, including love, pain, absence and loss, doubt, despair and mental anguish, and hope. Hardly any were published in her lifetime, and their true worth and originality were not appreciated for many years.

BACKGROUND NOTE

In 1955 an authoritative collection of Dickinson's work, *The Poems of Emily Dickinson*, was prepared by Thomas Johnson. The poems are dated, but as Johnson himself admitted, this is the result of educated guesswork. It is very difficult to be definite, since Dickinson never prepared the poems for publication and did not title them. Each poem that follows is headed with Johnson's number.

254

'Hope' is the thing with feathers –
That perches in the soul –
And sings the tune without the words –
And never stops – at all –

And sweetest – in the Gale – is heard –   5
And sore must be the storm –
That could abash the little Bird
That kept so many warm –

I've heard it in the chillest land –
And on the strangest Sea –   10
Yet, never, in Extremity,
It asked a crumb – of Me.

EXPLORATIONS

Before reading

1. Consider briefly what part 'hope' plays in your own day-to-day life.

2. If you had to represent hope figuratively in a painting or an image, how would you describe it?

First reading

3. How does the poet visualise hope?

4. a   Examine the analogy in detail. List the qualities or characteristics of hope suggested by each of the images in the first stanza. Pry beneath the obvious. For example, what does 'sings the tune without the words' suggest?

   b   What is the effect of the description of hope as the 'thing with feathers'?

5. a   What aspects of hope are suggested in the second stanza?

   b   What does the sound effect of the word 'abash' contribute to this picture?

   c   What is the effect of the adjective 'little'?

6. In the third stanza, which qualities of hope are a repetition of suggestions already encountered and which are new?

7. How do you interpret the last two lines? Do they indicate the strength or a weakness in the virtue of hope? It depends on whether you read the third line as part of the meaning of the previous two or read it with the last line. Experiment with both readings. Is there some ambiguity and does this show a weakness in the virtue of hope?

Second reading

8. Do you think the bird analogy is successful? Explain your views. What other metaphors for hope could you advance?

9. What insights into the nature of hope did you get from reading this poem?

10. How would you describe the mood of the poem? Suggest ways in which this mood is created in the text.

Third reading

11. What do you notice about the technical features of the poem: punctuation, sentences, capital letters, etc.? What is the effect of these?

12. Would you agree that the extraordinary imagery is one of the best features of this poem? Develop your answer with specific references.

13. Do you find this poem hopeful? Explain your views.

258

There's a certain Slant of light,
Winter Afternoons –
That oppresses, like the Heft
Of Cathedral Tunes –

Heavenly Hurt, it gives us –   5
We can find no scar,
But internal difference,
Where the Meanings, are –

None may teach it – Any –
'Tis the Seal Despair –   10
An imperial affliction
Sent us of the Air –

When it comes, the Landscape listens –
Shadows – hold their breath –
When it goes, 'tis like the Distance   15
On the look of Death –

EXPLORATIONS

Before reading

1. Try to recall the image of any wintry sunlit afternoon you have experienced. Describe the quality of the sunlight as best you remember it.

First reading

2. On a first reading, what do you notice about the quality of the sunlight described by the poet?

3. Attempt to describe this light. What can we say about it from the descriptive details in the poem? Is it possible to say very much? Explain.

4. Do you notice how we are made aware of the light? Is it described objectively or filtered through the speaker's feelings? Give an example.

Second reading

5. Explore in detail the speaker's attitude to this light. Pay particular attention to the images for what they reveal about the speaker's view and examine the connotations of similes and metaphors ('like the Heft/Of Cathedral Tunes', 'the Seal Despair', 'like the Distance/On the look of Death').

6. What do you think is meant by 'We can find no scar,/But internal difference, /Where the Meanings, are'?

7. What religious view or philosophy seems to lie behind this poem?

8. a How would you describe the tone of the poem? Refer to particular words and phrases.

   b What do you think the sounds of words contribute to the tone? Explain.

Third reading

9. Briefly set down your understanding of the theme of this poem.

10. Outline your general reaction to the poem. What is your evaluation of it as a nature poem?

11. Can you appreciate that the poem might be seen to reflect the poet's deep despair? In your own words, explain the nature of the despair felt by the speaker.

12. Explore the sound effects – echoes, rhymes, alliteration, etc. – used by the poet. Do you think these musical effects might serve to disguise the deep negative feelings in the poem?

13. What questions do you still have about the poem?

280

I felt a Funeral, in my Brain,
And Mourners to and fro
Kept treading — treading — till it seemed
That Sense was breaking through —

And when they all were seated,   5
A Service, like a Drum —
Kept beating — beating — till I thought
My Mind was going numb —

And then I heard them lift a Box
And creak across my Soul   10
With those same Boots of Lead, again,
Then Space — began to toll,

As all the Heavens were a Bell,
And Being, but an Ear,
And I, and Silence, some strange Race   15
Wrecked, solitary, here —

And then a Plank in Reason, broke,
And I dropped down, and down —
And hit a World, at every plunge,
And Finished knowing — then —   20

EXPLORATIONS

First reading

1. On a first reading, what images in particular hold your attention? What do these images suggest about the subject matter of the poem?

2. List the images suggestive of funerals as they occur throughout the poem. Do these conjure up for you the usual picture of a conventional funeral or is it somehow different? Comment on any unusual connotations.

3. Where is the speaker in this poem? What suggests this?

Second reading

4. If we read this poem as primarily about the process of dying, what insights about death does it convey?

5. Try a metaphorical reading of the poem. Examine the metaphor in the first line and then explore the poem as a psychological experience of breakdown. What insights does this reading bring to you?

6. Which view of the poem do you prefer to take? Could we hold both simultaneously?

Third reading

7. a Explore the speaker's feelings in the first stanza. What is suggested by the imagery and the repetitions?
    b How do you understand the fourth line?

8. Explore the connotations of the simile 'a Service, like a Drum' in the second stanza. What do the sounds of the words suggest about the speaker's state of mind in this stanza?

9. Explain the speaker's feelings in stanzas 2–3.

10. 'As all the Heavens were a Bell,/And Being, but an Ear'. What image does this conjure up for you and what does it suggest about the speaker's perception of her relationship with the heavens?

11. a Is the relationship between the speaker and the universe developed further in the following two lines? 'And I, and Silence, some strange Race /Wrecked, solitary, here –' Explain your understanding of this.
    b How does the speaker feel about her life, her position here?
    c Read the last line aloud. What does the rhythm, or lack of it, convey?

12. a Were you surprised by the actions of the last stanza or was it predictable?
    b Do you think it is an effective ending?

13. Experiment with different oral readings of the last line. What implications for meaning do the different readings have?

Fourth reading

14. Briefly list the principal themes and issues you found in the poem.

15. Decide on your own interpretation of the poem, grounding your views in the text.

16. Comment on the effectiveness of the imagery used to convey the ideas.

17. **a** How would you describe the tone of this poem: anguished, oppressed, lonely, helpless, coldly factual or something else?

    b What words, phrases or images do you think best indicate the poet's tone of voice?

18. Explore the writing technique, especially the repetitions, the sound effect of words, the truncated phrases, the use of single, isolated words, the effect of capitalisation and the punctuation.

- What is the effect of 'treading – treading', 'beating – beating' and other repetitions?

- What is the effect of the poet's continuous use of 'and'? Examine its use in the last stanza in particular.

- What is the effect when the dash is used for punctuation? Examine 'Kept beating – beating – till I thought'.

- What is the effect of the dash at the end of stanzas 4 and 5 in particular?

- Look at the poet's use of conventional punctuation – what is the effect in line 16? Read it aloud.

- List the capitalised words. Do they provide a guide through the poem? Trace it.

- What is the effect of the repeated sounds of words ('drum', 'numb';

'Soul', 'toll')? Explore the suggestions of the onomatopoeic 'creak'. What do these effects contribute to the creation of the atmosphere in the poem?

19. 'Dickinson treats the most tormented situations with great calm' (Helen McNeil). Would you agree with this statement on the evidence of this poem?

328

A Bird came down the Walk –
He did not know I saw –
He bit an Angleworm in halves
And ate the fellow, raw,

And then he drank a Dew   5
From a convenient Grass –
And then hopped sidewise to the Wall
To let a Beetle pass –

He glanced with rapid eyes
That hurried all around –   10
They looked like frightened Beads, I thought –
He stirred his Velvet Head

Like one in danger, Cautious,
I offered him a Crumb
And he unrolled his feathers   15
And rowed him softer home –

Than Oars divide the Ocean,
Too silver for a seam –
Or Butterflies, off Banks of Noon
Leap, plashless as they swim.   20

EXPLORATIONS

First reading

1. What do you notice about the nature drama unfolding on the walk?

2. Examine the bird's movements. What do they suggest about the creature?

3. Where is the speaker in this picture? When does she enter the 'camera shot'? What does she do and what is the bird's reaction?

Second reading

4. What does the speaker actually see and what does she create?

5. Examine how Dickinson creates the sense of the bird's flight in the last five lines of the poem. There is no actual description of the flight; rather, she proceeds by way of negative comparisons ('then', 'or'). What sense of the experience does she give us? What qualities of bird flight are evoked in this way? Refer to words or phrases in the text.

6. Step back or 'zoom out' from this picture and see the poet watching. What do you think is her attitude to this drama? What does she feel about the scene she is viewing? What words or phrases suggest this?

Third reading

7. What particular insights into the natural world does this poem offer you? Explain, with reference to the text.

8. Do you think Dickinson is being serious or humorous, or a combination of both here? Examine the tone of this poem.

9. 'Dickinson wickedly disturbs a clichéd vision of nature through her ornithological caricature' (Juhasz, Miller and Smith).
   Comment on this view in light of your own reading of the poem.

465

OL 2020

OL 2022

I heard a Fly buzz — when I died —
The Stillness in the Room
Was like the Stillness in the Air —
Between the Heaves of Storm —

The Eyes around — had wrung them dry —   5
And Breaths were gathering firm
For that last Onset — when the King
Be witnessed — in the Room —

I willed my Keepsakes — Signed away
What portion of me be   10
Assignable — and then it was
There interposed a Fly —

With Blue — uncertain stumbling Buzz —
Between the light — and me —
And then the Windows failed — and then   15
I could not see to see —

EXPLORATIONS

Before reading

1. Have you ever been present at a death, read about a deathbed scene or visited someone who was seriously ill and not expected to live? What did you notice and what were your thoughts?

First reading

2. What do you notice about the deathbed scene here? What elements do you think might be ordinary or common to any such scene? What would you consider unusual about the scene?

3. Who is the speaker in the poem?

Second reading

4. Comment on the atmosphere in the room. Would you consider it to be emotional or controlled, expectant, frightened, indifferent or something else? What words and phrases suggest this?

5. What is your impression of the onlookers?

6. How does the poet suggest that this is a dramatic moment?

Third reading

7. How is the prospect of death viewed (a) by the onlookers and (b) by the speaker?

8. 'There interposed a Fly'. What is your reaction to the fly and what do you think might be its significance in the poem? Refer to words or phrases.

9. In general, what understanding of death is conveyed by this poem? Explore the connotations of phrases such as 'Heaves of Storm', 'that last Onset', 'the King/Be witnessed', 'With Blue – uncertain stumbling Buzz', 'And then the Windows failed'.

10. Do you find the speaking voice effective? Comment on the tone and the style of speech. What part do the phrasing and punctuation play in this?

Fourth reading

11. 'Few poets have dealt with this all-engrossing subject with such intense feeling under such perfect control' (Richard Sewall).
Do you find intense feeling and perfect control here?

5I2

The Soul has Bandaged moments –
When too appalled to stir –
She feels some ghastly Fright come up
And stop to look at her –

Salute her – with long fingers –   5
Caress her freezing hair –
Sip, Goblin, from the very lips
The Lover – hovered – o'er –
Unworthy, that a thought so mean
Accost a Theme – so – fair –   I0

The soul has moments of Escape –
When bursting all the doors –
She dances like a Bomb, abroad,
And swings upon the Hours,

As do the Bee – delirious borne –   I5
Long Dungeoned from his Rose –
Touch Liberty – then know no more,
But Noon, and Paradise –

The Soul's retaken moments –
When, Felon led along,   20
With shackles on the plumed feet,
And staples, in the Song,

The Horror welcomes her, again,
These, are not brayed of Tongue –

NOTES

1	Soul:	psyche or spirit
3	Fright:	a personification of fear or horror
7	Goblin:	a small malevolent spirit
10	Accost:	speak to, question
14	swings upon the Hours:	an image of childlike play, lasting through all the hours of the day
16	his Rose:	the flower with its nectar, source of the bee's energy
18	Noon:	the term is used with different connotations in various Dickinson poems; here it probably symbolises the paradise of earthly love. The bee soul escapes from his dungeon, finds fulfilment in the rose and is transported into an ecstasy of love ('Noon, and Paradise').
20	Felon:	a criminal
21	the plumed feet:	could suggest freedom of flight, which is in this case curtailed with shackles. In Greek mythology the messenger of the gods, Mercury, had plumed feet. Perhaps poetic inspiration is the theme in question here.
22	staples:	metal fastenings, in this case restricting the song
24	These:	refers to the soul's 'retaken moments', the capturing horror

EXPLORATIONS

First reading

1. What images, phrases or sounds made the most impression on you on a first reading?

2. What is your first impression of the mood or moods of the speaker? What leads you to say this?

3. Is there a narrative line in this poem? Can you trace the sequence of events?

Second reading

4. Explore the following 'thinking points'. Make notes to yourself to clarify your thinking on them.

   a   'The Soul has Bandaged moments'. How do you visualise this? What does it suggest about the condition of the soul?

   b   What does the second line add to our picture of the soul?

   c   The soul is named as feminine. How do you perceive the scene in lines 3–4?

   d   The situation becomes more threatening in lines 5–6. Explain the nature of that threat. What is the impact of the adjective 'freezing'?

   e   Do you think there is a change of attitude by the speaker in line 7 ('Sip, Goblin')? Explain.

   f   'lips/The Lover – hovered – o'er'. What does 'hovered' mean? What does it suggest about the lover and the nature of the relationship? Is the use of the past tense significant?

   g   Do you think lines 9–10 refer to the thoughts of the lover or the speaker's present feelings? Could they refer to both? What implications does each interpretation have?

h   What is suggested about the speaker's state of mind by the first and second stanzas?

i   How would you describe the different mood of the third stanza? Do the verbs help create it?

j   Is there any suggestion that this mood is also perilous? Explain.

k   In the fourth stanza, this new mood is compared to the activities of a bee escaped from captivity. What does this simile convey about the nature of the mood? (Refer to the notes for the significance of 'Noon'.) Explore the effect of the many long vowel sounds in this stanza.

l   In the fifth stanza, how does the poet visualise the soul? Do you think this image is effective? Explain the mood in this stanza.

m   In the fifth stanza, do you think the true horror of captivity is hidden somewhat by the simple repetitive hymn metre and the musical rhyme of lines 20 and 22?

n   Is there any community support for the speaker's predicament? What is suggested in the last line about how this mental suffering must be borne? (Note: 'These' refers back to the 'retaken moments'.)

Third reading

5.   What are your impressions of the mental state of the speaker? Refer to the text.

6.   Explore the appropriateness of the different images and similes Dickinson uses to symbolise the soul.

7.   What do you consider to be the main issues and themes explored in this poem? Refer to the text.

8.   After some critical thinking, outline a reading you yourself find satisfactory and can substantiate with references to the poem.

Fourth reading

9.   What insights into the human condition does this poem offer?

10.   'This poem deals with the intimate aspects of pain and loss.' Comment on the poem in light of this statement.

11.   What part does the music of words – sound effects, metre, rhyme, etc. – play in creating the atmosphere of this poem?

697

I could bring You Jewels – had I a mind to –
But You have enough – of those –
I could bring You Odors from St. Domingo –
Colors – from Vera Cruz –

Berries of the Bahamas – have I –   5
But this little Blaze
Flickering to itself – in the Meadow –
Suits Me – more than those –

Never a Fellow matched this Topaz –
And his Emerald Swing –   10
Dower itself – for Bobadilo –
Better – Could I bring?

BACKGROUND NOTE

Despite her withdrawal from society, Dickinson kept up an active correspondence. Sometimes she sent flowers or gifts with her notes; other times she sent poems as gifts. She also sent poems as love tokens. She often used West Indian images as metaphors for the glories of summer, blooming flowers, poetic success, etc. Rebecca Patterson feels that these images were 'consistently playful rather than intense'.

NOTES

3	St. Domingo:	Santo Domingo, capital city of the Dominican Republic, on the Caribbean island of Hispaniola (so named by Columbus)
4	Vera Cruz:	a city and the main seaport of Mexico. The original settlement was founded in 1519 by Cortés and became the main link between the colony of Mexico and Spain.
5	the Bahamas:	islands in the West Indies, the first land touched by Columbus in 1492
9	Topaz:	a yellow sapphire (precious stone)
10	Emerald:	a precious stone of bright green colour
11	Bobadilo:	probably an allusion to Francisco Bobadilla, a tyrannical Spaniard and Columbus's enemy, who replaced Columbus as governor of the Indies and sent him back to Spain in chains. He 'seized the admiral's gold, plate, jewels and other valuables, plus an enormous treasure in gold wrested from the islanders'. Thus, jewels equal to a dower for Bobadilla would be priceless. We can assume that Dickinson had read Washington Irving's *Life of Columbus*, which contains the information about Bobadilla.

EXPLORATIONS

First reading

1. In this poem the speaker is presenting a gift. What do you understand about the gift she is describing? Examine lines 6–8 in particular.

2. What do we learn about her attitude to it?

3. a Could it be considered a love token? Explain how the poem might be read as a love poem.
   b Do you think this is a credible reading? Explain your own opinion.

Second reading

4. It has been said that Dickinson delighted in making her poems mysterious. For example, she sometimes structured them as riddles. Is there a sense of the mysterious about this poem?

5. What do you think this poem reveals about the writer?

6. Would you consider the tone playful or serious here? Explain your view, with reference to the poem.

986

A narrow Fellow in the Grass
Occasionally rides –
You may have met Him? – did you not
His notice sudden is –

The Grass divides as with a Comb –   5
A spotted Shaft is seen –
And then it closes at your feet
And opens further on –

He likes a Boggy Acre
A Floor too cool for Corn –   10
Yet when a Boy, and Barefoot –
I more than once at Noon

Have passed, I thought, a Whip lash
Unbraiding in the Sun
When stooping to secure it   15
It wrinkled And was gone –

Several of Nature's People
I know, and they know me –
I feel for them a transport
Of Cordiality   20

But never met this Fellow
Attended or alone
Without a tighter breathing
And Zero at the Bone.

BACKGROUND NOTE

On the other side of the street where Emily lived was the 'Dickinson Meadow', where she might have encountered the 'narrow Fellow' in a 'Boggy Acre'.

EXPLORATIONS

First reading

You might approach this poem as a sort of literary riddle and explore the clues carried by the connotations and sounds of words and images.

1. **a** Consider the 'narrow Fellow'. What is actually seen of him? Is this enough to identify the creature with any certainty?

    b What does the title lead you to expect?

2. There are incidental indications of his presence. Where are they and what do they add to our understanding of the 'narrow Fellow'?

3. How do you imagine the speaker? What persona or character does the speaker adopt for this narrative? (See the third stanza.) Do you think this is in any way significant?

Second reading

4. Consider the metaphorical descriptions of the creature. Perhaps the most exciting is 'Whip lash'. What are the connotations of the words? What does the term suggest about the creature? Do these connotations clash with the image of it 'Unbraiding in the Sun'?

5. How did it move when the speaker bent to pick it up?

6. In general, what is your impression of the qualities and nature of this creature?

7. Are there any attempts to make the creature seem less threatening? Refer to the text.

8. What does 'Barefoot' add to the atmosphere of the scene? Who is barefoot? When did this happen?

9. **a** Was the speaker less troubled by this when in her youth? What is the speaker's present or adult reaction to an encounter with the 'narrow Fellow'? Refer to the text.

    b What does 'Zero at the Bone' suggest about her feelings?

Third reading

10. What does the poem convey to us about the writer's attitude or attitudes to nature? Support your ideas with references to the text.

11. Do you think this is an effective evocation of a snake? Support your answer with references to the text.

12. Would you agree that there is real fear beneath the apparent casualness of this poem?

Fourth reading

13. 'When she opened her eyes to the real hidden beneath the daily, it was to the peculiarity, awesomeness, and mystery of it' (John Robinson). Would you agree with this interpretation of the poem?

214

I taste a liquor never brewed –
From Tankards scooped in Pearl –
Not all the Vats upon the Rhine
Yield such an Alcohol!

Inebriate of Air – am I –   5
And Debauchee of Dew –
Reeling – thro' endless summer days –
From inns of Molten Blue –

When 'Landlords' turn the drunken Bee
Out of the Foxglove's door –   10
When Butterflies – renounce their 'drams' –
I shall but drink the more!

Till Seraphs swing their snowy Hats –
And Saints – to windows run –
To see the little Tippler   15
Leaning against the – Sun!

EXPLORATIONS

First reading

1. **a** If you first approach the poem
as a riddle, does this help you to
decipher stanzas 1–2? For
example, can you suggest an
answer to any of the following
enigmas?

    • How could there be a liquor
that wasn't brewed?

    • How are tankards, or beer mugs,
the colour of pearl?

    • 'Inebriate of Air', 'Debauchee of
Dew' – who or what might she
be? Who or what gets drunk on
dew?

    • She is seen staggering from 'inns
of Molten Blue' – an unusual
colour for an inn as we know it.
What or where are the inns?

    b Is all revealed in the third
stanza? Examine the first two
lines. Explain your reading of
stanzas 1–2.

2. Now explain the central metaphor
of the poem.

3. Would you agree that the poet's
train of thought becomes more
whimsical as the poem progresses?

4. What do the first two stanzas
suggest about the speaker's attitude
to nature?

Second reading

5. What self-image does the poet
attempt to project in this poem?
Do you think she sees herself as
dissolute, rebellious, assertive
or something else? Explain, with
reference to phrases or images.

6. It is generally agreed that this is a
humorous poem. Comment on
some of the methods by which the
humour is achieved.

7. Do you think there is a substantial
theme beneath the whimsical
and humorous surface? Make
suggestions.

8. How would you describe the tone
of the poem? Refer to words and
phrases in the text.

Third reading

9. The literary critic David Porter spoke
of a 'tone of ecstatic assurance',
reflecting the attitude of the speaker
as victor over the pains of life.
Would you agree with this?

10. What is your own evaluation of this
poem?

341

After great pain, a formal feeling comes –
The Nerves sit ceremonious, like Tombs –
The stiff Heart questions 'was it He, that bore',
And 'Yesterday, or Centuries before'?

The Feet, mechanical, go round –   5
A Wooden way
Of Ground, or Air, or Ought –
Regardless grown,
A Quartz contentment, like a stone –

This is the Hour of Lead –   10
Remembered, if outlived,
As Freezing persons, recollect the Snow –
First – Chill – then Stupor – then the letting go –

EXPLORATIONS

Before reading

1. Have you ever experienced severe pain, such as from a broken bone or appendicitis, or a severe toothache or headache? Try to recollect how you felt as the pain ebbed away and you were free of it for the first moment in a long while. Were you elated or just exhausted, tired, numbed, etc.? Recapture how you felt in short phrases or images.

First reading

2. Explore the images in the poem for some indication of the speaker's feeling 'After great pain'.
   - What are the connotations of 'The Nerves sit ceremonious, like Tombs'?
   - What might 'The stiff Heart' indicate?
   - What does the heart's disorientation in lines 3–4 suggest about the strength of the pain?
   - What do the images of the second stanza intimate about the speaker's present mood and condition?
   - What does the image 'Hour of Lead' conjure up for you?
   - Are the references to snow comforting or threatening? Explain.

Second reading

3. a Is there a common thread running through any of these images that might give an overview of the speaker's condition? Consider, for instance, 'The Nerves sit ceremonious', 'The stiff Heart', 'The Feet, mechanical'.
   b Taken together, what do these external physical manifestations reveal about the speaker's inner feelings?
   c What do the natural references to wood, quartz and lead suggest about the speaker's condition?

4. Comment on the poet's own description of this condition as 'a formal feeling'. Is this unusual definition supported by any other evidence from the poem? Explain.

5. Can you express the central concern of this poem in one sentence?

6. Do you find the conclusion of this poem in any way hopeful or just totally bleak? Explain your reading of it.

Third reading

7. Do you think this poem is an effective evocation of the particular feeling? Comment.

8. What do you find most unusual or striking about it?

GERARD MANLEY HOPKINS

(1844–89)

Prescribed for Higher Level exams in 2019 and 2021

O n Saturday, 8 June 1889, at 85 St Stephen's Green, Dublin, a Jesuit priest died of typhoid. None of the other priests who shared the rat-infested building with the odd little man from England could have guessed that he would be commemorated a hundred years later as one of the most important poets in the English language.

Gerard Manley Hopkins was born into a prosperous Anglican family on 28 July 1844 at Stratford in Essex. He was the oldest of nine children. The Hopkins household had a great interest in poetry, drawing, music and architecture. In 1854, Gerard was sent to Highgate School as a boarder. One of his teachers described him as 'a pale young boy, very light and active, with a very meditative and intellectual face'. He was fiercely independent and an outstanding student, winning prizes for poetry and a scholarship to study Classics at Balliol College, Oxford. At Oxford, Hopkins converted to Catholicism and in 1868 he joined the Jesuit Order. He decided to destroy the poems that he had written because he wished to devote his life totally to the service of God (an act which he described as 'the slaughter of the innocents').

'In my salad days, in my Welsh days': St Beuno's College, North Wales, 1874–77

Hopkins was sent to St Beuno's College in North Wales to study theology. In 1875, he was encouraged by one of his superiors to write a poem to commemorate the death of five German nuns in a shipwreck. The result was 'The Wreck of the Deutschland', a poem of extraordinary brilliance and originality; in fact, it was so innovative in its use of language and rhythm that no editor would publish it. Undeterred by the unfavourable reaction, Hopkins continued to write poetry. He corresponded regularly with a friend from his days at Oxford, Robert Bridges. Despite Bridges's dislike for his technical experimentation, Hopkins sensed the importance of his own work. It was Bridges who first published Hopkins's work in 1918, almost thirty years after the poet's death.

The first five poems by Hopkins in this anthology were written in St Beuno's in 1877, between the months of March and August. This was one of the happiest times in the poet's adult life – he called them 'my salad days'. These poems are often referred to as the 'bright sonnets' because of the poet's optimistic mood and obvious delight in the beautiful Clwyd Valley and distant Snowdonia. They contrast starkly with the 'terrible sonnets' he wrote later.

'The encircling gloom': Liverpool and Glasgow, 1878–81

After his ordination, Hopkins spent time teaching Classics and doing some parish work. Towards the end of 1879, he was sent to work in a parish in Bedford Leigh, near Manchester, and then to St Francis Xavier's in the heart of industrial Liverpool. The poet who had such a love of nature was shocked to see the full impact of England's Industrial Revolution. The population of the city had increased dramatically as a result of immigration from famine-stricken Ireland and pollution from the factories was unregulated. He found some comfort in the warmth of the local people who made him feel welcome.

One of these local people, a 31-year-old farrier, died from consumption on 21 April 1880. His name was Felix Spencer. A week later, Hopkins wrote the poem 'Felix Randal', which is included in this anthology.

In 1881, Hopkins spent a few months working in St Joseph's Parish in Glasgow. Before he left Scotland, on 28 September, he paid a visit to Inversnaid, on the eastern shore of Loch Lomond. William Wordsworth's poem 'To a Highland Girl (At Inversnayde, upon Loch Lomond)' may well have prompted this visit. He wasn't very happy with the poem that he composed, 'Inversnaid'. It remained unseen until after his death.

'To seem the stranger lies my lot, my life': Dublin, 1884–89

Hopkins's appointment as Fellow of the Royal University of Ireland and Professor of Greek and Latin Literature at the Catholic University of Ireland was not the accolade one might think. The English Provincial of the Jesuits did not know where to employ the eccentric priest and the President of the University wanted a fellow Jesuit so that he could spend the annual salary of £400 on the upkeep of the college. Thus began the most miserable period in the poet's short life.

'Gerard Hopkins was at an opposite pole to everything around him: literary, political, social, etc. (a thorough John Bull incapable of understanding Rebel Ireland). No one took him seriously.' (Fr Joe Darlington, a colleague of Hopkins in the university).

To make matters worse, the poet's primary responsibility for the five years he lived in Dublin was correcting examination papers. Alienation and physical exhaustion took its toll on his spiritual wellbeing and he began to suffer from deep depression. The so-called 'terrible sonnets' – 'No worst, there is none' and 'I wake and feel the fell of dark, not day' – were written in 1885 and mark the nadir of his life.

Even though there is evidence of a spiritual recovery, his physical deterioration was hastened by the unsanitary conditions in which he lived. One of his last poems, 'Thou Art Indeed Just, Lord', was written on St Patrick's Day, 1889, a few months before he died at the relatively young age of forty-four. His final words were, 'I am so happy, I am so happy.' He is buried in Glasnevin Cemetery in Dublin.

GOD'S GRANDEUR

The world is charged with the grandeur of God.
    It will flame out, like shining from shook foil;
    It gathers to a greatness, like the ooze of oil
Crushed. Why do men then now not reck his rod?
Generations have trod, have trod, have trod;   5
    And all is seared with trade; bleared, smeared with toil;
    And wears man's smudge and shares man's smell: the soil
Is bare now, nor can foot feel, being shod.

And for all this, nature is never spent;
    There lives the dearest freshness deep down things;   10
And though the last lights off the black West went
    Oh, morning, at the brown brink eastward, springs –
Because the Holy Ghost over the bent
    World broods with warm breast and with ah! bright wings.

NOTES

This poem was written while Hopkins was studying in St Beuno's (pronounced 'Bíno') College in North Wales. The poet sent it as a birthday present to his mother on 3 March 1877.

1	charged:	as in electrically charged, suggesting a force rather than a substance: 'All things therefore are charged with love, are charged with God, and if we know how to touch them, give off sparks and take fire, yield drops and flow, ring and tell of him.' *Hopkins*
2	foil:	as in tin foil, a leaf of metal often used to set something off by contrast
3	ooze of oil:	a reference to the harvesting of fruit, compared with: 'Or by a cyder-press, with patient look, Thou watchest the last oozings hours by hours.' *Keats, 'Ode to Autumn'*
4	reck:	heed
4	rod:	authority
6	seared:	withered, scorched
9	spent:	used up, exhausted
12	brink:	brink of daylight

EXPLORATIONS

Before reading

1. Have you ever been startled by the beauty of a natural scene? Do you ever feel that development, 'progress', the work of mankind is destroying the beauty of the natural world? Discuss these ideas before reading the poem.

First reading

2. All poetry should be experienced 'through the ears' at first. This is especially true of Hopkins's poetry. Read the poem aloud several times. Experiment with the placing of stresses until you find a version that is satisfactory.

3. Pick out a phrase, image or even a word that appeals to you and say why you chose it. (Imagine that you are thinking up a name for a band, e.g. Crushed!)

4. This is the first of Hopkins's so-called 'bright sonnets'. Can you suggest a reason why the poem is considered 'bright'?

Second reading

5. What qualities of the natural world does the poet admire?

6. How does the poet contrast the different manifestations of God's grandeur?

7. At what point does the poet move from admiration to reflection?

8. What, according to the poet, has been the impact of mankind on the natural world?

9. Identify the ways in which mankind is perceived to have affected the physical world.

10. What is the effect of the last word of the image in line 8, 'nor can foot feel, being shod'? What does it suggest

about the poet's attitude to human development?

11. How does the mood of the poem change in the sestet?

12. Consider the possible meanings of the line, 'There lives the dearest freshness deep down things'. What word is missing from this statement? The omission of a word from a line is a stylistic device called ellipsis. Hopkins used it frequently. When you have encountered more examples of it, consider its effect.

13. Lines 11–12 state in an unusual way that the sun sets and rises again. How does the poet's manner of expressing this idea add greater significance to this mundane event? Does this image have any religious resonance?

14. What is the effect of the 'ah!' in the final line?

Third reading

15. Identify the changes of tone in the poem. Which one is predominant?

16. There is a great sense of energy in the first quatrain. How does the poet generate this energy? Pay close attention to rhythm and sound.

17. How does the second quatrain differ from the first in terms of sound and rhythm?

18. Carefully consider the implications of the final image of the poem. How is the Holy Ghost represented?

Fourth reading

19. How does the poet perceive the relationship between man, God and the natural world?

20. What words or phrases appeal to your senses?

21. How does this poem vary from the standard Petrarchan sonnet?

22. Carefully consider the meaning, the sound and the position of the word 'Crushed'. Would you agree that the poet draws attention to the word? Watch out for other words in later poems that are highlighted by their position in a similar way.

23. What peculiarities of style can you identify in this poem? Pay particular attention to the sound effects.

24. Is there a tension in the poem between the poet who loves beauty and the priest who feels a duty to moralise? Consider the manner in which the poet moves from joy in the contemplation of the natural world to dismay at the way mankind has abused the world, and finally to the assertion that the Holy Ghost will continue to nurture the world. Do you find this movement satisfying?

25. In what way are the poet's concerns relevant to today's world?

26. If you had to recommend this poem to a friend, what aspect or aspects of the poem would you choose to highlight?

SPRING

Nothing is so beautiful as Spring —
    When weeds, in wheels, shoot long and lovely and lush;
    Thrush's eggs look little low heavens, and thrush
Through the echoing timber does so rinse and wring
The ear, it strikes like lightnings to hear him sing;   5
    The glassy peartree leaves and blooms, they brush
    The descending blue; that blue is all in a rush
With richness; the racing lambs too have fair their fling.

What is all this juice and all this joy?
    A strain of the earth's sweet being in the beginning   10
In Eden garden. — Have, get, before it cloy,
    Before it cloud, Christ, lord, and sour with sinning,
Innocent mind and Mayday in girl and boy,
    Most, O maid's child, thy choice and worthy the winning.

NOTES

2	wheels:	an architectural term that describes a design similar to the wheel of a bicycle with spokes radiating from the centre
3	low heavens:	the eggs mirror the pattern of the clouds against the sky (a dappled effect)
4	timber:	tree or wood
4	rinse and wring:	the effect of the bird's song on the ear
6	leaves and blooms:	these nouns are used as verbs here
8	fair:	abundant
9	juice:	possibly meaning the essence or spirit of a thing
10	strain:	a musical term meaning a remembered melody and/or an inherited quality
11	cloy:	satiate, fill to the limit, lose its appeal (verb having 'innocent mind' and 'Mayday' as object)
12	cloud:	verb having 'innocent mind' and 'Mayday' as object
12	sour:	verb having 'innocent mind' and 'Mayday' as object
13	Mayday:	Hopkins associates May with the purity of Mary, the Blessed Virgin and Mother
14	maid's child:	Jesus

EXPLORATIONS

First reading

1. Read the poem aloud several times. Listen carefully to the rhythm or movement of the lines in order to pick up the mood of the poem. Is this a happy or sad poem? Pick out phrases or images that capture the mood of the first verse.

2. Does this poem remind you of 'God's Grandeur' in any way? Discuss the similarities briefly.

Second reading

3. The opening line of the poem is very simple. What is the effect of such a simple beginning? Does it draw you into the poem?

4. Does it surprise you that the poet enthuses about weeds in the second line? What qualities do weeds have that might appeal to the poet? Does his admiration for weeds tell us anything about his personality? How has your attitude to weeds been developed?

5. What does the poet mean by the phrase 'rinse and wring/The ear'? Consider carefully the meanings and associations attached to these two words. Do you think they are unusual words to describe the effect of the bird's song? Suggest a reason for the poet's choice of image.

6. In 'God's Grandeur', the poet described how God's grandeur 'will flame out'. Here, he describes the song of the bird striking him 'like lightning'. What effect is the poet creating with these images?

7. Would you agree that there is a great sense of startled delight in the octet? How does the poet achieve this?

8. a In the octet, the poet provides us with a rich array of movement, sounds, shapes, textures and colours. Identify each one of them.

   b How does the poet move from weeds to thrush's eggs, to the 'glassy peartree' and finally to the 'descending blue'? Would you agree that the movement follows the eye naturally?

   c How does the poet return from the sky to the lambs?

9. What is the tone of the sestet? How does it differ from the octet? Consider the effect of the question in line 9.

10. The poet seems to associate springtime with paradise, but it is only a strain that will soon disappear. Does the poet suggest any reason for this?

11. a Do you find the reflection in the sestet satisfying or an intrusion on the wonderful description of spring?

    b Does the complicated syntax (sentence structure) jar the ear after the vibrant octet?

Third reading

12. Look for examples of the following features: alliteration, assonance, rhyme, ellipsis. Explain how they contribute to the poem.

Fourth reading

13. Do you consider this an optimistic or pessimistic poem? Give reasons for your answer.

14. What is the theme of this poem?

15. Do you note any variations in the use of the Petrarchan sonnet?

16. What similarities have you discovered between this poem and 'God's Grandeur' in terms of theme and poetic technique?

17. Which poem do you prefer and why? Do you prefer the poet's descriptions of nature or his meditations on its significance? Or do you find the combination of description and reflection most satisfying?

AS KINGFISHERS CATCH FIRE, DRAGONFLIES DRAW FLAME

As kingfishers catch fire, dragonflies draw flame;
    As tumbled over rim in roundy wells
    Stones ring; like each tucked string tells, each hung bell's
Bow swung finds tongue to fling out broad its name;
Each mortal thing does one thing and the same: 5
    Deals out that being indoors each one dwells;
    Selves – goes itself; myself it speaks and spells,
Crying What I do is me: for that I came.

Í say more: the just man justices;
    Keeps gráce: thát keeps all his goings graces;   10
Acts in God's eye what in God's eye he is –
    Chríst. For Christ plays in ten thousand places,
Lovely in limbs, and lovely in eyes not his
    To the Father through the features of men's faces.

BACKGROUND NOTE

'All things therefore are charged with love, are charged with God, and if we know how to touch them give off sparks and take fire, yield drops and flow, ring and tell of him.' *Notebooks and papers of Hopkins*

NOTES

1	kingfishers:	birds with brilliant plumage
1	dragonflies:	insects
3	tucked:	plucked
6	indoors:	within
7	Selves:	(verb) asserts its own nature, individuality
9	justices:	(verb) acts in a way that promotes justice: 'acts in a godly manner, lives fully energised by grace, justness, sanctity' (R.V. Schoder SJ)

EXPLORATIONS

Before reading

1. 'I am what I am,' a politician once said in self-defence. What do you think he meant? Was it a declaration of apology or defiance? How many of us have the courage to be what we are? Do we express our individuality or hide it behind a veneer of conformity? Is there any other creature or object in existence that possesses such individuality as we do?

First reading

2. Read the poem aloud several times. What sounds dominate?

3. Pick out a phrase or image that you find appealing, intriguing or strange. Explain your choice.

Second reading

4. This poem can be quite difficult to grasp on a first reading. The language itself is not difficult; however, the poet has concentrated his meaning through the use of ellipsis (omission of words) and unusual syntax. It becomes easier to understand when you realise that the same idea is expressed in different ways throughout the octet. Consider the statement, 'What I do is me: for that I came.' It asserts not only the individuality of all things, but also the notion that everything and everyone has its role in God's creation. With this in mind, attempt an explanation of the first line of the poem.

5. Identify the images in lines 2, 3 and 4. What do they have in common?

6. What are all these creatures and things doing?

7. The poet seems to give a sense of destiny or purpose to animate and inanimate objects alike. Identify examples of each. Consider the significance of this idea.

8. Do you agree that there is an extraordinary intensity and sense of conviction to the octet? How is this intensity conveyed?

9. How does the sestet develop the thought in the octet? Would you agree that there is a change of emphasis from the philosophical to the religious?

10. **a** What is your reaction to a statement such as 'the just man justices'? Does it read well? Is it poetic? Can you think of a reason why the poet should express himself in such a way?

    b Are there any other expressions in the poem that strike you as odd or unusual?

11. In the last three lines, the poet suggests that the 'imprint' of Christ's love is evident in all aspects of God's creation. Everything in existence is unique and has its own essence, but each individual person and thing shares in God's design. The poet sees Christ in 'ten thousand places' and in 'men's faces'. This is the unifying and moral principle that governs the universe. This is how Hopkins sees the incarnation of Christ. Find out what you can about the word 'incarnation'. It is a very important word if you want to understand the way Hopkins relates to the world.

Third reading

12. How does this poem differ from 'God's Grandeur'? Would you agree that the nature imagery is employed in a different way in this poem?

13. This poem is believed to have been written as a defence of Scotism against Thomism. The teachings of Duns Scotus advocated the uniqueness of all things and the ability of the senses to perceive what is good and beautiful. In this philosophy there is a moral value to what is beautiful. This point of view has great significance for a priest who was made to doubt the value of poetry by his superiors. Thomas Aquinas, on the other hand, was suspicious of the senses and stressed the importance of reason. Try to relate these ideas to the poem. What is your own view on this debate, which is sometimes characterised as a debate between the emotions and reason, romance and pragmatism, the heart and the head?

THE WINDHOVER

To Christ our Lord

I caught this morning morning's minion, kingdom
    of daylight's dauphin, dapple-dawn-drawn Falcon, in his riding
    Of the rolling level underneath him steady air, and striding
High there, how he rung upon the rein of a wimpling wing
In his ecstasy! then off, off forth on swing,   5
    As a skate's heel sweeps smooth on a bow-bend: the hurl and gliding
    Rebuffed the big wind. My heart in hiding
Stirred for a bird, – the achieve of, the mastery of the thing!

Brute beauty and valour and act, oh, air, pride, plume, here
    Buckle! AND the fire that breaks from thee then, a billion   10
Times told lovelier, more dangerous, O my chevalier!

    No wonder of it: shéer plód makes plough down sillion
Shine, and blue-bleak embers, ah my dear,
    Fall, gall themselves, and gash gold-vermilion.

NOTES

Hopkins described this poem as 'the best thing I ever wrote'.

	Windhover:	a kestrel, common in the Clwyd area of Wales. At St Beuno's College there was a glass case of stuffed birds on which the following inscription was written: 'The Kestrel or Windhover: The commonest and most conspicuous of British falcons remarkable for its habit of remaining suspended in the air without changing position while it scans the ground for its prey.'
1	caught:	caught sight of (an example of ellipsis)
1	minion:	favourite
2	dauphin:	prince, heir apparent to the French throne (to the kingdom of daylight)
2	dapple-dawn-drawn:	a coined adjective meaning 'dappled and drawn out in front of the dawn' or 'dappled and attracted by the dawn'
4	rung upon the rein:	(i) a technical term of the riding school – 'to ring on the rein' is said of a horse that circles at the end of a long rein held by its trainer; (ii) 'to ring' in falconry means to rise in spirals
4	wimpling:	pleated
6	bow-bend:	as the skater forms the figure 8
6	hurl:	normally a verb, but here it is a noun meaning the vigorous forward motion
8	achieve:	verb used as noun meaning 'achievement'

10	Buckle:	this complex word is crucial to the meaning of the poem. There are several possible interpretations: (i) prepare for action, come to grips, engage the enemy; (ii) clasp, enclose, bring together as one; (iii) give way, bend, collapse under stress or pressure. Interpretations (i) and (ii) can be combined in the image of the chivalric knight putting on his armour in order to do battle. Perhaps the poet is pleading for the qualities mentioned to be united 'here' in his heart.
10	fire:	characteristic energy
11	chevalier:	a knight (French), a reference to Christ
12	shéer plód:	sheer hard work
12	sillion:	a strip of arable land
14	gall:	hurt
14	gold-vermilion:	a mixture of gold and red colour

EXPLORATIONS

Before reading

1. Some people erroneously regard poetry as a kind of cryptic puzzle to be solved, a sort of verbal Rubik's Cube. If the primary purpose in reading a poem is to 'find the meaning', then surely the poet would have been better employed writing his or her ideas in understandable prose. Clearly, there is more to a poem than 'meaning'. The way in which the 'meaning' is expressed provides the 'beauty' or aesthetic value of a poem. It is possible to enjoy the beauty of a poem without understanding the meaning. Discuss your attitude to poetry in general and how your view of it has been formed.

First reading

2. In a letter to Robert Bridges about this poem, Hopkins invited him to 'Take breath and read it with the ears, as I always wish to be read, and my verse becomes all right.'
    Read the first eight lines several times and try to get a sense of the rhythm. Pay particular attention to the changes of pace. Do you agree that the rhythm seems to capture the flight of the bird and that there is a sense of awe and breathlessness as one reaches the end of the octet? How is this achieved?

3. The poet gives a procession of titles to the kestrel, 'as in some royal proclamation of medieval pageantry' (Peter Milward SJ). What is the effect of this? How does it lead into the imagery of horseriding?

4. How does the poet convey the sense that the bird is in complete control of its environment?

5. a The poet uses imagery from the worlds of horseriding and skating to describe the movement of the bird. Look closely at these images and describe the movements of the bird in your own words.

    b Do you think the poet's use of imagery is effective in communicating the grace, elegance and energy of the bird?

6. Is there a paradox in the combination of 'hurl' and 'gliding'? Explain.

7. a Why is the poet's heart 'in hiding'? Is he afraid, ashamed, humbled, envious?

   b Why might a student priest feel envious of this magnificent bird in flight?

   c Why does he write 'for a bird' rather than 'for the bird'?

8. The first tercet begins with a list of qualities the bird embodies. Describe these qualities in your own words.

9. a Look at the possible meanings of 'Buckle' and arrive at your own conclusions on its meaning.

   b Does the capitalisation of the word 'and' imply a consequence of 'Buckle'?

   c What does 'thee' refer to? His heart? The bird? Christ? Consider the possibilities.

10. The second part of the tercet is addressed to 'my chevalier'. What connection does the poet see between the windhover and Christ our Lord? Is there a physical similarity between the bird with its outstretched wings and Christ on the Cross? Does the poet see the bird battling against the wind as a symbol of Christ battling against evil? Consider these possibilities.

Second reading

11. The poet uses quite a varied diction in this poem. At the start, the language is regal – 'minion', 'kingdom', 'dauphin'. What other categories of words are used in the poem? Note the contrast between words like 'Buckle', 'plód' and 'minion', 'sillion', 'billion', 'vermilion'. Describe the texture of these words.

12. The second tercet presents the reader with two images of beauty evolving out of what appears to be unpleasant. The drudgery of ploughing the land brings forth a radiant surface. The embers of a dying fire fall from the grate, breaking open to reveal the glowing interior. What resonances do these images create in the context of the whole poem? Do they connect with the image of Christ on the Cross in any way?

13. a Would you agree that there is a passionate intensity to this poem? How is this effect created?

   b Is there a mystical quality to this poem? Discuss your understanding of mysticism.

Third reading

14. a Compare this poem with the previous three poems under the following headings: theme, mood, development of thought, style and use of the sonnet form.

   b Would you agree that it is quite different in terms of development of thought and use of the sonnet form?

15. Find out what you can about the Spiritual Exercises of St Ignatius Loyola, in particular his 'Meditation on the Kingdom'.

16. Find out what you can about sprung rhythm, inscape and instress.

17. This poem is written in a remarkably original style. Consider the elements of that style, such as the use of alliteration, assonance, exclamation, ellipsis, inversion, compound adjectives, the use of verbs as nouns, sprung rhythm and rhyme. What is the primary purpose of all these poetic devices? It might be useful to consider their effect.

18. Do the difficulties of interpretation make 'The Windhover' a richer or more frustrating poem? Is it possible to enjoy the parts of the poem without a clear understanding of the whole? Consider this question in relation to poetry in general.

PIED BEAUTY

Glory be to God for dappled things –
     For skies of couple-colour as a brinded cow;
      For rose-moles all in stipple upon trout that swim;
Fresh-firecoal chestnut-falls; finches' wings;
     Landscape plotted and pieced – fold, fallow, and plough;   5
      And áll trádes, their gear and tackle and trim.

All things counter, original, spare, strange;
     Whatever is fickle, freckled (who knows how?)
      With swift, slow; sweet, sour; adazzle, dim;
He fathers-forth whose beauty is past change: 10
         Praise him.

NOTES

	Pied:	of different colours
1	dappled:	irregular patches of different colours. Hopkins was particularly fond of 'dappled' and uses the word often in his writings.
2	brinded:	brindled, brownish with streaks of another colour
3	rose-mole:	rose-like spots
3	stipple:	dotted
4	Fresh-firecoal:	In his journal (17 September 1868), Hopkins refers to 'Chestnuts as bright as coals or spots of vermilion' (a brilliant red pigment).
4	chestnut-falls:	see 'Fresh-firecoal' above
5	fold:	pasture for sheep to graze
5	fallow:	unused
5	and plough:	planted with crops
6	áll trádes ... tackle:	the variety of trades with their different implements
7	counter:	all things that stand in contrast with other things
7	spare:	rare

EXPLORATIONS

Before reading

1. a Make a class list of 'beautiful things' to see if there is any consensus on what constitutes beauty. Consider the view that 'beauty is in the eye of the beholder'.

   b Is there a social pressure to conform to or agree on a single type of physical beauty? If so, where does this pressure come from? Have you ever considered as beautiful someone or something no one else admires?

First reading

2. This poem seems to be very simple in its message. It is a celebration of 'pied beauty' or the beauty that comes from a variety of colour and/or contrast. List all the examples of such beauty to be found in the poem.

3. a Are all the poet's illustrations of beauty taken from the natural world?

   b What does the poet mean in line 6 by 'áll trádes, their gear and tackle and trim'?

4. a Does his appreciation of variety and contrast extend beyond the mere physical in the last four lines?

   b Do you find it unusual that a priest in the 19th century should celebrate 'All things counter, original, spare, strange'?

   c Have you noticed any other aspects of Hopkins's poetry that suggest his unconventionality? Take another look at the descriptive adjectives used in lines 7–8.

Second reading

5. How would you describe the tone of this poem?

6. Do you notice a difference between this poem and 'As kingfishers catch fire' on the one hand and 'God's Grandeur' and 'Spring' on the other?

7. Consider the significance of line 10. Who is 'He'? How is his beauty 'past change'?

8. What is the effect of the brief last line?

Third reading

9. The poem supports the views of the painter John Ruskin, for whom Hopkins had great admiration. Find out what you can about Ruskin's aesthetic theory.

10. The simple opening and conclusion echo the Ignatian mottoes *Ad Maiorem Dei Gloriam* (AMDG) and *Laus Deo Semper* (LDS). The poem thus becomes a kind of prayer of praise and a meditation on the glory of God. Consider the efficacy of the poem as a prayer.

11. This is a curtal sonnet, i.e. a sonnet that has been cut short. How has the sonnet been shortened? Why do you think the poet chose to write such a sonnet?

12. This is the last of the five poems on your course that were written during a seven-month period of Hopkins' life spent in North Wales. Write a summary of the poet's central concerns in these poems. Make a list of stylistic features that are characteristic of Hopkins's poetry.

FELIX RANDAL

Felix Randal the farrier, O is he dead then? my duty all ended,
Who have watched his mould of man, big-boned and hardy-handsome
Pining, pining, till time when reason rambled in it, and some
Fatal four disorders, fleshed there, all contended?

Sickness broke him. Impatient, he cursed at first, but mended   5
Being anointed and all; though a heavenlier heart began some
Months earlier, since I had our sweet reprieve and ransom
Tendered to him. Ah well, God rest him all road ever he offended!

This seeing the sick endears them to us, us too it endears.
My tongue had taught thee comfort, touch had quenched thy tears,   10
Thy tears that touched my heart, child, Felix, poor Felix Randal;

How far from then forethought of, all thy more boisterous years,
When thou at the random grim forge, powerful amidst peers,
Didst fettle for the great grey drayhorse his bright and battering sandal!

'The Village Blacksmith in his Smithy' by Herbert Dicksee (c. 1890)

NOTES

1	farrier:	a blacksmith or horse doctor
4	fleshed:	took hold of the flesh
4	contended:	competed
6	heavenlier:	more focused on the next world
7	sweet reprieve and ransom:	Holy Communion
8	all road:	in any way (colloquial Lancashire phrase)
12	How far from then forethought of:	how far away were the thoughts of death when you were in your prime
13	random:	an architectural term, meaning built with rough irregular stones; or it could refer to the untidiness of the forge
14	drayhorse:	a horse suitable for pulling heavy loads or dray carts

EXPLORATIONS

Before reading

1. One of the most challenging roles for a priest is to provide comfort to the sick and the dying. He must reconcile the existence of suffering with faith in a loving God. What must it be like to minister to the terminally ill? Does one become indifferent? Does it become a job? How important is faith in the afterlife? Imagine for a moment how you would cope in that role.

First reading

2. a   Read the poem through several times. Would you agree that the meaning of the poem is relatively easy to grasp?

    b   Write a summary of the thoughts in the poem.

3. a   The poet provides the reader with a vivid picture of the farrier. What do we learn about his physical appearance and the changes that took place as a result of illness?

    b   What do we learn about his personality? Does it undergo any change?

4. a   How would you describe the relationship between the poet/ priest and the farrier? Look at the opening statement and lines 9–11 in particular.

    b   Do you see any change or development in the poet's attitude to the farrier?

5. What is the effect of the questions in the first quatrain?

6. The first eight lines of the poem are primarily descriptive. How do the next six lines differ in mood?

7. In the first tercet (lines 9–11), how does the poet convey the idea that his relationship with the farrier was mutually rewarding?

8. In 'The Windhover', the student priest seemed to envy the bird's ability to 'achieve' something. Is there any hint in this poem to suggest that the poet finds satisfaction in his parish work?

9. a   The second tercet reflects another change of mood. The poet seems to be looking back to a time when the blacksmith was at his physical peak. What is the poet trying to achieve in these lines?

    b   How does the ending affect the overall mood of the poem?

10. Suggest reasons why the sandal is described as 'bright and battering'.

Second reading

11. The image of Holy Communion in line 7 ('our sweet reprieve and ransom') is a very rich one. Explore its connotations.

12. What is the effect created by the use of ellipsis (omission of words) in phrases such as 'my duty [is] all ended'?

13. a   Hopkins tended to use complex syntax in his poetry. The final sentence is a good example. What is the effect of such an unusual arrangement of words?

    b   Can you suggest a reason for this arrangement? Try arranging the sentence in a more normal manner and consider the merits of each arrangement.

14. Show how rhythm and imagery combine to create a powerful and triumphant conclusion to the poem.

15. Are there dramatic elements in this poem? Identify them.

Third reading

16. What elements of the sonnet form are recognisable in this poem? How does it differ from a conventional sonnet? How do the innovations contribute to the impact of the poem?

17. Is this a poem about death or a poem about religious faith? Explain your answer.

18. What significance is there in the phrase 'child, Felix, poor Felix Randal'? Does this phrase have a biblical resonance?

19. Return to your original summary. Would you agree that there is much more to this poem than you thought at first? Elaborate.

20. There is no record of a man named Felix Randal dying in Liverpool around this time, but there is a record for a man called Felix Spencer, who was a farrier. Look up the words 'felix' and 'rand' in the dictionary. Can you suggest a reason why the poet would have changed the man's name in this way?

21. Hopkins writes poetry that appeals to the senses. Discuss.

INVERSNAID

OL 2019

OL 2021

This darksome burn, horseback brown,
His rollrock highroad roaring down,
In coop and in comb the fleece of his foam
Flutes and low to the lake falls home.

A windpuff-bonnet of fáwn-fróth   5
Turns and twindles over the broth
Of a pool so pitchblack, féll-frówning,
It rounds and rounds Despair to drowning.

Degged with dew, dappled with dew
Are the groins of the braes that the brook treads through,   10
Wiry heathpacks, flitches of fern,
And the beadbonny ash that sits over the burn.

What would the world be, once bereft
Of wet and wildness? Let them be left,
O let them be left, wildness and wet;   15
Long live the weeds and the wilderness yet.

NOTES

1	burn:	a term frequently used by Scottish poets for a small stream. Arklet Water flows from Loch Arklet among the Trossachs and enters Loch Lomond near Inversnaid.
3	coop:	an enclosed space; suggests the idea of water trapped in pockets
3	comb:	the water combs over the rocks, in contrast to 'coop'
4	Flutes:	could describe the flute-like shape (an architectural term) of the water falling and/or the sound made by the waterfall
5	fáwn-fróth:	the froth is a fawn colour
6	twindles:	a verb coined from an obscure noun, 'twindle', meaning 'twin'. It is a combination of 'dwindle' and 'twitch' and describes the movement of the water.
6	broth:	one of the poet's favourite words to describe the seething water, suggestive of a witch's brew
7	féll-frówning:	'frowning' suggests the gloomy appearance of the scene. 'Fell' can mean a mountain, an animal's hide or ruthless. It could also come from the verb 'to fall' (with theological implications).
9	Degged:	sprinkled (Lancashire dialect)
9	dappled:	one of the poet's favourite words to describe patches of different (contrasting) colours
10	groins:	folds, another architectural term to describe the joints of vaulting in an arched roof or possibly a bodily metaphor
10	braes:	steep banks (Scottish term)
11	heathpacks:	patches of densely packed heather
11	flitches:	strips cut from a tree, i.e. ragged tufts
12	beadbonny ash:	refers to the beautiful (bonny) orange/red berries of the rowan tree or mountain ash

EXPLORATIONS

Before reading

1. Look carefully at the pictures of Inversnaid. Does the place appeal to you? Give reasons for your answer.

2. 'Long live the weeds and the wilderness yet.'
   Do you know any place that remains untouched by human development? Write a brief description of it.

First reading

3. Read the poem aloud several times in the classroom. What sounds are dominant?

4. Choose an image or phrase that appeals because of its sound or association. Explain your choice.

5. In general terms, what sort of scene is evoked by the words in the poem?

Second reading

6. With the aid of the glossary and in your own words, describe the actions and appearance of the water in the first two verses. Does the poet make it easy for you to visualise the scene? How does he do it? Comment on the effect of words such as 'horseback', 'rollrock', 'pitchblack' and 'féll-frówning'.

7. Would you agree that there is a great sense of energy in the first verse? How does the poet achieve this effect? Is the downward movement of the water echoed in the rhythm of the lines?

8. Is there a darkening of mood in the second verse? What words convey the change?

9. In the third verse, the poet describes the terrain the stream runs through. Describe the scene in your own words. How do the poet's words ('degged', 'groins', 'braes', 'beadbonny') flavour the description?

10. How is the fourth verse different from the previous three? In your own words, explain what aspect of Inversnaid appeals most to Hopkins.

Third reading

11. Now that your understanding of the poem has deepened, read it aloud again. Would you agree that this is a very simple poem once the difficulties of language are overcome?

12. Would it surprise you to learn that Hopkins once thought of being a landscape painter? Pick out examples of his attention to detail. Use the accompanying photographs to get a sense of the accuracy of his descriptions.

I WAKE AND FEEL THE FELL OF DARK, NOT DAY

I wake and feel the fell of dark, not day.
What hours, O what black hours we have spent
This night! what sights you, heart, saw; ways you went!
And more must, in yet longer light's delay.
    With witness I speak this. But where I say   5
Hours I mean years, mean life. And my lament
Is cries countless, cries like dead letters sent
To dearest him that lives alas! away.

    I am gall, I am heartburn. God's most deep decree
Bitter would have me taste: my taste was me;   10
Bones built in me, flesh filled, blood brimmed the curse.
    Selfyeast of spirit a dull dough sours. I see
The lost are like this, and their scourge to be
As I am mine, their sweating selves; but worse.

NOTES

1	fell:	an adjective meaning 'cruel'; or a noun meaning 'a stretch of moorland' or 'the skin of an animal'; or a verb meaning 'to strike down'; it could also be a play on the word 'fall'. Here, the word is used as a noun.
9	gall:	a bitter substance secreted in the liver
9	heartburn:	burning sensation in the lower part of the chest
12	Selfyeast:	yeast is a fungus substance used in baking bread; thus, it 'sours' a 'dull dough'. Originally, Hopkins used the phrase 'my selfstuff', i.e. the very stuff of my being or self.
13	The lost:	those in Hell

EXPLORATIONS

Before reading

1. Darkness, nightmares and terror, a sense of abandonment, self-disgust – these are the powerful forces at work in this poem. Which of these images do you find most terrifying? Give reasons for your answer.

First reading

2. How is the sense of darkness emphasised in the first quatrain?

3. What effect is created by the poet's address to his 'heart'?

4. How does the poet create a sense of spiritual desolation? Is it described in abstract terms or does he create a sense in which it is physical as well as spiritual?

5. To whom are his 'dead letters' sent? Why does he describe them as 'dead'?

6. In the sestet, there is a powerful impression of self-disgust. Identify the images used by the poet to create this effect.

7. **a** Hopkins changed the phrase 'God's most deep decree' to 'God's most just decree' and then changed it back to the original. How do the two phrases differ?

   b What do we learn about the poet's state of mind from this information?

8. Lines 11 – 12 are a kind of definition of self. His physical body is described in gruesome terms; his spirit, instead of lifting the dough, sours it and makes it worse. What is your reaction to this self-definition? Does it inspire shock or pity?

9. Does the poem end with despair or consolation? Who is 'worse'?

Second reading

10. Are we told why the poet feels such desolation? Does it matter?

11. Pick out examples of the poet's use of inversion (of normal word order). How does this device contribute to the sense of anguish in the poem?

NO WORST, THERE IS NONE. PITCHED PAST PITCH OF GRIEF

No worst, there is none. Pitched past pitch of grief,
More pangs will, schooled at forepangs, wilder wring.
Comforter, where, where is your comforting?
Mary, mother of us, where is your relief?
My cries heave, herds-long; huddle in a main, a chief –   5
Woe, world-sorrow; on an age-old anvil wince and sing
Then lull, then leave off. Fury had shrieked 'No ling-
ering! Let me be fell: force I must be brief.'

     O the mind, mind has mountains; cliffs of fall
Frightful, sheer, no-man-fathomed. Hold them cheap   10
May who ne'er hung there. Nor does long our small
Durance deal with that steep or deep. Here! creep,
Wretch, under a comfort serves in a whirlwind: all
Life death does end and each day dies with sleep.

NOTES

1	Pitched past pitch:	to pitch (verb) could mean 'to throw' and 'pitch' (noun) could either mean pitch-black, as in tar, or it could be used in a musical sense. There are other possible combinations of meaning. The sense of the line seems to be that the poet has been cast beyond what are considered to be the normal limits of human suffering.
2	forepangs:	previous experienced agonies
3	Comforter:	the Holy Spirit
5	herds-long:	a long line of cries, like a herd of cattle, huddled together
6	wince and sing:	words chosen as much for their sound as their meaning; they suggest the beating of a hammer against an anvil
7	Fury:	an avenging spirit sent to punish crime, or possibly the personification of a guilty conscience
8	fell:	cruel
8	force:	perforce, of necessity
10	no-man-fathomed:	(coinage) no man has fathomed or explored the depths of this mental abyss
10–11	Hold them cheap ... hung there:	those who ... anguish it causes
12	Durance:	endurance

EXPLORATIONS

Before reading

1. This is a poem about mental suffering and a struggle with despair. If you have ever experienced such feelings, try to describe them.

First reading

2. When you have read the poem several times, pick out the images or impressions that are most vivid. Discuss these with the rest of the class.

3. Does Hopkins use any of the poetic devices found in 'I wake and feel the fell of dark, not day'?

Second reading

4. The opening sentence is short and dramatic. Note carefully that the poet uses the superlative 'worst', not the comparative 'worse'. How does this change the meaning?

5. The second sentence seems to suggest that the agonies that are about to torment him have been 'schooled' by previous agonies and will therefore be even more skilled at inflicting pain. How does the poet's expression of this idea surpass this paraphrase? Would you agree that there is an extraordinary intensity in the line?

6. a In his address to the Holy Ghost, Hopkins repeats the word 'where'. What is the effect of this repetition?

   b Are there any other examples of this in the poem?

   c What is the cumulative effect of this technique?

7. a How does the second quatrain differ from the first? Is it easier or more difficult to comprehend? Give reasons for your answer.

   b Despite the obscurity of the lines, certain impressions are communicated. What are they?

8. How does the poet engage our senses in the octet?

9. In the sestet, the poet suggests that mental torment can feel like hanging onto the edge of a cliff. Is it a good image? Give reasons for your answer.

10. At the end of the poem, Hopkins seems to find some scrap of comfort in the idea that sleep brings the day to a close just as death brings life to a close. What does this 'comfort' say about his state of mind?

Third reading

11. Are we told at any stage in the poem what it is that is causing such anguish? Is the poet concerned more with the experience of suffering than the cause?

12. Do you ever get the feeling that the poet is just feeling sorry for himself? Or is his documentation of suffering a testament to his courage?

13. What variations in the use of the sonnet form are evident in this poem?

14. Consider the overall impact of such poetic devices as alliteration, assonance, ellipsis, repetition, compound words and onomatopoeia.

15. Compare this poem with 'I wake and feel the fell of dark, not day'. (They are usually referred to as 'the terrible sonnets'.) Which of the two is more effective in communicating the poet's suffering? Give reasons for your answer.

THOU ART INDEED JUST, LORD, IF I CONTEND

Justus quidem tu es, Domine, si disputem tecum; verumtamen justa loquar ad te: Quare via impiorum prosperatur? etc.

Thou art indeed just, Lord, if I contend
With thee; but, sir, so what I plead is just.
Why do sinners' ways prosper? and why must
Disappointment all I endeavour end?

   Wert thou my enemy, O thou my friend,   5
How wouldst thou worse, I wonder, than thou dost
Defeat, thwart me? Oh, the sots and thralls of lust
Do in spare hours more thrive than I that spend,

Sir, life upon thy cause. See, banks and brakes
Now, leavèd how thick! lacèd they are again   10
With fretty chervil, look, and fresh wind shakes

Them; birds build – but not I build; no, but strain,
Time's eunuch, and not breed one work that wakes.
Mine, O thou lord of life, send my roots rain.

BACKGROUND NOTE

The Latin quotation is taken from Jeremiah 12:1. The full text is: 'Thou indeed, O Lord, art just, if I plead with thee, but yet I will speak what is just to thee: why doth the way of the wicked prosper: why is it well with all of them that transgress and do wickedly? Thou hast planted them, and they have taken root: they prosper and bring forth fruit. Thou art near in their mouth and far from their reins. And thou, O Lord, hast known me, thou hast seen me, and proved my heart with thee.' It was customary for a Jesuit priest to repeat the phrase, '*Justus es, Domine, et rectum iudiciumtuum*' (You are just, O Lord, and your judgement is right), like a mantra. It signifies an acceptance of God's will, however unpalatable it may seem.

NOTES

7	sots:	drunkards
7	thralls:	slaves
9	brakes:	thickets
11	fretty:	fretted or interlaced
11	chervil:	cow parsley
13	eunuch:	castrated male employed in a harem
13	wakes:	comes to life

EXPLORATIONS

Before reading

1. Have you ever felt that life is unfair and that there seems to be no connection between effort and reward? Describe the circumstances and the feeling.

First reading

2. Read the poem aloud. Can you hear the sense of hurt, anger and frustration? Identify where you think the feelings are at their most intense.

Second reading

3. The first quatrain takes the words from Jeremiah and arranges them to suit the constraints of the sonnet form. Is there any tension in these lines or is the poet simply repeating the formula from the Bible?

4. Is there a tone of humility or anger in the first quatrain?

5. Is there any evidence in the second quatrain to suggest that the poet's feelings are becoming unmanageable? Look carefully at the metre and syntax.

6. What is the effect of the commas around 'Lord', 'sir', 'O thou my friend', 'O thou lord of life'?

7. It is difficult to separate the third stanza from the second. Is this deliberate? What does the poet intend to convey by this arrangement?

Third reading

8. What is the poet's complaint?

9. Is there a sense of growing anger as the poem progresses? Does it continue to build until the end of the poem?

10. To what extent does the syntax contribute to the expression of tortured innocence?

11. How does the imagery change in the sestet?

12. What sort of relationship exists between the poet and God?

13. What kind of 'work' does the poet want? Does he write as a poet or as a priest? Or both?

14. Hopkins included this poem in a letter to Robert Bridges. He suggested that it be read 'adagio molto' (a musical term meaning very slowly) 'and with great stress'. How would such a reading enhance the impact of the poem?

WILLIAM BUTLER
YEATS

(1865–1939)

Prescribed for Higher Level exams in 2019 and 2022

n 1865 William Butler Yeats was born in Dublin to a County Sligo family. His grandfather had been rector of the Church of Ireland at Drumcliff. His father, the portrait painter John Butler Yeats, had married Susan Pollexfen, who belonged to a family of substantial traders and ship-owners from County Sligo. His brother, Jack B. Yeats, was to become one of Ireland's best-known painters. William Yeats was educated intermittently at the Godolphin School in London, the High School in Dublin and the Dublin Metropolitan School of Art.

He was interested in mysticism and the supernatural and developed a great curiosity about Irish mythology, history and folklore. It became one of his life's great passions to develop a distinctive, distinguished Irish literature in English. His first long poem, 'The Wanderings of Oisin' (1889), established the tone of what became known as the Celtic Twilight. His early volumes of poetry reflect his interest in mysticism, theosophy and mythology but also deal with his hopeless love affairs, most notably that with Maude Gonne. In 1889 he had met and fallen in love with her, and though she would not marry him, he remained obsessed with her for most of his life. With Lady Gregory of Coole Park, Gort, County Galway and John Millington Synge he founded the Irish Literary Theatre Society in 1899 and later the Abbey Theatre in 1904.

By the end of the century Yeats had changed his decorative, symbolist style of poetry and began to write in a more direct style. From *The Green Helmet* (1910) onwards he shows a more realistic attitude to love and also begins to write about everyday cultural and political affairs. *Responsibilities* (1914) contains satires on the materialism of Dublin's middle class. Among the major themes of his mature years are the need for harmony in life, the search for perfection in life and art, and the mysteries of time and eternity. These are to be found particularly in the poems of the later volumes, *The Tower* (1928), *The Winding Stair* (1933) and *Last Poems* (1936–39).

Yeats was made a senator in 1922 and was very active in public life; he supervised the design of the new coinage in 1926. He was awarded the Nobel Prize for Literature in 1923. He died in Rome in 1939 and his body was not brought back to Ireland until after the war, when it was buried in Drumcliff.

THE LAKE ISLE OF INNISFREE

OL 2022

I will arise and go now, and go to Innisfree,
And a small cabin build there, of clay and wattles made:
Nine bean-rows will I have there, a hive for the honey-bee,
And live alone in the bee-loud glade.

And I shall have some peace there, for peace comes dropping slow,   5
Dropping from the veils of the morning to where the cricket sings;
There midnight's all a glimmer, and noon a purple glow,
And evening full of the linnet's wings.

I will arise and go now, for always night and day
I hear lake water lapping with low sounds by the shore;   10
While I stand on the roadway, or on the pavements grey,
I hear it in the deep heart's core.

NOTES

1	I will arise …:	this has echoes of the return of the Prodigal Son in Luke 15:18 – 'I will arise and go to my father' – so they were the words of another returning emigrant
1	Innisfree:	(in Irish, *Inisfraoich*: Heather Island) – a rocky island on Lough Gill, County Sligo
2	wattles:	rods interlaced with twigs or branches to make a fence

EXPLORATIONS

Before reading

1. Read only the title. What comes into your mind when you read the title?

First reading

2. What do you notice about Yeats's island?

3. What sights and sounds will the poet see and hear? List them.

4. Contrast this island with the poet's present surroundings.

Second reading

5. Do you think that the features of the island mentioned by the poet are the usual sights and sounds of everyday life in the country or will this place be special? Explain your thinking on this.

6. What kind of space or place is the poet attempting to create? What does that indicate about his needs and philosophy of life or values? Refer to the poem to support your theories.

7. What is the poet's attitude to nature as suggested in the poem? Refer to specific lines and phrases.

Third reading

8. The poet seems almost impelled or driven to go and create this ideal place. Where is the sense of compulsion in the poem and how is it created? Explore the style of language he uses, the syntax, the rhythms of his language and the repeated phrases in order to help you with this.

9. What do you think is the meaning and significance of the last line?

Fourth reading

10. State succinctly what you think the poem is about.

11. What mood do you think the poet creates here and how do the images and the sounds of words contribute to this?

12. Does anything about the poet's vision here appeal to you? Discuss this.

SEPTEMBER 1913

What need you, being come to sense,
But fumble in a greasy till
And add the halfpence to the pence
And prayer to shivering prayer, until
You have dried the marrow from the bone?   5
For men were born to pray and save:
Romantic Ireland's dead and gone,
It's with O'Leary in the grave.

Yet they were of a different kind,
The names that stilled your childish play,   10
They have gone about the world like wind,
But little time had they to pray
For whom the hangman's rope was spun,
And what, God help us, could they save?
Romantic Ireland's dead and gone,   15
It's with O'Leary in the grave.

Was it for this the wild geese spread
The grey wing upon every tide;
For this that all that blood was shed,
For this Edward Fitzgerald died,   20
And Robert Emmet and Wolfe Tone,
All that delirium of the brave?
Romantic Ireland's dead and gone,
It's with O'Leary in the grave.

Yet could we turn the years again,   25
And call those exiles as they were
In all their loneliness and pain,
You'd cry, 'Some woman's yellow hair
Has maddened every mother's son':
They weighed so lightly what they gave.   30
But let them be, they're dead and gone,
They're with O'Leary in the grave.

BACKGROUND NOTE

During 1913 Yeats spent a great deal of energy in support of Lady Gregory's nephew, Sir Hugh Lane, a wealthy art collector, who made a gift to the city of Dublin of an extraordinary collection of modern painting on condition that the city build a suitable gallery. There was a great deal of dispute about the structure, the location and the cost. Yeats was furious at what seemed a mean-spirited, penny-pinching, anti-cultural response to the project.

NOTES

8	O'Leary:	John O'Leary (1830–1907), a Fenian who was arrested in 1865 and sentenced to twenty years' imprisonment. After a number of years he was released on condition that he went into exile. Returning to Dublin in 1885 he was greatly influential in Yeats's developing views on Irish nationalism.
17	the wild geese:	Irish soldiers who were forced into exile after the Williamite victory of the 1690s. They served in the armies of France, Spain and Austria.
20	Edward Fitzgerald:	Lord Edward Fitzgerald (1763–98), one of the leaders of the United Irishmen, who died of wounds received while being arrested
21	Robert Emmet:	leader of the rebellion of 1803
21	Wolfe Tone:	Theobald Wolfe Tone (1763–98), leader of the United Irishmen. Captured and sentenced to death, he committed suicide in prison.

EXPLORATIONS

First reading

Stanza 1

1. 'What need you' – the 'you' here refers to the new Irish, relatively prosperous and Catholic middle classes, whom Yeats is addressing. What does he suggest are their main concerns or needs in life?

2. Explore the connotations of the images used in the first five lines, i.e. what is suggested by each of the pictures? List all the suggestions carried by each of the following and discuss them in groups: 'fumble', 'greasy till', 'add the halfpence to the pence', 'add … prayer to shivering prayer', 'dried the marrow from the bone'.

3. As a consequence of your explorations, what do you think is

Yeats's attitude to these people? What words do you think best convey the tone?

4. 'For men were born to pray and save'. Does the poet really mean this? If not, what does he mean? How should it be read? Try reading it aloud.

5. a Read aloud the last two lines of the stanza as you think the poet would wish it to be read.
   b How is this refrain different from the earlier lines of the stanza?
   c What do you understand by 'Romantic Ireland' and how does Yeats feel about it?

6. Now read the entire stanza aloud, differentiating between the sections that are sarcastic, bitter or condemnatory and the lines that are wistful, nostalgic or plaintive.

Second reading

Stanza 2

7. 'They' – the romantic generations of heroes – had great power and influence in society. How is this suggested? Explore all the possible suggestions carried by lines 10–11.

8. How were they different from the present generation?

9. Is there a suggestion that they were fated to act as they did? Examine line 13.

10. In groups, discuss the best possible way of reading this stanza aloud, then do it.

Third reading

Stanza 3

11. 'for this … For this … For this'. Through this repetition, Yeats punches out the contrast between past and present. His attitude to the present generation is quite clear by now. But what does this stanza say about his attitude to the heroes of Ireland's past? Explore in detail the suggestions carried by the images.

12. 'All that delirium of the brave'. Discuss what this implies about heroism.

Stanza 4

13. 'All Yeats's sympathy and admiration is with the past generations of heroes.'
Discuss this and refer to the text in support of your ideas.

14. 'You'd cry, "Some woman's yellow hair/Has maddened every mother's son".'
What do you think is meant by this?

Fourth reading

15. 'In this poem we find a quite grotesque portrayal of the middle classes in contrast to an unreal and highly romanticised portrayal of past patriots.'
Discuss this as an interpretation of the poem.

16. What do you think is the effect of the refrain?

17. Do you think this was a politically risky, even dangerous, poem to publish? Explain.

18. Are you surprised by the passion and strength of feeling here? Outline your reactions.

THE WILD SWANS AT COOLE

The trees are in their autumn beauty,
The woodland paths are dry,
Under the October twilight the water
Mirrors a still sky;
Upon the brimming water among the stones   5
Are nine-and-fifty swans.

The nineteenth autumn has come upon me
Since I first made my count;
I saw, before I had well finished,
All suddenly mount   10
And scatter wheeling in great broken rings
Upon their clamorous wings.

I have looked upon those brilliant creatures,
And now my heart is sore.
All's changed since I, hearing at twilight,   15
The first time on this shore,
The bell-beat of their wings above my head,
Trod with a lighter tread.

Unwearied still, lover by lover,
They paddle in the cold   20
Companionable streams or climb the air;
Their hearts have not grown old;
Passion or conquest, wander where they will,
Attend upon them still.

But now they drift on the still water,   25
Mysterious, beautiful;
Among what rushes will they build,
By what lake's edge or pool
Delight men's eyes when I awake some day
To find they have flown away?   30

NOTES

Coole:		Coole Park, outside Gort, County Galway, and home of Lady Augusta Gregory. She was a friend and benefactor to the poet and collaborated on many of his projects. Yeats regarded Coole Park as a second home and a welcoming refuge and retreat.
6	nine-and-fifty swans:	there actually were fifty-nine swans on the lake at Coole Park
7	The nineteenth autumn:	Yeats is referring to the summer and autumn of 1897, which was the first time he stayed for a lengthy period at Coole. At that time he was passionately involved with Maude Gonne and in a state of acute nervous exhaustion.
18	Trod with a lighter tread:	it is interesting that the poet chooses to recast 1897 as a hopeful and even carefree period, when this was not the case

EXPLORATIONS

First reading

Stanza 1

1. Notice all the details that draw Yeats's eyes and ears to the scene. Visualise them intently, with your eyes closed if you can. If you came upon this scene, what would your thoughts be?

2. How would you describe the atmosphere of this scene? What particular images or sounds contribute to this atmosphere? Explain.

Stanza 2

3. Read the second stanza with energy, aloud if possible, and see if you can make the swans come alive.

4. **a** Examine the description of the swans here. What attributes or qualities of these creatures does the poet wish to convey?

   b How are these qualities carried by the language? Look at images, verbs, adverbs, the sounds of words and the structure of the long single sentence.

Second reading

5. In the third stanza the poet introduces a personal note. What does he reveal about himself?

6. In stanzas 3–4 the poet Yeats explores the contrasts between the life and condition of the swans and his own life and condition. In your own words, explain the detail of these contrasts.

7. Do you think the poet envies the swans? If so, what exactly does he envy? Refer to phrases and lines to support your thinking.

8. Is this a logical or a poetic argument? Explain.

Third reading

9. If we read the first four stanzas as lamenting the loss of youth, passion and love, what particular loss frightens the poet in the final stanza? Explain.

10. What general issues or themes does Yeats deal with in this poem?

11. Do you think there is any sense of resolution of the personal issues raised by Yeats in this poem? Does

he come to any definite conclusion? Explain your thinking.

12. Examine how the poem is structured stanza by stanza, moving from the very particular local beginning to the general speculation about love in stanza 4, then opening up into the rather mysterious ending that seeks to look into the future. What is the effect of this?

13. The poem is built upon a series of antitheses: the swans and the poet, the poet then and the poet now, and contrasting moods. Show how these are developed.

14. What do you think the symbolism adds to the poem? Explore the elements of sky and water, trees and paths, great broken rings and of course the swans themselves.

Fourth reading

15. Would you agree that the poem creates a 'hauntingly evocative description of the swans'? Discuss or write about this.

16. 'Ageing and the diminution of visionary power are bitterly regretted' (Terence Brown).
    Discuss this view of the poem, referring in detail to the text to substantiate your argument.

AN IRISH AIRMAN FORESEES HIS DEATH

OL 2019

OL 2022

I know that I shall meet my fate
Somewhere among the clouds above;
Those that I fight I do not hate,
Those that I guard I do not love;
My country is Kiltartan Cross,   5
My countrymen Kiltartan's poor,
No likely end could bring them loss
Or leave them happier than before.
Nor law, nor duty bade me fight,
Nor public men, nor cheering crowds,   10
A lonely impulse of delight
Drove to this tumult in the clouds;
I balanced all, brought all to mind,
The years to come seemed waste of breath,
A waste of breath the years behind   15
In balance with this life, this death.

NOTES

An Irish Airman:		the speaker in the poem is Major Robert Gregory, the only son of Yeats's friend and mentor, Lady Augusta Gregory of Coole Park, near Gort, County Galway. He was a pilot in the Royal Flying Corps in the First World War and at the time of his death, on 23 January 1918, was on service in Italy. It emerged later that he had been accidentally shot down by the Italian allies.
3	Those that I fight:	the Germans
4	Those that I guard:	the English or possibly the Italians
5	Kiltartan Cross:	a crossroads near Robert Gregory's home at Coole Park, Gort, County Galway

EXPLORATIONS

Before reading

1. **a** Read only the title. What do you expect to find in this poem?

    b Imagine what this man's thoughts might be. How might he visualise his death? How might he feel about it? Jot down briefly the thoughts, pictures and feelings you imagine might go through his mind.

First reading

2. Who is the speaker in this poem? If in doubt, consult the note ('An Irish Airman') above.

3. Focus on lines 1–2. Are you surprised by how definite he is? Can you suggest any reasons why he might be so definite about his coming death? How would you describe his mood?

4. How do you think the speaker would say these first two lines? Experiment with various readings aloud.

5. Taking the first four lines as a unit, are you surprised that they are spoken by a military man, a pilot? In your own words, describe how he views his situation.

Second reading

6. In lines 5–8 the speaker talks about the people of his home area. How does he feel about them? Does he identify with them in any way? Have the people and the speaker anything in common? How does he think his death will affect their lives? Does he feel they will miss him? Do you think his attitude to them is uncaring or that he feels unable to affect their lives in any way? Discuss these questions and write down the conclusions you come to, together with evidence from the text.

7. What do you think is the purpose of mentioning his Kiltartan countrymen in the context of his explanation? How does it fit in with his reasoning?

8. In your own words, explain the further reasons in lines 9–10 that the speaker discounts as having had any influence on his decision to volunteer.

9. What is revealed about the character of the speaker in the lines you have explored so far?

Third reading

10. We get to the kernel of his motivation in lines 11–12. Examine the language very carefully.

    a 'A lonely impulse of delight': can you understand why he might feel this sense of delight? Explain how you see it.

    b 'Impulse': what does this tell us about the decision? 'A lonely impulse': what does this suggest about the decision and the man?

    c 'Drove': what does this add to our understanding of how he felt and of his decision?

    d 'Tumult in the clouds': in what other context might the words 'tumult' or 'tumultuous' be used? Suggest a few. What does the sound of the word suggest? What does it suggest about the speaker's view of flying?

11. In light of what you have discovered so far, and in the voice of the speaker, write a letter home explaining your decision to volunteer as a pilot. Try to remain true to the speaker's feelings as outlined in the poem.

12. 'In spite of his hint of excitement earlier, the speaker did not make a rash and emotional decision.' On the evidence of lines 13–16, would you agree with this statement? Write a paragraph.

13. 'The years to come seemed waste of breath … In balance with this life, this death.'
    Yet the speaker seemed to want this kind of life very much. Explore how the use of 'breath' and 'death' as rhyming words help to emphasise this.

Fourth reading

14. Having read this poem, what do you find most interesting about the speaker?

15. What appeals to you about the poem? Do you find anything disturbing about it?

16. Thousands of Irishmen fought and died in the British army during the First World War; others could not bring themselves to join that army while Ireland was governed by England. How does the speaker deal with this issue? Is the title significant?

17. As well as being a rhetorical device, the repetition of words and phrases emphasises certain ideas and issues. List the main ideas thus emphasised.

18. What are the principal themes or issues the poem deals with? Write a number of short paragraphs on this.

19. 'The pictures and images are sparsely used but very effective.' Comment on any two images.

20. To whom is this poem being spoken? Read it aloud. Is the tone more appropriate to a letter or to a public statement or speech? Explain your view with reference to phrases or lines in the text.

EASTER 1916

I have met them at close of day
Coming with vivid faces
From counter or desk among grey
Eighteenth-century houses.
I have passed with a nod of the head   5
Or polite meaningless words,
Or have lingered awhile and said
Polite meaningless words,
And thought before I had done
Of a mocking tale or a gibe   10
To please a companion
Around the fire at the club,
Being certain they and I
But lived where motley is worn:
All changed, changed utterly: 15
A terrible beauty is born.

That woman's days were spent
In ignorant good-will,
Her nights in argument
Until her voice grew shrill.   20
What voice more sweet than hers
When, young and beautiful,
She rode to harriers?
This man had kept a school
And rode our wingèd horse;   25
This other his helper and friend
Was coming into his force;
He might have won fame in the end,
So sensitive his nature seemed,
So daring and sweet his thought.   30
This other man I had dreamed
A drunken, vainglorious lout.
He had done most bitter wrong
To some who are near my heart,
Yet I number him in the song;   35
He, too, has resigned his part
In the casual comedy;
He, too, has been changed in his turn,
Transformed utterly:
A terrible beauty is born.   40

Hearts with one purpose alone
Through summer and winter seem
Enchanted to a stone
To trouble the living stream.
The horse that comes from the road, 45
The rider, the birds that range
From cloud to tumbling cloud,
Minute by minute they change;
A shadow of cloud on the stream
Changes minute by minute; 50
A horse-hoof slides on the brim,
And a horse plashes within it;
The long-legged moor-hens dive,
And hens to moor-cocks call;
Minute by minute they live: 55
The stone's in the midst of all.

Too long a sacrifice
Can make a stone of the heart.
O when may it suffice?
That is Heaven's part, our part 60
To murmur name upon name,
As a mother names her child
When sleep at last has come
On limbs that had run wild.
What is it but nightfall? 65
No, no, not night but death;
Was it needless death after all?
For England may keep faith
For all that is done and said.
We know their dream; enough 70
To know they dreamed and are dead;
And what if excess of love
Bewildered them till they died?
I write it out in a verse –
MacDonagh and MacBride 75
And Connolly and Pearse
Now and in time to be,
Wherever green is worn,
Are changed, changed utterly:
A terrible beauty is born. 80

NOTES

Easter 1916:		on Monday, 24 April 1916, a force of about 700 republicans who were members of the Irish Volunteers and the Irish Citizen Army took over the centre of Dublin in a military revolution and held out for six days against the British army. This was known as the Easter Rising.
1	them:	those republicans, in the pre-1916 days
3	grey:	built of granite or limestone
12	the club:	probably the Arts Club, where Yeats was a founder member in 1907
17	That woman:	Constance Gore-Booth (1868–1927) of Lissadell, County Sligo, who married the Polish Count Markiewicz. She became a fervent Irish nationalist and was actively involved in the Fianna and the Citizen Army. She was sentenced to death for her part in the Rising but the sentence was later commuted to penal servitude for life. She was released in 1917 under the general amnesty.
24	This man:	Padraig Pearse (1879–1916). Barrister, teacher and poet, he was the founder of St Enda's School and editor of *An Claidheamh Soluis*. He believed that a blood sacrifice was necessary to revolutionise Ireland. A member of the revolutionary IRB and the Irish Volunteers, he was the Commandant General and President of the Provisional Government during Easter week.
25	wingèd horse:	Pegasus, the winged horse, was a symbol of poetic vision
26	This other:	Thomas MacDonagh (1878–1916), poet and academic who taught at University College Dublin
31	This other man:	Major John MacBride, who had fought with the Boers against the British in South Africa and in 1903 married Maude Gonne, the woman Yeats loved. He too was executed for his part in the Rising.
33	He had done most bitter wrong:	reference to rumours of family violence and debauchery
34	To some who are near my heart:	Maude Gonne and her daughter

41–3	Hearts ... stone:	'stone' at its simplest is usually taken to be a symbol for the fanatical heart, i.e. those who devote themselves fanatically to a cause, become hardened and lose their humanness as a result
67–8	needless death ... England may keep faith:	the Bill for Irish Home Rule had been passed in the Westminster Parliament. In 1914, however, it was suspended on the outbreak of World War I, but with the promise that it would be put into effect after the war.
76	Connolly:	James Connolly (1870–1916). Trade union organiser and founder of the Citizen Army, he was military commander of the insurgents in Dublin, Easter 1916.

EXPLORATIONS

Before reading

1. First reread 'September 1913' and remind yourself how Yeats felt about the Irish middle class of his time.

First reading

Stanza 1

2. Concentrate on the first fourteen lines. These are the same people who feature in 'September 1913'. Yeats is no longer savagely angry, but he certainly has no respect for them. Visualise the encounter he describes – time of day, atmosphere, what the poet does, what he says, how he behaves. Share these ideas.

3. a What 'polite meaningless words' might he have said? Invent some dialogue for him.

   b As he speaks these 'polite meaningless words', what is he actually thinking? Script his thoughts and the 'tale' or 'gibe' he might tell later.

4. 'Where motley is worn': what does this tell us about how Yeats regarded Ireland at this time?

5. How would you describe the poet's feelings and mood in this first section?

6. The first fourteen lines are transformed by lines 15–16 and given a new context. Framed by use of the perfect tense – 'I have met them', 'I have passed' – the impression is given that that was then, this is now.

   a Reread the first section from this perspective.

   b Do you think Yeats is ashamed of his earlier treatment of these people? Discuss this with reference to lines or phrases in the poem.

7. 'A terrible beauty is born.' Explore all the implications of this phrase.

Second reading

Stanza 2

8. According to the poet, what are the effects on Constance Markiewicz of fanatical dedication to a political cause?

9. 'This other his helper'. In contrast to the portrait of Constance Markiewicz, which is somewhat masculine, this portrait of Thomas MacDonagh is quite

feminised. Would you agree?
Explain your thinking with reference
to words and phrases in the poem.

10. There is great emphasis on change in
this section. List all the instances and
comment on them.

11. There is a sense that this change or
transformation was not something
actually effected by these people,
but rather something that happened
to them: 'He, too, has been changed
in his turn,/Transformed utterly'.
They were changed by death and
by executions. Do you think Yeats is
exploring how ordinary people are
changed into heroes? What is he
suggesting? Discuss this.

Third reading

Stanza 3

12. Here Yeats is fascinated by flux and
the process of change.
    a   List all the examples he uses.
    b   Comment on the atmosphere
        created here. Is it an appealing
        picture?

13. In this section he is exploring the
paradox that only a stone (the
fanatical heart) can alter the flow of
a stream, i.e. the course of life. But
it can do this only at the expense of
losing humanness. What does this
indicate about Yeats's thinking on
revolutionary politics?

Fourth reading

Stanza 4

14. What is your initial impression of
the tone of this section? Is the poet
weary, worried, confused, giving up?
Refer in detail to the text.

15. 'our part/To murmur name upon
name'.
How does he see the poet's role
here?

16. 'sleep … not night but death …
needless death … excess of love/
Bewildered them'.
The poet is attempting to think
through his confusions and
uncertainties here. Trace his
thoughts in your own words.

17. Finally, at the end of the poem, Yeats
lists out the dead, almost as a sacred
act. What is the effect of this for
the poet, the reader and those who
died?

Fifth reading

18. Yeats had been severely
disillusioned by the new Irish
Catholic middle class, but he had to
rethink this view after 1916. Explain
the process of his rethinking as it
happens in the poem.

19. 'Despite his sense of awe and
admiration for the change brought
about, this poem does not represent
a totally unqualified approval of
revolutionary politics.'
Discuss this view of the poem,
supporting your answer with
references to the text.

20. Though written in 1916, Yeats did
not have this poem published until
October 1920. Speculate on his
possible reasons. Do you think they
were justified?

THE SECOND COMING

Turning and turning in the widening gyre
The falcon cannot hear the falconer;
Things fall apart; the centre cannot hold;
Mere anarchy is loosed upon the world,
The blood-dimmed tide is loosed, and everywhere   5
The ceremony of innocence is drowned;
The best lack all conviction, while the worst
Are full of passionate intensity.

Surely some revelation is at hand;
Surely the Second Coming is at hand.   10
The Second Coming! Hardly are those words out
When a vast image out of *Spiritus Mundi*
Troubles my sight: somewhere in sands of the desert
A shape with lion body and the head of a man,
A gaze blank and pitiless as the sun,   15
Is moving its slow thighs, while all about it
Reel shadows of the indignant desert birds.
The darkness drops again; but now I know
That twenty centuries of stony sleep
Were vexed to nightmare by a rocking cradle,   20
And what rough beast, its hour come round at last,
Slouches towards Bethlehem to be born?

NOTES

	The Second Coming:	in its Christian interpretation, this refers to the prediction of the second coming of Christ (see Matthew 24). In Yeats's occult and magical philosophy, it might also refer to the second birth of the Avatar, or great antithetical spirit, which Yeats and his wife felt certain would be reincarnated as their baby son, whose birth was imminent. In fact, the child turned out to be a girl, dashing that theory.
1–2	Turning … falconer:	the bird is rising in ever-widening circles and so making the pattern of an inverted cone, or gyre. These lines could be read as the trained bird of prey reverting to its wild state or, in a more religious sense, taken to represent Christian civilisation growing further away from Christ (the falconer).
12	Spiritus Mundi:	'the spirit of the world', which Yeats describes as 'a general storehouse of images which have ceased to be a property of any personality or spirit'
14	A shape with lion body and the head of a man:	instead of the second coming of Christ, Yeats imagines this horrific creature, a sort of Antichrist
20	rocking cradle:	the birth of Christ in Bethlehem began the then two-thousand-year period of Christian history

EXPLORATIONS

Before reading

1. Read Matthew 24:1–31 and some of the Book of Revelations, particularly chapters 12, 13, 20 and 21. Discuss these.

First reading

2. The trained falcon is released and it circles, looking for prey. What do you think might happen if the falcon cannot hear the falconer?

3. What do you see and imagine when you read (a) line 3 and (b) line 4?

4. 'The blood-dimmed tide is loosed'. What does this picture conjure up for you? Do you find it sinister, frightening or something else?

5. Lines 7–8 focus on people. What types of people do you think the poet has in mind? Discuss this.

Second reading

6. Taking the first stanza as a whole, what does it communicate about Yeats's view of civilisation as he saw it at that time?

7. 'The first stanza or section is full of the tension of opposites.'
Discuss or write about this.

8. In the second section of the poem Yeats is looking for some sufficiently weighty reason which would explain this collapse of civilisation. What occurs to him first?

9. His first short-lived thought is replaced by this 'vast image' that 'troubles' his sight. Read Yeats's description carefully.
    a Describe what you imagine.

b What particular qualities are exhibited by this 'rough beast'?

c What particular images or phrases help create the sense of revulsion?

10. Are you shocked by the association with Bethlehem? What is suggested here? Discuss this.

Third reading

11. Yeats is talking about the end of the Christian era, the end of innocence. This is encapsulated in particular in the horrific image of one of the holiest places in Christianity, Bethlehem, being defiled by this beast. What typically nightmarish elements do you notice in the second section of the poem?

12. In your own words, set out briefly what you think the poem is about.

13. Comment on the power of the imagery.

14. Though this was written primarily as a reaction to events in Europe, can you understand how it might be read as a commentary on the Irish situation of that time? Explain your views.

15. Could the poem be seen as prophetic in any way?

16. What did this poem make you think about? Describe the effect it had on you.

SAILING TO BYZANTIUM

I

That is no country for old men. The young
In one another's arms, birds in the trees
– Those dying generations – at their song,
The salmon-falls, the mackerel-crowded seas,
Fish, flesh, or fowl, commend all summer long   5
Whatever is begotten, born, and dies.
Caught in that sensual music all neglect
Monuments of unageing intellect.

II

An aged man is but a paltry thing,
A tattered coat upon a stick, unless   10
Soul clap its hands and sing, and louder sing
For every tatter in its mortal dress,
Nor is there singing school but studying
Monuments of its own magnificence;
And therefore I have sailed the seas and come   15
To the holy city of Byzantium.

III

O sages standing in God's holy fire
As in the gold mosaic of a wall,
Come from the holy fire, perne in a gyre,
And be the singing-masters of my soul.   20
Consume my heart away; sick with desire
And fastened to a dying animal
It knows not what it is; and gather me
Into the artifice of eternity.

IV

Once out of nature I shall never take   25
My bodily form from any natural thing,
But such a form as Grecian goldsmiths make
Of hammered gold and gold enamelling
To keep a drowsy Emperor awake;
Or set upon a golden bough to sing   30
To lords and ladies of Byzantium
Of what is past, or passing, or to come.

Mosaic from the church of Sant'Apollinare Nuovo in Ravenna showing a procession of saints carrying crowns – symbols of martyrs. (See note regarding line 17.)

NOTES

	Byzantium:	the Roman emperor Constantine, who became a Christian in 312 AD, chose Byzantium as his capital city, renaming it Constantinople in 330. Yeats idealised Byzantium, in particular at the end of the fifth century, as the centre of European civilisation – a place where all life was in harmony.
1	That:	Ireland
4	The salmon-falls, the mackerel- crowded seas:	all images of regeneration, new life, energy and plenty
5	commend:	praise, celebrate
17	O sages:	probably refers to the depiction of the martyrs being burned in a fire in a mosaic at the church of Sant'Apollinare Nuovo in Ravenna, which Yeats saw in 1907
19	perne in a gyre:	when Yeats was a child in Sligo he was told that 'pern' was another name for the spool or bobbin on which thread was wound. So the idea of circular movement is carried in the word 'perne', which Yeats constructs here as a verb. A gyre is a revolving cone of time in Yeats's cosmology. Here, Yeats is asking the sages to journey through the cone of time to come to him and teach him perfection and teach his soul to sing.
24	artifice of eternity:	artifice is something constructed, created – here, a work of art. The word can also have connotations of trickery or sleight of hand. In a certain sense art is outside time and has a sort of eternal quality about it. Yeats asks the sages to gather him into the eternity of art.
27	such a form:	Yeats wrote that he had read somewhere that there existed in the Emperors' Palace in Byzantium 'a tree made of gold and silver, and artificial birds that sang'. Here the golden bird is used as a metaphor for art, which is beautiful, perfect and unchanging.
32	Of what is past, or passing, or to come:	though Yeats wished to escape out of the stream of time into the eternity of art, ironically, the golden bird's song is about time

EXPLORATIONS

First reading

Stanza 1

1. Read the first stanza carefully for yourself, as many times as you feel necessary. In groups, try out different ways of reading the first sentence aloud. Why do you think it should be read in that way?

2. Notice the perspective. The poet has already left Ireland, either in reality or imagination, and is looking back.

    a   What does he remember about the country?

    b   Why is it 'no country for old men'?

3. The first stanza vividly portrays the sensuality of life. Explore how the poet does this. Consider the imagery, the sounds of words, repeated letters, the crowded syntax, the repetitions and rhythms of the sentence, etc.

4. How do you think the poet feels about this teeming fertility? Ostensibly he is renouncing the world of the senses, but do you think he dwells on these scenes a little too much if he dislikes or hates them? Consider phrases such as 'The young/In one another's arms, birds in the trees'; 'commend all summer long'; 'Caught in that sensual music'. Do you think there might be a hint of nostalgia and a sense of loss here? Discuss the tone of the stanza.

5. In the midst of all this energy and life, there are the seeds of death. Explain the paradox and word punning in 'dying generations'.

Where else in the first stanza is there an awareness of time?

6. What does the poet value that he feels is neglected in Ireland?

7. Reread the stanza and list all the reasons you can find for Yeats's departure or withdrawal.

8. Now read the first sentence aloud as you think the poet intended it.

Second reading

Stanza 2

9. In this stanza Yeats asserts that only the soul gives meaning to the human being.

    a   Explore the contrast between body and soul here.

    b   Do you think that the imagery used is effective? Explain.

10. 'Nor is there ... own magnificence'.

    a   Tease out the possible meanings of these two lines. Explore the following reading: the only way the spirit learns to sing (achieves perfection) is by studying monuments created by and for itself, i.e. works of art. In other words, art enriches the soul.

    b   Explain why the poet has come to Byzantium.

Third reading

Stanza 3

11. In the third stanza Yeats entreats the sages of the timeless city to teach his soul to sing, i.e. perfect his spirit. But perfection cannot be achieved without pain and sacrifice. Where in the stanza is this notion dealt with?

12. What is the poet's ultimate goal as expressed in the stanza?

13. Byzantium was renowned as the city of religion, philosophy and a highly formalised art. Where are these elements reflected in the second and third stanzas?

Fourth reading

Stanza 4

14. In the fourth stanza the poet wishes that his spirit would be transformed into the perfect work of art and so live on, ageless and incorruptible. What do you notice about this piece of art?

15. Do you think Yeats achieves the yearned-for escape from the flux of time into the 'immortality' of art? Carefully consider the irony of the final line.

16. Essentially, what is Yeats writing about in this poem?

17. 'This poem is built around essential contrasts and polarities.'
Discuss this with reference to relevant phrases and lines.

18. Can you appreciate Yeats's dilemma as experienced here as well as his deep yearning?

FROM MEDITATIONS IN TIME OF CIVIL WAR:

VI. THE STARE'S NEST BY MY WINDOW

The bees build in the crevices
Of loosening masonry, and there
The mother birds bring grubs and flies.
My wall is loosening; honey-bees,
Come build in the empty house of the stare.   5

We are closed in, and the key is turned
On our uncertainty; somewhere
A man is killed, or a house burned,
Yet no clear fact to be discerned:
Come build in the empty house of the stare.   10

A barricade of stone or of wood;
Some fourteen days of civil war;
Last night they trundled down the road
That dead young soldier in his blood:
Come build in the empty house of the stare.   15

We had fed the heart on fantasies,
The heart's grown brutal from the fare;
More substance in our enmities
Than in our love; O honey-bees,
Come build in the empty house of the stare.   20

NOTES

Stare's Nest:		'stare' is a term sometimes used in the West of Ireland for a starling
Meditations in Time of Civil War:		this is quite a lengthy poem structured in seven sections. The first was composed in England in 1921; the other sections were written in Ireland during the Civil War of 1922–23.
I	The bees:	there is a possible echo of the bees that were sent by the gods to perform certain tasks in Porphyry's mystical writing. At any rate, they may symbolise patient creative endeavour, as distinct from the destructive forces all around.
14	That dead young soldier:	this is based on an event that reputedly took place beside Yeats's Galway house, Thoor Ballylee, when a young soldier was dragged down a road, his body so badly battered and mutilated that his mother could only recover his head

EXPLORATIONS

Before reading

1. Read only the title. What might you expect to find in this poem?

First reading

Stanzas 1–3

2. Examine the detail of the first three lines of stanza 1. Write about what you see: the details, the sounds, the atmosphere.

3. In the actual historical context, many Big Houses of the establishment class were abandoned or evacuated for fear of reprisals. What do you imagine might have been the poet's thoughts when he first came upon this scene by the window?

4. There are two references to 'loosening' masonry or walls in the first stanza. Do you think these might be significant? Explain.

5. Read the second stanza carefully. What is the atmosphere in the house and what details contribute to this?

6. What single word do you find most powerful in the third stanza? Write about it.

Second reading

Stanza 4

7. Tease out the meaning of the fourth stanza in your own words.

8. Comment on the tones you find in the final stanza and suggest how these are created.

9. How do you think the repeated refrain should be read? Try it.

Third reading

10. Would you agree that Yeats is torn between a bitter disappointment and a desperate hope here? Discuss this.

11. 'The poem captures the atmosphere of war with vivid realism.' Discuss this statement with reference to the text.

12. Explore the music of this piece: the onomatopoeia, the effect of the rhyming, the haunting refrain, etc.

13. 'This poem is really a prayer.' Discuss.

Fourth reading

14. 'This poem could be read as a metaphor for the situation of the poet's traditional class, the Anglo-Irish Ascendancy.' Discuss this.

15. How did this poem affect you? Write about it.

IN MEMORY OF EVA GORE-BOOTH AND CON MARKIEWICZ

The light of evening, Lissadell,
Great windows open to the south,
Two girls in silk kimonos, both
Beautiful, one a gazelle.
But a raving autumn shears 5
Blossom from the summer's wreath;
The older is condemned to death,
Pardoned, drags out lonely years
Conspiring among the ignorant.
I know not what the younger dreams – 10
Some vague Utopia – and she seems,
When withered old and skeleton-gaunt,
An image of such politics.
Many a time I think to seek
One or the other out and speak 15
Of that old Georgian mansion, mix
Pictures of the mind, recall
That table and the talk of youth,
Two girls in silk kimonos, both
Beautiful, one a gazelle. 20

Dear shadows, now you know it all,
All the folly of a fight
With a common wrong or right.
The innocent and the beautiful
Have no enemy but time; 25
Arise and bid me strike a match
And strike another till time catch;
Should the conflagration climb,
Run till all the sages know.
We the great gazebo built, 30
They convicted us of guilt;
Bid me strike a match and blow.

BACKGROUND NOTE

Eva Gore-Booth (1870–1926; pictured below, left) was a poet and a reader of Eastern philosophy. She became involved in social work for the poor and was a member of the women's suffrage movement. Her sister, Constance Gore-Booth (1868–1927; below, right), married a Polish poet and landowner, Count Casimir Markiewicz. A committed socialist republican, she became involved in Irish revolutionary movements and joined the Citizen Army. She was sentenced to death for her part in the Easter Rising, but the sentence was commuted to life imprisonment and she was released in the general amnesty of 1917. She was appointed Minister for Labour in the first Dáil Éireann of 1919 and was the first Irish woman government minister. She took the anti-treaty side in the Civil War.

NOTES

1	Lissadell:	the County Sligo Georgian mansion built in the early part of the nineteenth century and home of the Gore-Booth family. Yeats visited in 1894–95.
3	kimonos:	traditional Japanese long robes
4	gazelle:	a small, delicately formed antelope. The reference is to Eva Gore-Booth.
7	The older:	Constance
8	lonely years:	Constance's husband returned to his lands in the Ukraine and she was separated from her children
16	old Georgian mansion:	Lissadell, an image of aristocratic elegance and good taste for Yeats
21	Dear shadows:	both women were dead at the time of writing
30	gazebo:	the scholar A.N. Jeffares gives three possible meanings: a summer house; a vantage point; and to make a fool of oneself or be conspicuous (in Hibernian English)

EXPLORATIONS

First reading

Lines 1–4

1.   Picture the scene in the first four lines – notice all the details. What do you learn about the lifestyle of the people living here?

2. What questions are you prompted to ask by these lines? Formulate at least three. Share your questions.

3. a Do you think Yeats treasured this memory?

   b What do the lines reveal about what Yeats valued or considered important in life?

Lines 5–6

4. Do you think these lines are an effective metaphor for the passage of time or a rather tired one? Discuss this.

Lines 7–13

5. Read these lines, consult the notes and then briefly state in your own words how the life paths or careers of these two women have developed.

6. Do you think Yeats approved of their careers? Explain your view with reference to words and phrases in the text.

Second reading

7. 'Two girls in silk kimonos, both/ Beautiful, one a gazelle.'
   These lines are repeated at the end of the first section. Do you think the refrain here should be spoken in the same tone as lines 3–4 or have intervening lines coloured the poet's feeling? Explain your opinion on this. Read the first section aloud as you think Yeats would want it read.

8. Lines 21–25 carry the kernel of the poet's insight, which he feels certain the spirits ('Dear shadows') of the two sisters will understand.

   a What is this wisdom or insight?

   b Is there a certain weariness of tone here? Explain.

9. What do you understand by Yeats's animated wish at the end of the poem to light a bonfire?

Third reading

10. What are the main issues or themes that Yeats deals with in this poem? Support your view with detailed reference.

11. What could one discern about the poet's philosophy of life from a reading of this poem? Refer to the detail of the text.

12. Yeats felt that the Anglo-Irish Ascendancy class, with their great houses and wealth, had a duty to set an example of graciousness and cultured living.

    a Do you think he felt that Eva and Constance had let the side down? Where and how might this be suggested?

    b Do you think he may have considered their activities unfeminine?

13. 'The off-rhymes that Yeats employs from time to time give the poem a conversational naturalism and reinforce the theme of imperfection.' Discuss this with reference to the details of the poem.

14. Many of Yeats's poems about time are structured on quite violent contrasts. Do you think this is an effective device here? Comment.

15. Think or talk about your personal reactions to this poem. What did it make you think about? What insights did it give you?

SWIFT'S EPITAPH

Swift has sailed into his rest;
Savage indignation there
Cannot lacerate his breast.
Imitate him if you dare,
World-besotted traveller; he   5
Served human liberty.

BACKGROUND NOTE

Jonathan Swift (1667–1745) was the most famous dean of St Patrick's Cathedral, Dublin. Poet, political pamphleteer and satirist, he was the author of such well-known works as *The Drapier Letters, A Modest Proposal, A Tale of a Tub* and *Gulliver's Travels*. Politically conservative, Swift voiced the concerns and values of Protestant Ireland with an independence of mind and a courage that Yeats admired.

This poem is a translation, with some alterations, of the Latin epitaph on Swift's burial stone in St Patrick's Cathedral, Dublin. Yeats changed the first line and added the adjective 'World-besotted' in the penultimate line. The original epitaph, which is in Latin, runs as follows:

Here is laid the Body of
JONATHAN SWIFT
Doctor of Divinity,
Dean of this Cathedral Church,
Where savage indignation
can no longer
Rend his heart,
Go traveller, and imitate,
if you can,
This earnest and dedicated
Champion of Liberty.
He died on the 19th day of Oct.,
1745 a.d. aged 78 years.

EXPLORATIONS

First reading

1. What does the first line suggest about Swift's death?

2. What can we learn about Swift's life from this epitaph?

3. What qualities of Swift's do you think Yeats admired?

4. Comment on the tone of the epitaph. Do you think it is unusual? Refer in detail to words and phrases.

Second reading

5. How do Yeats's alterations in lines 1 and 5 change the epitaph?

6. Contrast Swift's original epitaph with Yeats's own epitaph.

AN ACRE OF GRASS

Picture and book remain,
An acre of green grass
For air and exercise,
Now strength of body goes;
Midnight, an old house   5
Where nothing stirs but a mouse.

My temptation is quiet.
Here at life's end
Neither loose imagination,
Nor the mill of the mind   10
Consuming its rag and bone,
Can make the truth known.

Grant me an old man's frenzy,
Myself must I remake
Till I am Timon and Lear   15
Or that William Blake
Who beat upon the wall
Till Truth obeyed his call;

A mind Michael Angelo knew
That can pierce the clouds,   20
Or inspired by frenzy
Shake the dead in their shrouds;
Forgotten else by mankind,
An old man's eagle mind.

NOTES

2–5	An acre of green grass … an old house:	the reference is to Riversdale, a farmhouse with orchards and fruit gardens at the foot of the Dublin Mountains in Rathfarnham which in 1932 Yeats leased for thirteen years
9	loose imagination:	unstructured imagination
11	rag and bone:	the leftover, discarded bric-a-brac of life. Lines 10–11 might refer to the imagination's everyday, casual focus on life's bric-a-brac.
15	Timon:	an Athenian who died in 399 BC who was satirised by the comic writers of his time for his marked misanthropy, or strong dislike of humanity. Shakespeare dramatised the story in Timon of Athens.
15	Lear:	Shakespeare's King Lear, who couldn't accept old age gracefully, lost his reason and lived wild on the heath

| 16 | William Blake: | (1757–1827) by profession an engraver, Blake is best known for his more accessible poems 'Songs of Innocence' and 'Songs of Experience'. Lesser known is a great body and range of work which shows him as a mystic, apocalyptic visionary, writer of rude verses and an independent thinker who challenged the accepted philosophies and values of his age. He was considered mad by his contemporaries. Yeats admired him greatly and co-edited his *Prophetic Books* in 1893. He also wrote an interpretation of Blake's mythology. |
| 19 | Michael Angelo: | Michelangelo Buonarroti (1475–1564) was one of the premier figures of the Italian Renaissance – sculptor, architect, painter and poet. Among his most famous creations are the statue of David and the ceiling of the Sistine Chapel in Rome. |

EXPLORATIONS

First reading

1. Explore the images and sounds of the first stanza.
   a   What do we learn about the condition of the poet?
   b   How would you describe the atmosphere created in this stanza? What words and sounds contribute most to that?

2. In the second stanza, the poet is still thinking of poetry despite his age. In your own words, describe his dilemma.

3. Examine the metaphor for the mind used in lines 10–1. What do you think of it?

4. Comment on the tones found in stanzas 1–2. Do you think there is a sense of emptiness at the end of the second stanza? Explore how the sounds of the words contribute to this.

Second reading

5. 'Grant me an old man's frenzy.' This is a very unusual prayer. Does the remainder of stanza 3 help to explain this intercession? Consult the textual notes and try to outline in your own words what Yeats is actually praying for.

6. What is the connection that Yeats is making between poetry, madness and truth?

7. There is evidence of a new energy in both language and imagery in stanzas 3–4. Comment in detail on this.

8. This extraordinary change or metamorphosis culminates in the final image of 'An old man's eagle mind'. Trace how this conceit (or startling comparison) has been prepared for earlier in the fourth stanza.

Third reading

9. Would you agree that this poem is a most unusual response to the theme of old age?

10. Yeats's theories of creativity (partly inspired by the works of the German philosopher Nietzsche) included the need for continual transformation of the self. Trace the transformation that occurs here.

FROM UNDER BEN BULBEN

V

Irish poets, learn your trade,
Sing whatever is well made,
Scorn the sort now growing up
All out of shape from toe to top,
Their unremembering hearts and heads   5
Base-born products of base beds.
Sing the peasantry, and then
Hard-riding country gentlemen,
The holiness of monks, and after
Porter-drinkers' randy laughter;   10
Sing the lords and ladies gay
That were beaten into the clay
Through seven heroic centuries;
Cast your mind on other days
That we in coming days may be   15
Still the indomitable Irishry.

VI

Under bare Ben Bulben's head
In Drumcliff churchyard Yeats is laid,
An ancestor was rector there
Long years ago; a church stands near,   20
By the road an ancient cross.
No marble, no conventional phrase;
On limestone quarried near the spot
By his command these words are cut:

> *Cast a cold eye*   25
> *On life, on death.*
> *Horseman, pass by!*

September 4, 1938

BACKGROUND NOTE

The final draft of this poem is dated 4 September 1938, about five months before the poet's death. Parts of it were published in 1939. 'Under Ben Bulben' as a whole can be seen as Yeats's poetic testimony, an elegy for himself, defining his convictions and the poetic and social philosophies that motivated his life's work.

Section V: Yeats urges all artists, poets, painters and sculptors to promote the necessary heroic images that nourish civilisation.

Section VI: rounds his life to its close and moves from the mythologies associated with the top of Ben Bulben to the real earth at its foot in the Drumcliff churchyard.

NOTES

Section V

2	whatever is well made:	comments on the great tradition of art and letters (see also the note for line 14 below)
3–6	Scorn the sort ... products of base beds:	Yeats had joined the Eugenics Society in London in 1936 and became very interested in its literature and in research on intelligence testing. (Eugenics is the science of improving the human race through selective breeding.)
11–12	Sing the lords ... beaten into the clay:	refers to the Cromwellian settlement of 1652, which evicted the majority of Irish landowners to Clare and Connaught to make room for new English settlers
13	centuries:	the centuries since the Norman invasions
14	other days:	a reference to the great tradition in European art and letters valued by Yeats, but it could also be a reference to Ireland's literary tradition, particularly of the eighteenth century

Section VI

17	Ben Bulben:	a mountain north of Sligo connected with Irish mythology
18	Drumcliff:	at the foot of Ben Bulben, the site of a sixth century monastery founded by St Colmcille
19	ancestor was rector there:	the Revd John Yeats (1774–1846), Yeats's grandfather, was rector there and is buried in the graveyard
20–1	a church stands near ... ancient Cross:	as well as the remains of a round tower, there is a high cross and part of an older cross in the churchyard
27	Horseman:	has echoes of the fairy horseman of folk belief, but might also have associations with the Irish Ascendancy class

First reading

Section V

1. Yeats's advice to Irish poets to write about the aesthetically pleasing ('whatever is well made') is quite understandable, but what do you think of his advice on what they should scorn? Consult the textual notes.
   a   What exactly is he saying?
   b   What is your reaction to this rant?

2. In your own words, what does Yeats consider to be the proper subjects for poetry?

3. What image of 'Irishry' does Yeats wish to celebrate? Do you think he is being elitist and superior?

Second reading

4. Would you agree that this section exhibits an abhorrence for the present at the expense of a romanticised past? Explain your opinion with reference to the details of the verse.

5. This reads like an incantation. What features of poetic technique do you think contribute to this? Consider the metre, the rhyming scheme, the choice of diction, etc.

6. Write about the poet's attitude of mind as you detect it from these lines.

7. Professor Terence Brown has written of 'Under Ben Bulben': 'Skill (i.e. poetic) here is complicit with a repulsive politics and a deficient ethical sense.'

On the evidence of the extract, would you agree with this?

Third reading

Section VI

8. Yeats visualised the details of his last resting place very carefully. Without checking back, what details of the churchyard can you remember?

9. How would you describe the atmosphere of the churchyard? What details in the verse contribute particularly to this?

Fourth reading

10. What do these lines reveal about the poet, how he sees himself and how he wishes to be remembered?

11. Discuss the epitaph in the last three lines. How does it differ from most epitaphs you have read?

12. The scholar A.N. Jeffares felt that the epitaph embodied Yeats's essential attitude to life and death, 'which he thought must be faced with bravery, with heroic indifference and with the aristocratic disdain of the horseman'.
   Consider this as a possible reading of the lines and write a response to it.

POLITICS

'In our time the destiny of man presents its meanings in political terms.' (Thomas Mann)

How can I, that girl standing there,
My attention fix
On Roman or on Russian
Or on Spanish politics?
Yet here's a travelled man that knows   5
What he talks about,
And there's a politician
That has read and thought,
And maybe what they say is true
Of war and war's alarms,   10
But O that I were young again
And held her in my arms.

BACKGROUND NOTE

Written in May 1938, this poem was composed as an answer to an article about Yeats that had praised his public language but suggested that he should use it on political subjects.

NOTES

Thomas Mann: a German novelist (1875–1955)

EXPLORATIONS

First reading

1. In your own words, state the dilemma or conflict that Yeats is experiencing here.

2. 'And maybe what they say is true/ Of war'.
   From the context of the poem, what do you suppose 'they' say? Examine Thomas Mann's epigraph for suggestions.

3. 'That girl standing there'.
   To whom or to what do you think the poet might be referring?

Second reading

4. Write about the essential conflicts that are set up here: politics versus love, public life versus private, public devotion versus private satisfaction, etc.

5. 'For all its simplicity of language, this is a very well-crafted poem.'
   Discuss this statement with reference to the text.

6. State what you think this poem is about.

7. 'The vision in this poem is that of an old man.'
   Argue about this.

ROBERT
FROST

(1874–1963)

Prescribed for Higher Level exams in 2020 and 2021

Robert Lee Frost was born in San Francisco on 26 March 1874. Following his father's death in 1885, he moved with his younger sister Jeanie and his mother to Lawrence, Massachusetts, where his grandparents lived. Robert entered Lawrence High School in 1888, where he studied Latin, Greek, ancient and European history and mathematics. From high school he went to Dartmouth College and Harvard, but left the two colleges without graduating. On 19 December 1895 he married Elinor White, a former classmate. For health reasons he took up farming. In later years he recalled that his favourite activities were 'mowing with a scythe, chopping with an axe and writing with a pen'. He supplemented his income by teaching and lecturing.

Frost devoted his free time to reading the major poets in order to perfect his own writing. Shakespeare, the English Romantics (Wordsworth, Keats and Shelley) and the Victorian poets (Hardy, Kipling and Browning) all influenced his work. The many biblical references in his poems reflect his studies of scripture, while his classical education enabled him to write with confidence in traditional forms. He followed the principles laid down in Wordsworth's 'Preface to the Lyrical Ballads', basing his poetry on incidents from common life described in 'language really used by men'.

Frost and his family emigrated to England in 1912, where he published two collections, *A Boy's Will* (1913) and *North of Boston* (1914). The books were well received and he was introduced into the literary circles in London, where he met W. B. Yeats. After the outbreak of World War I, Frost returned to America and wrote his next collection, *Mountain Interval*. This book contains some of his best-known poems, including 'Birches', 'Out, Out—' and 'The Road Not Taken', with their characteristic themes of isolation, fear, violence and death. Frost bought another farm in Franconia, New Hampshire, and supported his family by college teaching, readings, lectures, book royalties and reprint fees. In January 1917 he became Professor of English at Amherst, Massachusetts. By 1920 he could afford to move to Vermont and devote himself to apple-farming and writing poetry. In recognition of his work he won the Pulitzer Prize four times, in 1924, 1931, 1937 and 1943.

In contrast to his public life, Frost's personal life was dogged by tragedy. His sister Jeanie was committed to a mental asylum. His daughter Lesley had an emotionally disturbed life and blamed her father for her problems. His favourite child, Marjorie, had a nervous breakdown, developed tuberculosis and died in 1934 aged 29. Irma, his third daughter, suffered from mental illness throughout her adult life. Elinor, his wife, died of a heart attack on 20 March 1938 and his only son, Carol, committed suicide in 1940. Frost survived the turbulence of these years with the support of his friend, secretary and manager, Kay Morrison. In his final years, Frost enjoyed public acclaim. He recited 'The Gift Outright' at John F. Kennedy's inauguration, watched on television by over 60 million Americans. He travelled as a celebrated visitor to Brazil, Ireland and Russia. On his 88th birthday he received the Congressional Gold Medal from President Kennedy and in the same year, 1962, published his final volume, *In the Clearing*. On 29 January 1963, two months before his 89th birthday, Robert Frost died peacefully in a Boston hospital.

THE TUFT OF FLOWERS

`OL 2020`

`OL 2021`

I went to turn the grass once after one
Who mowed it in the dew before the sun.

The dew was gone that made his blade so keen
Before I came to view the levelled scene.

I looked for him behind an isle of trees;   5
I listened for his whetstone on the breeze.

But he had gone his way, the grass all mown,
And I must be, as he had been, – alone,

'As all must be,' I said within my heart,
'Whether they work together or apart.'   10

But as I said it, swift there passed me by
On noiseless wing a bewildered butterfly,

Seeking with memories grown dim o'er night
Some resting flower of yesterday's delight.

And once I marked his flight go round and round,   15
As where some flower lay withering on the ground.

And then he flew as far as eye could see,
And then on tremulous wing came back to me.

I thought of questions that have no reply,
And would have turned to toss the grass to dry;   20

But he turned first, and led my eye to look
At a tall tuft of flowers beside a brook,

A leaping tongue of bloom the scythe had spared
Beside a reedy brook the scythe had bared.

I left my place to know them by their name,   25
Finding them butterfly weed when I came.

The mower in the dew had loved them thus,
By leaving them to flourish, not for us,

Nor yet to draw one thought of ours to him,
But from sheer morning gladness at the brim.   30

The butterfly and I had lit upon,
Nevertheless, a message from the dawn,

That made me hear the wakening birds around,
And hear his long scythe whispering to the ground,

And feel a spirit kindred to my own;   35
So that henceforth I worked no more alone;

But glad with him, I worked as with his aid,
And weary, sought at noon with him the shade;

And dreaming, as it were, held brotherly speech
With one whose thought I had not hoped to reach.   40

'Men work together,' I told him from the heart,
'Whether they work together or apart.'

NOTES

1	to turn the grass:	to toss the cut grass so that it will dry
3	keen:	sharp-edged, eager
6	whetstone:	a stone used for sharpening edged tools by friction
23	scythe:	a long, curving, sharp-edged blade for mowing grass

EXPLORATIONS

First reading

1. Describe the scene in the first five couplets. What do you see? Who is present? What is he doing?

2. Explore the mood in these opening lines. How does the speaker feel? Do you think you would feel the same way?

3. How does the speaker feel after he discovers the butterfly weed? What words or phrases suggest a change in his mood?

4. According to the poem, why did the mower not cut these flowers?

5. What images or phrases caught your attention on a first reading? Why?

Second reading

6. In your opinion, what is the 'message from the dawn'?

7. What do you think the poet means when he says 'henceforth I worked no more alone'?

Third reading

8. Briefly outline the themes of this poem.

9. Shifts of mood and tone are marked by the word 'but'. Trace these changes in the poem.

10. The speaker describes the mower as a 'spirit kindred to my own'. In what sense is this true?

Fourth reading

11. Frost introduces the concept of 'turning' three times in the poem. Examine the changes that occur with each of them.

12. Follow the development of the main ideas. Examine the images that convey these ideas and state whether or not you find them effective.

13. 'Frost rejects ornate, poetic diction, preferring a language that is conversational and relaxed.' Examine Frost's use of language in the poem.

14. 'Frost's decision to write in conventional forms, using traditional rhythms and rhymes and syntax, reflects his belief that poetry should be accessible to the ordinary man.' Assess this poem in light of the above statement.

MENDING WALL

Something there is that doesn't love a wall,
That sends the frozen-ground-swell under it
And spills the upper boulders in the sun;
And makes gaps even two can pass abreast.
The work of hunters is another thing: 5
I have come after them and made repair
Where they have left not one stone on a stone,
But they would have the rabbit out of hiding,
To please the yelping dogs. The gaps I mean,
No one has seen them made or heard them made,   10
But at spring mending-time we find them there.
I let my neighbor know beyond the hill;
And on a day we meet to walk the line
And set the wall between us once again.
We keep the wall between us as we go.   15
To each the boulders that have fallen to each.
And some are loaves and some so nearly balls
We have to use a spell to make them balance:
'Stay where you are until our backs are turned!'
We wear our fingers rough with handling them.   20
Oh, just another kind of out-door game,
One on a side. It comes to little more:
There where it is we do not need the wall:
He is all pine and I am apple orchard.
My apple trees will never get across   25
And eat the cones under his pines, I tell him.
He only says, 'Good fences make good neighbours.'
Spring is the mischief in me, and I wonder
If I could put a notion in his head:
'Why do they make good neighbours? Isn't it   30
Where there are cows? But here there are no cows.
Before I built a wall I'd ask to know
What I was walling in or walling out,
And to whom I was like to give offence.
Something there is that doesn't love a wall,   35
That wants it down.' I could say 'Elves' to him,
But it's not elves exactly, and I'd rather
He said it for himself. I see him there
Bringing a stone grasped firmly by the top
In each hand, like an old-stone savage armed.   40
He moves in darkness as it seems to me,
Not of woods only and the shade of trees.
He will not go behind his father's saying,
And he likes having thought of it so well
He says again, 'Good fences make good neighbors.'   45

EXPLORATIONS

First reading

1. If you were asked to paint a picture based on this poem where would you place the wall and the two men? What are the men doing? Are they looking at each other? Describe their postures and their facial expressions. What other details would you include?

2. How are the gaps in the wall created?

3. What do you think the poet means when he describes wall–building as 'just another kind of outdoor game'?

4. Outline the arguments Frost uses against building walls.

Second reading

5. In what sense is the neighbour 'all pine and I am apple orchard'?

6. 'He moves in darkness'.
   What forms of darkness overshadow the neighbour?

7. Describe as clearly as possible your image of the neighbour as Frost portrays him.

Third reading

8. Walls unite and divide. How is this illustrated within the poem?

9. 'Good fences make good neighbors.' Do you think the speaker agrees with this proverb? Explain your answer.

10. The neighbour repeats the proverb because 'he likes having thought of it so well'. Why is this comment ironic?

11. What do we learn about the narrator's personality in the poem?

Fourth reading

12. What themes and issues are raised in this poem?

13. How does Frost achieve a sense of mystery in the poem? Are any of the images mysterious or magical? What effect do they have on the poem?

14. Follow the development of the main ideas. Examine the images that convey these ideas and state whether or not you find them effective.

15. This poem is concerned with unity and division, communication and isolation, hope and disappointment. Do you agree? Where are these tensions most obvious? Are they resolved at the end?

16. 'Human nature, not Mother Nature, is the main concern in Frost's poetry.' Would you agree with this statement based on your reading of this poem?

AFTER APPLE-PICKING

My long two-pointed ladder's sticking through a tree
Toward heaven still,
And there's a barrel that I didn't fill
Beside it, and there may be two or three
Apples I didn't pick upon some bough.　　　　　5
But I am done with apple-picking now.
Essence of winter sleep is on the night,
The scent of apples: I am drowsing off.
I cannot rub the strangeness from my sight
I got from looking through a pane of glass　　　10
I skimmed this morning from the drinking trough
And held against the world of hoary grass.
It melted, and I let it fall and break.
But I was well
Upon my way to sleep before it fell,　　　　　15
And I could tell
What form my dreaming was about to take.
Magnified apples appear and disappear,
Stem end and blossom end,
And every fleck of russet showing clear.　　　20
My instep arch not only keeps the ache,
It keeps the pressure of a ladder-round.
I feel the ladder sway as the boughs bend.
And I keep hearing from the cellar bin
The rumbling sound　　　　　　　　　　　　25
Of load on load of apples coming in.
For I have had too much
Of apple-picking: I am overtired
Of the great harvest I myself desired.
There were ten thousand thousand fruit to touch,　30
Cherish in hand, lift down, and not let fall.
For all
That struck the earth,
No matter if not bruised or spiked with stubble,
Went surely to the cider-apple heap　　　　　35
As of no worth.
One can see what will trouble
This sleep of mine, whatever sleep it is.
Were he not gone,
The woodchuck could say whether it's like his　　40
Long sleep, as I describe its coming on,
Or just some human sleep.

EXPLORATIONS

First reading

1. Imagine the orchard as Frost describes it in the opening lines. What details does he include? How would you describe the scene now that the apple-picking is over?

2. Explain in your own words what happened at the drinking trough in the morning.

3. Why did the apple-picker have to be so careful with the apples?

4. What connects the woodchuck and the harvester?

Second reading

5. The fruit has been harvested. How does the speaker feel now?

6. What is it that will trouble his sleep?

7. Select your favourite image in the poem and explain your choice.

8. Does the poet successfully capture the sensations of picking apples? Examine his use of images and the language used.

Third reading

9. There are moments of confusion in the poem. Is this deliberate? Why? Refer closely to the text in your answer.

10. In the poem, autumn is seen as a season of abundance rather than a time of decay. How does the poet re-create the richness of the harvest for the reader?

11. A dream-like quality pervades the poem. How is this achieved? Consider the language used, the imagery, descriptions, metre and rhyme.

Fourth reading

12. Frost's language is sensuously evocative and rich in imagery. Discuss his use of tactile, visual and auditory imagery in the poem as a whole.

13. What part do sounds and rhythm play in the creation of the mood in the poem?

14. Briefly explain your personal reaction to 'After Apple-Picking'.

THE ROAD NOT TAKEN

Two roads diverged in a yellow wood,
And sorry I could not travel both
And be one traveler, long I stood
And looked down one as far as I could
To where it bent in the undergrowth;   5

Then took the other, as just as fair,
And having perhaps the better claim,
Because it was grassy and wanted wear;
Though as for that, the passing there
Had worn them really about the same,   10

And both that morning equally lay
In leaves no step had trodden black.
Oh, I kept the first for another day!
Yet knowing how way leads on to way,
I doubted if I should ever come back.   15

I shall be telling this with a sigh
Somewhere ages and ages hence:
Two roads diverged in a wood, and I –
I took the one less traveled by,
And that has made all the difference.   20

EXPLORATIONS

First reading

1. On a first reading, what do you notice about the setting of the poem? What details made the deepest impression on you? Explain.

2. What is the main focus of the speaker's attention throughout the poem?

3. Why does he choose the second road? Are his reasons convincing?

4. Why will the speaker talk about this moment 'ages and ages hence'?

5. What is the difference referred to by Frost in the last line?

Second reading

6. Comment on the title of the poem. What does it lead you to expect? Does the poem fulfil your expectations?

7. On a surface level, the speaker is faced with a choice between two paths. On a deeper level, what do the roads symbolise?

8. What is the dominant mood of the poem? What words, phrases and images suggest this mood?

Third reading

9. What images create an autumnal atmosphere in the poem? Why did Frost choose this time of year?

10. What themes or issues can you identify in 'The Road Not Taken'?

11. Do you find the imagery in this poem effective in conveying the theme? Refer to specific images in your answer.

12. The poem opens and closes on a note of regret. Trace the development of thought and mood throughout the poem.

Fourth reading

13. Doubt is replaced by certainty in this poem. Examine the movement from one state to the other.

14. What appeals to you about this poem? Consider the theme, images, sounds and particular words or phrases in your answer.

BIRCHES

When I see birches bend to left and right
Across the lines of straighter darker trees,
I like to think some boy's been swinging them.
But swinging doesn't bend them down to stay
As ice storms do. Often you must have seen them   5
Loaded with ice a sunny winter morning
After a rain. They click upon themselves
As the breeze rises, and turn many-colored
As the stir cracks and crazes their enamel.
Soon the sun's warmth makes them shed crystal shells   10
Shattering and avalanching on the snow crust –
Such heaps of broken glass to sweep away
You'd think the inner dome of heaven had fallen.
They are dragged to the withered bracken by the load,
And they seem not to break; though once they are bowed   15
So low for long, they never right themselves:
You may see their trunks arching in the woods
Years afterwards, trailing their leaves on the ground
Like girls on hands and knees that throw their hair
Before them over their heads to dry in the sun.   20
But I was going to say when Truth broke in
With all her matter of fact about the ice storm,
I should prefer to have some boy bend them
As he went out and in to fetch the cows –
Some boy too far from town to learn baseball,   25
Whose only play was what he found himself,
Summer or winter, and could play alone.
One by one he subdued his father's trees
By riding them down over and over again
Until he took the stiffness out of them,   30
And not one but hung limp, not one was left
For him to conquer. He learned all there was
To learn about not launching out too soon
And so not carrying the tree away
Clear to the ground. He always kept his poise   35
To the top branches, climbing carefully
With the same pains you use to fill a cup
Up to the brim, and even above the brim.
Then he flung outward, feet first, with a swish,
Kicking his way down through the air to the ground.   40
So was I once myself a swinger of birches.
And so I dream of going back to be.

It's when I'm weary of considerations,
And life is too much like a pathless wood
Where your face burns and tickles with the cobwebs   45
Broken across it, and one eye is weeping
From a twig's having lashed across it open.
I'd like to get away from earth awhile
And then come back to it and begin over.
May no fate willfully misunderstand me   50
And half grant what I wish and snatch me away
Not to return. Earth's the right place for love:
I don't know where it's likely to go better.
I'd like to go by climbing a birch tree,
And climb black branches up a snow-white trunk   55
Toward heaven, till the tree could bear no more,
But dipped its top and set me down again.
That would be good both going and coming back.
One could do worse than be a swinger of birches.

EXPLORATIONS

Before reading

1. Have you ever climbed a tree? Discuss your experience, explaining where you were, how difficult it was and what skills you needed to climb up and down.

First reading

2. On a first reading, what do you see? Visualise the trees, the ice, the sky and the boy. What sounds can you hear? Are there any other details you should include?

3. What images caught your imagination?

4. How would you describe the general mood of the poem?

Second reading

5. Based on the details given by Frost, describe the character of the boy.

6. Would you agree that the boy is a skilled climber? What details support this point of view?

7. Do you think the speaker really intends to climb trees again? What makes him long to be a 'swinger of birches' once more?

8. What do you understand by the line 'And life is too much like a pathless wood'?

9. Is the speaker's wish to escape from earth a death wish? Explain your answer.

10. Explain clearly what you think Frost means in the last eight lines of the poem.

Third reading

11. Frost uses the image of girls drying their hair in the sun. Why? How effective is this image?

12. 'One could do worse than be a swinger of birches.'
    Does the poet present a convincing argument in support of this claim?

13. How does Frost achieve a conversational tone in the poem? Why does he adopt this voice?

Fourth reading

14. In what way do the boy's actions resemble those of a poet?

15. How does the music in the poem – sounds, metre, etc. – contribute to the atmosphere?

16. Comment on the poet's contrasting use of light and darkness.

17. 'Though much of Frost's poetry is concerned with suffering, he is also capable of capturing moments of unearthly beauty and joy in his work.'
    Comment on the poem in light of this statement.

'OUT, OUT—'

OL 20

OL 20

The buzz saw snarled and rattled in the yard
And made dust and dropped stove-length sticks of wood,
Sweet-scented stuff when the breeze drew across it.
And from there those that lifted eyes could count
Five mountain ranges one behind the other   5
Under the sunset far into Vermont.
And the saw snarled and rattled, snarled and rattled,
As it ran light, or had to bear a load.
And nothing happened: day was all but done.
Call it a day, I wish they might have said   10
To please the boy by giving him the half hour
That a boy counts so much when saved from work.
His sister stood beside them in her apron
To tell them 'Supper'. At the word, the saw,
As if to prove saws knew what supper meant,   15
Leaped out at the boy's hand, or seemed to leap –
He must have given the hand. However it was,
Neither refused the meeting. But the hand!
The boy's first outcry was a rueful laugh,
As he swung toward them holding up the hand   20
Half in appeal, but half as if to keep
The life from spilling. Then the boy saw all –
Since he was old enough to know, big boy
Doing a man's work, though a child at heart –
He saw all spoiled. 'Don't let him cut my hand off –   25
The doctor, when he comes. Don't let him, sister!'
So. But the hand was gone already.
The doctor put him in the dark of ether.
He lay and puffed his lips out with his breath.
And then – the watcher at his pulse took fright.   30
No one believed. They listened at his heart.
Little – less – nothing! – and that ended it.
No more to build on there. And they, since they
Were not the one dead, turned to their affairs.

NOTES

'Out, Out—':   the title is taken from William Shakespeare's famous tragedy, *Macbeth*: 'Out, Out brief candle; life's but a walking shadow, a poor player that struts and frets his hour upon the stage, and then is heard no more: it is a tale told by an idiot, full of sound and fury, signifying nothing.'

28   ether: an anaesthetic

EXPLORATIONS

First reading

1. Read the poem aloud. What words and phrases made the greatest impact on your ear? What animals are suggested in the opening line? How are these animals evoked?

2. Why does Frost describe the scenery?

3. Frost refers repeatedly to 'they' and 'them'. Who do you think these people are? What is your impression of them?

4. The poem turns on the word 'supper'. What happens? Is it an appropriate word in the context?

5. 'He saw all spoiled'. In what sense is all spoiled?

6. What is the boy's immediate fear? Refer to the poem to support your answer.

Second reading

7. Trace the narrative line in this poem. Were you surprised by the ending? Do you think it is an effective conclusion?

8. Comment on the title. Is it a suitable one? Could you suggest another?

9. 'Little – less – nothing!' Read this line aloud and comment on the rhythm. What is the effect of the exclamation mark?

Third reading

10. How effectively does the poet evoke the terror felt by the boy? Examine the techniques used by Frost in your answer.

11. Would you describe the poet as a detached or a sympathetic observer? Is he angered by the incident? How do we know? Comment on the tone.

12. How does the poet engage the reader's sympathies for the boy? Examine the details given, the use of emotive language and the comments made throughout the poem.

Fourth reading

13. What themes and issues are explored in the poem?

14. Sound plays an important role in the poem. Examine the use of assonance, alliteration and onomatopoeia in 'Out, Out—'.

15. 'In his poetry, Frost confronts the reader with the harsh realities of life.' Discuss this statement in light of your reading of this poem.

16. Identify and discuss some of the distinctive qualities of Frost's style that are evident in this poem.

SPRING POOLS

These pools that, though in forests, still reflect
The total sky almost without defect,
And like the flowers beside them, chill and shiver,
Will like the flowers beside them soon be gone,
And yet not out by any brook or river,   5
But up by roots to bring dark foliage on.

The trees that have it in their pent-up buds
To darken nature and be summer woods –
Let them think twice before they use their powers
To blot out and drink up and sweep away   10
These flowery waters and these watery flowers
From snow that melted only yesterday.

NOTE

6	foliage:	the leaves of a tree or plant

EXPLORATIONS

First reading

1. What do the pools and the flowers have in common?

2. What do you notice about the trees? What characteristic of the trees does the poet focus on, especially in the second stanza? Why?

3. Why should the trees think twice before they drain the pools and overshadow the flowers?

Second reading

4. Outline the argument of the poem. Would you agree that it is condensed with considerable skill? What is the effect of this on the reader?

5. What image made the greatest impression on you? Explain your choice.

6. How important are the sounds of words in creating the atmosphere in this poem?

Third reading

7. What mood is evoked by this scene? How is this mood created?

8. 'The beauty of this poem lies in the aptness of the descriptions and the clarity of the language.'
Do you agree? Explain your answer.

Fourth reading

9. Fragility and strength are contrasted in the poem. Where is this contrast most evident? What is the effect? How is this effect achieved?

10. Discuss the techniques Frost uses in this poem to depict the changing nature of the world. Support your answer by quotation or reference.

11. 'Frost is a master of the lyric form, his images are sensuous, his language clear and his tone controlled.'
Examine 'Spring Pools' in light of this statement.

12. Give your personal reaction to the poem.

ACQUAINTED WITH THE NIGHT

I have been one acquainted with the night.
I have walked out in rain – and back in rain.
I have outwalked the furthest city light.

I have looked down the saddest city lane.
I have passed by the watchman on his beat   5
And dropped my eyes, unwilling to explain.

I have stood still and stopped the sound of feet
When far away an interrupted cry
Came over houses from another street,

But not to call me back or say good-by;   10
And further still at an unearthly height,
One luminary clock against the sky

Proclaimed the time was neither wrong nor right.
I have been one acquainted with the night.

NOTE

12   luminary: something that gives light, especially a heavenly body

EXPLORATIONS

First reading

1. Describe the scene in your own words.

2. Examine the images used. What do they have in common? Do they provide an insight as to the central idea of the poem?

3. How would you describe the poet's mood?

Second reading

4. What do you think is the main theme of the poem? Explain your answer.

5. Do you think the imagery used is effective in illustrating the theme? Which images are most appropriate, in your opinion?

6. What feelings does the poem arouse in you? How does it do this?

Third reading

7. What do you notice about the verbs in the poem? What tense is it written in? What purpose might this serve?

8. This poem can be read at more than one level. Suggest another reading of 'Acquainted with the Night'.

Fourth reading

9. Note the repetitions in the poem. What effect do they have?

10. How does Frost evoke the atmosphere of the urban landscape?

11. There is a deep sense of isolation in this poem. Do you agree? Where is it most evident, in your opinion?

12. '"Acquainted With the Night" is a tribute to the triumph of the human spirit in the face of adversity, rather than a record of the defeat of the soul at its darkest hour.'
Discuss the poem in light of this statement.

DESIGN

I found a dimpled spider, fat and white,
On a white heal-all, holding up a moth
Like a white piece of rigid satin cloth –
Assorted characters of death and blight
Mixed ready to begin the morning right,   5
Like the ingredients of a witches' broth –
A snow-drop spider, a flower like a froth,
And dead wings carried like a paper kite.

What had that flower to do with being white,
The wayside blue and innocent heal-all?   10
What brought the kindred spider to that height,
Then steered the white moth thither in the night?
What but design of darkness to appall? –
If design govern in a thing so small.

NOTE

2   heal-all: a common flower used for medicinal purposes, usually blue or violet in
                      colour

EXPLORATIONS

First reading

1. What do you normally associate with the word 'dimpled'?

2. What images in the octave captured your attention? What do they suggest about the subject matter of the poem?

3. The poet raises several issues in the sestet. What are these issues and what conclusion, if any, does he reach?

4. Jot down the words or phrases that best describe your response to this poem on a first reading.

Second reading

5. How does the octet–sestet division mark the development of thought in the poem?

6. Describe the poet's mood in the sestet.

7. What is the effect of the scene on the speaker? Does he find it repulsive, horrifying, interesting, puzzling? Refer to the text to support your answer.

Third reading

8. Briefly outline the main argument in this poem.

9. Discuss the poet's use of colour.

10. Would you describe this as a nature poem? Explain your answer.

Fourth reading

11. What view of life and death is expressed in the poem? Where is this most evident?

12. Comment on the way the imagery in the poem forges the link between evil and beauty, innocence and death.

13. What is your own reaction to 'Design'?

14. Briefly compare the portrayal of nature in this poem with its portrayal in another poem by Frost on your course.

PROVIDE, PROVIDE

The witch that came (the withered hag)
To wash the steps with pail and rag
Was once the beauty Abishag,

The picture pride of Hollywood.
Too many fall from great and good   5
For you to doubt the likelihood.

Die early and avoid the fate.
Or if predestined to die late,
Make up your mind to die in state.

Make the whole stock exchange your own!   10
If need be occupy a throne,
Where nobody can call you crone.

Some have relied on what they knew,
Others on being simply true.
What worked for them might work for you.   15

No memory of having starred
Atones for later disregard
Or keeps the end from being hard.

Better to go down dignified
With boughten friendship at your side   20
Than none at all. Provide, provide!

NOTES

1	hag:	an ugly old woman, a witch
3	Abishag:	(I Kings 1:2-4) 'Having searched for a beautiful girl throughout the territory of Israel, they found Abishag of Shunem and brought her to the king. The girl was of great beauty. She looked after the king and waited on him …'
12	crone:	a withered old woman

EXPLORATIONS

Before reading

1. Read the title only. Jot down what you imagine the poem is about before reading the poem itself.

First reading

2. The idea that youth rapidly fades is introduced in the opening stanza. What images convey this?

3. What advice does Frost offer as to how to avoid the worst aspects of old age?

4. How can one avoid being called a 'crone'?

5. Imagine you are the old woman in the poem. Write your response to 'Provide, Provide'.

Second reading

6. Can memories offer comfort to the old?

7. Has 'boughten friendship' any advantages according to the poet? What is his tone here?

8. What do you think is meant by the title of the poem?

Third reading

9. Is the poem intended to teach us a lesson? Comment on the moral.

10. Do you think Frost is being serious or humorous here? Examine the tone throughout the poem.

Fourth reading

11. Do you think there is an important theme in the poem? Explain your answer.

12. Examine the contrasts in the poem. State what they are and whether or not you think they are effective.

13. Did you enjoy this poem? Why?

14. 'Realism rather than pessimism is a hallmark of Frost's poetry.' Discuss this statement in light of your reading of this poem.

DAVID HERBERT
LAWRENCE

(1885–1930)

Prescribed for Higher Level exams in 2019, 2020, 2022

David Herbert Lawrence was born in 1885 in the coal-mining town of Eastwood, Nottinghamshire England. The son of a coal miner, Lawrence had always been a sickly child. He had missed a lot of school in his childhood due to illness but still managed to gain a scholarship to Nottingham High School in 1898.

By 1901 he was working as a junior clerk in Haywood's surgical appliance factory but this ended with a severe bout of pneumonia. He began writing poetry around this time and started drafts of some of his published early work. Between 1902 and 1906 he worked as a pupil-teacher at the British School in Eastwood and in 1908 received his teaching Certificate from University College Nottingham. He then moved to Croydon in London to start his first teaching job. In 1910 Lawrence's first novel, *The White Peacock*, was published, but this was also the year his mother died, which had a profound impact on the writer. After another bout of pneumonia, he eventually abandoned teaching to be a full-time writer.

Lawrence had numerous romantic entanglements in his early twenties, including a brief engagement to Louie Burrows. In 1912 he was introduced to Frieda Weekley, *nee* von Richthofen, the wife of his former university professor, Ernest Weekley, with whom she had three young children. Six years his senior, Frieda made a big impression on the young writer and after an exchange of letters and an intense affair, they ran away to Germany together. Their time in Europe was spent travelling from place to place, starting in Germany, moving through the Alps and into Italy. They eventually returned to England and settled in Cornwall for a time. They were married in 1914.

Following the success of his next novel *Sons and Lovers*, which was published in 1913 to excellent reviews *The Rainbow* was published in 1915. However, it was very quickly condemned by reviewers due to its frank descriptions of sexual desires. By November the publishers were prosecuted on an obscenity charge and remaining copies of the book were seized and burned. For the young Lawrence this was a devastating blow. The possibility of publishing future novels was now doubtful and publishers rejected his works of fiction. In 1917 he managed to publish *Look! We have come through!* a collection of poetry that charted his life with Frieda, and he followed this with a number of short stories.

Once the war ended, the couple left England and started their years of exile. They travelled through Italy, Sardinia, Switzerland and settled for a brief time in Taormina in Sicily. It was during this time that he wrote many of the poems that became *Birds, Beasts and Flowers* (1923) including 'Snake' and 'The Mosquito'. His next novel, *Women in Love*, was published in 1920 with numerous edits and revisions demanded by the publishers. Lawrence foresaw that his work would never be well received in England and set his sights on America. The Lawrences travelled to Ceylon (Sri-Lanka) and Australia before settling for a time in Taos, New Mexico.

His relationship with Frieda was tempestuous and they were both known for their infidelities. They had numerous arguments that sometimes resulted in brief separations.

From 1924 onwards, Lawrence's health increasingly deteriorated. He was diagnosed with tuberculosis and in early 1925 suffered from a combination of typhoid, malaria and influenza. When he had sufficiently recovered the couple returned to Europe and settled in Italy. By 1926 Lawrence had started what became his most famous novel, *Lady Chatterley's Lover*, and had also started painting. His paintings were exhibited in the Warren Gallery in London in the summer of 1929. However, the gallery was raided by policemen in July and thirteen of the paintings were seized on the grounds of obscenity. Lawrence was outraged and started a collection of poetry called *Nettles*, which consisted of a series of stinging attacks on the perceived hypocrisy. A heavily censored version of *Lady Chatterley's Lover* was published in America in 1928 and in Britain in 1932 after the author's death, but the full version of the text was banned until 1960.

Lawrence's health continued to decline and he eventually agreed to be admitted to a sanatorium in Vence, France. But, in typical Lawrence style, when he failed to recover he discharged himself, refusing to succumb to the pressure of his illness. He decided to die as he lived, on his own terms. Under the care of Frieda and a nurse, Lawrence died on 2 March 1930, aged 44.

CALL INTO DEATH

Since I lost you, my darling, the sky has come near,
And I am of it, the small sharp stars are quite near,
The white moon going among them like a white bird
    among snow-berries,
And the sound of her gently rustling in heaven like a
    bird I hear.

And I am willing to come to you now, my dear,   5
As a pigeon lets itself off from a cathedral dome
To be lost in the haze of the sky; I would like to come
And be lost out of sight with you, like a melting foam.

For I am tired, my dear, and if I could lift my feet,
My tenacious feet, from off the dome of the earth   10
To fall like a breath within the breathing wind
Where you are lost, what rest, my love, what rest!

NOTES

3	snow-berries:	species of honeysuckle shrub with white berries
10	tenacious:	keep ng a firm grip, not easily letting go

EXPLORATIONS

First reading

1. What does the title of the poem 'Call into Death' suggest to you? Who could be calling? Is it a fearful call?

2. What are the initial feelings of the poet? Do they change as the poem progresses? What words or phrases suggest the mood of the poet?

3. What images stand out to you in the poem? What do they suggest to you? Can you think why the poet might have chosen them?

Second reading

4. What do you think are Lawrence's views on death as revealed in this poem?

5. Lawrence uses contrasting images to illustrate tension. Identify some of those images and outline the tensions they reveal.

6. What does the poet miss about his mother? What words or phrases in the poem suggest this to you?

Third reading

7. The language of the poem is deceptively simple, belying the depth of the themes explored. Write a paragraph on Lawrence's use of language in this poem.

8. Death, love and loss are central to this poem. How does Lawrence explore these themes here? How is this similar to or different from other poems by Lawrence you have studied?

PIANO

Softly, in the dusk, a woman is singing to me;
Taking me back down the vista of years, till I see
A child sitting under the piano, in the boom of the tingling strings
And pressing the small, poised feet of a mother who smiles as she sings.

In spite of myself, the insidious mastery of song   5
Betrays me back, till the heart of me weeps to belong
To the old Sunday evenings at home, with winter outside
And hymns in the cosy parlour, the tinkling piano our guide.

So now it is vain for the singer to burst into clamour
With the great black piano appassionato. The glamour   10
Of childish days is upon me, my manhood is cast
Down in the flood of remembrance, I weep like a child for the past.

'Sous la Table' (Under the table) by Chantal Roux (2015)

NOTES

2	vista:	a distant view, or broad expanse
4	poised:	graceful, elegant
5	insidious:	deceptive, cunning, manipulative
10	appassionato:	musical term: with passion or great feeling
10	glamour:	appealing or attractive but can also mean bewitched or enchanted

EXPLORATIONS

First reading

1. Have you ever had the experience of a piece of music sparking a vivid memory? How did it make you feel?

2. What does the word 'dusk' make you think of?

3. What image from his childhood is the poet reminded of by the music?

4. How does the poet envision his mother? What words or phrases stand out in his description?

5. How does the poet create a sense of a home in the second stanza?

6. How has his recollection of the past affected the poet in the last stanza?

Second reading

7. How does the poet create the sense of the child's perspective in the first stanza?

8. Reread the second stanza. What words or phrases suggest that he is not comfortable with this return to memory?

9. What contrasting images does Lawrence utilise in the poem to show the contrast and tensions between the past and present?

10. Read the poem aloud and note where the line pauses and where the rhyme and rhythm have an impact on how the line is said. What effect does the changing rhythm and rhyme have on the poem?

Third reading

11. In your opinion, is this a poem about nostalgia, loss or something else? What words or phrases in the poem support this view?

12. What insight into the poet have you gained from this poem?

13. As a poet, Lawrence can capture the universality of emotion while focusing on a personal moment. How well do you think this poem exemplifies this trait?

THE MOSQUITO

When did you start your tricks,
Monsieur?

What do you stand on such high legs for?
Why this length of shredded shank,
You exaltation?   5

Is it so that you shall lift your centre of gravity upwards
And weigh no more than air as you alight upon me,
Stand upon me weightless, you phantom?

I heard a woman call you the Winged Victory
In sluggish Venice.   10
You turn your head towards your tail, and smile.

How can you put so much devilry
Into that translucent phantom shred
Of a frail corpus?

Queer, with your thin wings and streaming legs,   15
How you sail like a heron, or a dull clot of air,
A nothingness.

Yet what an aura surrounds you;
Your evil little aura, prowling, and casting a numbness on my mind.

That is your trick, your bit of filthy magic: 20
Invisibility, and the anaesthetic power
To deaden my attention in your direction.

But I know your game now, streaky sorcerer.
Queer, how you stalk and prowl the air
In circles and evasions, enveloping me,   25
Ghoul on wings
Winged Victory.

Settle and stand on long thin shanks
Eyeing me sideways, and cunningly conscious that I am aware,
You speck.   30

I hate the way you lurch off sideways into the air
Having read my thoughts against you.

Come then, let us play at unawares,
And see who wins in this sly game of bluff.
Man or mosquito.   35

You don't know that I exist, and I don't know that you exist.
Now then!

It is your trump,
It is your hateful little trump,
You pointed fiend,   40
Which shakes my sudden blood hatred of you:
It is your small, high, hateful, bugle in my ear.

Why do you do it?
Surely it is bad policy.

They say you can't help it.   45

If that is so, then I believe a little in Providence protecting the innocent.
But it sounds so amazingly like a slogan,
A yell of triumph as you snatch my scalp.

Blood, red blood
Super-magical   50
Forbidden liquor.

I behold you stand
For a second enspasmed in oblivion,
Obscenely ectasied
Sucking live blood,   55
My blood.

Such silence, such suspended transport,
Such gorging,
Such obscenity of trespass.

You stagger   60
As well you may.
Only your accused hairy frailty,
Your own imponderable weightlessness
Saves you, wafts you away on the very draught my anger makes in its snatching.

Away with a paean of derision,   65
You winged blood-drop.

Can I not overtake you?
Are you one too many for me,
Winged Victory?
Am I not mosquito enough to out-mosquito you?   70

Queer, what a big stain my sucked blood makes
Beside the infinitesimal faint smear of you!
Queer, what a dim dark smudge you have disappeared into!

Siracusa

NOTES

4	shank:	part of the leg between the knee and ankle, but also can refer to part of an implement like a knife
5	exaltation:	raising someone in power or rank or extreme happiness.
9	Winged Victory:	Refers to a statue the Winged Victory of Samothrace (c.220–185 BC; pictured) now in the Louvre. The statue is of a winged female figure – the messenger goddess Victory (or Nike) and a base in the shape of the prow of a ship on a pedestal. The statue is missing several features including its head, which means the shape now resembles that of the mosquito. In Greek mythology, Victory spread the news of victory in athletic competition or battle and brought the victor his crown. Once on earth she participated in the libation or sacrifice made by the victor to the gods.
38	trump:	can mean to trumpet or make a loud sound; in a card game the trump is the suit which is required to win but it also can refer to a winning move or final resource
46	Providence:	manifestation of the protective care of God
65	paean:	a song of praise or victory

EXPLORATIONS

First reading

1. What do you think about when you read the title of the poem? What emotions, memories, sights and sounds do you think of when imagining a mosquito?

2. Why do you think the poet calls the mosquito 'Monsieur'?

3. Why does he compare the mosquito to the statue Winged Victory (see picture)?

4. What words or phrases in the poem suggest that the mosquito is supernatural?

5. What do you think the poet's feelings are towards the mosquito throughout the poem? What words or phrases in the poem suggest this? Do his feelings change as the poem progresses?

Second reading

6. How does the poet build the tension between himself and the mosquito?

7. The poet focuses on sounds and imagery throughout the poem. Identify some of the more striking sounds and images. How do these sounds and imagery add to the impact of the poem?

8. The physical aspects of the mosquito hold a fascination for the poet. How does Lawrence detail the physical aspects throughout these poem? How do they reveal his attitude to the mosquito?

9. The battle between poet and insect is built to an epic scale. What techniques does the poet use to create this effect? Do you think he is entirely serious in displaying this in such a manner or has his anger escalated to such an extent that it is now epic?

10. The bite of the mosquito is graphically depicted. What words or phrases stand out to you in this depiction? What do they suggest to you?

11. Who is ultimately victorious in this battle? Explain your answer.

Third reading

12. How does the structure of this poem reflect the subject matter?

13. Do you think this poem may represent more than just a battle with a mosquito? If so, what?

14. What does this poem reveal about the character of Lawrence? How does this fit with the impression you have of him from your reading of his other poems on the course?

The Winged Victory of Samothrace (c.220–185 BCE), on display in the Louvre

SNAKE

A snake came to my water-trough
On a hot, hot day, and I in pyjamas for the heat,
To drink there.

In the deep, strange-scented shade of the great dark carob-tree
I came down the steps with my pitcher   5
And must wait, must stand and wait, for there he was at the trough before me.

He reached down from a fissure in the earth-wall in the gloom
And trailed his yellow-brown slackness soft-bellied down, over the edge of the stone
    trough
And rested his throat upon the stone bottom,
And where the water had dripped from the tap, in a small clearness,   10
He sipped with his straight mouth,
Softly drank through his straight gums, into his slack long body,
Silently.

Someone was before me at my water-trough,
And I, like a second comer, waiting.   15

He lifted his head from his drinking, as cattle do,
And looked at me vaguely, as drinking cattle do,
And flickered his two-forked tongue from his lips, and mused a moment,
And stooped and drank a little more,
Being earth-brown, earth-golden from the burning bowels of the earth   20
On the day of the Sicilian July, with Etna smoking.

The voice of my education said to me
He must be killed,
For in Sicily the black, black snakes are innocent, the gold are venomous.

And voices in me said, If you were a man   25
You would take a stick and break him now, and finish him off.

But must I confess how I liked him,
How glad I was he had come like a guest in quiet, to drink at my water-trough
And depart peaceful, pacified, and thankless,
Into the burning bowels of this earth?   30

Was it cowardice, that I dared not kill him?
Was it perversity, that I longed to talk to him?
Was it humility, to feel so honoured?
I felt so honoured.

And yet those voices: 35
If you were not afraid, you would kill him!

And truly I was afraid, I was most afraid,
But even so, honoured still more
That he should seek my hospitality
From out the dark door of the secret earth.   40

He drank enough
And lifted his head, dreamily, as one who has drunken,
And flickered his tongue like a forked night on the air, so black,
Seeming to lick his lips,
And looked around like a god, unseeing, into the air,   45
And slowly turned his head,
And slowly, very slowly, as if thrice adream,
Proceeded to draw his slow length curving round
And climb again the broken bank of my wall-face.

And as he put his head into that dreadful hole,   50
And as he slowly drew up, snake-easing his shoulders, and entered farther,
A sort of horror, a sort of protest against his withdrawing into that horrid black hole,
Deliberately going into the blackness, and slowly drawing himself after,
Overcame me now his back was turned.

I looked around, I put down my pitcher,   55
I picked up a clumsy log
And threw it at the water-trough with a clatter.

I think it did not hit him,
But suddenly that part of him that was left behind convulsed in undignified haste,
Writhed like lightning, and was gone   60
Into the black hole, the earth-lipped fissure in the wall-front,
At which, in the intense still noon, I stared with fascination.

And immediately I regretted it.
I thought how paltry, how vulgar, what a mean act!
I despised myself and the voices of my accursed human education.   65

And I thought of the albatross,
And I wished he would come back, my snake.

For he seemed to me again like a king,
Like a king in exile, uncrowned in the underworld,
Now due to be crowned again.   70
And so, I missed my chance with one of the lords
Of life.

And I have something to expiate;
A pettiness.

Taormina

NOTES

| 21 | Etna: | Mount Etna, active volcano on the east coast of Sicily |
| 73 | expiate: | to make amends, to pay the penalty for something |

EXPLORATIONS

First reading

1. The poem describes a simple event. Outline what happens in the poem in a few sentences.

2. What does the poet feel at the sight of the snake? How does he convey his emotions?

3. How is the movement of the snake described by the poet?

4. What do the voices in his head tell him to do?

5. Why does the poet regret his actions?

Second reading

6. The poem was written in Taormina in Sicily. How does the poet convey a sense of place in the poem?

7. The poet reveals his thought process while deciding how to respond to the snake. What does this process reveal about the poet? Support your answer with details from the poem.

8. How does the structure reflect the action of the poem?

9. The most famous story involving a meeting of a man and a snake is the biblical story of Adam and Eve and their exile from the Garden of Eden. How does 'Snake' reflect this biblical story? What aspects are similar or different?

Third reading

10. The voices in his head tell the poet he should kill the snake. How does Lawrence explore the idea of social conditioning (or doing what society expects you to do) in this poem?

11. The poet says 'If you were a man you would take a stick and break him now, and finish him off.'
What does this reveal about society's views of masculinity? How does Lawrence react to this view?

12. How does Lawrence's views on masculinity here reflect the views expressed in some of his other poems you have studied?

13. The imagery in this poem is very sensual. Write a note on Lawrence's use of imagery in this poem.

HUMMING-BIRD

I can imagine, in some otherworld
Primeval-dumb, far back
In that most awful stillness, that only gasped and hummed,
Humming-birds raced down the avenues.

Before anything had a soul, 5
While life was a heave of Matter, half inanimate,
This little bit chipped off in brilliance
And went whizzing through the slow, vast, succulent stems.

I believe there were no flowers then,
In the world where the humming-bird flashed ahead of creation. 10
I believe he pierced the slow vegetable veins with his long beak.

Probably he was big
As mosses, and little lizards, they say, were once big.
Probably he was a jabbing, terrifying monster.

We look at him through the wrong end of the long telescope of Time, 15
Luckily for us.

Española

NOTE

2   Primeval-dumb: relating to the earliest stages of the world or human history, ancient

EXPLORATIONS

First reading

1. Find a clip of a humming-bird in flight. What characteristics of the bird stand out?

2. What words or phrases would you use to describe the bird? Are any of your choices similar to those used by the poet?

3. The poet imagines what the world looked like millions of years ago when creatures were beginning to evolve. What strikes you about his description?

Second reading

4. How does the poet describe the flight of the bird?

5. What do you think the poem means by 'Before anything had a soul'?

6. How does the poet use contrast throughout the poem? What effect does this have?

7. How could the humming-bird be described as 'a jabbing, terrifying monster'?

8. What impact do the last two lines of the poem have on the rest of the poem?

Third reading

9. How could the humming-bird represent creativity for the poet? What words or images in the poem might support this view?

10. How does the structure of the poem reflect the world he is depicting? Look in particular at the length of the lines and the way the rhythm varies. Read the poem aloud to help to identify the stresses and pauses.

11. What does this poem reveal Lawrence's attitude towards the natural world?

Personal response

12. You decide to create a short video to capture the mood of this poem for YouTube. Describe how you might use setting, lighting, soundtrack, music, etc. to communicate the mood clearly. Explain your choices based on your knowledge of the poem.

INTIMATES

Don't you care for my love? she said bitterly.

I handed her the mirror, and said:
Please address these questions to the proper person!
Please make all requests to head-quarters!
In all matters of emotional importance   5
please approach the supreme authority direct!
So I handed her the mirror.

And she would have broken it over my head,
but she caught sight of her own reflection
and that held her spellbound for two seconds   10
while I fled.

EXPLORATIONS

First reading

1. What is your initial reaction to the events in this poem?

2. Who do you think is speaking? What relationship do they have?

3. The mirror is often used as a literary device to symbolise other things. What might the mirror symbolise here?

4. Look again at the title. How does this reflect the events in the poem?

Second reading

5. What is the poet suggesting about vanity?

6. Is there a serious undertone here regarding the need to reflect on yourself first in a relationship?

7. What impact does the rhyming scheme and rhythm have on this poem?

8. What words or images stand out for you in this poem? Explain your choices.

Third reading

9. Do you think this poem is Lawrence reflecting on his own relationship or could he be reflecting on society in general? Explain your answer.

10. What does this poem reveal about the poet? Explain your answer.

11. Imagine you are the woman in this poem. What might your reaction to the poem be?

12. What message could this poem hold for a generation obsessed with social media?

DELIGHT OF BEING ALONE

I know no greater delight than the sheer delight of being alone.
It makes me realise the delicious pleasure of the moon
that she has in travelling by herself: throughout time,
or the splendid growing of an ash-tree
alone, on a hill-side in the north, humming in the wind.   5

EXPLORATIONS

First reading

1.   Is being alone usually described as being a 'sheer delight'? What are the usual words associated with being alone? How are these different to Lawrence's interpretation?

2.   Are there times you like being alone? What is it about being alone that is appealing?

3.   The moon is often used as a symbol in poetry. Can you think of other poems where the moon is used as a symbol? What is associated with the moon?

4.   What does the phrase 'the splendid growing of an ash-tree' suggest to you?

Second reading

5.   Lawrence uses many words in the poem to show his delight in being alone, 'sheer delight', 'no greater delight' and 'delicious pleasure'. What effect do these words have on the poem?

6.   How is the image of the ash tree different to the other images in the poem? What do you think Lawrence might have meant by it?

7.   What other contrasts can be found in the poem? What effect do they have?

Third reading

8.   What does this poem reveal about the poet? How is this similar to or different from his earlier poems?

9.   Comment on the poet's use of symbolism in the poem.

10. What are the emotions expressed in this poem? How has the poet displayed these emotions?

11. Are there elements of Lawrence's style evident here that you have found in his other poems? Explain.

ABSOLUTE REVERENCE

I feel absolute reverence to nobody and to nothing human
neither to persons nor things nor ideas, ideals nor religions nor institutions,
to these things I feel only respect, and a tinge of reverence
when I see the fluttering of pure life in them.

But to something unseen, unknown, creative   5
from which I feel I am a derivative
I feel absolute reverence. Say no more!

NOTES

| 1 | reverence: | deep respect for someone or something |
| 6 | derivative: | based on another source, imitates something else |

EXPLORATIONS

First reading

1. What does the title suggest to you? What might you associate these words with?

2. Examine the list of things Lawrence feels no reverence for in lines 1 and 2. Do you think they demand reverence?

3. Are there institutions or people or ideas that you revere? What inspires this reverence?

4. What is the difference between reverence and respect? Why does Lawrence make that distinction?

5. What is his attitude towards creativity?

Second reading

6. What do you think he means by 'the fluttering of pure life'?

7. The word 'derivative' is often used as an insult to artists, meaning that they are mere copies of a greater artist and lack originality. Why do you think Lawrence refers to himself as derivative?

8. What effect does the exclamation 'Say no more!' have on the poem?

Third reading

9. What impact does the structure, including the line length and use of enjambment, have on the poem?

10. Would you consider this a protest poem? If so, to whom or about what is Lawrence protesting?

11. How would you describe the tone of this poem?

WHAT HAVE THEY DONE TO YOU?

What have they done to you, men of the masses, creeping back and forth to work?

What have they done to you, the saviours of the people, oh what have they saved you
   from, while they pocketed the money?

Alas, they have saved you from yourself, from your own frail dangers
and devoured you with the machine, the vast maw of iron.

They saved you from your squalid cottages and poverty of hand to mouth   5
and embedded you in workmen's dwellings, where your wage is the dole of work,
   and the dole is your wage of nullity.

They took away, oh they took away your man's native instincts and intuitions
   and gave you a board-school education, newspapers, and the cinema.

They stole your body from you, and left you an animated carcass
to work with, and nothing else: 10
unless goggling eyes, to goggle at the film
and a board-school brain, stuffed up with the ha'penny press.

Your instincts gone, your intuitions gone, your passions dead
Oh carcass with a board-school mind and a ha'penny newspaper intelligence,
what have they done to you, what have they done to you, Oh what have they
   done to you?   15

Oh look at my fellow-men, oh look at them
the masses! Oh, what has been done to them?

NOTES

4	maw:	the gaping, mouth and throat of a greedy animal
6	dole:	modern meaning is a state benefit given to the unemployed, which was introduced by the British government in 1918, but can also mean one's lot or destiny, to dole out is to distribute or share out portions
6	nullity:	of no importance or worth
9	carcass:	the remains of a dead animal, a dead body
12	Ha'penny press:	short for halfpenny, cheap press (newspapers)

EXPLORATIONS

First reading

1. What images are conjured up by the poet in the first line? How do you think he feels about what he sees? What gives you that impression?

2. Who do you think the poet is addressing in the poem?

3. From reading the third stanza, how does the poet feel about industrialisation and mechanisation?

4. What was life like for workers before the factories? Is life any better now?

5. What is the poet's attitude towards 'board-school education, newspapers and the cinema'? What words or phrases in the poem give you that impression?

6. Why might board-school education, newspapers and the cinema be viewed as negative? What are the modern equivalents?

Second reading

7. Who does 'they' represent in the poem? What is the poet's attitude towards them? How is it expressed?

8. Look at the use of repetition in the poem. What effect does it have? How does it contribute to the tone?

9. How does the use repetition reflect factory life?

Third reading

10. This poem was written in 1929 when Lawrence was gravely ill. How might this context have influenced his writing? Explain your answer.

11. The theme of man in conflict with machine has been explored by many writers. Does Lawrence hold any hope for man in this exploration? Explain your answer.

BABY-MOVEMENTS II, "TRAILING CLOUDS"

As a drenched, drowned bee
Hangs numb and heavy from the bending flower,
     So clings to me,
My baby, her brown hair brushed with wet tears
     And laid laughterless on her cheek,   5
Her soft white legs hanging heavily over my arm
     Swinging to my lullaby.
My sleeping baby hangs upon my life
     As a silent bee at the end of a shower
     Draws down the burdened flower.   10
She who has always seemed so light
     Sways on my arm like sorrowful, storm-heavy boughs,
Even her floating hair sinks like storm-bruised young leaves
Reaching downwards:
     As the wings of a drenched, drowned bee   15
     Are a heaviness, and a weariness.

NOTE

"Trailing Clouds":	The title of this poem is a quote from the Wordsworth poem 'Ode: Intimations of Immortality from Recollections of Early Childhood' (1804). In this poem Wordsworth, in a very stylised format, asserts that children possess a divine wisdom that adults no longer have. The poem charts the journey from the joy of childhood to the limitations of adulthood. The full quote reads: 'But trailing clouds of glory do we come/From God, who is out home: Heaven lies about us in our infancy'

EXPLORATIONS

First reading

1. The poem begins with a simile. How is the child compared to the bee?

2. Describe the simple scene depicted in the poem.

3. What features of the child are emphasised in the poem? Why do you think Lawrence does this?

4. Identify some of the repeated images used by Lawrence in the poem. What effect do they have?

Second reading

5. Read the poem aloud. How do the run-on lines and pauses emphasise certain aspects of the poem?

6. Throughout the poem, Lawrence uses alliterative phrases (where words in a phrase begin with the same letter). Why do you think he places stresses on these phrases? What impact does it have?

7. This poem was written early in Lawrence's career, what aspects of his early style are evident here?

Third reading

8. The title is taken from a Wordsworth poem that asserts that children are closer to God than adults. What elements of childhood innocence and divinity can be found in this poem?

9. In your opinion, what does the bee symbolise in the poem?

10. What is revealed about Lawrence's personality in this poem? Explain your answer.

Personal reading

11. You decide to create a short video to capture the mood of this poem for YouTube. Describe how you might use setting, lighting, soundtrack, music, etc. to communicate the mood clearly. Explain your choices based on your knowledge of the poem.

12. Imagine you are Lawrence. Write a letter to the baby of the poem, now that she has grown up, detailing what you remember about the incident.

BAVARIAN GENTIANS

Not every man has gentians in his house
In soft September, at slow, sad Michaelmas.
Bavarian gentians, tall and dark, but dark
darkening the daytime torch-like with the smoking blueness of Pluto's gloom,
ribbed hellish flowers erect, with their blaze of darkness spread blue   5
blown flat into points, by the heavy white draught of the day.

Torch-flowers of the blue-smoking darkness, Pluto's dark-blue blaze
black lamps from the halls of Dis, smoking dark blue
giving off darkness, blue darkness, upon Demeter's yellow-pale day
whom have you come for, here in the white-cast day?   10

Reach me a gentian, give me a torch!
let me guide myself with the blue, forked torch of a flower
down the darker and darker stairs, where blue is darkened on blueness
down the way Persephone goes, just now, in first-frosted September,
to the sightless realm where darkness is married to dark,   15
and Persephone herself is but a voice, as a bride,
a gloom invisible enfolded in the deeper dark
of the arms of Pluto as he ravishes her once again
and pierces her once more with his passion of the utter dark
among the splendour of black-blue torches, shedding fathomless darkness
   on the nuptials.   20

Give me a flower on a tall stem, and three dark flames,
for I will go to the wedding, and be wedding-guest
at the marriage of the living dark.

NOTES

Bavarian Gentians:		Small blue trumpet-shaped flower
2	Michaelmas:	feast of St Michael, 29 September
4	Pluto:	Greek god of the underworld, sometimes called Hades
8	Dis:	short for *Dis Pater*, Roman god of riches and ruler of the underworld (a place where the gods went to await spring)
9	Demeter:	Greek goddess associated with fertility and grain, corn and the harvest, mother of Persephone
14	Persephone:	Greek goddess and Queen of the underworld, daughter of Zeus and Demeter. She was abducted to the underworld by Pluto and tricked into eating pomegranate seeds, which obliged her to return to the underworld for four months each year to be with Pluto. While in the underworld, the earth could not grow and produce crops (winter). Her return to the earth marked a time of rebirth and growth (spring).

EXPLORATIONS

First reading

1. Examine the image of the Bavarian Gentians flower. Try to accurately describe it.

2. Read the first two stanzas. How does your description of the flower echo Lawrence's?

3. Describe the atmosphere created by the rhyming couplet at the beginning of the poem.

4. How does Lawrence develop this atmosphere as the poem progresses? What words or phrases help to create this atmosphere?

Second reading

5. The poem describes a journey into the underworld. Does the poet seem scared or determined throughout the poem? Do his emotions change?

6. Flowers are often used as symbols in poetry. What does the image of this flower mean to Lawrence in this poem?

7. Read the poem aloud. How does the line structure and rhythm add to the atmosphere and tone of the poem?

8. Identify the numerous references to light and darkness in the poem. What do you think Lawrence is trying to suggest by this?

9. What other contrasts can be found in the poem?

Third reading

10. This poem was written in the last year of his life, when Lawrence knew he was approaching death. What do you think his views on death are based on your reading of the poem?

11. Mythology is often used in poetry to bring a personal experience greater universal significance. Do you think the use of the Persephone myth has that impact here or does the poem remain entirely personal?

12. Death is the end of the physical being. How does Lawrence focus on the loss of physicality in the poem?

ELIZABETH
BISHOP

(1911–79)

Prescribed for Higher Level exams in 2019, 2021 and 2022

Elizabeth Bishop was born on 8 February 1911 in Worcester, Massachusetts. Her father died when she was eight months old. Her mother never recovered from the shock and for the next five years was in and out of mental hospitals. In 1916 she was institutionalised and separated from her daughter, whom she was never to see again – she died in 1934.

Elizabeth was reared for the most part by her grandparents in Great Village, Nova Scotia. The elegy 'First Death in Nova Scotia' draws on some childhood memories. 'Sestina' also evokes the sadness of this period. Yet her recollections of her Nova Scotia childhood were essentially positive and she had great affection for her maternal grandparents, aunts and uncles in this small agricultural village.

She went to boarding school and then attended Vassar College, a private university in New York, from 1930 to 1934. She graduated in English literature (but also took Greek and music), always retaining a particular appreciation for Renaissance lyric poetry and for the works of Gerard Manley Hopkins. It was at Vassar that she first began to publish stories and poems in national magazines and where she met the poet Marianne Moore, who became an important influence on her career as a poet and with whom she maintained a lifelong friendship and correspondence. It was also at Vassar that she formed her first lesbian relationship, and here too, on her own admission, her lifelong problem with alcohol addiction began.

In 1939 she moved to Key West, Florida, a place she had fallen in love with over the previous years. 'The Fish' reflects her enjoyment of the sport of fishing at that time. Key West became a sort of refuge and base for Bishop over the next fifteen years. In 1945 she won the Houghton Mifflin Poetry Award. In 1946 her first book of poetry, *North and South*, was published and was well received by the critics. 'The Fish' is among its thirty poems.

The years 1945 to 1951, when her life was centred on New York, were very unsettled. She felt under extreme pressure in a very competitive literary circle and drank heavily. 'The Bight' and 'The Prodigal' reflect this dissolute period of her life.

In 1951 she left for South America on the first stage of a writer's trip round the world. She was fascinated by Brazil and by Lota Soares, on old acquaintance with whom she began a relationship that was to last until the latter's death in 1967. 'Questions of Travel' and 'The Armadillo' reflect this period of her life. In 1970 she was appointed poet in residence at Harvard, where she taught advanced verse writing and studies in modern poetry for her first year and, later, poets and their letters. She began to do a good many public readings of her poetry to earn a living. She continued to do public readings, punctuated by spells in hospital with asthma, alcoholism and depression. She died suddenly of a brain aneurysm on 6 October 1979.

THE FISH

OL 2019
OL 2021
OL 2022

I caught a tremendous fish
and held him beside the boat
half out of water, with my hook
fast in a corner of his mouth.
He didn't fight.   5
He hadn't fought at all.
He hung a grunting weight,
battered and venerable
and homely. Here and there
his brown skin hung in strips   10
like ancient wallpaper,
and its pattern of darker brown
was like wallpaper:
shapes like full-blown roses
stained and lost through age.   15
He was speckled with barnacles,
fine rosettes of lime,
and infested
with tiny white sea-lice,
and underneath two or three   20
rags of green weed hung down.
While his gills were breathing in
the terrible oxygen
– the frightening gills,
fresh and crisp with blood,   25
that can cut so badly –
I thought of the coarse white flesh
packed in like feathers,
the big bones and the little bones,
the dramatic reds and blacks   30
of his shiny entrails,

and the pink swim-bladder
like a big peony.
I looked into his eyes
which were far larger than mine   35
but shallower, and yellowed,
the irises backed and packed
with tarnished tinfoil
seen through the lenses
of old scratched isinglass.   40
They shifted a little, but not
to return my stare.
– It was more like the tipping
of an object toward the light.
I admired his sullen face,   45
the mechanism of his jaw,
and then I saw
that from his lower lip
– if you could call it a lip –
grim, wet, and weaponlike,   50
hung five old pieces of fish-line,
or four and a wire leader
with the swivel still attached,
with all their five big hooks
grown firmly in his mouth.   55
A green line, frayed at the end
where he broke it, two heavier lines,
and a fine black thread
still crimped from the strain and snap
when it broke and he got away.   60
Like medals with their ribbons
frayed and wavering,
a five-haired beard of wisdom
trailing from his aching jaw.
I stared and stared   65
and victory filled up
the little rented boat,
from the pool of bilge
where oil had spread a rainbow
around the rusted engine   70
to the bailer rusted orange,
the sun-cracked thwarts,
the oarlocks on their strings,
the gunnels – until everything
was rainbow, rainbow, rainbow!   75
And I let the fish go.

NOTE

40   isinglass: a semi-transparent form of gelatine extracted from certain fish and used in making jellies, glue, etc.

EXPLORATIONS

First reading

1. How do you visualise the fish? Think of it as a painting or a picture. What details strike you on a first reading?

2. What is your initial impression of the speaker in this poem?

Second reading

3. Consider in detail the description of the fish. Which elements of the description could be considered objective or factual? Which elements could be seen as purely subjective on the part of the poet? Which are imagined or aesthetic elements in the description?

4. Do you think the poet's re-creation of the fish is a good one? Explain your views.

Third reading

5. Explore the attitude of the speaker towards the fish over the entire length of the poem. What changes do you notice, and where?

6. Why do you think she released the fish? Explore the text for possible reasons.

7. Do you think this is an important moment for the poet? What does she learn or discover? Where in the text is this suggested?

8. Is the poet excited by this experience? Where in the text is this suggested? Comment on the tone of the poem.

Fourth reading

9. What issues does this poem raise? Consider what the poem has to say about:
    - Our relationship with the natural world
    - The nature of creativity
    - Moments of insight and decision
    - Other themes hinted at

10. Do you think the imagery is effective in getting across a real understanding of the fish and an awareness of the poet's mood? Explore any two relevant images and explain how they function.

11. This is quite a dramatic poem. Explain how the dramatic effect is created. Consider such elements as the way the narrative builds to a climax, the ending, the effect of the short enjambed lines and the speaker's interior debate.

12. What did you like about this poem?

THE BIGHT

On my birthday

At low tide like this how sheer the water is.
White, crumbling ribs of marl protrude and glare
and the boats are dry, the pilings dry as matches.
Absorbing, rather than being absorbed,
the water in the bight doesn't wet anything,   5
the color of the gas flame turned as low as possible.
One can smell it turning to gas; if one were Baudelaire
one could probably hear it turning to marimba music.
The little ocher dredge at work off the end of the dock
already plays the dry perfectly off-beat claves.   10
The birds are outsize. Pelicans crash
into this peculiar gas unnecessarily hard,
it seem to me, like pickaxes,
rarely coming up with anything to show for it,
and going off with humorous elbowings.   15
Black-and-white man-of-war birds soar
on impalpable drafts
and open their tails like scissors on the curves
or tense them like wishbones, till they tremble.
The frowsy sponge boats keep coming in   20
with the obliging air of retrievers,
bristling with jackstraw gaffs and hooks
and decorated with bobbles of sponges.
There is a fence of chicken wire along the dock
where, glinting like little plowshares,   25
the blue-gray shark tails are hung up to dry
for the Chinese-restaurant trade.
Some of the little white boats are still piled up
against each other, or lie on their sides, stove in,
and not yet salvaged, if they ever will be, from the last bad storm,   30
like torn-open, unanswered letters.
The bight is littered with old correspondences.
Click. Click. Goes the dredge,
and brings up a dripping jawful of marl.
All the untidy activity continues,   35
awful but cheerful.

NOTES

Bight:		recess of coast, bay
2	marl:	soil composed of clay and lime, sometimes used as fertiliser
3	pilings:	heavy beams driven into the sea bed as support for a jetty or dock
7	Baudelaire:	Charles-Pierre Baudelaire (1821–67), French lyric poet, author of *Les Fleurs du Mal*
8	marimba:	type of xylophone used in African or South American music
9	ocher [ochre]:	orange-brown colour
10	claves [clefs]:	symbols of musical notation; there are three clefs, C, G and F, which, when placed on a particular line of a stave of music, show the pitch of the notes
17	impalpable:	not easily grasped; imperceptible to touch
20	frowsy:	slovenly, unkempt

EXPLORATIONS

First reading

1. Think of the poem as a painting. Describe it as you see it laid out: background, foreground, centre, left side, right side.

2. What mood is suggested by the scene? Explain.

Second reading

3. In what ways do you think it differs from a chocolate-box painting?

4. Is the reader-viewer encouraged to view the scene in a new and fresh way? Where and how does this happen? Examine the details of the descriptions. What is unusual about them?

Third reading

5. What do you think is the impact of the subtitle, 'On my birthday'? Might it be significant that she marks her birthday in this way, viewing this scene? How might she identify with the scene? From the evidence of the text, what do you think her mood is?

Fourth reading

6. Consider the style of the versification. Concentrate on such aspects as metre, rhyme or the lack of it, the organisation of sentence or sense units, etc. What does the form of the poem contribute to its effectiveness?

7. Would you consider it accurate to suggest that the poem moves along in bursts of poetic intensity, punctuated by more prosaic reflections? Discuss.

AT THE FISHHOUSES

Although it is a cold evening,
down by one of the fishhouses
an old man sits netting,
his net, in the gloaming almost invisible,
a dark purple-brown,   5
and his shuttle worn and polished.
The air smells so strong of codfish
it makes one's nose run and one's eyes water.
The five fishhouses have steeply peaked roofs
and narrow, cleated gangplanks slant up   10
to storerooms in the gables
for the wheelbarrows to be pushed up and down on.
All is silver: the heavy surface of the sea,
swelling slowly as if considering spilling over,
is opaque, but the silver of the benches,   15
the lobster pots, and masts, scattered
among the wild jagged rocks,
is of an apparent translucence
like the small old buildings with an emerald moss
growing on their shoreward walls.   20
The big fish tubs are completely lined
with layers of beautiful herring scales
and the wheelbarrows are similarly plastered
with creamy iridescent coats of mail,
with small iridescent flies crawling on them.   25
Up on the little slope behind the houses,
set in the sparse bright sprinkle of grass,
is an ancient wooden capstan,
cracked, with two long bleached handles
and some melancholy stains, like dried blood,   30
where the ironwork has rusted.
The old man accepts a Lucky Strike.
He was a friend of my grandfather.
We talk of the decline in the population
and of codfish and herring   35
while he waits for a herring boat to come in.
There are sequins on his vest and on his thumb.
He has scraped the scales, the principal beauty,
from unnumbered fish with that black old knife,
the blade of which is almost worn away.   40

Down at the water's edge, at the place
where they haul up the boats, up the long ramp
descending into the water, thin silver
tree trunks are laid horizontally
across the gray stones, down and down   45
at intervals of four or five feet.

Cold dark deep and absolutely clear,
element bearable to no mortal,
to fish and to seals … One seal particularly
I have seen here evening after evening.   50
He was curious about me. He was interested in music;
like me a believer in total immersion,
so I used to sing him Baptist hymns.
I also sang 'A Mighty Fortress Is Our God.'
He stood up in the water and regarded me   55
steadily, moving his head a little.
Then he would disappear, then suddenly emerge
almost in the same spot, with a sort of shrug
as if it were against his better judgment.
Cold dark deep and absolutely clear,   60
the clear gray icy water … Back, behind us,
the dignified tall firs begin.
Bluish, associating with their shadows,
a million Christmas trees stand
waiting for Christmas. The water seems suspended   65
above the rounded gray and blue-gray stones.
I have seen it over and over, the same sea, the same,
slightly, indifferently swinging above the stones,
icily free above the stones,
above the stones and then the world.   70
If you should dip your hand in,
your wrist would ache immediately,
your bones would begin to ache and your hand would burn
as if the water were a transmutation of fire
that feeds on stones and burns with a dark gray flame.   75
If you tasted it, it would first taste bitter,
then briny, then surely burn your tongue.
It is like what we imagine knowledge to be:
dark, salt, clear, moving, utterly free,
drawn from the cold hard mouth   80
of the world, derived from the rocky breasts
forever, flowing and drawn, and since
our knowledge is historical, flowing, and flown.

'Nova Scotia Landscape', a watercolour by Elizabeth Bishop

EXPLORATIONS

First reading

1. On a first reading, what do you notice about the setting of the poem? List the things that make an immediate impression on you.

2. Examine in detail what is being described in the first section. What is your impression of the atmosphere of the place?

3. What do you suppose is the writer's attitude to that scene in the first section? Does she find it repulsive, or awe-inspiring, or is she completely unaffected by it? Comment, with reference to the text.

4. What aspect of the scene draws the poet's main focus of attention during the entire poem?

Second reading

5. List all the characteristics or facets of the sea alluded to or reflected on by the poet throughout the poem.

6. Do you think she manages to effectively evoke the mysterious power of the sea? Comment.

Third reading

7. Bishop's poetic technique involved
   a   detailed description and
   b   making the familiar strange or unusual so that we see it afresh.
   Comment under these headings on her description of the sea.

8. How would you assess the mood of this poem? Take into consideration both the landscape and the poet.

9. The poem is written in free verse. What does this contribute to the effect of the poem? What else do you notice about the technique of this poem?

Fourth reading

10. The poem builds to a moment of insight for the poet. Where is this and what is the insight? Describe, in as much depth as you can, what she comes to learn from the sea.

11. Outline the main issues raised by this poem.

12. Do you find any trace of the personality or feelings of the poet in this poem? Comment.

THE PRODIGAL

OL 2019
OL 2021
OL 2022

The brown enormous odor he lived by
was too close, with its breathing and thick hair,
for him to judge. The floor was rotten; the sty
was plastered halfway up with glass-smooth dung.
Light-lashed, self-righteous, above moving snouts,   5
the pigs' eyes followed him, a cheerful stare –
even to the sow that always ate her young –
till, sickening, he leaned to scratch her head.
But sometimes mornings after drinking bouts
(he hid the pints behind a two-by-four),   10
the sunrise glazed the barnyard mud with red;
the burning puddles seemed to reassure.
And then he thought he almost might endure
his exile yet another year or more.

But evenings the first star came to warn.   15
The farmer whom he worked for came at dark
to shut the cows and horses in the barn
beneath their overhanging clouds of hay,
with pitchforks, faint forked lightnings, catching light,
safe and companionable as in the Ark.   20
The pigs stuck out their little feet and snored.
The lantern – like the sun, going away –
laid on the mud a pacing aureole.
Carrying a bucket along a slimy board,
he felt the bats' uncertain staggering flight,   25
his shuddering insights, beyond his control,
touching him. But it took him a long time
finally to make his mind up to go home.

NOTE

23   aureole: a halo of light around the sun or moon

EXPLORATIONS

Before reading

1. What does the title of the poem lead you to expect?

First reading

2. Were any of your expectations met on reading the poem?

3. How do you see the character in this poem?
   - What is he doing? How does he live?
   - Why is he there?
   - Does he find any satisfaction in his work?
   - What helps him endure his exile?

4. What details of the scene affected you most?

Second reading

5. Examine the final five lines. What do you think the 'shuddering insights, beyond his control' might be? Re-create his thoughts as you imagine them here.

6. Bishop appeals to a range of senses – smell, sight, sound, touch – to re-create the atmosphere of the place. Examine a sample of each type of image and discuss the effect.

7. How would you describe the atmosphere of the place? Is it one of unrelieved misery or is there some contentment in it? Refer to the text.

8. Examine the poet's attitude to the prodigal. Do you think she is condemnatory, sympathetic or neutral? Discuss, with reference to the text.

9. What is your own attitude to the prodigal?

Third reading

10. What are the main human issues raised by this poem?

11. Briefly express the theme of the poem.

12. Bishop's poetic technique involved really looking at the detail of her subject matter. Where do you think this works best in 'The Prodigal'?

QUESTIONS OF TRAVEL

There are too many waterfalls here; the crowded streams
hurry too rapidly down to the sea,
and the pressure of so many clouds on the mountaintops
makes them spill over the sides in soft slow-motion,
turning to waterfalls under our very eyes.   5
— For if those streaks, those mile-long, shiny, tearstains,
aren't waterfalls yet,
in a quick age or so, as ages go here,
they probably will be.
But if the streams and clouds keep travelling, travelling,   10
the mountains look like the hulls of capsized ships,
slime-hung and barnacled.

Think of the long trip home.
Should we have stayed at home and thought of here?
Where should we be today?   15
Is it right to be watching strangers in a play
in this strangest of theatres?
What childishness is it that while there's a breath of life
in our bodies, we are determined to rush
to see the sun the other way around?   20
The tiniest green hummingbird in the world?
To stare at some inexplicable old stonework,
inexplicable and impenetrable,
at any view,
instantly seen and always, always delightful?   25
Oh, must we dream our dreams
and have them, too?
And have we room
for one more folded sunset, still quite warm?

But surely it would have been a pity   30
not to have seen the trees along this road,
really exaggerated in their beauty,
not to have seen them gesturing
like noble pantomimists, robed in pink.
— Not to have had to stop for gas and heard   35
the sad, two-noted, wooden tune
of disparate wooden clogs
carelessly clacking over
a grease-stained filling-station floor.

(In another country the clogs would all be tested.   40
Each pair there would have identical pitch.)
– A pity not to have heard
the other, less primitive music of the fat brown bird
who sings above the broken gasoline pump
in a bamboo church of Jesuit baroque: 45
three towers, five silver crosses.

– Yes, a pity not to have pondered,
blurr'dly and inconclusively,
on what connection can exist for centuries
between the crudest wooden footwear   50
and, careful and finicky,
the whittled fantasies of wooden cages.
– Never to have studied history in
the weak calligraphy of songbirds' cages.
– And never to have had to listen to rain   55
so much like politicians' speeches:
two hours of unrelenting oratory
and then a sudden golden silence
in which the traveller takes a notebook, writes:

'Is it lack of imagination that makes us come   60
to imagined places, not just stay at home?
Or could Pascal have been not entirely right
about just sitting quietly in one's room?

Continent, city, country, society:
the choice is never wide and never free.   65
And here, or there ... No. Should we have stayed at home,
wherever that may be?'

'Brazilian Landscape', a watercolour by Elizabeth Bishop

NOTES

45	baroque:	the style of art that developed in the 17th century after the Renaissance, characterised by massive, complex and ornate design
62	Pascal:	Blaise Pascal (1623–62), French mathematician, physicist and philosopher, author of *Pensées*, who commented, 'I have discovered that all human evil comes from this, man's being unable to sit still in a room.'

EXPLORATIONS

First reading

1. This is a travel poem with a difference. What are the elements found here that one would normally expect of a travel poem and what elements do you find different or unusual?

2. Follow the traveller's eye. What does she notice in particular about the geography and culture of Brazil?

3. What impression of Brazilian culture do you get? Examine the references in detail.

Second reading

4. Do you think the poet feels comfortable in this place? What is her attitude to what she sees? Do you think she is just the usual tired, grumpy traveller or something else?

5. One critic has said that Bishop is essentially a poet of the domestic because she feels estranged in the greater world. Comment on that statement in light of your reading of this poem.

6. What bothers her about travel? Jot down your ideas on this.

Third reading

7. List the main issues raised in this poem.

8. What do you notice about the style in which the poem is written? Comment critically on it.

THE ARMADILLO

for Robert Lowell

This is the time of year
when almost every night
the frail, illegal fire balloons appear.
Climbing the mountain height,

rising toward a saint   5
still honored in these parts,
the paper chambers flush and fill with light
that comes and goes, like hearts.

Once up against the sky it's hard
to tell them from the stars –   10
planets, that is – the tinted ones:
Venus going down, or Mars,

or the pale green one. With a wind,
they flare and falter, wobble and toss;
but if it's still they steer between   15
the kite sticks of the Southern Cross,

receding, dwindling, solemnly
and steadily forsaking us,
or, in the downdraft from a peak,
suddenly turning dangerous.   20

Last night another big one fell.
It splattered like an egg of fire
against the cliff behind the house.
The flame ran down. We saw the pair

of owls who nest there flying up   25
and up, their whirling black-and-white
stained bright pink underneath, until
they shrieked up out of sight.

The ancient owls' nest must have burned.
Hastily, all alone,   30
a glistening armadillo left the scene,
rose-flecked, head down, tail down,

and then a baby rabbit jumped out,
short-eared, to our surprise.
So soft! – a handful of intangible ash   35
with fixed, ignited eyes.

Too pretty, dreamlike mimicry!
O falling fire and piercing cry
and panic, and a weak mailed fist
clenched ignorant against the sky!   40

NOTES

3	fire balloons:	St John's Day (24 June) was celebrated by releasing these fire balloons in a type of local religious worship. Air currents took them up the mountainside, where they sometimes became a hazard to houses. Bishop's partner, Lota Soares, had a sprinkler system installed on the roof to counter the danger.
16	Southern Cross:	a constellation of stars in the southern hemisphere

EXPLORATIONS

First reading

1. Trace the sequence of events in the poem.

2. What images strike you most forcibly?

3. What is your first impression of the location in this poem? How do you imagine it?

Second reading

4. Do you think it would be correct to say that the poet is ambivalent in her attitude to the fire balloons? Discuss.

5. Trace the development of the fire imagery throughout the poem. How does the poet link it with the natural world?

6. Where do you think the poet's sympathies lie in this poem? Explain.

Third reading

7. Examine the poet's outlook on life here. What image of the local people is presented? What view of humanity in general informs this poem? Can you discern a philosophy of life behind it? Note your impressions, however tentative, then formulate your thoughts in a more organised way.

8. Would you say the poet is uncharacteristically emotional here? Explain your views.

9. What else do you notice about the style of this poem?

Fourth reading

10. Why do you think this might be considered an important poem?

SESTINA

September rain falls on the house.
In the failing light, the old grandmother
sits in the kitchen with the child
beside the Little Marvel Stove,
reading the jokes from the almanac,   5
laughing and talking to hide her tears.

She thinks that her equinoctial tears
and the rain that beats on the roof of the house
were both foretold by the almanac,
but only known to a grandmother.   10
The iron kettle sings on the stove.
She cuts some bread and says to the child,

It's time for tea now; but the child
is watching the teakettle's small hard tears
dance like mad on the hot black stove,   15
the way the rain must dance on the house.
Tidying up, the old grandmother
hangs up the clever almanac

on its string. Birdlike, the almanac
hovers half open above the child,   20
hovers above the old grandmother
and her teacup full of dark brown tears.
She shivers and says she thinks the house
feels chilly, and puts more wood in the stove.

It was to be, says the Marvel Stove.   25
I know what I know, says the almanac.
With crayons the child draws a rigid house
and a winding pathway. Then the child
puts in a man with buttons like tears
and shows it proudly to the grandmother   30

But secretly, while the grandmother
busies herself about the stove,
the little moons fall down like tears
from between the pages of the almanac
into the flower bed the child   35
has carefully placed in the front of the house.

Time to plant tears, says the almanac.
The grandmother sings to the marvellous stove
and the child draws another inscrutable house.

NOTES

	Sestina:	a fixed verse form consisting of six stanzas of six lines each, normally followed by three lines
5	almanac:	an annual publication that includes information such as weather forecasts, farmers' planting dates, tides tables and information arranged according the year's calendar
7	equinoctial:	happening at or near the time of an equinox

EXPLORATIONS

First reading

1. What is the prevailing atmosphere in this poem? What elements chiefly contribute to this?

2. What are the recurring elements in this poem?

Second reading

3. How do you see the grandmother?

4. How do you see the child here?

5. Is the child completely unhappy? Are there any alleviating soft elements in her life?

6. What do you think is absent from the child's picture of life?

Third reading

7. Do you understand how the poem is constructed? Explain briefly.

8. Trace the progression of the tear imagery throughout the poem, from the reference to 'September rain' in the first stanza. How do you interpret this in the context of the statement the poet is making about her childhood?

9. Examine the references to her drawings of the house. What do they suggest to you about the child and her environment?

Fourth reading

10. What thoughts does this poem spark off about childhood and about domestic relationships?

11. Do you think Bishop has made a successful re-creation of a child's world? Examine the actions and the diction in particular.

12. Would you consider this to be a sentimental poem? The term 'sentimental' can be read neutrally as 'emotional thought expressed in literature' or more negatively as 'showing emotional weakness, mawkish tenderness'. Which, if either, description applies? Discuss.

FIRST DEATH IN NOVA SCOTIA

In the cold, cold parlor
my mother laid out Arthur
beneath the chromographs:
Edward, Prince of Wales,
with Princess Alexandra,   5
and King George with Queen Mary.
Below them on the table
stood a stuffed loon
shot and stuffed by Uncle
Arthur, Arthur's father.   10

Since Uncle Arthur fired
a bullet into him,
he hadn't said a word.
He kept his own counsel
on his white, frozen lake,   15
the marble-topped table.
His breast was deep and white,
cold and caressable;
his eyes were red glass,
much to be desired.   20

'Come,' said my mother,
'Come and say good-bye
to your little cousin Arthur.'
I was lifted up and given
one lily of the valley   25
to put in Arthur's hand.
Arthur's coffin was
a little frosted cake,
and the red-eyed loon eyed it
from his white, frozen lake.   30

Arthur was very small.
He was all white, like a doll
that hadn't been painted yet.
Jack Frost had started to paint him
the way he always painted   35
the Maple Leaf (Forever).
He had just begun on his hair,
a few red strokes, and then
Jack Frost had dropped the brush
and left him white, forever.   40

The gracious royal couples
were warm in red and ermine;
their feet were well wrapped up
in the ladies' ermine trains.
They invited Arthur to be   45
the smallest page at court.
But how could Arthur go,
clutching his tiny lily,
with his eyes shut up so tight
and the roads deep in snow?   50

NOTES

3	chromographs:	printed reproduction of a colour photograph
8	loon:	a diver, a kind of bird, noted for its clumsy gait on land
36	Maple Leaf:	national emblem of Canada
42	ermine:	white fur with black spots, from a type of stoat, used in monarchs' robes

EXPLORATIONS

First reading

1. First decide who is speaking. Where and when was the event depicted and what age is the speaker?

2. What do you find unusual or confusing on a first reading?

3. If we consider the speaker to be a young child, does this help you come to grips with the poem? Reread it.

Second reading

4. What is most noticeable about the scene here?

5. What is the atmosphere in the parlour?

6. How do you think the child speaker feels? Discuss.

Third reading

7. Examine the title. Why 'first death'? Discuss the many possible connotations of this.

8. Comment on the use of colour in the poem.

9. Comment on the versification.

Fourth reading

10. Do you think the poet has managed to successfully re-create the young child's experience?

11. What did you learn about Elizabeth Bishop from reading this poem?

FILLING STATION

Oh, but it is dirty!
– this little filling station,
oil-soaked, oil-permeated
to a disturbing, over-all
black translucency.   5
Be careful with that match!

Father wears a dirty,
oil-soaked monkey suit
that cuts him under the arms,
and several quick and saucy   10
and greasy sons assist him
(it's a family filling station),
all quite thoroughly dirty.

Do they live in the station?
It has a cement porch   15
behind the pumps, and on it
a set of crushed and grease-
impregnated wickerwork;
on the wicker sofa
a dirty dog, quite comfy.   20

Some comic books provide
the only note of color –
of certain color. They lie
upon a big dim doily
draping a taboret   25
(part of the set), beside
a big hirsute begonia.

Why the extraneous plant?
Why the taboret?
Why, oh why, the doily?   30
(Embroidered in daisy stitch
with marguerites, I think,
and heavy with gray crochet.)

Somebody embroidered the doily.
Somebody waters the plant,   35
or oils it, maybe. Somebody
arranges the rows of cans

so that they softly say:
ESSO–SO–SO–SO
to high-strung automobiles.   40
Somebody loves us all.

EXPLORATIONS

Before reading

1. Think about the title. What do you see?

First reading

2. Describe the atmosphere this poem creates for you. What details do you think are significant in creating this? Discuss them.

Second reading

3. Plan the shots you would use if you were making a film of this scene. Describe what you see in each shot and explain your choice in detail.

4. Is there any progression, development of complexity, etc. in this film? How do you understand it?

5. What do the doily, the taboret and the begonia add to the atmosphere?

Third reading

6. What is it about this scene that fascinates the poet: the forecourt, the domestic details or something else? Discuss.

7. How do you understand the 'somebody' in stanza 6?

Fourth reading

8. Do you think the poet is discovering a truth and making a statement about life? If so, what? Discuss.

9. Write up your own notes on the theme of the poem, the poet's philosophy of life, her poetic method and the style and tone of the poem.

10. 'The details of Bishop's poems are always compelling but never the whole point.'
Discuss, with reference to the text.

11. 'This is a poem that manages to create poignancy and wit simultaneously.'
Discuss.

IN THE WAITING ROOM

In Worcester, Massachusetts,
I went with Aunt Consuelo
to keep her dentist's appointment
and sat and waited for her
in the dentist's waiting room.   5
It was winter. It got dark
early. The waiting room
was full of grown-up people,
arctics and overcoats,
lamps and magazines.   10
My aunt was inside
what seemed like a long time
and while I waited I read
the *National Geographic*
(I could read) and carefully   15
studied the photographs:
the inside of a volcano,
black, and full of ashes;
then it was spilling over
in rivulets of fire.   20
Osa and Martin Johnson
dressed in riding breeches,
laced boots, and pith helmets.
A dead man slung on a pole
– 'Long Pig,' the caption said.   25
Babies with pointed heads
wound round and round with string;
black, naked women with necks
wound round and round with wire
like the necks of light bulbs.   30
Their breasts were horrifying.
I read it right straight through.
I was too shy to stop.
And then I looked at the cover:
the yellow margins, the date.   35
Suddenly, from inside,
came an oh! of pain
– Aunt Consuelo's voice –
not very loud or long.
I wasn't at all surprised;   40
even then I knew she was

a foolish, timid woman.
I might have been embarrassed,
but wasn't. What took me
completely by surprise   45
was that it was *me*:
my voice, in my mouth.
Without thinking at all
I was my foolish aunt,
I – we – were falling, falling,   50
our eyes glued to the cover
of the *National Geographic*,
February, 1918.

I said to myself: three days
and you'll be seven years old.   55
I was saying it to stop
the sensation of falling off
the round, turning world
into cold, blue-black space.
But I felt: you are an *I*,   60
you are an *Elizabeth*,
you are one of *them*.
Why should you be one, too?
I scarcely dared to look
to see what it was I was.   65
I gave a sidelong glance
– I couldn't look any higher –
at shadowy gray knees,
trousers and skirts and boots
and different pairs of hands   70
lying under the lamps.
I knew that nothing stranger
had ever happened, that nothing
stranger could ever happen.

Why should I be my aunt,   75
or me, or anyone?
What similarities –
boots, hands, the family voice
I felt in my throat, or even
the *National Geographic*   80
and those awful hanging breasts –
held us all together
or made us all just one?
How – I didn't know any

word for it – how 'unlikely' …   85
How had I come to be here,
like them, and overhear
a cry of pain that could have
got loud and worse but hadn't?

The waiting room was bright   90
and too hot. It was sliding
beneath a big black wave,
another, and another.

Then I was back in it.
The War was on. Outside,   95
in Worcester, Massachusetts,
were night and slush and cold,
and it was still the fifth
of February, 1918.

BACKGROUND NOTE

This poem was probably written around 1970 and was published in the *New Yorker* on 17 July 1971. It is the opening poem of Bishop's collection *Geography III*, published in 1976.

NOTE

21	Osa and Martin Johnson:	American photographers and explorers; Bishop first saw the Johnsons' jungle film *Baboons* in the winter of 1935

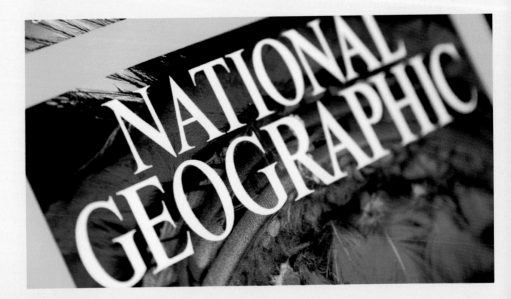

EXPLORATIONS

Before reading

1. What might you expect from this title?

2. Do you remember what it was like as a child to sit in a dentist's waiting room? Re-create such an experience. Make brief notes for yourself.

First reading

3. In the poem, what elements of the waiting room experience are all too familiar to you?

4. Who is the speaker in this poem? Assemble as much information, factual and impressionistic, as you can.

Second reading

5. After the familiar, what is encountered by the child?

6. Which event most unnerves her? Can you suggest why she is unnerved?

7. What is the child's reaction to this experience?

Third reading

8. What is your understanding of the experience described in this poem? Comment briefly.

9. What view of women does Bishop project in this poem?

10. Comment on the experience of childhood reflected here.

Fourth reading

11. What themes or issues are raised by this poem? Explain how the poet deals with some of the following:

- A child's realisation of selfhood
- The poet's uncomfortable connection with the rest of humanity
- The variety and strangeness of the world of which one is a part
- That we are always at risk of being ambushed by the unfamiliar, even in the security of the domestic
- That the chief lessons of childhood are learning to deal with pain and mortality and accepting unity in spite of difference
- Any others

12. What is your own reaction to this poem? Structure your thoughts in the form of questions.

13. Comment on the structure of the poem (five sections) and the type of verse used.

ADRIENNE RICH

(1929–2012)

Prescribed for Higher Level exams in 2020 and 2022

Adrienne Rich was born in Baltimore, USA on 16 May 1929, the elder of two daughters. Her father, Arnold, was a doctor and a pathology professor at Johns Hopkins University, while her mother, Helen, had been a talented pianist and composer before devoting herself to raising her two daughters.

Adrienne was a bright child and was educated at home by her parents prior to entering the school system. It was her father who was to have the greater influence on her. Indeed, it was under his guidance that she began to write poetry. As she developed, Rich was to experience a sense of conflict as she tried to break away from her father's influence both in her writing and in her life.

In 1951 Adrienne graduated from Radcliffe College with an excellent degree. In the same year she received the Yale Younger Poets award for her first book of poetry. In 1953 she married a Harvard economist, Alfred Conrad, and had three sons. Adrienne continued to write, but she felt increasingly unhappy with the direction of her life. The 1960s were a time of great political upheaval in the United States and both Rich and her husband became involved with movements for social justice, with her interest focusing on the women's movement.

Her experiences as a lesbian and a feminist led her to develop an empathy with all those groups in society who are considered less equal, and her poetry became increasingly politicised as she sought to give a voice to those who are not normally heard. Although Rich has won many prizes for her writing, in 1997 she declined the National Medal for the Arts from the then president, Bill Clinton, saying, 'A president cannot meaningfully honour certain token artists while the people at large are so dishonoured.'

Adrienne Rich published her latest book of poems, *Telephone Ringing in the Labyrinth: Poems 2004–2006*, at the age of seventy-eight. She died in 2012.

AUNT JENNIFER'S TIGERS

Aunt Jennifer's tigers prance across a screen,
Bright topaz denizens of a world of green.
They do not fear the men beneath the tree;
They pace in sleek chivalric certainty.

Aunt Jennifer's fingers fluttering through her wool   5
Find even the ivory needle hard to pull.
The massive weight of Uncle's wedding band
Sits heavily upon Aunt Jennifer's hand.

When Aunt is dead, her terrified hands will lie
Still ringed with ordeals she was mastered by.   10
The tigers in the panel that she made
Will go on prancing, proud and unafraid.

'Tyger/Tyger' by Francis Broomfield (2002)

NOTES

1	prance:	to spring forward on back legs with front legs raised; to walk arrogantly
2	topaz:	a yellow/gold gem
2	denizens:	inhabitants
4	chivalric:	courtly, knightly
10	ordeals:	painful or horrifying experiences

EXPLORATIONS

First reading

1. Imagine that you are a director preparing to film this scene. Using the clues given in the poem, write the instructions that you would give to :

   a The set designer, regarding how the sets should look; and

   b The cameraman/woman, describing the camera shots that he/she should use.

2. Divide a copy page into two short columns. Put the heading 'Tigers' at the top of one column and 'Aunt Jennifer' at the top of the second. Put the answers to the following questions side by side in the relevant columns. Leave a one-line gap after each pair of answers:

   a What verbs are associated with the tigers in the first and third stanzas? What verbs are associated with Aunt Jennifer in the second and third stanzas?

   b What colours are associated with the tigers in the first stanza? What colours are associated with Aunt Jennifer in the second stanza?

   c What emotions are associated with the tigers in the first and third stanzas? What emotions are associated with Aunt Jennifer in the second and third stanzas?

3. **Class Discussion:**

   a Discuss the differences between the two lists of verbs in Question 2.

   b Is there a feeling of power in one list and powerlessness in the other?

   c Can you decide who was having more fun in life – the tigers or Aunt Jennifer? Give reasons for your decision.

4. **Paired Discussion:** The colour yellow/gold is suggested in connection with the tigers and Aunt Jennifer. Using the list you made in Question 2 (a), discuss the following questions:

   a Are there any differences in the way the colour is used with the tigers and with Aunt Jennifer?

   b Consider the colours that appear alongside the yellow/gold in each case. Do they change how you see the yellow/gold?

   Individual Writing: Using the points that arose in the discussion, answer the following question. How does Rich use colour to convey that the tigers have very different lives from Aunt Jennifer's?

5. **Group Discussion:**

   a Using your lists of emotions from Question 2, discuss the mood created in the images of the tigers and the mood created in the descriptions of Aunt Jennifer.

   b Would you rather be with the tigers or with Aunt Jennifer? Why?

Second reading

6. **Paired Discussion:**

   a Do you find it surprising that Aunt Jennifer was the creator of the tiger screen? Why?

   b Can you suggest what might have driven Aunt Jennifer to make this screen?

   c What do you think she was trying to say?

Paired Writing:

With one of you as Aunt Jennifer and one as a reporter, write an interview with Aunt Jennifer about her tiger screen.

7. **Class Discussion:**

   a Discuss the different ways in which the male figures interact with the tigers and with Aunt Jennifer.

   b What is the poet's attitude to the male figures in the poem?

   c Do you think that this is a fair attitude, bearing in mind that Rich wrote this poem as a woman living in the early 1950s?

Individual Writing: Using the points that arose in the discussion, how are men portrayed in this poem?

Third reading

8. a Can you explain the theme of the poem?

   b Do you agree or disagree with the attitude expressed in the theme? Give reasons for your answer.

9. Physically, the tigers are suggested as whole bodies, while Aunt Jennifer is represented only by her hands. How does Rich use this method to reveal the differing lives of Aunt Jennifer and the tigers?

10. 'Power lies at the heart of this poem.'
    Discuss this statement, using references from the poem to support your views.

THE UNCLE SPEAKS IN THE DRAWING ROOM

I have seen the mob of late
Standing sullen in the square,
Gazing with a sullen stare
At window, balcony, and gate.
Some have talked in bitter tones,   5
Some have held and fingered stones.

These are follies that subside.
Let us consider, none the less,
Certain frailties of glass
Which, it cannot be denied,   10
Lead in times like these to fear
For crystal vase and chandelier.

Not that missiles will be cast;
None as yet dare lift an arm.
But the scene recalls a storm   15
When our grandsire stood aghast
To see his antique ruby bowl
Shivered in a thunder-roll.

Let us only bear in mind
How these treasures handed down   20
From a calmer age passed on
Are in the keeping of our kind.
We stand between the dead glass-blowers
And murmurings of missile-throwers.

'Uncle and Niece' by Edgar Degas (c. 1876)

NOTES

7	follies:	foolish activities
16	aghast:	dismayed

EXPLORATIONS

First reading

1.　**Class Discussion:**

　a　What image does the word 'mob' suggest to you?

　b　How would you describe the mood of the mob in the first stanza?

　c　Pick out two words that really help you to understand their mood.

2.　a　'These are follies that subside.' What does this line tell you about the uncle's attitude to the mob?

　b　'Not that missiles will be cast'. Do you think the uncle truly believes what he is saying?

　c　Is he really as calm and confident as the two quotations in this question suggest? Refer to the second and third stanzas to support your view.

3.　**Group Discussion:** The uncle is concerned about the 'crystal vase and chandelier'. Would you be concerned about items such as these if your house were under threat of attack?

Individual Writing: Using the points that arose in the discussion, answer the following question. What do the uncle's reactions reveal about the type of person he is?

4.　**Paired Discussion:**

　a　Is it significant that the uncle speaks in 'the drawing room'?

　b　Would the effect be the same if the uncle were in the kitchen or the bedroom? Why/why not?

Individual Writing: Using the points that were discussed, imagine that you were visiting the house when this incident occurred. Write a letter to your friend describing what happened and how you felt about it.

Second reading

5.　a　What do the 'crystal vase and chandelier' and the 'ruby bowl' suggest about the uncle's lifestyle?

　b　Pick out any other words in the poem that give further clues about the type of house that the uncle lives in.

　c　How do you think the mob feel about the way that he lives?

6.　**Class Discussion:**

　a　What qualities do 'the mob' in the first stanza and the 'thunder-roll' in the third stanza have in common?

　b　Might they have similar effects on the glass objects?

　c　How are the 'glassblowers' in the final stanza different from them?

7. a What does the final stanza tell us about the uncle's attitude to the glass objects?

   b Pick out the key phrases that you feel reveal his attitude.

   c Do you agree with his opinion? Why?

Third reading

8. **Individual Writing:**

   a This poem comes from Rich's book entitled *A Change of World*. How could this poem be seen as representing a possible 'change of world'?

   b What could
   (i) the uncle,
   (ii) the glass objects and
   (iii) the mob
   represent in this context?
   You might like to share your thoughts with the class when you have finished.

9. **Group Discussion:** Where do you think Rich's sympathies lie: with the uncle or with the mob? Refer to the poem to support your viewpoint.

   Individual Writing: Using the points that were discussed, how does the poem reveal Rich's loyalties?

10. 'In "The Uncle Speaks in the Drawing Room" and "Aunt Jennifer's Tigers", Rich skilfully uses everyday language to create poems that are both elegant and vivid.'
    Discuss this statement with regard to her use of (a) rhyme and rhythm, alliteration, assonance and onomatopoeia; (b) clear and effective images.

POWER

Living   in the earth-deposits   of our history
Today a backhoe divulged   out of a crumbling flank of earth
one bottle   amber   perfect   a hundred-year-old
cure for fever   or melancholy   a tonic
for living on this earth   in the winters of this climate   5

Today I was reading about Marie Curie:
she must have known she suffered   from radiation sickness
her body bombarded for years   by the element
she had purified
It seems she denied to the end   10
the source of the cataracts on her eyes
the cracked and suppurating skin   of her finger-ends
till she could no longer hold   a test-tube or a pencil

She died   a famous woman   denying
her wounds   15
denying
her wounds   came   from the same source as her power

NOTES

2	backhoe:	a mechanical digger
2	flank:	side of the body between ribcage and hip
4	melancholy:	a thoughtful sadness
6	Marie Curie (1867–1934):	discovered the radioactive elements plutonium and radium that are used in medicine today. First person to win two Nobel prizes. Died of leukaemia caused by exposure to high levels of radiation.
11	cataracts:	condition where the lens of the eye becomes opaque so that light cannot pass through
12	suppurating:	oozing pus

EXPLORATIONS

First reading

1. **Class Discussion:**

    a   What is your reaction to the way that this poem is arranged on the page?

    b   Did this arrangement encourage or discourage you from reading the poem? Why?

2. **Paired Discussion:**

    a   What is the discovery that triggers the poet's thoughts?

    b   What senses does Rich appeal to in her description of this discovery in lines 2–5?

    c   Why do you think the bottle was thrown away with its contents apparently unused?

Paired Writing: Using the points that were discussed, answer the following question. You are visiting Rich when she discovers the bottle. With one of you writing as Rich and the other as yourself, write out the conversation you have.

3. Do you find the first five lines of this poem interesting or confusing? Give reasons for your opinion.

Second reading

4. The poet's thoughts move on to the woman scientist Marie Curie.
   a   What effects did Curie's work have on her life?
   b   Would you like to live a life such as Marie Curie's? Why?

5. **Class Discussion:**
   a   How does Marie Curie react to the 'radiation sickness'?
   b   Can you suggest any reasons for her behaviour?
   c   As a woman, Curie was very unusual in the male-dominated scientific world. Do you think that this factor played a part in her denial of her sickness?

Individual Writing: Using the points that arose in the discussion, answer the following question. Imagine that you are interviewing Marie Curie for a newspaper. Using your work on this question and Question 4, write out the questions you would ask her and the answers she might give.

6. **Group Discussion:**
   a   Do you find the movement of the poem from describing the discovery of the 'bottle' to writing about Marie Curie confusing?

   b   Might the idea of a 'cure' connect the two images in some way?

Third reading

7. a   Obviously, Curie had physical wounds from the radiation sickness, but could she have also been 'wounded' by the society in which she lived? In what ways?
   b   Why would Rich be unhappy about Curie denying the fact that, as a woman, society inflicted 'wounds' on her?

8. Do you find Rich's use of the 'stream of consciousness' method successful in 'Power', or is it all rather confusing? Use quotations from the poem to support your opinion.

9. Compare 'Power' with 'Aunt Jennifer's Tigers'. Which poem do you prefer? Give reasons for your preference.

10. Consider how Rich explores the concept of 'Power' in three of the poems you have studied. Use quotations to support your answer.

STORM WARNINGS

The glass has been falling all the afternoon,
And knowing better than the instrument
What winds are walking overhead, what zone
Of gray unrest is moving across the land,
I leave the book upon a pillowed chair   5
And walk from window to closed window, watching
Boughs strain against the sky

And think again, as often when the air
Moves inward toward a silent core of waiting,
How with a single purpose time has traveled   10
By secret currents of the undiscerned
Into this polar realm. Weather abroad
And weather in the heart alike come on
Regardless of prediction.

Between foreseeing and averting change   15
Lies all the mastery of elements
Which clocks and weatherglasses cannot alter.
Time in the hand is not control of time,
Nor shattered fragments of an instrument
A proof against the wind; the wind will rise,   20
We can only close the shutters.

I draw the curtains as the sky goes black
And set a match to candles sheathed in glass
Against the keyhole draught, the insistent whine
Of weather through the unsealed aperture.   25
This is our sole defense against the season;
These are the things that we have learned to do
Who live in troubled regions.

'Storm Clouds' by K. F. Nordström (1893)

NOTES

11	undiscerned:	unperceived by thought or senses
14	prediction:	forecast
15	averting:	preventing
23	sheathed:	enclosed, protected by
25	aperture:	gap

EXPLORATIONS

Before reading

1. How do you feel about storms: the wind, rain, thunder and lightning? Are you afraid of them or do you feel exhilarated by them? Take one minute and write a list of all the words that come into your head when you think of the word 'Storms'. Don't try to control the words or leave out words that seem to have no sensible connection. When the minute is up, review your list. You could use it as a basis for a short descriptive piece of writing, either in prose or poetry, about your perception of 'Storms'.

First reading

2. **Group Discussion:**
   a What do you think of Rich's description of a developing storm?
   b Are there any similarities between her poem and your written piece?
   c Did any of her images or phrases express something of what you felt about storms? If so, try to explain what she was able to express for you.

3. 'Weather abroad/And weather in the heart alike/come on/ Regardless of prediction.'

   a What thoughts does the impending storm trigger in Rich?
   b Do you feel that the connection she makes actually works? Why?

4. **Class Discussion:** The third stanza outlines the level of power that we humans have in the face of impending storms, be they emotional or meteorological. How effective does Rich think our power is? Choose one phrase or one image from this stanza that you feel clearly conveys this view.

5. **Individual Writing:**
   a In your own words, outline the actions that Rich takes in the final stanza.
   b Do these actions actually succeed in keeping the storm out of her house?

Second reading

6. Examine the structure of this poem and compare it to 'Aunt Jennifer's Tigers' and 'The Uncle Speaks in the Drawing Room'.
   a What similarities do you notice between the three poems?
   b What would you consider to be the main difference?
   c Can you suggest why Rich altered her approach to structure in this way?

7. **Class Discussion:**
    a   What does the weather suggest to you about Rich's emotions?
    b   How do you interpret her actions of closing the curtains and lighting the candles?
    c   Can you think of another poem by Rich where a woman contains her emotions?

Third reading

8. 'Rich uses language in this poem with the skill of a sculptor. Rhythm and metre, metaphor, assonance and alliteration have all been chiselled into a smoothly flowing form.' Discuss this statement using quotations to illustrate your points.

9. A lyric poem is one in which a single speaker communicates a mood, an attitude or a state of mind to the reader. A lyric poem does not seek to tell a story, but rather to express an individual feeling or thought. Consider whether 'Storm Warnings' could be described as a lyric. Support your arguments with relevant quotations and references.

10. 'These are the things that we have learned to do/Who live in troubled regions.'
    Taking any three of Rich's poems, discuss how she conveys her view that women have learned to do certain 'things' in order to 'live in troubled regions'.

11. Review the short descriptive piece that you wrote on 'Storms'.
    a   Does it suggest anything about your emotional state?

b   Having read Rich's poem, would you like to add anything to it or are you happy with your work?

LIVING IN SIN

She had thought the studio would keep itself;
no dust upon the furniture of love.
Half heresy, to wish the taps less vocal,
the panes relieved of grime. A plate of pears,
a piano with a Persian shawl, a cat   5
stalking the picturesque amusing mouse
had risen at his urging.
Not that at five each separate stair would writhe
under the milkman's tramp; that morning light
so coldly would delineate the scraps   10
of last night's cheese and three sepulchral bottles;
that on the kitchen shelf among the saucers
a pair of beetle-eyes would fix her own –
envoy from some village in the moldings . . .
Meanwhile, he, with a yawn,   15
sounded a dozen notes upon the keyboard,
declared it out of tune, shrugged at the mirror,
rubbed at his beard, went out for cigarettes;
while she, jeered by the minor demons,
pulled back the sheets and made the bed and found   20
a towel to dust the table-top,
and let the coffee-pot boil over on the stove.
By evening she was back in love again,
though not so wholly but throughout the night
she woke sometimes to feel the daylight coming   25
like a relentless milkman up the stairs.

NOTES

I	studio:	studio flat/apartment: a flat with a room used as an artist's studio, a one-roomed flat
3	heresy:	contrary to doctrine or what is normally accepted
6	picturesque:	beautiful, as in a picture
10	delineate:	draw
11	sepulchral:	like a tomb, gloomy
14	moldings:	mouldings, strips of decorative wood
26	relentless:	persistent

EXPLORATIONS

First reading

I. **Class Discussion:**
    a   Have you ever heard the phrase

'living in sin' before?

b   What do you understand it to
mean?

c   In the 1950s and 1960s this
phrase suggested a relationship

that was rather shocking, yet exciting, because the couple were not married. Do you think the phrase has lost its impact nowadays?

2. **Paired Discussion:**
   a What picture of the studio does the girl have in her imagination in lines 4–7?
   b What is the studio like in reality?

Individual Writing: Using the points that arose in the discussion, imagine that you are the girl in the poem. Describe how you feel about the studio in which you are living.

3. Consider the description of the man in lines 15–18.
   a Does he seem like a man who would tempt a woman to 'live in sin'? Why?
   b From the clues in these lines, describe him in your own words.

4. **Group Discussion:**
   a How does the woman spend her time when she first gets up?
   b Consider the phrase 'jeered by the minor demons'. Does it help you to understand what urges the woman to do these things?

5. **Class Discussion:**
   a Why do you think that it is she who tidies up the 'studio' while he does not?
   b Do you think that this is a realistic portrayal of male/female behaviour? Why?

Presentation to the Class: Using the points that were discussed, write and present a short speech on the following topic: 'Women are too concerned with housework, while

men are not concerned enough.'

6. 'By evening she was back in love again,'
   a Can you suggest what might make the woman fall in love again with the man as the day progresses?
   b This line implies a happy ending to the poem. Do you think that there is, indeed, a happy ending? Why?

Second reading

7. **Paired Writing:** Imagine that either the man or the woman writes to a 'problem page' in a magazine about their relationship. With one of you writing as the man/woman and the other writing as the 'agony aunt/ uncle', write the letters that you think would pass between the two. You might like to read your work out to the class so as to see some different approaches to the situation.

8. What do you think that Rich is trying to communicate about love in the poem? Do you agree with her? Refer to the poem in your answer.

Third reading

9. **Group Discussion:**
   a The woman's decision to tidy the studio is a significant one. How could it be seen as a metaphor for women in society?
   b Is Rich suggesting that women are trained, or forced, by society to behave in a certain way?

Individual Writing: Using the points that arose in the discussion, explain in your own words the themes of this poem. Use quotations to support your points.

10. Rich wrote this poem in the 1950s.
Do you think that the message
the poem carries is relevant in the
twenty-first century?

THE ROOFWALKER

– for Denise Levertov

Over the half-finished houses
night comes. The builders
stand on the roof. It is
quiet after the hammers,
the pulleys hang slack.   5
Giants, the roofwalkers,
on a listing deck, the wave
of darkness about to break
on their heads. The sky
is a torn sail where figures   10
pass magnified, shadows
on a burning deck.

I feel like them up there:
exposed, larger than life,
and due to break my neck.   15
Was it worth while to lay –
with infinite exertion –
a roof I can't live under?
– All those blueprints,
closings of gaps,   20
measurings, calculations?
A life I didn't choose
chose me: even
my tools are the wrong ones
for what I have to do.   25
I'm naked, ignorant,
a naked man fleeing
across the roofs
who could with a shade of difference
be sitting in the lamplight   30
against the cream wallpaper
reading – not with indifference –
about a naked man
fleeing across the roofs.

NOTE

Denise Levertov (1923–1997): poet who was born in England but moved to America after she married. Feminism and activism became important elements in her writing. She developed a style in which the thinking process was reflected in line and image.

EXPLORATIONS

Before reading

1. Have you ever walked along a high narrow wall, or a narrow track on a hillside, or across a bridge where you felt uncomfortable about your situation? Take a moment to remember, then write a short passage describing your feelings.

First reading

2. **Class Discussion:**
   a   What mood is created in the first section of the poem?
   b   How do you think the builders feel about being up on the roof?

   Individual Writing: Using the points that were discussed, that you are one of the builders. Using the information in the first section of the poem, describe in your own words your thoughts and feelings at this time.

3. **Paired Discussion:** 'Giants, the roofwalkers, /on a listing deck'
   a   The speaker imagines the builders on something other than a roof. Can you explain what it is?
   b   What does this imagery tell you about the speaker's attitude to the builders?

   Individual Writing: Using the points that were discussed, choose one image that you find particularly vivid from the first section and explain in your own words what it helps you to 'see'.

4. 'I feel like them up there:/exposed, larger than life,/and due to break my neck.'
   a   In what way do these lines signal a change in the speaker's attitude towards the roofwalkers?
   b   Do you think that she is afraid, or worried, or both?

5. **Class Discussion:**
   a   How does the speaker feel about her life?
   b   Pick out one image or phrase that you think clearly suggests these feelings.
   c   Do you think she has put a lot of effort into trying to make this life work? Why?

6. **Individual Writing:** Remembering the piece that you wrote before reading this poem, and using your work for Questions 3 and 4, write a short piece expressing what you would say to this woman if you met her.

Second reading

7. 'I'm naked, ignorant,/a naked man fleeing/across the roofs'.
   a   What emotions do you feel when you read these lines?
   b   What do you think the word 'fleeing' suggests about the man's actions?

c   Does this image help you to understand how the speaker feels, or do you find it confusing?

8. **Class Discussion:** Read lines 30–34.
   a   What mood is created in this final image?
   b   Do you find the mood surprising, given the feelings that the speaker expressed earlier on in the poem?
   c   Is the speaker actually 'sitting in the lamplight', or is she just imagining the scene?

9. **Class Discussion:**
   a   Do you think the speaker would be truly happy if she could manage to change and sit in a room with 'cream wallpaper'?
   b   Which phrases or images reveal her realisation that, even if she changed, she would not be happy in such a situation?

Individual Writing: Using your work on Questions 7, 8 and 9, answer the following:
   a   Can you explain the final thirteen lines of this poem in your own words?
   b   Do you find the final thirteen lines of this poem a successful conclusion to the piece? Give reasons for your viewpoint.

Third reading

10. **Group Discussion:**
    a   How is the appearance of this poem different from poems such as 'Aunt Jennifer's Tigers' and 'Storm Warnings'?
    b   What effect does this appearance have on the way you read the poem?

c   Can you suggest why Rich decided to try a new approach with this poem?

Individual Writing: Using the points that were discussed, answer the following question. 'When we read "The Roofwalker", it is as if we are inside Rich's head listening to her thoughts.'
Discuss, with reference to the poem.

11. Choose two poems that you feel show Rich's efforts to use her 'tools' of writing to the best of her ability. In your answer, examine her use of everyday language, images, rhyme, rhythm, assonance and alliteration.

OUR WHOLE LIFE

Our whole life a translation
the permissible fibs

and now a knot of lies
eating at itself to get undone

Words bitten thru words   5

meanings burnt-off like paint
under the blowtorch

All those dead letters
rendered into the oppressor's language

Trying to tell the doctor where it hurts   10

like the Algerian
who has walked from his village, burning

his whole body a cloud of pain
and there are no words for this

except himself   15

NOTES

2	permissible:	allowable
8	dead letters:	undelivered letters
9	oppressor:	one who governs harshly and cruelly

EXPLORATIONS

Before reading

1. Have you ever been somewhere where you and your family did not speak the language and had difficulty making yourself understood? Or did you find the first days in Irish college very difficult because you could not understand or be understood? Recount your experience to the class.

First reading

2. Did this poem remind you in any way of the experiences that were described in the 'Before Reading' exercise?

3. **Class Discussion:** Rich uses the word 'translation' in the opening line of the poem.
   a Look it up in a dictionary and write down the definitions given.
   b Suggest situations where you might be involved in translating words.
   c How are the 'fibs', 'lies' and 'meanings' connected to the act of 'translation'?

Individual Writing: Using the points that arose in the discussion, answer the following question. What aspects of language is Rich concerned with in lines 1–7 of this poem?

4. **Group Discussion:** 'All those dead letters/rendered into the oppressor's language'.
    a   Imagine that you had sent letters to someone and they had never been delivered; how would you feel?
    b   Do you think that Rich is suggesting similar emotions by using the phrase 'dead letters' here?
    c   Think back to Ireland's past. How did the Irish people feel when they were forced to speak English?
    d   Do you think that Rich uses the phrase 'the oppressor's language' to convey similar feelings?

    Individual Writing: Using the points that were discussed, answer the following question. In your own words, describe the emotions that Rich is trying to communicate in the two lines quoted above.

5. Imagine that you are the Algerian in lines 10–15. Write a short passage expressing your feelings and thoughts as you go through the experience that Rich describes. You might like to share your work with the class.

6. **Class Discussion:** Using your work for Questions 3, 4 and 5, discuss the following:
    a   Can you see any connections between your three answers?
    b   Do you think that Rich is happy with the language she uses?
    c   What clues in the poem lead you to your conclusion?

Second reading

7. **Class Discussion:** Rich uses the phrase 'the oppressor's language'.
    a   Has the 'oppressor' figure appeared in any of Rich's other poems that you have studied?
    b   Can you sum up how this 'oppressor' figure is portrayed?
    c   In the light of this, whom do you think the 'Our' in the first line of the poem refers to?

    Individual Writing: Using the points that arose in the discussion, answer the following question. What is Rich trying to say in this poem about the language that women use?

8. **Class Debate:** Write a short speech either for or against the motion: 'The English language is a male-centred language.'

9. **Individual Writing:**
    a   In your own words, explain the theme of this poem.
    b   What is your reaction to this theme?

Third reading

10. How do you feel about the way Adrienne Rich portrays the male figure in her poetry? Use references from at least four of her poems to support your viewpoint.

11. Rich uses the 'stream of consciousness' approach in this poem to suggest the way in which her thoughts and feelings spontaneously develop. Using references from this poem and one other poem by Rich, discuss the advantages and disadvantages of such an approach.

TRYING TO TALK WITH A MAN

Out in this desert we are testing bombs,
that's why we came here.

Sometimes I feel an underground river
forcing its way between deformed cliffs
an acute angle of understanding   5
moving itself like a locus of the sun
into this condemned scenery.

What we've had to give up to get here—
whole LP collections, films we starred in
playing in the neighborhoods, bakery windows   10
full of dry, chocolate-filled Jewish cookies,
the language of love-letters, of suicide notes,
afternoons on the riverbank
pretending to be children

Coming out to this desert   15
we meant to change the face of
driving among dull green succulents
walking at noon in the ghost town
surrounded by a silence

that sounds like the silence of the place   20
except that it came with us
and is familiar
and everything we were saying until now
was an effort to blot it out—
Coming out here we are up against it   25

Out here I feel more helpless
with you than without you
You mention the danger
and list the equipment
we talk of people caring for each other   30
in emergencies—laceration, thirst—
but you look at me like an emergency

Your dry heat feels like power
your eyes are stars of a different magnitude
they reflect lights that spell out: EXIT   35
when you get up and pace the floor
talking of the danger

as if it were not ourselves
as if we were testing anything else.

NOTES

4	deformed:	misshapen
5	acute angle:	an angle less than 90°
6	locus:	the defined motion of a point
17	succulents:	thick, fleshy plants
31	laceration:	torn flesh

EXPLORATIONS

First reading

1.   **a**   What is your reaction to the opening two lines of the poem?
    b   Did they make you want to read the rest of the poem? Why?

2. **Individual Writing:**
    a   In your own words, describe the scene that you imagine from the clues in lines 1–7 and lines 15–19.
    b   How would you feel in such an environment? You might like to share your thoughts with the class.

3. **Class Discussion:**
    a   What sort of environment did the people live in before they came to the desert?
    b   Are there any indications in the poem as to why they left this world for the desert?

4. **Group Discussion:**
    a   Examine lines 1–7 and 15–19, where Rich describes the desert. What do you notice about her use of punctuation in these lines?
    b   Now look at lines 8–14. What do you notice about the punctuation in these lines?

c   Why do you think she changes her use of punctuation?

Individual Writing: Using the points that were discussed, answer the following question. How does Rich use punctuation to strengthen her descriptions in this poem?

Second reading

5.   **Paired Discussion:** 'surrounded by a silence that sounds like the silence of the place except that it came with us . . .'

a   Can you explain the two types of silence that Rich is referring to here?

b   Why do you think there is silence between the two people?

6.   **Class Discussion:**

a   What do the couple do in response to the silence?

b   Why do you think they react in this way?

Individual Writing: Based on the behaviour you considered in Questions 5 and 6, do you think the couple are happy or unhappy together? Use quotations from the poem to prove your viewpoint.

7.   'Out here I feel more helpless with you than without you'.

a   What do these lines tell you about how the speaker feels when she is with her partner?

b   Does the title of the poem make it easier for you to understand why she feels 'helpless'?

c   Can you now suggest what the theme of this poem is?

8.   **Class Discussion:** Do the last twelve lines of the poem indicate a happy or unhappy ending for the couple?

Individual Writing: Using the points that were discussed, do you find the conclusion to the poem a satisfactory one? Support your opinion by reference to the poem.

Third reading

9.   This poem is based on two areas of imagery: a) the testing of bombs in the desert; and b) the nature of the couple's relationship.
Trace how Rich weaves the two together in order to convey the theme of this poem. Before you answer this question you might find it helpful to set out the relevant points in two columns, following the method used for 'Aunt Jennifer's Tigers'.

10.   The lyric poem is one in which a single speaker communicates a mood, an attitude or a state of mind to the reader. Discuss the following statement with reference to 'Trying to Talk with a Man' and one other poem: 'Rich takes the lyric poem and gives it a political twist so that the single speaker communicates not only about herself, but also about the society that she lives in.'

DIVING INTO THE WRECK

First having read the book of myths,
and loaded the camera,
and checked the edge of the knife-blade,
I put on
the body-armor of black rubber   5
the absurd flippers
the grave and awkward mask.
I am having to do this
not like Cousteau with his
assiduous team   10
aboard the sun-flooded schooner
but here alone.

There is a ladder.
The ladder is always there
hanging innocently   15
close to the side of the schooner.
We know what it is for,
we who have used it.
Otherwise
it's a piece of maritime floss   20
some sundry equipment.

I go down.
Rung after rung and still
the oxygen immerses me
the blue light   25
the clear atoms
of our human air.
I go down.
My flippers cripple me,
I crawl like an insect down the ladder   30
and there is no one
to tell me when the ocean
will begin.

First the air is blue and then
it is bluer and then green and then   35
black I am blacking out and yet
my mask is powerful
it pumps my blood with power
the sea is another story

the sea is not a question of power   40
I have to learn alone
to turn my body without force
in the deep element.

And now: it is easy to forget
what I came for   45
among so many who have always
lived here
swaying their crenellated fans
between the reefs
and besides   50
you breathe differently down here.

I came to explore the wreck.
The words are purposes.
The words are maps.
I came to see the damage that was done   55
and the treasures that prevail.
I stroke the beam of my lamp
slowly along the flank
of something more permanent
than fish or weed   60

the thing I came for:
the wreck and not the story of the wreck
the thing itself and not the myth
the drowned face always staring
toward the sun   65
the evidence of damage
worn by salt and sway into this threadbare beauty
the ribs of the disaster
curving their assertion
among the tentative haunters.   70

This is the place.
And I am here, the mermaid whose dark hair
streams black, the merman in his armored body
We circle silently
about the wreck   75
we dive into the hold.
I am she: I am he

whose drowned face sleeps with open eyes
whose breasts still bear the stress

whose silver, copper, vermeil cargo lies   80
obscurely inside barrels
half-wedged and left to rot
we are the half-destroyed instruments
that once held to a course
the water-eaten log   85
the fouled compass

We are, I am, you are
by cowardice or courage
the one who find our way
back to this scene   90
carrying a knife, a camera
a book of myths
in which
our names do not appear.

NOTES

1	myths:	legends, folklore
9	Cousteau:	Jacques-Yves Cousteau, famous for his underwater films and TV programmes. He worked tirelessly to increase public awareness of the oceans.
10	assiduous:	hard-working
11	schooner:	a type of ship
20	maritime:	connected with the sea
20	floss:	thread
21	sundry:	various pieces
48	crenellated:	lacy, with irregular edges
56	prevail:	triumph, exist
67	threadbare:	worn, ragged
69	assertion:	statement
70	tentative:	cautious, uncertain
80	vermeil:	a bright, beautiful red, as in vermilion

EXPLORATIONS

Before reading

1. Rich's poems work on a number of interwoven levels and this can sometimes cause confusion, particularly in a longer poem such as this. For this poem, use an A4 or double copy page. Rule out five equal columns. Use the following five headings: 'Setting'; 'Activity'; 'Emotional Setting'; 'Emotional Activity'; 'Political Messages'. As you answer the questions, fill in the appropriate columns with points summarising your thinking. In this

way, the interrelationship between the layers should become clearer.

First reading

2. **Class Discussion:** This discussion will help you to fill in the 'Setting' and 'Activity' columns in Question 1.
   a   Where is this poem set?
   b   What is the speaker going to do?
   c   What preparations does she make?
   d   What does she use to move down to the water?
   e   Is her journey down the ladder an easy one or does it take a lot of effort?
   f   Is there anyone with her?

   Individual Writing: Using the answers that arose out of your discussion, begin to fill in the columns headed 'Setting' and 'Activity' in point form.

3. **Class Discussion:** This discussion will help you to fill in the 'Setting' and 'Activity' columns.
   a   What does the diver have to learn to do in the water?
   b   Why does she go to the wreck?
   c   How do you imagine the wreck from the description in the poem?
   d   Who does the diver meet at the wreck?

   Individual Writing: Using the answers you discussed, finish filling in the columns headed 'Setting' and 'Activity' in point form.

Second reading

4. **Class Discussion:** This discussion will help you to fill in the 'Emotional Setting' column in Question 1.

   a   How do you think the diver feels as she prepares for the dive?
   b   Consider what her checking of the knife edge and putting on the 'body-armor' convey about the emotional setting of the poem.
   c   Read lines 22–37 and consider her emotions during these experiences.

   Individual Writing: Using the answers that arose out of your discussion, fill in the column headed 'Emotional Setting' in point form.

5. **Class Discussion:** This discussion will help you to fill in the 'Emotional Activity' column in Question 1.
   a   How does the diver's mood change when she learns how to move in 'the deep element'?
   b   What are her feelings when she reaches the wreck?
   c   How does she feel when she meets the mermaid and merman?
   d   What is her mood in the final eight lines of the poem, when she becomes one with the mermaid and merman?

   Individual Writing: Using the answers that arose out of your discussion, fill in the column headed 'Emotional Activity' in point form.

6. **Class Discussion:** This discussion will help you to fill in the final column, 'Political Messages'. This poem tells of a heroic quest for treasure in an old wreck and the transformation that occurs to the

heroine when she succeeds in her quest.

a   Consider what the quest represents: is the diver trying to learn something about being a woman, or is she questioning 'the book of myths' that contain all the accepted inequalities of our society?

b   What do you think the treasure represents: is it self-knowledge, or knowledge about why men have most of the power in society?

c   What might the wreck represent: the diver's own unsatisfactory life as a woman, or the outdated rules of society that reinforce inequality?

d   What could her transformation into an androgynous figure (partly male, partly female) represent: the achievement of true personal power through surviving all the injustices, or could it stand for society, doomed to destruction because it is based on inequality?

Individual Writing: Using the answers that arose out of your discussion, fill in the column 'Political Messages' in point form.

Third reading

7. **Paired Discussion:** Referring back to the relevant columns should prove helpful.

a   How does the physical setting at the beginning of the poem influence the diver's emotional setting?

b   What effects do the physical activities in which the diver engages have on her emotional activities?

Individual Writing: Using the answers that arose out of your discussion, answer the following question. Trace how the diver's emotions change as she goes through the different experiences described in the poem. Use quotations to support your points.

8. **Group Discussion:** Referring back to the relevant column should prove helpful.

a   What message does this poem communicate about Rich's attitude to being a woman?

b   What message is conveyed about the society that Rich lived in?

Individual Writing: Using the answers that arose out of your discussion, explain in your own words the major themes of this poem.

9. 'Rich has the ability to create images that are stunningly vivid.'
Discuss this statement, using quotations from 'Diving into the Wreck' and two other poems by Rich that you have studied.

10. 'The words are purposes. The words are maps.'
Consider how Rich conveys her belief that language traps people in inequality, with reference to two of her poems on your course.

FROM A SURVIVOR

The pact that we made was the ordinary pact
of men & women in those days

I don't know who we thought we were
that our personalities
could resist the failures of the race   5

Lucky or unlucky, we didn't know
the race had failures of that order
and that we were going to share them

Like everybody else, we thought of ourselves as special

Your body is as vivid to me   10
as it ever was: even more

since my feeling for it is clearer:
I know what it could and could not do

it is no longer
the body of a god   15
or anything with power over my life

Next year it would have been 20 years
and you are wastefully dead
who might have made the leap
we talked, too late, of making   20

which I live now
not as a leap
but a succession of brief, amazing movements

each one making possible the next

'Hotel by a Railroad' by Edward Hopper (1952)

NOTE

Rich wrote this poem to her husband, Alfred Conrad, who committed suicide in 1970.

EXPLORATIONS

Before reading

1. Have you ever been a bridesmaid
    or a groomsman at a wedding?
    What can you remember about the
    day? How did the couple who were
    getting married feel about their
    wedding? Did the experience make
    you feel positive or negative about
    getting married?

First reading

2. a   From your first reading of the
        poem, can you suggest a phrase
        that sums up Rich's feelings for
        her late husband?
    b   Do you find some of the
        feelings expressed in this poem

surprising when set against the
other poems on your course?
Why?

3. **Class Discussion:**
    a   Can you explain what the
        'ordinary pact' was that Rich
        made with her husband?
    b   Look up the word 'pact' in
        the dictionary and note the
        definitions of the word.
    c   Do you think that it is a good
        word to describe the marriage
        of a man and a woman? Why?

Individual Writing: Using the
points that were discussed, answer
the following question. What does
Rich's use of the word 'pact' to
describe marriage suggest about

her attitude to this connection between men and women?

4. **Class Discussion:**

   a What do you think she means by the phrase 'the failures of the race'?

   b Can you suggest a connection between the 'pact' and these 'failures'?

5. a How does Rich's attitude towards her husband's body change during their marriage?

   b Do you think that such a change is natural in a long–term relationship? Why?

   c In your opinion, would such a change make the couple's love stronger or weaker? Give reasons for your answer.

6. Adrienne Rich believes that 'Young readers need to learn that a poem is not a letter, or a diary entry, it's a crafted work which may begin in a personal experience but always evolves into something else if it has any value as art at all.' As the poem develops, what themes does Rich draw out of her starting point of 'personal experience'? You may find it helpful to consider some of the themes that you have already encountered in her work.

Second reading

7. **Class Discussion:**

   a Can you suggest what the 'leap' in lines 19 and 22 might represent?

   b Do Rich's other poems give you any indication of what this 'leap' might involve?

8. 'but a succession of brief, amazing movements/each one making possible the next'

   a Why do you think that Rich does not use a full stop at the end of the poem?

   b What do these final lines suggest to you about Rich's attitude to her life?

   c Is there a connection between these lines and the poem's title?

Third reading

9. **Group Discussion:** Rich uses very little punctuation in this poem.

   a Read the poem aloud as it is and listen to it carefully.

   b Put in the correct punctuation and read the poem again.

   c What effect does the added punctuation have on the way the poem is read?

   d Which version do you prefer, the unpunctuated or the punctuated one? Why?

10. **Class Presentation:** Prepare a piece for presentation to the class either agreeing or disagreeing with the statement: 'Rich has a depressingly negative view of male/female relationships.'
    Use quotations from at least three of her poems to support your argument.

11. Survival is an important concept in Rich's poetry. With reference to two of her poems featuring women who are successful survivors and two of her poems featuring women who are unsuccessful survivors, explain the factors that Rich believes make women successful or unsuccessful survivors.

SYLVIA
PLATH

(1932–63)

Prescribed for Higher Level exams in 2019 and 2021

Sylvia Plath was born in Boston, Massachusetts, on 27 October 1932 to Aurelia Schober Plath and Otto Plath, professor of biology and German at Boston University. In 1940 Otto died after a long illness, a tragedy that haunted Sylvia throughout her life. From a young age, Sylvia wanted above all else to be a writer. Already writing at the age of five, she had her first poem published in the children's section of the *Boston Herald* at the age of eight. She was a brilliant high school student, consistently earning A grades, and also led a busy social life. She had a number of stories and poems published – and also got many rejection slips; this pattern recurred throughout her writing life. In 1950 she entered the prestigious women's university, Smith College, Massachusetts.

In 1952 Plath was selected to work as one of twenty 'guest editors' with *Mademoiselle* magazine in New York City. On her return to Wellesley she suffered a serious bout of depression, for which she was given electric shock treatment. However, this seems to have deepened her depression and she attempted suicide in August, leading to a four-month spell in a psychiatric hospital. She resumed her studies in Smith College in January 1953, graduating with honours in 1955, and winning a Fulbright scholarship to study in Cambridge, England. There she met Ted Hughes, a young English poet, whom she married in June 1956.

Sylvia and Ted worked and wrote in the US for two years and returned to London in December 1959. 'Black Rook in Rainy Weather' and 'The Times Are Tidy' date from this period. Her first book, *The Colossus and Other Poems*, was published in February 1960 but received disappointing reviews. April 1960 saw the birth of their daughter, Frieda. The following year they moved to Devon, where their son, Nicholas, was born in January 1962. Throughout this time, Sylvia was writing poetry (including 'Morning Song', 'Finisterre', 'Mirror', 'Pheasant' and 'Elm'), some of which was published in magazines in Britain and the US. Her semi-autobiographical novel, *The Bell Jar*, was published in 1963.

Shortly after Nicholas's birth, Ted and Sylvia separated. She remained in Devon, caring for her children and writing despite poor health and recurring depression. She completed most of the poems that made up her second book, *Ariel* (published posthumously), among them 'Poppies in July' and 'The Arrival of the Bee Box'. In mid-December 1962, she moved to London with her children. The poems she wrote at this time include 'Child', written on 28 January 1963. However, unable to cope with the many difficulties facing her, she took her own life on 11 February 1963. Since her death her writing has received wide acclaim, including the prestigious Pulitzer Prize, an award rarely bestowed posthumously.

BLACK ROOK IN RAINY WEATHER

On the stiff twig up there
Hunches a wet black rook
Arranging and rearranging its feathers in the rain.
I do not expect a miracle
Or an accident   5

To set the sight on fire
In my eye, nor seek
Any more in the desultory weather some design,
But let spotted leaves fall as they fall,
Without ceremony, or portent.   10

Although, I admit, I desire,
Occasionally, some backtalk
From the mute sky, I can't honestly complain:
A certain minor light may still
Lean incandescent   15

Out of kitchen table or chair
As if a celestial burning took
Possession of the most obtuse objects now and then –
Thus hallowing an interval
Otherwise inconsequent   20

By bestowing largesse, honor,
One might say love. At any rate, I now walk
Wary (for it could happen
Even in this dull, ruinous landscape); skeptical,
Yet politic; ignorant   25

Of whatever angel may choose to flare
Suddenly at my elbow. I only know that a rook
Ordering its black feathers can so shine
As to seize my senses, haul
My eyelids up, and grant   30

A brief respite from fear
Of total neutrality. With luck,
Trekking stubborn through this season
Of fatigue, I shall
Patch together a content   35

Of sorts. Miracles occur,
If you care to call those spasmodic
Tricks of radiance miracles. The wait's begun again,
The long wait for the angel,
For that rare, random descent.   40

NOTES

2	rook:	crow
8	desultory:	without method, disjointed
10	portent:	omen of some possibly calamitous event
15	incandescent:	glowing, brilliant
19	hallowing:	making sacred
21	largesse:	a generously given present
25	politic:	prudent
31	respite:	brief period of relief

EXPLORATIONS

Before reading

1. What picture does the title create for you? Does it suggest a particular mood?

First reading

2. The poem is set against a very definite landscape: read the poem and describe the scene as accurately as you can. Build your picture from the poet's words and phrases.

3. What does the narrator seem to be doing in this poem? What thoughts does this lead to?

4. Describe the atmosphere the poem creates for you. What details are most important in setting this atmosphere?

Second reading

5. There is an abrupt change between lines 3 and 4. What is it?

6. The narrator claims that 'I do not expect ... nor seek' (lines 4–7). What does she neither expect nor seek?

7. What does she 'admit' to desiring? How does she convey the idea that it may not be possible to get what she desires?

8. Can you find other places in the poem where she makes a statement and then qualifies it – 'neutralises' it? What do such statements tell us about the narrator's frame of mind?

9. The 'minor light' of line 14 'may' have an extraordinary effect: read lines 14–22 carefully and explain this effect in your own words.

10. Can you explain how the 'rook/ Ordering its black feathers can [...] grant/A brief respite' to the speaker? A brief respite from what?

11. In the final lines, the poet is waiting for the 'rare, random descent' of the angel. What might the angel bring? What examples of this has she already given?

12. The angel's 'rare, random descent' is a metaphor: what do you think it represents? Look at references to other heavenly phenomena before answering.

Third reading

13. Comment on the effect of the repetition of the sound 'rain' in line 3.

14. Look through the poem again and pick out words connected with darkness and light. Compare the images or words used. Can you find any pattern?

15. The narrator does not 'seek ... design' in things around her. How does the language reflect that lack of design, the accidental nature of what happens? A good starting point might be to identify the words associated with time or chance.

16. There is a mixture of the everyday/ earthly and the extraordinary/ miraculous here. How is this effect achieved? You might find it helpful to contrast concrete descriptions with references to the sacred.

Fourth reading

17. Examine the rhyme scheme. What pattern do you find? What is the effect of this careful sound pattern?

18. Write a note on the style of the poem, looking at tone, language, imagery and structure.

19. Throughout her life, Plath was preoccupied with the conflict between her ambitions to be a poet and the expectations of a society that defined women as homemakers. Reread this poem with this in mind. Would you agree that this could be one theme of the poem? Are there other possibilities? Write about what you consider to be the main themes of this poem.

THE TIMES ARE TIDY

Unlucky the hero born
In this province of the stuck record
Where the most watchful cooks go jobless
And the mayor's rôtisserie turns
Round of its own accord.   5

There's no career in the venture
Of riding against the lizard,
Himself withered these latter-days
To leaf-size from lack of action:
History's beaten the hazard.   10

The last crone got burnt up
More than eight decades back
With the love-hot herb, the talking cat,
But the children are better for it,
The cow milks cream an inch thick.   15

EXPLORATIONS

Before reading

1. Think back to folk tales or legends you have read or heard involving knights in armour, witches and monsters. What can you remember about their world or the adventures described?

2. Jot down whatever comes into your mind when you hear the word 'tidy'.

First reading

3. The poem puts two eras side by side. What can you learn from the poem about each of them?

4. Which era sounds more appealing to you? Why? Which does the author seem to favour? Refer to the poem to support your impression.

Second reading

5. Try to mentally recapture the effect of listening to a stuck record. What do you think the poet is telling you about 'this province' when she uses this image? Do you think this links in any way with 'tidy'?

6. The poem was written about a particular phase in American political life. In light of this, suggest what the 'mayor's rôtisserie' might represent. Who might the 'cooks' be?

7. We are told that the jobless cooks are the 'most watchful': why then are they jobless? By choice? Because they have been sacked?

8. What mythical creature does the lizard resemble? Think of medieval knights and the creatures they did battle with. What is there in this stanza to show that the poet intends this connection to be made?

9. In what way has 'History' 'beaten the hazard'?

10. What association exists between the crone and the 'love-hot herb', the 'talking cat' and the 'cream an inch thick'?

11. What do the crone, the hero and the lizard have in common? How does their absence affect the 'times'?

12. Most of the poem focuses on what this age has lost: the last two lines suggest a gain. What is this? Do you think the poet is being serious here or is she being ironic? Explain your answer.

Third reading

13. Two eras are contrasted in the poem. How do they differ? Be precise – refer to the text for each point you make.

14. Choose the image(s) you consider to be most effective. Explain your choice.

15. Keeping in mind the title, the images used and the comparisons made, write a note on the tone of the poem.

Fourth reading

16. 'This poem is an ironic commentary on an era of smug, self-satisfied complacency in American life.' Discuss this statement, referring to imagery, language and tone.

MORNING SONG

Love set you going like a fat gold watch.
The midwife slapped your footsoles, and your bald cry
Took its place among the elements.

Our voices echo, magnifying your arrival. New statue.
In a drafty museum, your nakedness   5
Shadows our safety. We stand round blankly as walls.

I'm no more your mother
Than the cloud that distills a mirror to reflect its own slow
Effacement at the wind's hand.

All night your moth-breath   10
Flickers among the flat pink roses. I wake to listen:
A far sea moves in my ear.

One cry, and I stumble from bed, cow-heavy and floral
In my Victorian nightgown.
Your mouth opens clean as a cat's. The window square   15

Whitens and swallows its dull stars. And now you try
Your handful of notes;
The clear vowels rise like balloons.

EXPLORATIONS

Before reading

1. Look at the title of this poem: jot down the ideas you associate with both words. What mood do they evoke?

First reading

2. Stanzas 1–3 centre on the infant taking her place in the world. How do others respond to her? Which emotions come across most clearly?

3. How do you understand the image of the baby as a 'New statue' taking its place in a 'drafty museum'? How does nakedness 'shadow' the safety of the onlookers? (There are a number of possibilities.)

4. Explain in your own words what happens in stanzas 4–6. Do you find the description realistic?

Second reading

5. What emotions does the opening line suggest to you? Look at the first word, the image, the rhythm. Do you think it is an effective opening line? Why?

6. Identify the noises named in the poem. Name the source of each sound. Who is listening to them? What impression do they create? How do they contribute to the texture of the poem?

Third reading

7. This poem is rich in vivid imagery and word-pictures. Identify these.

8. Say what each image or word-picture suggests about the baby, about the mother and about the world they inhabit. How is this suggested? Refer to the language, the juxtaposition of images and the associations implied.

9. Explain the cloud/mirror/wind image used in stanza 3. What does the comparison suggest about the narrator's feelings about motherhood?

Fourth reading

10. 'Morning Song' is a tender evocation of a simple, daily event. Examine how the writer conveys the mood of tenderness while avoiding sentimentality.

11. Compare this poem with 'Child' in terms of theme, tone, language and imagery. Which of the two poems do you prefer? Why?

FINISTERRE

This was the land's end: the last fingers, knuckled and rheumatic,
Cramped on nothing. Black
Admonitory cliffs, and the sea exploding
With no bottom, or anything on the other side of it,
Whitened by the faces of the drowned.   5
Now it is only gloomy, a dump of rocks –
Leftover soldiers from old, messy wars.
The sea cannons into their ear, but they don't budge.
Other rocks hide their grudges under the water.

The cliffs are edged with trefoils, stars and bells   10
Such as fingers might embroider, close to death,
Almost too small for the mists to bother with.
The mists are part of the ancient paraphernalia –
Souls, rolled in the doom-noise of the sea.
They bruise the rocks out of existence, then resurrect them.   15
They go up without hope, like sighs.
I walk among them, and they stuff my mouth with cotton.
When they free me, I am beaded with tears.

Our Lady of the Shipwrecked is striding toward the horizon,
Her marble skirts blown back in two pink wings.   20
A marble sailor kneels at her foot distractedly, and at his foot
A peasant woman in black
Is praying to the monument of the sailor praying.
Our Lady of the Shipwrecked is three times life size,
Her lips sweet with divinity.   25
She does not hear what the sailor or the peasant is saying –
She is in love with the beautiful formlessness of the sea.

Gull-colored laces flap in the sea drafts
Beside the postcard stalls.
The peasants anchor them with conches. One is told: 30
'These are the pretty trinkets the sea hides,
Little shells made up into necklaces and toy ladies.
They do not come from the Bay of the Dead down there,
But from another place, tropical and blue,
We have never been to.   35
These are our crêpes. Eat them before they blow cold.'

NOTES

Finisterre:		the westernmost tip of Brittany – literally 'land's end'
3	Admonitory:	giving a warning
10	trefoils:	three-leaved plants
13	paraphernalia:	belongings, bits and pieces, ornaments
14	doom:	judgement, punishment
30	conches:	spiral shells
36	crêpes:	light, lacy, crisp pancakes – a speciality of Brittany

EXPLORATIONS

Before reading

1. What kind of landscape/seascape do the place names 'Finisterre' and 'land's end' suggest? How do you visualise it – the colours, shapes, sounds, weather, etc.?

First reading

Stanza 1

2. Read stanza 1. What overall picture do you form of the scene? What words or images do you find most striking? Is the personification effective?

3. How is language used to create the impression of an attack, a battle? Does this description of a headland create a familiar picture for you?

Stanza 2

4. What does stanza 2 describe? How does it connect with stanza 1? Notice how language and imagery are used to create links.

5. What qualities do you usually associate with mist? Which of these qualities does this mist share? What other qualities does the narrator attribute to it? Do these add anything new?

6. What is your impression of the atmosphere in this place? How is it created?

Second reading

Stanza 3

7. Describe in your own words the scene depicted in stanza 3. What connection is there with the first two stanzas?

8. The perspective in this stanza has changed: the poet is showing us things from a different angle. How is this indicated?

9. This stanza tells a little story within the poem. Tell it in your own words.

Stanza 4

10. The stalls in stanza 4 are suggested through a few precise details. Look at the description – can you picture them?

11. This stanza differs remarkably from the preceding stanzas. In what way?

12. Identify the ideas/words/images that link stanza 4 with the earlier stanzas. Explain the connection.

13. We now learn that the bay is named the Bay of the Dead: does the name fit, in your opinion? Why do you think the poet did not name it until the end of the poem?

Third reading

14. Comment on the effect of the image in lines 1–2. How is this image developed in the rest of this stanza and in stanza 2?

15. Stanza 3 opens with a description of the monument. Contrast the 'I' of stanza 2 with Our Lady of the Shipwrecked. What is the impact of the contrast? What is the narrator's attitude to Our Lady?

16. Comment on the language used to describe the scene – the details given and the intentions or qualities attributed to each figure. Where does the narrator fit into this scene? What does she seem to be saying about prayer?

17. The author broadens the scope of the poem through the stall-keeper's comments, which reflect quite a different response to the bay. How? What is the effect of the wider canvas?

18. How does the final line strike you? Would you agree that there is a slightly ironic note here? What effect does this have on your reading of the poem?

Fourth reading

19. Write a note on the tone of the poem. Be aware of the gradual change in tone, reflected in the language and imagery. Note the differences between the narrator's attitude and that of the other figures in the poem.

20. Trace the progress of thought from the opening line to the end of the poem. Focus on how the author moves from the inner thoughts of the narrator to a more objective view. Note where the changes occur.

21. Plath once commented that 'a poem, by its own system of illusions, can set up a rich and apparently living world within its particular limits'. Write about 'Finisterre' in light of this comment, looking at her choice of words, images, sound effects and point of view.

MIRROR

I am silver and exact. I have no preconceptions.
Whatever I see I swallow immediately
Just as it is, unmisted by love or dislike.
I am not cruel, only truthful –
The eye of a little god, four-cornered.   5
Most of the time I meditate on the opposite wall.
It is pink, with speckles. I have looked at it so long
I think it is a part of my heart. But it flickers.
Faces and darkness separate us over and over.

Now I am a lake. A woman bends over me,   10
Searching my reaches for what she really is.
Then she turns to those liars, the candles or the moon.
I see her back, and reflect it faithfully.
She rewards me with tears and an agitation of hands.
I am important to her. She comes and goes.   15
Each morning it is her face that replaces the darkness.
In me she has drowned a young girl, and in me an old woman
Rises toward her day after day, like a terrible fish.

NOTE

11   reaches: stretch of water, depths

EXPLORATIONS

Before reading

1. Think for a minute about a mirror. Write down quickly all the words, ideas and associations that come to mind.

First reading

2. Read this poem a number of times. What is it saying?

3. Write a note on the form of the poem: number of stanzas, number of lines, etc.

4. Pick out all the 'I' statements. How many are there? What effect do they have?

5. Identify the qualities the mirror claims to possess. What overall impression is created by these attributes?

6. Notice the position of the words 'a little god': they are at the exact centre of stanza 1. Can you suggest why the poet placed them just there?

7. What impression is created by the description of 'the opposite wall'?

8. In stanza 2, the mirror states that it is now 'a lake'. What similarities are there between a lake and a mirror? What differences are there? How does this new image expand the mirror image?

9. Why do you think the narrator describes the candles and the moon as 'liars'?

10. What might cause the woman's tears and agitation? How does this point broaden the scope of the poem?

11. The mirror/lake contains three phases of the woman's life: what are these?

Second reading

12. The focus – the point of view – changes between stanzas 1 and 2. How has the centre of consciousness changed? What is the effect of this?

13. Write a note about what you think the 'terrible fish' might be.

14. 'I am important to her': this is a very strong statement. How could a mirror be important to the woman? What do you think the mirror may represent to the narrator? (Try to move beyond the most obvious points.)

Third reading

15. Compare the opening lines (1–3) with the final lines. Trace the progress of thought through the poem, showing how the narrator moves from the opening statement to the conclusion. Note the changes in tone that occur.

16. The poem concludes on a note of desperation. How is this prepared for in the poem as a whole?

17. Do you agree that the narrator has 'no preconceptions', as stated in line 1? What evidence can you find to support your opinion? Look especially at phrases like 'I think', 'those liars', etc.

18. While the poem is unrhymed, Plath uses a variety of sound effects. Identify some of these and say what effect they create.

Fourth reading

19. Many writers and artists use the mirror as a symbol – for example, of the self, the alter ego, the 'dark side of the soul'. Reread the poem with this idea in mind. How does it colour your reading of the poem? Does it fit the poem?

20. It has been argued that in this poem, Plath is addressing the conflict between what a woman was expected to be (smooth, unruffled, reflecting the image the world wanted to see) and her true nature (struggling to be heard, seen for what it is: the 'terrible fish'). Reread the poem in light of this and write your response.

PHEASANT

You said you would kill it this morning.
Do not kill it. It startles me still,
The jut of that odd, dark head, pacing

Through the uncut grass on the elm's hill.
It is something to own a pheasant,   5
Or just to be visited at all.

I am not mystical: it isn't
As if I thought it had a spirit.
It is simply in its element.

That gives it a kingliness, a right.   10
The print of its big foot last winter,
The tail-track, on the snow in our court –

The wonder of it, in that pallor,
Through crosshatch of sparrow and starling.
Is it its rareness, then? It is rare.   15

But a dozen would be worth having,
A hundred, on that hill – green and red,
Crossing and recrossing: a fine thing!

It is such a good shape, so vivid.
It's a little cornucopia.   20
It unclaps, brown as a leaf, and loud,

Settles in the elm, and is easy.
It was sunning in the narcissi.
I trespass stupidly. Let be, let be.

NOTES

| 14 | crosshatch: | criss-cross pattern |
| 20 | cornucopia: | a mythical horn, always full of flowers and fruit. A symbol of plenty. |

EXPLORATIONS

First reading

1. The poem opens very abruptly: it plunges the reader right into the narrator's preoccupation. What is this? Why do you think she repeats the word 'kill'?

2. Lines 3–4 present a graphic picture. What scene is evoked?

3. The speaker's attitude towards the pheasant is clearly signalled in lines 5–6. What is it? Can you find any further echo of this feeling in the poem?

4. In stanzas 4–5 the poet pictures the pheasant. How does she underline its difference from the other birds that visit her yard?

5. Stanza 7 moves back to the present: the pheasant's 'clap' draws her attention. What was it doing before it flew up into the elm?

6. She loves the colour, the shape, the sound of the pheasant. Identify where each of these is praised.

Second reading

7. In stanza 3 the narrator explains why she feels so honoured by the visit of the pheasant. Identify what 'it is' and what 'it isn't' that touches her. Why do you think she tells us that she is 'not mystical'?

8. In what sense is she trespassing? What does this word suggest about her attitude to the pheasant?

9. How do the final words link back to the opening statement and request? Do you feel the narrator has got her way at the end? Explain.

10. What is the tone/mood of the poem? Use the text to support your points, paying attention to the narrator's relationship with 'you'.

Third reading

11. Plath describes the pheasant as 'vivid'. The same word could apply to this poem: it is strong, vigorous and sinewy. Write about this quality of the poem. Look at language – verbs, nouns, adjectives – as well as imagery, structure, rhythm and rhyme.

ELM

For Ruth Fainlight

I know the bottom, she says. I know it with my great tap root:
It is what you fear.
I do not fear it: I have been there.

Is it the sea you hear in me,
Its dissatisfactions? 5
Or the voice of nothing, that was your madness?

Love is a shadow.
How you lie and cry after it
Listen: these are its hooves: it has gone off, like a horse.

All night I shall gallop thus, impetuously, 10
Till your head is a stone, your pillow a little turf,
Echoing, echoing.

Or shall I bring you the sound of poisons?
This is rain now, this big hush.
And this is the fruit of it: tin-white, like arsenic. 15

I have suffered the atrocity of sunsets.
Scorched to the root
My red filaments burn and stand, a hand of wires.

Now I break up in pieces that fly about like clubs.
A wind of such violence 20
Will tolerate no bystanding: I must shriek.

The moon, also, is merciless: she would drag me
Cruelly, being barren.
Her radiance scathes me. Or perhaps I have caught her.

I let her go. I let her go 25
Diminished and flat, as after radical surgery.
How your bad dreams possess and endow me.

I am inhabited by a cry.
Nightly it flaps out
Looking, with its hooks, for something to love. 30

I am terrified by this dark thing
That sleeps in me;
All day I feel its soft, feathery turnings, its malignity.

Clouds pass and disperse.
Are those the faces of love, those pale irretrievables?   35
Is it for such I agitate my heart?

I am incapable of more knowledge.
What is this, this face
So murderous in its strangle of branches? –

Its snaky acids hiss.   40
It petrifies the will. These are the isolate, slow faults
That kill, that kill, that kill.

NOTES

15	arsenic:	lethal poison
18	filaments:	thread-like conductors of electrical current
24	scathe:	to hurt or injure, especially by scorching
35	irretrievables:	cannot be recovered or won back

EXPLORATIONS

First reading

1. Read to the poem a number of times. What sounds are most striking? Which words stay in your mind? Jot down your impressions.

2. What attitude does 'I' seem to adopt towards 'you' in stanza 3?

3. Stanzas 5–8 introduce rain, sunset, wind and moon. How is each one presented? How do they affect 'I'?

4. What change seems to occur in 'I' in stanzas 9–14? Can you identify at what point the change began?

5. Would you agree that the latter half of the poem powerfully conveys a nightmare world? Which images and phrases are most effective in building this impression?

Second reading

6. 'Elm' opens on a confident, objective note, as if the narrator is quite detached from 'you'. How is this achieved?

7. Trace the references to love in the poem. How does the narrator view love? Is it important to her?

8. There are several references to violence, both physical and mental. Select those you consider most powerful. What is the source of the violence?

9. Compare the force of love with the force of evil. Which comes across as the more powerful? Explain how this is achieved.

Third reading

10. Plath uses many rich and powerful images. The central image is the elm, the 'I' persona. Trace the elm's feelings and mood through the poem. What do you think the elm may symbolise to the poet? In answering this, reflect on the tone, the utter weariness, the feelings of anguish, the growing terror and the role 'you' plays in generating these feelings.

11. The moon is another important image in the poem. Reread the stanzas describing it (8, 9, 13). What qualities are attributed to it? What do you think it symbolises? Can you explain the seeming contradictions?

Fourth reading

12. The poet uses rich sound effects throughout the poem. Note where she uses rhyme, assonance, repetition, cacophony and soft sounds. How do these affect the reader/listener?

13. The poem opens with a calm, confident voice and a sense of control: 'I know …/I do not fear'. It closes on a note of hysterical despair and total loss of control: 'It petrifies the will. These are the isolate, slow faults/That kill, that kill, that kill.'
Trace the change through the poem. Describe how this transformation is achieved.

Fifth reading

14. 'Plath infuses this poem with a strong sense of vulnerability pitted against destructive energy.'
What is your response to this statement? Use detailed reference to the poem in support of each point you make.

15. '"Elm" is a powerful, urgent statement spoken by a narrator who has been abandoned by the person she loves.'
Discuss this view of the poem.

16. 'This poem has the surreal quality of a nightmare in which the smallest objects seem fraught with hidden significance.'
Discuss how this effect is achieved, basing each point you make on specific reference to the poem.

POPPIES IN JULY

OL 2
OL 2

Little poppies, little hell flames,
Do you do no harm?

You flicker. I cannot touch you.
I put my hands among the flames. Nothing burns.

And it exhausts me to watch you   5
Flickering like that, wrinkly and clear red, like the skin of a mouth.

A mouth just bloodied.
Little bloody skirts!

There are fumes that I cannot touch.
Where are your opiates, your nauseous capsules?   10

If I could bleed, or sleep! –
If my mouth could marry a hurt like that!

Or your liquors seep to me, in this glass capsule,
Dulling and stilling.

But colorless. Colorless.   15

NOTES

10	opiates:	narcotics, drugs that induce sleep, dull feelings
10	nauseous:	causing vomiting or illness

EXPLORATIONS

Before reading

1. Imagine a poppy. What qualities do you associate with it? Think of colour, texture and shape.

First reading

2. The poem opens with a question. What does it suggest to you?

3. Describe what the narrator is doing in this poem. What thoughts are triggered by her actions?

4. Identify the words associated with fire in lines 1–6. What is the narrator's feeling about this fire/ these poppies? What does fire symbolise? Do you see any of these qualities reflected here?

5. Which qualities of the poppies might make the narrator think of a mouth?

6. What could 'bloody' a mouth? Do any of the other words suggest violence?

7. Lines 9–15 focus on another aspect of poppies. What is this?

8. Looking at the various descriptions of the poppies, try to explain the author's attitude to them.

Second reading

9. What feelings does the narrator convey in this poem? Say how each feeling is suggested, referring to specific words and images.

10. There is a strong contrast between lines 1–8 and lines 9–15. How is this effected? Look at how words, images and tone contribute to the contrast.

11. The narrator seems to imply an answer to the question posed in stanza 1. How does she answer it?

Third reading

12. While there is no end rhyme in this poem, the poet uses quite intricate sound effects, including repetition. Trace these, noting the effect they have.

13. Write a paragraph about the poet's use of colour in the poem, noting how she moves from the vividness of the early stanzas to the final repeated 'colorless'. What might the loss of colour say about the narrator's feelings?

14. The poem moves from the outside world to the inner world of the narrator. Chart this movement through the poem. How does she connect one to the other?

Fourth reading

15. Do you think the intensity of the feeling conveyed is consistent with a simple description of poppies? What underlying emotion do you think might cause such intense anguish? Discuss this point, referring to the text in support of your arguments.

16. In 'Poppies in July' and 'Elm', Plath takes a simple natural object and invests it with intense feelings, creating a metaphor for personal suffering – the inner struggle to come to terms with an overwhelming problem. Write a comparison of the two poems.

THE ARRIVAL OF THE BEE BOX

I ordered this, this clean wood box
Square as a chair and almost too heavy to lift.
I would say it was the coffin of a midget
Or a square baby
Were there not such a din in it.   5

The box is locked, it is dangerous.
I have to live with it overnight
And I can't keep away from it.
There are no windows, so I can't see what is in there.
There is only a little grid, no exit.   10

I put my eye to the grid.
It is dark, dark,
With the swarmy feeling of African hands
Minute and shrunk for export,
Black on black, angrily clambering.   15

How can I let them out?
It is the noise that appalls me most of all,
The unintelligible syllables.
It is like a Roman mob,
Small, taken one by one, but my god, together!   20

I lay my ear to furious Latin.
I am not a Caesar.
I have simply ordered a box of maniacs.
They can be sent back.
They can die, I need feed them nothing, I am the owner.   25

I wonder how hungry they are.
I wonder if they would forget me
If I just undid the locks and stood back and turned into a tree.
There is the laburnum, its blond colonnades,
And the petticoats of the cherry.   30

They might ignore me immediately
In my moon suit and funeral veil.
I am no source of honey
So why should they turn on me?
Tomorrow I will be sweet God, I will set them free.   35

The box is only temporary.

NOTES

22	Caesar:	Roman emperor
28	turned into a tree:	a reference to the Greek myth of Daphne, who was chased by Apollo. She pleaded with the gods to help her escape and they changed her into a tree.
32	moon suit and funeral veil:	protective clothing worn by beekeepers

EXPLORATIONS

First reading

1. Stanza 1 gives the background to the arrival of the bee box and the narrator's reaction. Which feeling is most obvious? Have you ever felt this way about bees, wasps, etc.?

2. How does she seem to relate to the bees in stanzas 3–5?

3. Stanza 5 concludes with the statement 'They can die'. Do you actually believe she means this? How does she undermine her statement? Be precise.

4. How does she propose to escape the bees' wrath if she releases them?

5. She describes her clothing as a 'moon suit'. What ideas does this image suggest?

6. Comment on the contradiction between 'I am no source of honey' and 'I will be sweet God'. Note the play on words – what is the tone of these lines? How can she be 'sweet God' to the bees?

7. What happens in this poem? What part does the 'I' of the poem play in the event?

Second reading

8. The language used to describe the bee box is strong, suggesting something sinister and dangerous. Select the words or images that help to create this impression.

9. There is a contradiction between the image of a coffin and the intense life within the box. Which idea – death or life – is implied with more strength in the rest of the poem? Be precise.

10. In stanza 3 the writer creates a graphic metaphor for the bees and their sound. Identify these and note the common link between them. What do they tell us about the narrator?

11. In stanzas 4–5 the bees have become a metaphor for the narrator's words. Explain the image, trying to convey some of the feeling she captures. What relationship is suggested between the narrator and her words in these two stanzas?

12. The image of turning into a tree is associated with the Greek myth of the god Apollo and Daphne: she turned into a tree to escape his attentions. What does this association say about the narrator's attitude to the bees?

13. Write a detailed description of the changes in the narrator's attitude between stanza 1 and stanza 7.

14. The final line stands alone, separated from the rest of the poem, which is arranged in five-line stanzas. What does the line suggest? How does it colour the reader's response to the poem as a whole?

Third reading

15. Plath makes extensive use of internal rhyme, assonance and word play. One example is 'Square as a chair'. Here, 'chair' suggests the homely and ordinary, while 'square' implies honest, straightforward, exact. The rhyme almost echoes the box's shape – its regularity and squareness. Identify other examples of sound effects and word play in the poem. Comment on their use.

16. This poem moves between the real and familiar world and the symbolic. Can you identify what is real and ordinary, what happens on the surface?

17. On the symbolic level, what is suggested by the poem? Look at the metaphors used for the bee box, the bees and the 'I' persona. Be aware of the feelings conveyed throughout.

18. There is a touch of dark humour and self-mockery running through the poem. Where is this most obvious? What effect does it have on the reader?

Fourth reading

19. What do you consider to be the central theme of the poem? In answering, refer to the writer's tone and the images used. Look also at your answers to Questions 16 and 17.

CHILD

Your clear eye is the one absolutely beautiful thing.
I want to fill it with color and ducks,
The zoo of the new

Whose names you meditate –
April snowdrop, Indian pipe,   5
Little

Stalk without wrinkle,
Pool in which images
Should be grand and classical

Not this troublous   10
Wringing of hands, this dark
Ceiling without a star.

EXPLORATIONS

First reading

1. Read this poem aloud and listen to its lyrical tone. What is your first impression of the speaker's feeling for her child? Try to imagine the speaker and child – what image do you see?

2. What pictures does she create for the child's 'eye'?

3. Which words here remind you of childlike things? What mood is usually associated with these?

4. How do you interpret the final stanza? Does it affect your reading of the rest of the poem?

Second reading

5. What feelings does the narrator display towards the child in the opening stanzas?

6. Does the narrator's focus remain consistent throughout the poem? Where do you think the change occurs? Look at the verb tenses used when answering this.

7. How is the adult/narrator/mother contrasted with the child?

Third reading

8. What is the effect of line 1 on the reader? Examine how this is achieved.

9. Write a paragraph showing how this contrasts with the final lines. Look at language, imagery and tone.

10. The language of the poem is fresh, clear and simple. What is the effect of this?

11. Write a note about the impressions created by this poem for you.

BRENDAN
KENNELLY

(1936–)

Prescribed for Higher Level exams in 2019 and 2022

Brendan Kennelly was born in Ballylongford, County Kerry, on 17 April 1936. He was one of eight children born to Tim Kennelly and Bridie Ahern. The family owned a pub at the village crossroads where the young Kennelly first encountered the richness and variety of country pub culture – gossip, banter, storytelling, singing and dancing. Perhaps it was here that he first developed an unerring ear for the rhythms of language that is so evident in his poetry. Perhaps it was here too that that he was influenced by the oral tradition of poetry that he practised throughout his career; and possibly where he was first introduced to the role of cultural commentator, which is also present in his poetry.

Kennelly was educated at the local national school and at St Ita's College in Tarbert, which was run by an inspired educator, Miss Jane Agnes McKenna, who taught him French, Irish, Latin and Greek culture and instilled in him a love of literature. He went on to study English and French at Trinity College, Dublin, where he edited *Icarus*, the college literary magazine, and was also captain of the college Gaelic football club. He graduated from Trinity with a first-class honours degree in 1961 and a PhD in 1966, on 'Modern Irish Poets and the Irish Epic'. Kennelly was a member of the School of English at Trinity College for over forty years, first as a Junior Lecturer in English in 1963, and was appointed to a personal chair in Modern Literature at Trinity College in 1973, where he taught until his retirement in 2005.

Kennelly has had a prolific literary output as a poet; dramatist; novelist; translator from Irish, Spanish, Latin and Greek; prose writer of literary criticism; and editor of various anthologies, including *The Penguin Book of Irish Verse* (1970), *Love of Ireland: Poems from the Irish* (1989) and *Dublines* with Katie Donovan (1996).

He has produced more than thirty collections of poetry. It was the culture, history, characters and customs of his native Ballylongford region that inspired much of his early poetry, in volumes such as *My Dark Fathers* (1964), *Good Souls to Survive* (1967), *Dream of a Black Fox* (1968) and the sonnets of *Love Cry* (1972). Three epics stand out among his corpus of work: *Cromwell* (1983), which explored the fraught concept of Irish identity as a post-colonial nation; *The Book of Judas* (1991), which explored the fractured nature of the self through the voice of that reviled biblical character whose name has been a byword for betrayal for over two thousand years.

Both *The Book of Judas* and the third epic, *Poetry My Arse* (1995), are driven also by cultural criticism, in particular, politics, religion and even the poetry industry itself. Kennelly's later works include *The Man Made of Rain* (1998), *Glimpses* (2001), *Martial Art* (2003), *Reservoir Voices* (2009) and *Guff* (2013).

Throughout his career, he has been awarded many prizes, among them the 1996 International IMPAC Dublin Literary Award and the Irish PEN Award for Contribution to Irish Literature in 2010.

The popular image of Brendan Kennelly is that of the people's poet, walking the streets of Kerry towns or Dublin having 'the craic', appearing on talk shows or car ads. But above all these he is known and valued for his public recitations of his poetry – on air, on YouTube, and in school halls and venues around the country, where his poetry has resonated with many.

OL 2019

OL 2022

BEGIN

Begin again to the summoning birds
to the sight of light at the window,
begin to the roar of morning traffic
all along Pembroke Road.
Every beginning is a promise   5
born in light and dying in dark
determination and exaltation of springtime
flowering the way to work.
Begin to the pageant of queuing girls
the arrogant loneliness of swans in the canal   10
bridges linking the past and future
old friends passing though with us still.
Begin to the loneliness that cannot end
since it perhaps is what makes us begin,
begin to wonder at unknown faces   15
at crying birds in the sudden rain
at branches stark in the willing sunlight
at seagulls foraging for bread
at couples sharing a sunny secret
alone together while making good.   20
Though we live in a world that dreams of ending
that always seems about to give in
something that will not acknowledge conclusion
insists that we forever begin.

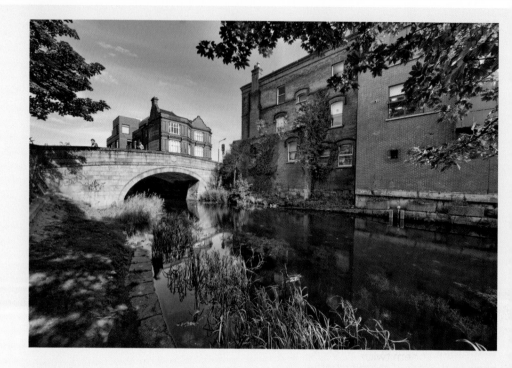

NOTES

4	Pembroke Road:	located in Ballsbridge, Dublin 4
7	determination:	persistent drive (of Spring)
7	exaltation:	can mean to praise highly, to raise up, or to make noble
9	pageant:	a spectacular performance (often used to illustrate historical events)
10 & 11	canal… bridges:	the bridge referred to is Baggot Street Bridge over the Grand Canal, Ballsbridge, Dublin. This is the area Patrick Kavanagh lived in and wrote about. Brendan Kennelly lived in nearby Raglan Road at the time of this poem.
17	stark:	bare, desolate

EXPLORATIONS

Before reading

1. **a** Think about a time or event in your life when you experienced disappointment or any kind of failure, or when you thought life was unfair or didn't make sense. What happened? What thoughts or people helped you to 'pick yourself up' and start again? Jot down your thoughts on the experience.

    b You may wish to share your experience in pairs or small groups.

First reading

2. Read the poem twice, in silence, or listen to it being read.

3. Do a class round of 'I noticed that…' i.e. everybody, in turn, contributes one sentence on something that they noticed in the poem. Each person begins with the phrase 'I noticed that…' (This can by anything that comes to mind as you read or listened; no need to look for something special; there are no 'correct' answers; everybody's contribution adds to the class reading of the poem.)

Second reading

Preparing to read aloud

4. You will have noticed that the first half of the poem is structured as three quatrains (four-line sections or sentences). Working in pairs or groups of four, take one quatrain and discuss how best it might be read aloud. Nominate a reader to represent the group. The following questions may help kick start the discussion.

First quatrain (lines 1–4)

*   What is happening in these four lines?

*   Do you think that the word 'again' is significant? Talk about how the first line might be read aloud.

*   The birds are described as 'summoning'. Talk about the choice of that word and what it may suggest about the sleeper's attitude?

*   How do the words 'the sight of light' create a noticeable lift of mood?

*   'the roar… all along' What do the sounds of these words suggest?

*   Are there stages of waking in the first quatrain? Discuss this.

Second quatrain (lines 5–8)

*   'Every beginning is a promise' Use a dictionary to explore the different nuances of meaning in the word 'promise'. What tone of voice do you think is appropriate for this line?

*   'born in light and dying in dark' Does this line change the mood a little? Discuss the possible meanings of this line.

*   'determination and exaltation of springtime' Explore the nuances of meaning in these words. In what tone of voice would you read lines 7 and 8?

*   Talk about the images and the feelings that lines 7 and 8 create for you.

Third quatrain (lines 9–12)

- What does the word 'pageant' suggest? What does this tell us about how the poet sees the queuing girls?

- Does the image of the swans strike a contrasting note and how might that be conveyed in the reading? Do the swans have reason to be arrogant?

- When you read the first two lines of the quatrain 'bridges…with us still', how do they make you feel? What do you think of when you read them?

- The images of time in these lines are different from the clichéd image of Old Father Time carrying a great scythe to mow us all down. Discuss the images of time that are conjured up here.

5. **a** Each group, in turn, produces a 'best effort' reading of one quatrain, so that the first half of the poem is read around the class.

   b Have a class discussion on what you have discovered about the poem through the readings and discussions so far. Make notes on the main discoveries.

6. Lines 13–20 run together as a section, followed by the final quatrain in lines 21–24. Divide the class into two. One half of the class groups will focus on reading lines 13–20 and the other half on reading lines 21–24. The following questions will help to provoke discussion among your group and will influence the way you read your lines.

Lines 13–20

- 'Begin to the loneliness that cannot end/since it perhaps is what makes us begin'.
  Do you think that there is, of necessity, a loneliness in every individual human being? Can there be a positive aspect to this? What is the poem suggesting?

- 'begin to wonder'
  In your own words, what exactly is the poet encouraging us to do? Share your interpretations of this wondering with your group.

- Explore the imagery in the poem. What are the different aspects of the city that he encourages us to engage with?

- Choose one image. Describe the details you see and explain how exactly it works for you. How does it make you feel? What does it make you think about?

- How will you read this section aloud? Does it have a certain energy?

Lines 21–24

- 'a world that dreams of ending'
  Do you think this may refer to an apocalyptic, man-made or natural catastrophe? How might the world end? Discuss the use of the word 'dreams' in this context.

- 'that always seems about to give in'
  List and discuss some examples of ways it seems about to begin.

- What are your ideas on this 'something' that refuses to 'acknowledge conclusion' and 'insists that we forever begin'? What is it? Where is it?

- What tone of voice do you consider appropriate for the reading of this final section? Explain your reasoning.

7. **a** Produce 'best effort' group readings of lines 13–24 as you did for lines 1–12 and have a class forum to gather what you have discovered. Make notes on your insights.

   b Listen to Brendan Kennelly reading this poem in your eBook. Talk about his reading. Would you like to add anything to your notes?

Third reading

8. As you listened to the poem could you hear the repeated rhythms, somewhat like a chant? Could the poem be read as a wish or a prayer? And for what?

9. In the preface, entitled 'Echoing Note', to his volume of poetry *Begin* (1999) Kennelly says:

   '*Poetry is a land and sea of echoes connecting with each other and with listening hearts as the years work and dream themselves into extinction.*'

   Among the examples of the 'echopower' of poetry he includes is 'the recurring hints of some hope in self-renewal, of recognising that the real tragedy is simply giving up, of refusing the shaky hope of beginning again.'

   a What echoes from this poem make a connection with you? Write about them.

b Would you agree that this is a poem of great wisdom? Explain your thinking in 150–200 words.

10. In the preface to *A Time for Voices: Selected Poems 1960–1990* Kennelly wrote: 'We write out of blindness; sometimes a poem becomes a shareable moment of light'. Discuss 'Begin' in the context of this statement.

BREAK 🔊

Someone else cut off my head
In a golden field.
Now I am re-created

By her fingers. This
Moulding is more delicate   5
Than a first kiss,

More deliberate than her own
Rising up
And lying down,

I am fine   10
As anything in
This legendary garden

Yet I am nothing till
She runs her fingers through me
And shapes me with her skill.   15

The form that I shall bear
Grows round and white.
It seems I comfort her

Even as she slits my face
And stabs my chest.   20
Her feeling for perfection is

Absolute.
So I am glad to go through fire
And come out

Shaped like her dream.   25
In my way
I am all that can happen to men.
I came to life at her finger-ends.
I will go back into her again.

EXPLORATIONS

First reading

1. What is your first reaction to the speaking voice in this poem? Is it different from other poetry you have read? In what way? Do you like it? What does it make you think of? Discuss your first reactions.

2. Listen to Brendan Kennelly reading the poem in your eBook. Is there anything you would like to add to your first thoughts on the poem?

3. a From listening to the voice in this poem, what do we learn about the bread?

   b What does the voice reveal about the woman? Make a list of these revelations.

4. Do you think the voice of the poem is male or female? Explain your thinking.

Second reading

5. The process of bread-making is described in very sensuous, even sensual, terms. Examine these descriptions and discuss what they might suggest.

6. a Describe the interaction and the relationship between the bread and the woman. Support your ideas with references.

   b Do you think this could be read as a love poem? Explain your views.

Third reading

7. Though the task involved here is the mundane one of bread-making, the portrayal of the woman that emerges is that of artist and, even more radical, of creator in this 'legendary garden'. Write about your views of women as presented in this poem.

8. How do you read/understand the mood and attitude of the bread-voice? Jot down your thoughts.

9. This is a very graphic poem. Imagine you are asked to film it:

   a   Consider which images you think would best carry the story.

   b   Write instructions for the cameraperson on what each shot should capture.

10. 'This poem offers us a unique perspective into an ordinary, everyday event'.
    Write about the poem in light of this statement.

Fourth reading

11. Read the section 'Bread: Context of the Poem' in the critical notes, where we can explore something of the poet's rationale for these poems. What do you learn from this that helps deepen your understanding of the poem 'Bread' and of poetry in general?

12. In the introduction to *Breathing Spaces* (1992) Kennelly wrote:

    > For me, poetry is an entering into the lives of things and people, dreams and events, images and mindtides. This passion for 'entering into' is, I believe, the peculiar vitality of the imagination.

    Using the 'entering into' approach, write a first draft for a poem where you enter into the life of a school book or a school bag or a biro or a favourite poem or another object. Donald Graves's rules for getting a first draft down will help you begin:

    i.   Lower your standards

    ii. Write quickly

    iii. Change nothing

    When you have a first draft, the fear recedes; then you can explore, experiment and reshape it until you hear it say something you feel to be true.

'DEAR AUTUMN GIRL' 🔊

(From *Love Cry*)

Dear Autumn girl, these helter-skelter days
When mad leaf-argosies drive at my head,
I try but fail to give you proper praise
For the excitement you've created
In my world: an islander at sea,   5
A girl with child, a fool, a simple king,
Garrulous masters of true mockery –
My hugest world becomes the littlest thing

Whenever you walk smiling through a room
And your flung golden hair is still wet   10
Ready for September's homaged rays;
I see what is, I wonder what's to come,
I bless what you remember or forget
And recognise the poverty of praise.

NOTES

1	helter-skelter:	rhyming jingle usually referring to disorderly haste or headlong confusion. It is also the name of the circular slide in a fun-fair.
2	leaf-argosies:	an argosy was the name of a very large merchant sailing ship of the sixteenth century. Shakespeare used the term in *The Merchant of Venice*. Here, the squalls of wind-blown leaves call to mind a fleet of argosies.
5 and 6		the references here are to characters in other poems by Kennelly
6	fool:	unwise person. In Shakespeare the word refers to a professional clown or jester; also to a simpleton or someone born with a mental disability. It is used in this last sense, in this poem.
6	Simple:	this word has many nuances or shades of meaning. It can mean: easily understood, uncomplicated; unsophisticated; childlike; humble; modest; foolish or feeble-minded.
7	Garrulous:	talkative, loquacious
7	Garrulous master of true mockery:	his world of literature produces overtalkative characters that are a false or absurdly inadequate representation of reality
11	homaged:	homage in feudal law was a public declaration of allegiance and service given to an overlord or king. In general terms, it means an expression of reverence.

EXPLORATIONS

First reading

I. **a** In your own words, list all the qualities of the Autumn Girl that you find in the poem.

b Working in pairs, share your findings and discuss any differences of opinion or confusions about meaning that you might have.

2. Examine closely the imagery in the first two lines. What is suggested about the state of mind of the writer?

3. What does the writer love about this girl and what concerns does he have? Discuss these.

Second reading

4. The poet speaks about 'the excitement you've created/ In my world'.

a When people say 'in my world' what do they usually mean? What type of world do you think the poet is speaking about here?

b See the critical notes on this poem. What are your initial thoughts on the world revealed here? Discuss in pairs or small groups.

5. **a** Think about how you act in any developing relationship or friendship. How much do you reveal about yourself and when?

b 'This is a courageously transparent and honest love poem'. Would you agree? Write your thoughts on this.

Third reading

6. 'I try but fail to give you proper praise'.
In your opinion, does the poet fail or succeed and to what degree? Discuss this and then write up your thoughts.

7. What questions do you still have about the poem? What issues are still unclear to you? Do a class 'round', i.e. each person contributes one sentence beginning with 'A question I still have is ...'

POEM FROM A THREE YEAR OLD

And will the flowers die?

And will the people die?

And every day do you grow old, do I
grow old, no I'm not old, do
flowers grow old?   5

Old things – do you throw them out?

Do you throw old people out?

And how you know a flower that's old?

The petals fall, the petals fall from flowers,
and do the petals fall from people too,   10
every day more petals fall until the
floor where I would like to play I
want to play is covered with old
flowers and people all the same
together lying there with petals fallen   15
on the dirty floor I want to play
the floor you come and sweep
with the huge broom.

The dirt you sweep, what happens that,
what happens all the dirt you sweep   20
from flowers and people, what
happens all the dirt? Is all the
dirt what's left of flowers and
people, all the dirt there in a
heap under the huge broom that   25
sweeps everything away?

Why you work so hard, why brush
and sweep to make a heap of dirt?
And who will bring new flowers?
And who will bring new people? Who will   30
bring new flowers to put in water
where no petals fall on to the
floor where I would like to
play? Who will bring new flowers

that will not hang their heads   35
like tired old people wanting sleep?
Who will bring new flowers that
do not split and shrivel every
day? And if we have new flowers,
will we have new people too to   40
keep the flowers alive and give
them water?

And will the new young flowers die?

And will the new young people die?

And why?   45

EXPLORATIONS

Before reading

1. Recruit someone who took care of you when you were about three years old such as a parent, grandparent, aunt, uncle, or childminder. What do they remember about you at this age? What were your likes and dislikes? What did you like to play at? What worried you? Did you ask questions and about what? Do you have any memories from when you were three to five years old?

First reading

2. Listen to Brendan Kennelly's reading of the poem in your eBook. What are your first thoughts about the poem? Share and discuss these.

3. What have you discovered about the child in this poem? In small groups, share your findings.

4. Following from your research into your own childhood, what elements in this poem would you say are typical of this stage of childhood?

Second reading

5. a This poem is structured as a torrent of questions from the young child. Working in pairs, make lists or categories of the questions, according to what they are about.

   b Write about the issues that preoccupy this child.

6. 'Why you work so hard, why brush/ and sweep to make a heap of dirt?' This is both a simple and a profound question.

   a In your own words, express the profound question.

   b Compose an answer for the child, using language and imagery that a three year old would understand.

Third reading

7. There is a dramatic energy in this poem. This rhythm is created by the repetition of words, phrases, images and by the repetition and torrent of questions. It is also created by the run-on lines where the sense is carried over three, five or even eight lines – see the section beginning 'every day more petals fall... the huge broom.' In contrast, we get eight separate lines – 1, 2, 6, 7, 8, 43, 44 and 45 – each printed in its own space.

   a What do you think is the effect of these separate lines?

   b Prepare and read the poem aloud, so that the different rhythms of the poem come across.

8. The composer Jane O'Leary wrote of this poem: 'Its attraction lies in its blend of simplicity and depth, innocence and perception.' Discuss this view of the poem in about 500 words.

9. Some people read this poem as expressing a desire for agelessness and perfection. Others say that the imagery overwhelms this theme. What do you think of these views? Structure your response, with appropriate references, in about 500 words.

10. What appeals to you about this poem? Write your thoughts on it, in about 500 words.

OLIVER TO HIS BROTHER

Loving brother, I am glad to hear of your welfare
And that our children have so much leisure
They can travel far to eat cherries.
This is most excusable in my daughter
Who loves that fruit and whom I bless.   5
Tell her I expect she writes often to me
And that she be kept in some exercise.
Cherries and exercise go well together.
I have delivered my son up to you.
I hope you counsel him; he will need it;   10
I choose to believe he believes what you say.
I send my affection to all your family.
Let sons and daughters be serious; the age requires it.
I have things to do, all in my own way.
For example, I take not kindly to rebels.   15
Today, in Burford Churchyard, Cornet Thompson
Was led to the place of execution.
He asked for prayers, got them, died well.
After him, a Corporal, brought to the same place
Set his back against the wall and died.   20
A third chose to look death in the face,
Stood straight, showed no fear, chilled into his pride.
Men die in their different ways
And girls eat cherries
In the Christblessed fields of England.   25
Some weep. Some have cause. Let weep who will.
Whole floods of brine are at their beck and call.
I have work to do in Ireland.

NOTES

15–22	rebels:	The Levellers were a popular political movement that demanded legal and political reforms in how the country was being governed. They gained support in Cromwell's New Model Army. Cromwell viewed their activities as rebellion and had three of the leaders – Cornet James Thompson, Corporal Perkins and Private John Church – executed in Burford Churchyard, Oxfordshire on 17 May 1649.
16	Cornet:	A Cornet was a junior officer who carried the colours in a troop of cavalry. (See note on Cromwell in the critical notes on this poem.)
27	brine:	salt water; also used to refer to tears, as here

EXPLORATIONS

Before reading

1. Research the life and work of Oliver Cromwell, in particular his campaign in Ireland 1649–50. Share and discuss your findings.

First reading

Lines 1–14

2. What do you discover about Cromwell in these lines? Consider his relationship with his children, his relationship with his brother, and his views on how children should be reared and anything else you notice about the character of Cromwell in these lines.

3. Are you surprised by the picture of Cromwell in these lines? Discuss.

Second reading

Lines 15–28

4. Examine carefully Cromwell's report on the deaths of the three Levellers (lines 16–22). What does it reveal about his thinking on death? Explain your views with references to the text.

5. 'The Cromwell of the second half of this poem is a very different person to the man we met in the first.' Write your views on this.

6. Do you find this a dramatic poem? Explore the elements of drama found here.

7. See the critical notes on this poem. What points would you now wish to add to your own notes on the poem?

Third reading

8. How far do you think this poem succeeds in rehabilitating Cromwell as a human being rather than as a *bête noire* (hated figure, literally 'black beast') of Irish history? Discuss this and then write up your argument.

9. In his Preface to *The Book of Judas*, Kennelly wrote about 'Cromwell':

   In a long poem, Cromwell (1983), I tried to open my mind, heart and imagination to the full, fascinating complexity of a man I was from childhood taught, quite simply, to hate. A learned hate is hard to unlearn.

   Using the poem 'Oliver to His Brother' as evidence, to what extent do you think Kennelly has managed to unlearn his hatred of Oliver Cromwell? Explore this issue, in about 800 words.

I SEE YOU DANCING, FATHER

No sooner downstairs after the night's rest
And in the door
Than you started to dance a step
In the middle of the kitchen floor.

And as you danced   5
You whistled.
You made your own music
Always in tune with yourself.

Well, nearly always, anyway.
You're buried now   10
In Lislaughtin Abbey
And whenever I think of you

I go back beyond the old man
Mind and body broken
To find the unbroken man.   15
It is the moment before the dance begins,

Your lips are enjoying themselves
Whistling an air.
Whatever happens or cannot happen
In the time I have to spare   20
I see you dancing, father.

NOTES

3	dance a step:	Irish dancing consists of particular patterns of steps and movements
11	Lislaughtin Abbey:	the ruins of a Franciscan friary dating back to the sixteenth century and situated on the south bank of the Shannon estuary about three miles from Ballylongford, Kennelly's home village. The modern cemetery for the region is situated in the grounds.

EXPLORATIONS

Before reading

1. Personal thinking time: If you had to compose an obituary or a funeral speech for a parent, what would you like to say? Write it in about 200 words. You don't have to share this work.

2. Discussion: Do you think it is difficult for boys to have really personal conversations with their fathers? Why? Discuss this.

First reading

3. What are your first thoughts on reading this poem? Jot them down.

4. What qualities of the father come across in the poem?

Second reading

5. From the evidence in the poem, what do you think are the poet's feelings towards his father?

6. Explore the use of language in the poem. What does it contribute to the atmosphere?

7. The poet refers to 'Whatever happens or cannot happen' (line 19) in the time he has to spare. Discuss the possible meanings of this line.

Third reading

8. Writing about this poem, another Kerry author John B. Keane said, 'In this poem there is concern, love and anguish – the anguish of memory and compassion. Discuss 'I See You Dancing, Father' in the light of this statement (in about 500 words).

9. Brendan Kennelly has said: 'A writer is not interested in explaining reality; he's interested in capturing it.' Discuss the poem in light of this statement.

A CRY FOR ART O'LEARY

(from the Irish of Eiblín Dubh Ní Chonaill)

My love
The first time I saw you
From the top of the market
My eyes covered you
My heart went out to you   5
I left my friends for you
Threw away my home for you

What else could I do?

You got the best rooms for me
All in order for me   10
Ovens burning for me
Fresh trout caught for me
Choice meat for me

In the best of beds I stretched
Till milking-time hummed for me   15

You made the whole world
Pleasing to me

White rider of love!

I love your silver-hilted sword
How your beaver hat became you   20
With its band of gold
Your friendly homespun suit
Revealed your body
Your pin of glinting silver
Glittered in your shirt   25

On your horse in style
You were sensitive pale-faced
Having journeyed overseas
The English respected you
Bowing to the ground   30
Not because they loved you
But true to their hearts' hate

They're the ones who killed you
Darling of my heart

My lover   35
My love's creature
Pride of Immokelly
To me you were not dead
Till your great mare came to me
Her bridle dragging ground   40
Her head with your startling blood
Your blood upon the saddle
You rode in your prime
I didn't wait to clean it
I leaped across my bed   45
I leaped then to the gate
I leaped upon your mare
I clapped my hands in frenzy
I followed every sign
With all the skill I knew   50
Until I found you lying
Dead near a furze bush
Without pope or bishop
Or cleric or priest
To say a prayer for you   55

Only a crooked wasted hag
Throwing her cloak across you

I could do nothing then
In the sight of God
But go on my knees   60
And kiss your face
And drink your free blood

My man!
Going out the gate
You turned back again   65
Kissed the two children
Threw a kiss at me
Saying, 'Eileen, woman, try
To get this house in order,
Do your best for us   70
I must be going now
I'll not be home again.'

I thought that you were joking
You my laughing man

My man!   75
My Art O'Leary
Up on your horse now
Ride out to Macroom
And then to Inchigeela
Take a bottle of wine   80
Like your people before you
Rise up
My Art O'Leary
Of the sword of love

Put on your clothes   85
Your black beaver
Your black gloves
Take down your whip
Your mare is waiting
Go east by the thin road   90
Every bush will salute you
Every stream will speak to you
Men and women acknowledge you

They know a great man
When they set eyes on him   95

God's curse on you, Morris,
God's curse on your treachery
You swept my man from me
The man of my children
Two children play in the house   100
A third lives in me

He won't come alive from me

My heart's wound
Why was I not with you
When you were shot   105
That I might take the bullet
In my own body?
Then you'd have gone free
Rider of the grey eye
And followed them   110

Who'd murdered me

My man!
I look at you now
All I know of a hero
True man with true heart 115
Stuck in a coffin
You fished the clean streams
Drank nightlong in halls
Among frank-breasted women

I miss you 120

My man!
I am crying for you
In far Derrynane
In yellow-appled Carren
Where many a horseman 125
And vigilant woman
Would be quick to join
In crying for you
Art O'Leary
My laughing man 130

O crying women
Long live your crying
Till Art O'Leary
Goes back to school
On a fateful day 135
Not for books and music

But for stones and clay

My man!
The corn is stacked
The cows are milking 140
My heart is a lump of grief
I will never be healed
Till Art O'Leary
Comes back to me

I am a locked trunk 145
The key is lost
I must wait till rust
Devours the screw

O my best friend
Art O'Leary   150
Son of Conor
Son of Cadach
Son of Lewis
East from wooded glens
West from girlish hills   155
Where rowanberries grow
Yellow nuts budge from branches
Apples laugh like small suns
As once they laughed
Throughout my girlhood   160
It is no cause for wonder
If bonfires lit O'Leary country
Close to Ballingeary
Or holy Gougane Barra
After the clean-gripping rider   165
The robust hunter
Panting towards the kill
Your own hounds lagged behind you
O horseman of the summoning eyes
What happened you last night?   170
My only whole belief
Was that you could not die
For I was your protection

My heart! My grief!

My man! My darling!   175

In Cork
I had this vision
Lying in my bed:
A glen of withered trees
A home heart-broken   180
Strangled hunting-hounds
Choked birds
And you
Dying on a hillside
Art O'Leary   185
My one man
Your blood running crazily
Over earth and stone

Jesus Christ knows well
I'll wear no cap   190
No mourning dress
No solemn shoes
No bridle on my horse
No grief-signs in my house
But test instead   195
The wisdom of the law
I'll cross the sea
To speak to the King
If he ignores me
I'll come back home   200
To find the man
Who murdered my man

Morris, because of you
My man is dead

Is there a man in Ireland   205
To put a bullet through your head

Women, white women of the mill
I give my love to you
For the poetry you made
For Art O'Leary   210
Rider of the brown mare
Deep women-rhythms of blood
The fiercest and the sweetest
Since time began
Singing of this cry I womanmake   215
For my man

NOTES

18	White rider of love:	Art O'Leary's horse, which has been described as a very pale colour with a white forehead
28	Having journeyed overseas:	Art O'Leary served as a Captain of Hussars in the Austrian Army. (See section on 'Historical context' in the critical notes on this poem on.)
37	Immokelly (or Imokilly):	One of the twenty-four baronies in the county of Cork
52	furze bush:	yellow flowering gorse that spreads widely in the countryside, if not controlled
56	hag:	old woman
78	Macroom:	a town in Co. Cork
79	Inchigeela:	A village near Macroom, Co. Cork, in what was hereditary O'Leary land
86	beaver:	a reference to his hat, which would have been made of beaver skin and fur. They were very expensive and were sometimes worn by the military.
96	Morris:	Abraham Morris was the Sheriff of Cork
123	Derrynane:	Derrynane House, near Cahir-Daniel, Co. Kerry. It was Eileen's homeplace.
134–137	Goes back to school:	His family wished that Art should be buried in the monastery of Kilcrea, Co. Cork, which was the family burial place. Due to some dispute, probably connected with the Penal Laws, this was contested and his body was first buried outside the churchyard in Killnamartyr until it could be interred in Kilcrea. Monasteries in Ireland were well known for their schools, hence the references to 'back to school' and 'books and music'.
151–153	Son of Conor… Cadach… Lewis:	the beginning of the genealogy, listing Art's father, grandfather and great grandfather
163	Ballingeary:	a village in the Shehy mountains, Co. Cork
164	Gougane Barra:	scenic countryside of mountains and lakes, west of Macroom. It is the site of the sixth century Oratory of St Finbarr. Because of its remoteness it became a popular place for the celebration of Mass during the time of the Penal Laws, in the seventeenth and eighteenth centuries.

EXPLORATIONS

Before reading

1. Read the 'Historical context' section on this poem in the critical notes on this poem.

First reading

2. Read this long poem carefully. Also listen to the poet reading it in your eBook. You may need to do this a number of times.

a   Work out both the storyline of the poem and the timeline, as Eileen tells it. (It may be a good idea to make a photocopy of the poem so that you can mark your attempts and change if necessary).

b Working in pairs or small groups, swap your storylines and timelines. Discuss any differences, confusions or questions.

c Bring any confusions and questions to a full class discussion.

3. Working in pairs, list everything about Eileen that you discover from this poem. Leave space to add to your notes later.

4. Again in pairs, list everything you have learned about Art O'Leary. Again leave space for notes.

Second reading

5. What attracted Eileen to O'Leary when they first met and what did she love about him? Jot down your ideas with textual references to support them. Discuss in pairs.

6. Collect all the epithets or endearment phrases that Eileen uses for her husband, e.g. 'my love', 'my man'. What do all of these indicate to you about her feelings and the depth and quality of their relationship? Write about this in 500 words.

7. Working in pairs, make an outline of the changing moods of the speaker (mark the poem if it helps). Talk about what Eileen must have been feeling in each situation and what indicates this. Add your notes to the portrait of Eileen from question 2 above.

8. Read the poem again, focusing on Art O'Leary. Isolate the points in the poem where he is mentioned and imagine what he may have been thinking at these moments. Write these thoughts in diary form or a blog.

Third reading

9. 'This is a poem of both grief and love'. Write about the intensity of the emotions as expressed in the poem. (500 words).

10. Do you think the imagery in this poem is striking and effective? Write about the imagery as you experienced it? (500 words).

11. Did you find this a very dramatic poem to read? Discuss how the sense of drama is created, in about 800 words.

Fourth reading

12. Rehearse and perform a class reading or a number of group readings of the poem. Discuss and note any new insights.

13. Compose an epitaph for Eibhlín Dubh Ní Chonaill or compose a shorter lament, to be spoken.

THINGS I MIGHT DO 🔊

I thought of things I might do with my heart.
Should I make it into a month like October,
A chalice for the sad madness of leaves
That I might raise in homage to the year's end?

Should I make it into a small white church in   5
A country-place where bells are childhood prayers?
Or a backroom of a brothel in Dublin
Where the trade of somethinglikelove endures?

Should I make it a judge to judge itself?
Or a caring face in a memory-storm?   10
Or a bed

For Judas dreaming of the tree:
    'There now, there now, rest as best you can,
    Darling, rest your treacherous head
    And when you've rested, come home to me.'   15

NOTES

The speaker in this poem is Judas Iscariot, one of the Twelve Apostles who disclosed Jesus'
whereabouts to the chief priests for thirty pieces of silver. He identified Jesus with a kiss.
According to tradition he later hanged himself from a tree.

3	chalice:	a drinking cup or goblet used at the time of the Roman Empire and now used in the ceremony of the Eucharist
4	homage:	an expression of reverence

EXPLORATIONS

Before reading

1. Have you ever experienced or read the term 'Judas' used in present-day speech? What does it call to mind? Share your experiences in the class.

First reading

2. **a** List the things Judas considers he might do with his heart.

   b What are your first thoughts on these?

3. Explore the first stanza in some detail. Do you think his first thought of making his heart into a month like October might be an apt one? Outline your thinking.

4. In the second stanza, two different possibilities for the heart are outlined. What is suggested about each location? What do you think is the effect of placing the two together?

5. The other possibilities listed are: 'a judge to judge itself'; 'a caring face in a memory storm'; 'Or a bed/ For Judas dreaming of the tree'. Discuss the value there might be for Judas in each of these.

Second reading

6. Think about the voice at the end of this poem.

   a What tone of voice do you think this should be spoken in? What leads you to think that? Who do you think may be speaking?

   b Try it out; read it aloud.

   c Do you think this voice brings Judas some comfort? Write down your thoughts.

7. Examine the images used as metaphors for the heart. Do you find them outrageous, appropriate, thought-provoking, bizarre or other? Write up your thoughts on these.

Third reading

8. Read the first three stanzas again. Have your thoughts on Judas's voice changed? Is there a possibility that he is putting on an act here, pretending to be the big guy? Could all this just be an act of bravado, another show of pretence, the final lie? Discuss.

9. Have a look at the section 'A reading of the poem' in the critical notes on this poem. Does this prompt any questions you could explore further? Discuss them.

10. Can you see any way in which this poem may be about us? Discuss this and then write up your thoughts.

(If you would like further information on *The Book of Judas* there is a brief overview in the critical notes on this poem.)

A GREAT DAY 🔊

She was all in white.

Snow
Suggests itself as a metaphor

But since this has been so often said
I may be justified in considering it dead.   5
Something about snow is not quite right.

Therefore, she was all in white.

He was most elegant too
All dickied up in dignified blue.

They came together, as is habitual   10
In that part of the world,
Through a grave ritual,

Listening
With at least a modicum of wonder –
What God has joined together   15
Let no man put asunder.

Man in woman, woman in man.
Soon afterwards, the fun began.

It was a great day –
Long hours of Dionysiac festivity.   20

Songs poured out like wine.
Praises flowed as they had never done.

The people there
Seemed to see each other in a new way.
This added to the distinction of the day.   25

And all the time she was all in white
Enjoying every song and speech
Enjoying every sip and every bite.

Such whiteness seems both beautiful and true
He thought, all dickied up in dignified blue.   30

He looks so good in blue
(This warmed her mind)
Blue suits him
Down to the ground.

At the table where they sat   35
Things seemed to fit.

And the loud crowd sang and danced
The whole day long, the whole night long.
There could never be anything but dance and song.

I must change, she whispered,   40
I must change my dress.

He never saw the white dress again.

In the train, the trees wore their rainy veils
With a reticent air.

It's good to get away, she whispered,   45
Touching her beautiful hair.

She closed her eyes, the trees were silent guests,
A tide of thoughts flowed in her head,
In his head.

'Darling, it was a great day,' she said.   50

NOTES

9	All dickied up:	Irish slang for 'dressed in best clothes'
15, 16	What God has…:	quote from St Matthew's Gospel 19:6 and used in the religious ceremony of marriage
20	Dionysiac:	relating to the ancient Greek God Dionysus, god of the harvest and fertility. His festival was reputed to be celebrated with drunken, uninhibited sensual dancing.

EXPLORATIONS

Before reading

1. **a**   In a class brain-storming session, list all the events or experiences that you would describe as being 'a great day'. What do they all have in common?

   b   Is this a phrase used more by older people than younger people? Have a chat with the older members of your family and ask them about the contexts in which they have used the phrase 'a great day'.

First reading

2.   List everything you find out about the bride, linking each discovery to a reference in the poem.

3.   List everything you find out about the groom. Again, link each item on the list to a reference in the poem.

4.   Do you think we get to know the bride and groom very well? Discuss this, in pairs or groups, and then write down your views.

5.   From the evidence in the poem, what do you think the guests would have considered as the main elements of 'a great day'.

Second reading

6.   'He never saw the white dress again' (line 42).
     What does this say to you about the 'great day'?

7.   'In the train, the trees wore their rainy veils/With a reticent air' (lines 43–44). What does this contribute to our understanding of the poem?

8.   The voice or presence of the poet intrudes into this poem, at times. Where does this happen and what do you think is the effect?

Third reading

9.   'She closed her eyes, the trees were silent guests,/A tide of thoughts flowed in her head,/ In his head.'

   a   Working in pairs, decide who takes the roles of the bride and of the groom. Then each writes the thoughts about the day that could possibly be flowing in her head or his. These thoughts need to be consistent with the bride and groom in the poem.

   b   Read your thought-voices to each other. Discuss what you learned about the characters.

   c   Have a class discussion on any new insights into the poem.

10.   Read 'A reading of the poem' in the critical notes on this poem. Which ideas do you agree with and which do you have doubts about? Add your thoughts to your notes on the poem.

11.   '"A Great Day" is a very subtle and well-crafted poem'.
      Write about the poem in the light of this statement.

12.   What does this poem add to your understanding of Brendan Kennelly's poetry? Write about this in 500 words.

FRAGMENTS

What had he to say to her now?
Where was the woman he believed he had known
In a street, out walking, by the sea,
In bed, working, dancing, loving the sun

And saying so, always for the first time?   5
Who was this stranger with the graven face?
What led to the dreaming-up of a home?
And what was he, at sixty? Who was

That man lifting the blackthorn stick
With the knobbed top from its place   10
At the side of the fire, quietly dying?

He listened to his own steps in the walk
Past the reedy mud where plover rose
And scattered, black fragments, crying.

NOTES

6	graven:	sculptured or carved on a surface; an archaic form of 'engraved'. It can also be used in the sense of 'to fix indelibly on' something – 'memory' for instance.
13	plover:	a wading bird. The grey plover, a winter visitor from Siberia, is often seen on large muddy estuaries and sloblands.

EXPLORATIONS

Before reading

1. Think back to when you were in primary school:

   a   What were your main likes and dislikes about food, clothes, football teams, music, etc?

   b   What words would best describe you then – shy, outgoing, confident, careful, carefree, ambitious, lazy or other?

   c   Back then, what did you want to do or be in life?

   d   Have you changed, and if so, in what ways?

First reading

2. At the beginning of the poem a man thinks back to the early years of a relationship.

   a   What does he remember about the woman?

   b   Do you think they were very much in love? What leads you to your conclusions?

   c   What do you learn about the man in this poem?

   d   In pairs or groups, discuss the speaker's frame of mind.

Second reading

3. What do you think may have happened? Discuss this in small groups and then share your ideas with the class.

4. Write a diary entry, letter or poem that the woman might have written expressing her views and feelings.

5. What would you say to the speaker if you met him on his walk? Write up your thoughts.

Third reading

6. What do you think is the central issue in this poem? Discuss it and then write your thoughts.

7. Do you think the title is apt for the poem? Explain your thinking.

8. Even though the poem doesn't provide any answers to the big questions, do you think it still gives us valuable insights into life? Write your thoughts on this (around 500 words).

9. 'The imagery in this poem carries the story'.
   Discuss this view (500 words).

10. 'No man ever steps in the same river twice, for it's not the same river and he's not the same man.' (Heraclitus)
   Write a story, a letter, a poem or a blog on this theme.
   Note: Heraclitus was a sixth-century BCE philosopher who used metaphysics (the branch of philosophy dealing with the nature of existence, truth and knowledge) to attempt to explain the world around him. He concluded that all the universe was in a state of constant change and used the river as an example.

THE SOUL'S LONELINESS 🔊

it's nothing to go on about
but when I hear it
in the ticking of the clock

beside the books and photographs
or see it in the shine   5
of an Eason's plastic bag at midnight

or touch it in the tree I call
Christ there outside my window
swaying in the day's afterglow

I shiver a little at the strangeness   10
of my flesh, the swell of sweat,
the child's poem I'll never forget

and find my eyes searching the floor
for a definition of grace
or a trace of yourself I've never noticed before.   15

NOTE

14   grace: probably meant in its religious sense as 'the unmerited favour of
                    God' in the sense of receiving compassion, forgiveness, love, mercy,
                    etc. or being given the strength by God to endure trials and sorrows

EXPLORATIONS

First reading

1. Consider the words of the title. What does this suggest to you? Discuss it.

2. In the first three stanzas there are images of sound and sight and touch. In your own words briefly describe what each image suggests to you. (200 words)

3. In stanzas four and five, what are the effects of loneliness on the speaker? Discuss this in pairs or groups and then write down your thoughts.

4. How does this poem make you feel or what do you think of when you read it? Write down your thoughts.

Second reading

5. Loneliness is a very difficult topic to write about. What do you think of the way the poet treats the issue here? Write up your ideas, then share them in small groups.

6. Brendan Kennelly wrote about the difference between loneliness and solitude, saying: 'In loneliness we are severed; in solitude we may grow strong.'
   Discuss this idea. Does it help your reading of the poem?

7. Do you find this poem unrelentingly bleak or do you think there are some grounds for hope? Write about this. (300 words)

8. What would you like to say to the speaker in this poem? Write a letter to him.

Third reading

9. Read the critical notes section on this poem and the section on the context of this poem in the epic *Poetry My Arse*. What questions do you have as a result? Discuss them.

10. What does this poem add to your understanding of Kennelly's poetry? Write your thoughts in 500 words.

SAINT BRIGID'S PRAYER 🔊

(from the Irish)

I'd like to give a lake of beer to God.
  I'd love the Heavenly
Host to be tippling there
  for all eternity.

I'd love the men of Heaven to live with me,   5
  to dance and sing.
If they wanted, I'd put at their disposal
  vats of suffering.

White cups of love I'd give them
  with a heart and a half;   10
sweet pitchers of mercy I'd offer
  to every man.

I'd make Heaven a cheerful spot
  because the happy heart is true.
I'd make the men contented for their own sake.   15
  I'd like Jesus to love me too.

I'd like the people of Heaven to gather
  from all the parishes around.
I'd give a special welcome to the women,
  the three Marys of great renown.   20

I'd sit with the men, the women and God
  there by the lake of beer.
We'd be drinking good health forever
  and every drop would be a prayer.

NOTES

2/3	Heavenly Host:	multitude of angels
8	vats:	large tanks or containers
20	the three Marys:	probably Mary the mother of Jesus, Mary Magdalene and Mary of Cleophas who were present at the Crucifixion

EXPLORATIONS

Before reading

1. a   If you believe in a heaven, describe how you visualise it.
   b   If you don't believe in a heaven, create a heaven and describe what it would be like.
   c   Discuss the different ideas of heaven around the class.

First reading

2. What's different about the picture of Heaven in this poem from any you have heard or read about before? Discuss this in pairs or groups in a full class discussion.

3. The first six lines are all in party-time mood but what do you understand by lines seven and eight? What do you think is the effect of those lines on the mood of the poem?

Second reading

4. 'Love and mercy are the two most fundamental needs for a happy life.' Debate this.

5. 'Happiness is our natural condition.' Debate this.

6. How can we be contented for our own sake? Discuss this in pairs or small groups. Then write a blog on the topic.

Third reading

7. In an earlier version of this poem, entitled 'The Things Brigit wished for', from A Book of Saints and Wonders by Lady Gregory (1907), the piece ends with:
'And it is what her desire was, to satisfy the poor, to banish every hardship, and to save every sorrowful man.'
Do you think Brendan Kennelly's version of her poem or version of Heaven would fulfil her desire? Write about this in 500 words.

8. What did you get from this poem? What did it contribute to your thinking about what's important in life? Write a personal response to the poem in 500 words.

SEAMUS HEANEY

(1939–2013)

Prescribed for Higher Level exams in 2019 and 2021

Seamus Heaney was born on 13 April 1939 on the family farm at Mossbawn, near Bellaghy, County Derry. From 1945 to 1951 he attended Anahorish primary school; in the period 1951–57 he was educated at St Columb's College in Derry and during the period 1957–61 at Queen's University, Belfast, where he achieved a first-class degree in English language and literature. In 1961 and 1962 he took a teacher training diploma at St Joseph's College of Education in Belfast. In 1966 he was appointed lecturer in English at Queen's University.

Heaney's first volume of poetry, *Death of a Naturalist*, was published in 1966. Filled mostly with the characters, scenes, customs, flora and fauna of the countryside that formed him, this volume, which includes 'Twice Shy' and 'Valediction', explores Heaney's cultural and poetic origins. *Door in the Dark*, Heaney's second volume, was published in 1969. While the first collection dealt mainly with childhood, coming of age, and the poet's relationship with the somewhat heroic figure of his father, *Door in the Dark* deals with more adult relationships. A few poems, such as 'The Forge', hark back to the style of the first volume in the celebration of local skills and in the poet's discovery in them of metaphors for his own craft. But the poet's Irish focus broadens out from local considerations to a more general awareness of geography, history and archaeology in such poems as 'Bogland'.

Heaney's third volume of poetry, *Wintering Out*, was published in 1972. The year 1969 had seen riots, bombs and sectarian killings. The Provisional IRA became a powerful force and the British army was deployed on the streets. Yet Heaney hardly ever addresses these contemporary political issues directly; instead he makes a journey back into the past of prehistoric humankind. In 'The Tollund Man' Heaney finds an oblique way of examining the sacrificial killings, the power of religion and the deadly demands of myth in our society. Heaney spent the academic year 1970–71 as guest lecturer at the University of California in Berkeley and found it difficult to settle back into life in Northern Ireland when he returned, a transition he described as 'like putting an old dirty glove on again'. He found the daily ritual of roadblocks, arrests, vigilante patrols, explosions and killings deeply disturbing. Heaney decided that it was time to leave Belfast and devote himself entirely to his writing. He resigned his post as lecturer in English at

Queen's University and moved with his family, his wife Marie and his sons Michael and Christopher, to a cottage at Glanmore, County Wicklow, during the summer of 1972, determined to go it alone as a poet and freelance writer. Their daughter, Catherine Ann, was born the following year.

Heaney's fourth volume of poetry, North, was published in 1975: Part I ranges over three thousand years of European civilisation, from the myths of Classical Greece to nineteenth-century Irish history, examining stories of conquest, cultural conflict and deeds of violence. Part 2 focuses on the pressures and prejudices in play in Northern Ireland at the time. Also in this section, he attempts to chart the milestones in his own development as a poet and as a member of his tribe: the Northern Catholic. In 'A Constable Calls' he recalls, from a child's perspective, his fear of an alien law. This collection of conflict poems in North is prefaced by two totally different poems: two peaceful poems outside the stream of history and time recalling the security of childhood, the holistic nature of the old ways of life, the peacefulness of the countryside, and the stability and certainty provided by family love and values. These two poems are 'Mossbawn: Two Poems in Dedication', of which the first is 'Sunlight'.

In 1976, when Heaney became Head of English at Carysfort College, the family moved to Sandymount, Dublin, which would be their family home for the rest of his life. There followed a prolific period in his writing. Field Work (1979) contains the poems 'The Skunk' and 'The Harvest Bow'. This was followed by Station Island (1984); The Haw Lantern (1987); and Seeing Things (1991), from which the poem 'Lightenings VIII' is taken. Among the most notable of his later works were: The Spirit Level (1996), winner of the Whitbread Book of the Year Award; Beowulf (1999), a translation and also a Whitbread winner; District and Circle (2006) and Human Chain (2010).

Heaney was an international literary figure who was a professor at Harvard University (1981–97) and was elected Professor of Poetry at Oxford (1989–94). His lectures from Oxford were published under the title The Redress of Poetry (1995). His work received worldwide recognition and renown when he was awarded the Nobel Prize for Literature in 1995. He was declared a Saoi of Aosdána and was also a member of the Royal Irish Academy. Among the many other accolades for his poetry were: The Golden Wreath of Poetry (2001); the T. S. Eliot Prize (2006) and the Griffin Trust for Excellence in Poetry Life Award (2012).

Seamus Heaney died on 30 August 2013 and was buried at the Cemetery of St Mary's Church, Bellaghy, Co. Derry.

THE FORGE

All I know is a door into the dark.
Outside, old axles and iron hoops rusting;
Inside, the hammered anvil's short-pitched ring,
The unpredictable fantail of sparks
Or hiss when a new shoe toughens in water.   5
The anvil must be somewhere in the centre,
Horned as a unicorn, at one end square,
Set there immovable: an altar
Where he expends himself in shape and music.
Sometimes, leather-aproned, hairs in his nose,   10
He leans out on the jamb, recalls a clatter
Of hoofs where traffic is flashing in rows;
Then grunts and goes in, with a slam and flick
To beat real iron out, to work the bellows.

EXPLORATIONS

Before reading

1. Read the title only. Jot down all the images that come into your head of what you might expect to see in the forge.

First reading

2. What do you actually see in this picture of the forge?

3. Where is the speaker standing in this poem? Do you think this might be significant? Why? What can he see? What can he not see?

Second reading

4. What can we say about the smith from his appearance and manner? Refer to the text.

5. How do you think the smith views his work? Read lines 13 and 14 again.

6. How does the poet view the smith's work? Read lines 6–9 again.

Third reading

7. What do you think is the poet's theme here?

8. Could the poem be read in a symbolic way, i.e. as dealing with a subject other than the surface one of the work of a blacksmith? If so, how?

9. Comment on the appropriateness of the imagery in this poem.

10. Would you agree with the following criticism by another poet, James Simmons? "'The Forge' . . . is shapely and vivid at first but fails to stand as a metaphor for the creative act. It becomes a cliché portrait of the village smithy. The smith has hairs in his nose and remembers better times. He retreats from the sight of modern traffic to beat real iron out, to work the bellows.' Give your opinion on both the metaphor and the portrait of the village forge.

Fourth reading

11. Comment on the style of language used. Is it poetic, prosaic, conversational, or what?

12. Do you think Heaney brings a sense of concrete realism to his art? Comment, with reference to the text.

13. What elements of the poem do not work very well for you? Explain, with reference to the text.

BOGLAND 🔊

For T. P. Flanagan

We have no prairies
To slice a big sun at evening —
Everywhere the eye concedes to
Encroaching horizon,

Is wooed into the cyclops' eye   5
Of a tarn. Our unfenced country
Is bog that keeps crusting
Between the sights of the sun.

They've taken the skeleton
Of the Great Irish Elk   10
Out of the peat, set it up
An astounding crate full of air.

Butter sunk under
More than a hundred years
Was recovered salty and white.   15
The ground itself is kind, black butter

Melting and opening underfoot,
Missing its last definition
By millions of years.
They'll never dig coal here,   20

Only the waterlogged trunks
Of great firs, soft as pulp.
Our pioneers keep striking
Inwards and downwards,

Every layer they strip   25
Seems camped on before.
The bogholes might be Atlantic seepage.
The wet centre is bottomless.

'Boglands' (for Seamus Heaney), an oil painting by T. P. Flanagan

NOTES

| 5 | cyclops: | in Greek mythology a Cyclops was one of a race of one-eyed giants |
| 6 | tarn: | a small mountain lake |

EXPLORATIONS

First reading

1. Explain the contrast between the prairies and the Irish landscape, as described in the first two stanzas.

2. Where else in the poem is this cultural contrast referred to?

3. What properties of bogland are dwelt on in stanzas 3–6?

4. Who do you see as the speaking voice in this poem?

Second reading

5. What queries are raised in your mind by a further reading? List at least three.

6. What do you think this poem is about?

Third reading

7. If we accept that the bog is a metaphor for Irishness, what is the poet saying on this theme? Refer to the text to substantiate your views.

8. Comment on the tone of this poem. Do you think the poet is pessimistic, excited, neutral, nostalgic, or what? Refer to the text.

9. Do you think this poem asks you to think in a different way about what it means to be Irish? Explain.

10. Consider the following critical comment made by James Simmons: 'As a man and poet in his life and philosophy Heaney is not geared to progress and reform. He wants to wallow and look back. He is going through a door into the dark, inward and downward, a kind of Jungian ground he will call it.' Which elements of this criticism do you think are justified? Do you think any element is unwarranted? Justify your comments with reference to the text.

Fourth reading

11. What questions would you like to ask Seamus Heaney about this poem?

12. In the form of headings, or a flow chart, or a spider diagram, bring together your ideas on the theme and imagery of this poem.

THE TOLLUND MAN 🔊

I

Some day I will go to Aarhus
To see his peat-brown head,
The mild pods of his eye-lids,
His pointed skin cap.

In the flat country near by   5
Where they dug him out,
His last gruel of winter seeds
Caked in his stomach,

Naked except for
The cap, noose and girdle,   10
I will stand a long time.
Bridegroom to the goddess,

She tightened her torc on him
And opened her fen,
Those dark juices working   15
Him to a saint's kept body,

Trove of the turfcutters'
Honeycombed workings.
Now his stained face
Reposes at Aarhus.   20

II

I could risk blasphemy,
Consecrate the cauldron bog
Our holy ground and pray
Him to make germinate

The scattered, ambushed   25
Flesh of labourers,
Stockinged corpses
Laid out in the farmyards,

Tell-tale skin and teeth
Flecking the sleepers   30
Of four young brothers, trailed
For miles along the lines.

III

Something of his sad freedom
As he rode the tumbril
Should come to me, driving,　　　　　35
Saying the names

Tollund, Grauballe, Nebelgard,

Watching the pointing hands
Of country people,
Not knowing their tongue.　　　　　40

Out there in Jutland
In the old man-killing parishes
I will feel lost,
Unhappy and at home.

EXPLORATIONS

First reading

1. Listen to a reading of part I. What do you see? What words or phrases make images for you?

2. Now read it. Describe the poet's subject. What details do you find most interesting? Why?

3. Identify the speaker in the poem. Identify the 'he' and 'she' referred to.

4. Explain the incident described. What do you think happened?

Second reading

5. Now read part I again. What is still unclear?

6. Read part II. What is the poet writing about here, and when do you think it occurred?

7. What do you think is the connection between part II and part I?

Third reading

8. What is happening in part III?

9. How does the poet feel? Read the second-last stanza aloud. Listen to the sounds of the words. Picture the scene in your mind.

10. Explain why you think the poet feels 'lost, unhappy and at home'.

Fourth reading

11. Examine the parallels and contrasts between Tollund Man and modern people as Heaney pictures them in this poem.

12. Is the poem making a political statement? If so, what?

13. Discuss the political imagery in this poem.

14. Make brief notes on the themes dealt with in this poem.

15. Comment on the variety of imagery used throughout the poem.

16. Do you think Heaney manages to create a feeling of sympathy for Tollund Man? How does he manage to achieve this?

17. Michael Parker described this poem as 'a potent combination of historical analogy and myth and intense emotion which exhibits the depth of Heaney's religious nature'. Discuss this analysis, substantiating your view by reference to the text.

MOSSBAWN: TWO POEMS IN DEDICATION
(1) SUNLIGHT 🔊

For Mary Heaney

There was a sunlit absence.
The helmeted pump in the yard
heated its iron,
water honeyed

in the slung bucket   5
and the sun stood
like a griddle cooling
against the wall

of each long afternoon.
So, her hands scuffled   10
over the bakeboard,
the reddening stove

sent its plaque of heat
against her where she stood
in a floury apron   15
by the window.

Now she dusts the board
with a goose's wing,
now sits, broad-lapped,
with whitened nails   20

and measling shins:
here is a space
again, the scone rising
to the tick of two clocks.

And here is love   25
like a tinsmith's scoop
sunk past its gleam
in the meal-bin.

EXPLORATIONS

First reading

1. What is described here?

2. What details stand out on a first reading?

Second reading

3. Think of the poem as a picture in two panels: the yard and the kitchen.
   a Study the detail of each scene, and discuss the significance of each piece of detail. What era is evoked by the detail?
   b Examine the portrait of Mary Heaney. What kind of person is she?
   c Describe the atmosphere created in each scene, and explain how it is created.

Third reading

4. This is the opening poem in a volume that deals for the most part with violence, conflict and conquest. Does this surprise you? Explain.

5. In that context, what do you think is the significance of the poem? What does this poem suggest about the poet's values and attitudes to living?

6. Do you think there is any significance in the change from past tense to present tense that occurs from stanza 5 onwards?

7. Explain your own reaction to this poem.

A CONSTABLE CALLS 🔊

His bicycle stood at the window-sill,
The rubber cowl of a mud-splasher
Skirting the front mudguard,
Its fat black handlegrips

Heating in sunlight, the 'spud'   5
Of the dynamo gleaming and cocked back,
The pedal treads hanging relieved
Of the boot of the law.

His cap was upside down
On the floor, next his chair.   10
The line of its pressure ran like a bevel
In his slightly sweating hair.

He had unstrapped
The heavy ledger, and my father
Was making tillage returns   15
In acres, roods, and perches.

Arithmetic and fear.
I sat staring at the polished holster
With its buttoned flap, the braid cord
Looped into the revolver butt.   20

'Any other root crops?
Mangolds? Marrowstems? Anything like that?'
'No.' But was there not a line
Of turnips where the seed ran out

In the potato field? I assumed   25
Small guilts and sat
Imagining the black hole in the barracks.
He stood up, shifted the baton-case

Further round on his belt,
Closed the domesday book,   30
Fitted his cap back with two hands,
And looked at me as he said goodbye.

A shadow bobbed in the window.
He was snapping the carrier spring
Over the ledger. His boot pushed off   35
And the bicycle ticked, ticked, ticked.

EXPLORATIONS

First reading

1. What descriptive details of the bicycle did you notice as you read this poem? Did they seem to you in any way significant?

2. What details of the policeman's description did you think significant? What type of character is suggested by these details?

Second reading

3. What do you think is the boy's attitude to the bicycle, as described in the poem? Where and how is this attitude communicated to the reader?

4. What is the relationship between the participants in this encounter: the policeman, the boy and his father? Examine the imagery and dialogue and the actions of those involved.

Third reading

5. Can you understand how the boy feels? Explain.

6. Do you think the poem faithfully represents how a child might actually feel in this situation? Examine your own experiences to test the truth of the poem.

7. Outline the main themes of this poem, as you understand them.

8. From your reading of this poem, would you agree that one of Heaney's strengths as a poet is his ability to create realistic descriptions in minute detail?

Fourth reading

9. What is your evaluation of this poem's truth and significance?

THE SKUNK

Up, black, striped and damasked like the chasuble
At a funeral mass, the skunk's tail
Paraded the skunk. Night after night
I expected her like a visitor.

The refrigerator whinnied into silence.   5
My desk light softened beyond the verandah.
Small oranges loomed in the orange tree.
I began to be tense as a voyeur.

After eleven years I was composing
Love-letters again, broaching the word 'wife'   10
Like a stored cask, as if its slender vowel
Had mutated into the night earth and air

Of California. The beautiful, useless
Tang of eucalyptus spelt your absence.
The aftermath of a mouthful of wine   15
Was like inhaling you off a cold pillow.

And there she was, the intent and glamorous,
Ordinary, mysterious skunk,
Mythologized, demythologized,
Snuffing the boards five feet beyond me.   20

It all came back to me last night, stirred
By the sootfall of your things at bedtime,
Your head-down, tail-up hunt in a bottom drawer
For the black plunge-line nightdress.

EXPLORATIONS

First reading

1. What images do you notice in particular? What sounds or smells? How would you describe the atmosphere?

2. The poem is set in two separate places, at two different times. Where is that division reflected in the stanzas? What are the two distinct times and places?

3. What image is associated with both locations? Explain the connection.

Second reading

4. How would you describe the poet's mood or state of mind in the first five stanzas?

5. What part does the skunk play here? What are your reactions to this analogy?

6. What is the poet saying in stanza 5?

Third reading

7. Examine the nature of the poet's relationship with his wife, as it comes across in this poem.

Fourth reading

8. Examine the sensuous language in this poem.

9. What does the imagery contribute to the effectiveness of the poem?

10. Do you think the transmutation of wife and skunk works well?

11. What exactly is the poet saying about love and relationships?

Fifth reading

12. Give a considered response to the following evaluation of the poem by the critic Neil Corcoran: "The Skunk" is characteristic of these marriage poems, which are one of the highest points of Heaney's career: tender without being cosy, personal without being embarrassingly self-revealing. They are poems of a deeply disinterested maturity, managing an intensely difficult tone: honest and quite without self-regard.'
Deal separately with each point.

THE HARVEST BOW

As you plaited the harvest bow
You implicated the mellowed silence in you
In wheat that does not rust
But brightens as it tightens twist by twist
Into a knowable corona,   5
A throwaway love-knot of straw.

Hands that aged round ashplants and cane sticks
And lapped the spurs on a lifetime of gamecocks
Harked to their gift and worked with fine intent
Until your fingers moved somnambulant: 10
I tell and finger it like braille,
Gleaning the unsaid off the palpable.

And if I spy into its golden loops
I see us walk between the railway slopes
Into an evening of long grass and midges,   15
Blue smoke straight up, old beds and ploughs in hedges,
An auction notice on an outhouse wall —
You with a harvest bow in your lapel,

Me with the fishing rod, already homesick
For the big lift of these evenings, as your stick   20
Whacking the tips off weeds and bushes
Beats out of time, and beats, but flushes
Nothing: that original townland
Still tongue-tied in the straw tied by your hand.

The end of art is peace   25
Could be the motto of this frail device
That I have pinned up on our deal dresser —
Like a drawn snare
Slipped lately by the spirit of the corn
Yet burnished by its passage, and still warm.   30

NOTES

	Harvest Bow:	a knot woven from wheat straw, a symbol of a fruitful harvest, embodying the spirit of the corn
5	corona:	halo of light round the sun
10	somnambulant:	sleep-walking (here, performing unconsciously, as in sleep)
12	palpable:	capable of being touched, felt, or readily perceived

EXPLORATIONS

First reading

1. As you read, visualise the poem in your mind's eye. What colours predominate? Which images strike you in particular? How do you imagine the setting?

Second reading

2. 'As you plaited the harvest bow' — who do you think is the 'you' addressed in the poem: a person older or younger than the poet, living in the town or in the country? What type of person?

3. Where is the poem set? Are there a number of settings in it? Examine the imagery again.

4. Examine the time frames in the poem. Is it set in the present or the past, or both? Read the verses in the order 5, 1, 2, 3, 4. Does this help to clarify which is the present, which is the recent past, and which are distant memories?

5. In your own words, briefly reconstruct the narrative.

Third reading

6. Trace the various references to the harvest bow that are scattered throughout the poem. Examine each image and say what it suggests to you about the significance of the bow.

7. How does the poet regard the bow? Is it important to him? What does it enable him to do?

8. How do you think the father viewed the bow?

9. How does the poet regard his father? Examine the images used about him and the tone of the utterances referring to him.

10. If the father was a better communicator, what do you think he might have said in stanza 4?

Fourth reading

11. What do you imagine he might mean by the motto 'The end of art is peace'?

12. What lines, phrases or images are still unclear to you? Discuss interpretations.

13. What does the poem reveal about Heaney's attitude to his rural heritage?

14. What does the poet feel about the value of art and poetry in society?

Fifth reading

15. What is your own reaction to 'The Harvest Bow'? Does it say anything of significance to you?

16. What questions would you like to ask the poet if you could?

THE UNDERGROUND

There we were in the vaulted tunnel running,
You in your going-away coat speeding ahead
And me, me then like a fleet god gaining
Behind you before you turned to a reed

Or some new white flower japped with crimson   5
As the coat flapped wild and button after button
Sprang off and fell in a trail
Between the Underground and the Albert Hall.

Honeymooning, mooning around, late for the Proms,
Our echoes die in that corridor and now   10
I come as Hansel came on the moonlit stones
Retracing the path back, lifting the buttons

To end up in a draughty lamplit station
After the trains have gone, the wet track
Bared and tensed as I am, all attention   15
For your step following and damned if I look back.

NOTES

The Underground:		the underground train system in London
3	fleet:	fleet of foot, swift, nimble
5	japped:	possibly means varnished or lacquered
4	before you turned to a reed:	this is a reference to the classical myth of Pan and Syrinx. The nymph Syrinx was being pursued by the god Pan and in order to preserve her virginity she appealed to the river nymphs for help. Just as Pan reached for her she was transformed into a bed of reeds, which he was left clutching. He made his music pipes from these reeds and called them syrinx in memory of her.
11	Hansel:	refers to a Grimms' fairy tale about two inseparable children, Hansel, a woodcutter's son, and Gretel, a young girl found in the forest. The family fell on bad times and were starving so the wife persuaded the father to abandon the children in the forest. But Hansel marked the trail with pebbles so they found their way home.
16	damned if I look back:	refers to the classical myth of Orpheus and Eurydice. In Greek legend Orpheus was a Thracian poet and a very skilled musician. When his wife Eurydice died, he travelled down to the underworld, the kingdom of the dead, and by his music persuaded King Pluto to free her. However, this was on the condition that Orpheus would not look back until they reached the earth. Just as they came towards the light at the mouth of the tunnel, because of his love for Eurydice, Orpheus could not prevent himself glancing back to look at her face. She immediately vanished down to Hades again. Because he loved her too much Orpheus lost her forever.

EXPLORATIONS

Before reading

1. Make a list of all the connotations, real and imaginary, that occur to you about the word 'underground'.

First reading

2. In your own words, describe what happens in this poem.

3. What details in particular catch your eye?

4. How would you describe the atmosphere?

5. Retell the narrative from the woman's perspective.

Second reading

6. Do you think the speaker is as carefree as you might expect him to be on his honeymoon? Develop your ideas on this.

7. If this is a love poem, what is it saying about love?

8. Do you think the setting is appropriate to a love poem? Explain. What would you like to ask the poet about this?

POSTSCRIPT

And some time make the time to drive out west
Into County Clare, along the Flaggy Shore,
In September or October, when the wind
And the light are working off each other
So that the ocean on the one side is wild   5
With foam and glitter, and inland among stones
The surface of a slate-grey lake is lit
By the earthed lightning of a flock of swans,
Their feathers roughed and ruffling, white on white,
Their fully grown headstrong-looking heads   10
Tucked or cresting or busy underwater.
Useless to think you'll park and capture it
More thoroughly. You are neither here nor there,
A hurry through which known and strange things pass
As big soft buffetings come at the car sideways   15
And catch the heart off guard and blow it open.

EXPLORATIONS

First reading

1. **a** Have you ever seen flashes of scenery on a car journey that you can still remember, even though you only saw them for a moment?

   b Does this poem in any way remind you of your experience?

Second reading

2. This poem is set in County Clare in 'September or October'. What images are there in lines 3–7 that help you to picture what County Clare is like at this time of year?

3. 'The surface of a slate-grey lake is lit/By the earthed lightning of a flock of swans,/Their feathers roughed and ruffling, white on white'
   Can you suggest why Heaney describes the swans as 'earthed lightning'? You might find it helpful to consider the colour and texture of the lake and the swans.

4. Do you find Heaney's description of the swans a realistic one? Why? Use quotations from the poem to support your answer.

5. Heaney decided not to use any full stops until line 11 of this poem.

   a What effect does this have on the way that you read the poem?

   b Does the effect that he is trying to create have anything to do with the fact that he is describing a car journey?

6. 'You are neither here nor there,/A hurry through which known and strange things pass'.
   What do you think Heaney is trying to suggest about travelling in a car when he uses the phrases 'neither here nor there' and 'A hurry through'?

Third reading

7. What do the final two lines of the poem reveal about how the glimpses of the scenery affected Heaney?

8. From your readings of the poem, can you work out how Seamus Heaney feels about County Clare? You will find it useful to consider the tone, or the emotion, of his words.

9. **a** Why do you think Heaney decided to give this poem the title 'Postscript'?

   b Do you think that it is a successful title, or can you suggest another title that you would consider more suitable?

10. Imagine that you have been asked to prepare a short film to be shown as Seamus Heaney reads this poem. Describe the images that you would show and the camera angles that you would use to capture how you 'see' this poem.

A CALL

'Hold on,' she said, 'I'll just run out and get him.
The weather here's so good he took the chance
To do a bit of weeding.'
   So I saw him
Down on his hands and knees beside the leek rig,   5
Touching, inspecting, separating one
Stalk from the other, gently pulling up
Everything not tapered, frail and leafless,
Pleased to feel each little weed-root break,
But rueful also . . .   10
   Then found myself listening to
The amplified grave ticking of hall clocks
Where the phone lay unattended in a calm
Of mirror glass and sunstruck pendulums . . .

And found myself then thinking: if it were nowadays,   15
This is how Death would summon Everyman.

Next thing he spoke and I nearly said I loved him.

NOTE		
16	Everyman:	the main character in a famous English morality play of the early sixteenth century. When Everyman is summoned by Death he invites all his acquaintances (who include Kindred, Good Deeds, Goods, Knowledge, Beauty and others) to go with him, but only Good Deeds agrees to go.

EXPLORATIONS

Before reading

1. When you last made a phone call to a landline and someone went away to get whoever you were trying to reach, what thoughts went through your mind as you waited? Share the results in groups.

First reading

2. What thoughts were going through the poet's mind as he waited?

3. The poet has a very clear visual image of his father. What aspects of the man does he highlight?

4. Reread the section describing the hallway as the speaker waits.
   a If you close your eyes and picture the scene, what do you see and hear?
   b What thoughts come to your mind?
   c How would you describe the atmosphere in the hallway? Refer to words and images to support your answer.

5. Now read the next two lines. Does it come as a complete surprise that the poet is thinking about death? Explain your thinking.

6. a Suggest some possible reasons why the poet did not say he loved his father.
   b Do you think he might now regret that?

Second reading

7. What are the main ideas/issues dealt with in this poem?

8. a Do you think it was important to write about these issues? Explain your thinking.
   b Do you think he does it well? What aspects or sections do you find particularly effective? Explain.

9. There is some ambiguity about the title. Suggest a couple of different ways in which the title might be understood.

10. Phone a friend. Listen, think and write it up.

TATE'S AVENUE

Not the brown and fawn car rug, that first one
Spread on sand by the sea but breathing land-breaths,
Its vestal folds unfolded, its comfort zone
Edged with a fringe of sepia-coloured wool tails.

Not the one scraggy with crusts and eggshells   5
And olive stones and cheese and salami rinds
Laid out by the torrents of the Guadalquivir
Where we got drunk before the corrida.

Instead, again, it's locked-park Sunday Belfast,
A walled back yard, the dust-bins high and silent   10
As a page is turned, a finger twirls warm hair
And nothing gives on the rug or the ground beneath it.

I lay at my length and felt the lumpy earth,
Keen-sensed more than ever through discomfort,
But never shifted off the plaid square once.   15
When we moved I had your measure and you had mine.

NOTES

3	vestal:	chaste, virginal. Vesta was the Roman goddess of hearth and home and vowed to chastity.
4	sepia-coloured:	brown-coloured
6	salami:	a kind of sausage
7	Guadalquivir:	a river in Spain
8	corrida:	bullfight

EXPLORATIONS

First reading

1. Make a list of the images you remember after a first reading. Are they all of a similar kind or are there differences or contrasts?

2. Examine the experience described in the first stanza. Do you think it was a happy experience? Explain your thinking, making reference to the text.

3. Do you think that experience was enjoyable? Explain your thinking, referring to the poem.

Second reading

4. Now read the fourth stanza and describe the experience there.

5. The third stanza gives a rationale for the difference of experience. Examine this closely and from the evidence here, describe what it may have been like to live in 'locked-park Sunday Belfast'.

6. Using the contrasting romantic experiences on rugs, the poet is making a point about ways of life and cultural differences. In groups discuss what these might be and write up the opinions in a coherent form.

THE PITCHFORK

Of all implements, the pitchfork was the one
That came near to an imagined perfection:
When he tightened his raised hand and aimed with it,
It felt like a javelin, accurate and light.

So whether he played the warrior or the athlete   5
Or worked in earnest in the chaff and sweat,
He loved its grain of tapering, dark-flecked ash
Grown satiny from its own natural polish.

Riveted steel, turned timber, burnish, grain,
Smoothness, straightness, roundness, length and sheen.   10
Sweat-cured, sharpened, balanced, tested, fitted.
The springiness, the clip and dart of it.

And then when he thought of probes that reached the farthest,
He would see the shaft of a pitchfork sailing past
Evenly, imperturbably through space,   15
Its prongs starlit and absolutely soundless –

But has learned at last to follow that simple lead
Past its own aim, out to an other side
Where perfection – or nearness to it – is imagined
Not in the aiming but the opening hand.   20

EXPLORATIONS

Before reading

1. Talk to a farmer or go online to find out all you can about the uses of a pitchfork.

2. If possible, see if you can find a pitchfork to examine in detail. Hold it, weigh it, handle it, try using it. Or examine a picture of one. Think about its uses.

First reading

3. What does the farmer in the poem love about the pitchfork? Examine the text in detail and write three paragraphs on the qualities of a good pitchfork.

4. Apart from its value as an agricultural implement, what else does the pitchfork contribute to the life and consciousness of the farmer?

Second reading

5. Consider the final stanza and, in pairs or groups, share your thoughts or possible meanings.

6. This poem is taken from a volume entitled *Seeing Things*. Explore the different kinds of 'seeing' that occur in this poem.

7. What does this poem say about farmers and farming? Write about it.

LIGHTENINGS VIII

The annals say: when the monks of Clonmacnoise
Were all at prayers inside the oratory
A ship appeared above them in the air.

The anchor dragged along behind so deep
It hooked itself into the altar rails   5
And then, as the big hull rocked to a standstill,

A crewman shinned and grappled down the rope
And struggled to release it. But in vain.
'This man can't bear our life here and will drown,'

The abbot said, 'unless we help him.' So   10
They did, the freed ship sailed, and the man climbed back
Out of the marvellous as he had known it.

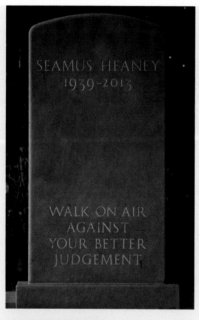

EXPLORATIONS

First reading

1. On a first reading, what do you
    notice about this narrative? What
    do you find exciting or arresting or
    amusing?

2. 'This man can't bear our life
    here and will drown'. Explore the
    significance of this statement.

3. 'The man climbed back/Out of
    the marvellous as he had known it.'
    Imagine the incident as seen from
    the point of view of the crewman.
    Tell it.

Second reading

4. What is real here and what is
    fabulous or imaginary?

5. What do you see as the point of the
    anecdote? Is it making a statement
    about poetry, about imagined reality,
    about knowledge? Explain your
    thinking.

6. Comment on the form or structure
    of the poem.

7. What do you notice about the style
    of the language? Do you find it
    effective for this poem?

8. Do you like this poem? Elaborate.

EILÉAN
NÍ CHUILLEANÁIN

(1942–)

Prescribed for Higher Level exams in 2019 and 2020

iléan Ní Chuilleanáin was born in Cork in 1942, the eldest of three children. Her father was Cormac Ó Cuilleanáin, a noted academic and professor of Irish at University College Cork. Her mother was Eilis Dillon, who wrote over fifty books, including detective stories, historical novels and children's stories. On leaving school, Eiléan Ní Chuilleanáin attended University College Cork and was awarded a BA in English and History in 1962, a Master's degree in 1964 and a Bachelor of Letters in 1968, following a period of study in Oxford.

She won her first prize for poetry in 1966, the *Irish Times* Award for Poetry. This was followed in 1973 by the Patrick Kavanagh Poetry Award for her first collection of poetry. In 1975, her commitment to the Irish literary scene led her to co-found the literary magazine *Cyphers* with Macdara Woods, Leland Bardwell and Pearse Hutchinson, which is still being published today. She has continued to win prizes for her poetry and in 2010 she won the International Griffin Poetry Prize.

Eiléan Ní Chuilleanáin has worked as an academic in Trinity College Dublin since 1966, when she was appointed to a Junior Lectureship in English, specialising in Renaissance literature, and she is now a Fellow Emeritus. In 1978 she married fellow poet Macdara Woods and they have a son, Niall, who is a musician.

LUCINA SCHYNNING IN SILENCE OF THE NICHT

Moon shining in silence of the night
The heaven being all full of stars
I was reading my book in a ruin
By a sour candle, without roast meat or music
Strong drink or a shield from the air   5
Blowing in the crazed window, and I felt
Moonlight on my head, clear after three days' rain.

I was washed in cold water; it was orange, channelled down bogs
Dipped between cresses.
The bats flew through my room where I slept safely.   10
Sheep stared at me when I woke.

Behind me the waves of darkness lay, the plague
Of mice, plague of beetles
Crawling out of the spines of books,
Plague shadowing pale faces with clay   15
The disease of the moon gone astray.

In the desert I relaxed, amazed
As the mosaic beasts on the chapel floor
When Cromwell had departed, and they saw
The sky growing through the hole in the roof.   20

Sheepdogs embraced me; the grasshopper
Returned with lark and bee.
I looked down between hedges of high thorn and saw
The hare, absorbed, sitting still
In the middle of the track; I heard   25
Again the chirp of the stream running.

NOTES

Lucina Schynning in Silence of the Nicht:		this is a line taken from a poem by a Scottish poet, William Dunbar, who died before 1530. Lines 1–2 of Ní Chuilleanáin's poem are a modern English translation of this line and another line from Dunbar's poem. Lucina is another name for Diana, the goddess of the moon.
6	crazed:	possibly marked with fine surface cracks; possibly made insane
9	cresses:	a plant with edible leaves
12	plague:	around 1650, many people in Ireland died from the plague
14	Crawling out:	a reference to spontaneous generation, i.e. the belief that life could suddenly appear from sources that were not parents, eggs or seeds, such as mud or books. This was accepted as fact until the late Renaissance.
19	Cromwell:	Oliver Cromwell, who landed in Ireland in 1649 with a large army. The war that followed his arrival led to great destruction, many deaths and famine in Ireland.

EXPLORATIONS

Before reading

1. In this poem, nature is shown as having a positive effect on human emotions. Do you agree or disagree with this idea? Why?

First reading

2. What is your first reaction to this poem? Do you like or dislike it? Why? Refer to the text to support your opinion.

3. **a** How do the images in lines 3–6 convey the speaker's negative and depressed emotions?

   b Line 7 suggests that her emotions begin to change. In what way have they changed? What has caused this change?

4. **a** 'I washed in cold water; it was orange, channelled down bogs/ Dipped between cresses.' What senses are appealed to in this image?

   b What does this image suggest to you about the state of the speaker's emotions at this point?

   c How do the images that follow in lines 10–11 also convey this state?

5. Although she has now put her negative and depressed emotions behind her, in lines 12–16 the speaker uses a series of images to show just how nightmarish they were. Choose one image from these lines that you feel is particularly effective in doing this. Explain the reasons for your choice.

Second reading

6. In lines 17–20, the speaker compares her 'amazed' feelings to the 'mosaic beasts on the chapel floor'. In your own words, explain how this comparison works.

7. **a** How would you describe the effect that the world of nature has on the speaker's feelings in lines 21–26?

    b   Do you think this is an effective ending for this poem? Why?

Third reading

8. 'I was reading my book in a ruin/By a sour candle, without roast meat or music', 'the plague/Of mice, plague of beetles/Crawling out of the spines of books'.

    a   What impression do you get of the speaker's attitude to books and their contents from these lines?

    b   Do you think this is a fair representation of books? Why?

9.   Discuss how the world of nature is shown to have a positive effect on human emotions in 'Lucina Schynning in Silence of the Nicht'.

10.   Having explored this poem, do you still have the same reaction to this poem as you did for Question 2? Why?

THE SECOND VOYAGE

Odysseus rested on his oar and saw
The ruffled foreheads of the waves
Crocodiling and mincing past: he rammed
The oar between their jaws and looked down
In the simmering sea where scribbles of weed defined   5
Uncertain depth, and the slim fishes progressed
In fatal formation, and thought
                              If there was a single
Streak of decency in these waves now, they'd be ridged
Pocked and dented with the battering they've had,   10
And we could name them as Adam named the beasts,
Saluting a new one with dismay, or a notorious one
With admiration; they'd notice us passing
And rejoice at our shipwreck, but these
Have less character than sheep and need more patience.   15

I know what I'll do he said;
I'll park my ship in the crook of a long pier
(And I'll take you with me he said to the oar)
I'll face the rising ground and walk away
From tidal waters, up riverbeds   20
Where herons parcel out the miles of stream,
Over gaps in the hills, through warm
Silent valleys, and when I meet a farmer
Bold enough to look me in the eye
With 'where are you off to with that long   25
Winnowing fan over your shoulder?'
There I will stand still
And I'll plant you for a gatepost or a hitching-post
And leave you as a tidemark. I can go back
And organise my house then.   30
                              But the profound
Unfenced valleys of the ocean still held him;
He had only the oar to make them keep their distance;
The sea was still frying under the ship's side.
He considered the water-lilies, and thought about fountains   35
Spraying as wide as willows in empty squares,
The sugarstick of water clattering into the kettle,
The flat lakes bisecting the rushes. He remembered spiders and frogs
Housekeeping at the roadside in brown trickles floored with mud,
Horsetroughs, the black canal, pale swans at dark: 40
His face grew damp with tears that tasted
Like his own sweat or the insults of the sea.

NOTES

1	Odysseus:	the King of Ithaca and hero of Homer's 'The Odyssey'. Because he offends Poseidon, the god of the sea, Odysseus encounters many difficulties on his sea journey back home after the Trojan War. On one occasion, he goes down into the underworld and speaks to the spirit of the blind seer, Tiresias. Tiresias tells Odysseus that when he is once again King of Ithaca he must take an oar and walk away from Ithaca until he meets a man who knows nothing about the sea. This man will think that the oar is a winnowing fan used to separate grain from the husks. Odysseus should stick the oar into the ground at this place and make offerings to the god Poseidon. If he does this, Odysseus will live a long life as King of Ithaca. This quest has been referred to as Odysseus' 'Second Voyage'.
3	Crocodiling:	possibly as when used to describe the surface of paint cracking so that it looks like the scales of crocodile skin; possibly as when used to describe a line of paired children walking one after the other; possibly linking to 'foreheads' (line 2) to suggest the movement of a hunting crocodile through water with only the bumps of his eyes and upper head above water
3	mincing:	walking in an exaggerated and affected way in small short steps
10	Pocked:	pockmarked with spots from chickenpox or smallpox
12	notorious:	known for being bad
17	crook:	a curve, as at the top of a shepherd's crook
24	Bold:	brave, courageous
26	Winnowing fan:	a fan used to blow air to separate wheat grains from the outer dry husks
28	hitching-post:	a post to which animals are tied to stop them from wandering off
29	tidemark:	a mark left by the tide at its highest point
31	profound:	stretching to a great depth
37	sugarstick:	a striped candy stick
38	bisecting:	cutting into two equal parts

EXPLORATIONS

First reading

1. This is a poem that is filled with vivid images that appeal to the reader's senses. Choose two images from the poem that you find particularly striking and explain the reasons for your choices.

2. What do Odysseus' actions in lines 1–6 suggest to you about his attitude to the sea? Refer to the poem in your answer.

3. Explain in your own words how lines 8–15 convey that Odysseus wants to gain power over the waves and the sea and also that Odysseus feels contempt for the waves. Support your answers by reference to the poem.

Second reading

4. Both Odysseus and the sea are established as the two key characters in this poem. What qualities of Odysseus' personality are conveyed in lines 1–15? What qualities of the sea are conveyed in lines 1–15? Support your answers by reference to the poem.

5. a Based on your work for Questions 2–4, can you suggest why Odysseus decides that his second voyage will be on land?

   b How is his attitude to the land, described in lines 16–29, different to his attitude to the sea? Refer to the poem in your answers.

6. 'But the profound/Unfenced valleys of the ocean still held him; He had only the oar to make them keep their distance'.

   a What do these lines tell you about the true state of the balance of power between Odysseus and the sea?

   b What phrases or images in these lines convey Odysseus' lack of power to you?

7. How do the images that Odysseus recalls in lines 35–40 suggest that he believes that water is more easily controlled on land?

Third reading

8. 'His face grew damp with tears that tasted/Like his own sweat or the insults of the sea.'
   Examine the different ways in which the final two lines of this poem can be interpreted. Do you find these lines a satisfactory conclusion to the poem? Why?

9. Discuss how Eiléan Ní Chuilleanáin uses changes in the focus of this poem to increase the effect that it has on the reader. Support your answers by reference to the poem.

10. 'Eiléan Ní Chuilleanáin's poetry reminds us that the past, in the forms of folktales, fairytales and myths, can still have an influence on our lives in the present.'
    Write your response to this statement, supporting your answer with suitable reference to the poems 'To Niall Woods and Xenya Ostrovskaia, married in Dublin on 9 September 2009' and 'The Second Voyage'.

DEATHS AND ENGINES 🔊

We came down above the houses
In a stiff curve, and
At the edge of Paris airport
Saw an empty tunnel
– The back half of a plane, black   5
On the snow, nobody near it,
Tubular, burnt-out and frozen.

When we faced again
The snow-white runways in the dark
No sound came over   10
The loudspeakers, except the sighs
Of the lonely pilot.

The cold of metal wings is contagious:
Soon you will need wings of your own,
Cornered in the angle where   15
Time and life like a knife and fork
Cross, and the lifeline in your palm
Breaks, and the curve of an aeroplane's track
Meets the straight skyline.

The images of relief: 20
Hospital pyjamas, screens round a bed
A man with a bloody face
Sitting up in bed, conversing cheerfully
Through cut lips:
These will fail you some time.   25

You will find yourself alone
Accelerating down a blind
Alley, too late to stop
And know how light your death is;
You will be scattered like wreckage,   30
The pieces every one a different shape
Will spin and lodge in the hearts
Of all who love you.

NOTES

7	Tubular:	shaped like a tube
13	contagious:	able to spread to others
23	conversing:	in conversation

EXPLORATIONS

Before reading

1. **a**   The title of this poem is 'Deaths and Engines'. Working in pairs and without reading the poem, discuss the possible connections between deaths and engines that could be explored in this poem. Share your ideas with the class and write up bullet-point summaries of them on the board.

    b   Based on this title and your ideas, do you think this will be a happy poem or a sad poem? Why?

First reading

2. Select an image or a phrase from the poem that you think is particularly effective in suggesting a feeling or a sensation and explain the reasons for your choice.

3. From your reading of lines 1–12, what impression do you get of the effect that seeing the plane wreckage had on those who were landing in 'Paris airport'? Support your answer by referring to the poem.

4. **a**   'Soon you will need wings of your own'. Explain in your own words what the poet is referring to in this line.

b   Choose one of the images that the poet uses in lines 15–19. Write the image down and discuss how it refers to death.

5. a   'The images of relief'. How can the images in lines 21–4 be interpreted as 'images of relief'?

    b   What do you think the poet is suggesting about these 'images of relief' in the line 'These will fail you some time'? Support your answers by reference to the poem.

Second reading

6. a   What emotions do you think the poet wants her readers to feel when they read lines 26–8? Refer to the particular word or image that you think creates each of the emotions that you have suggested.

    b   What emotions do you think she wants her readers to feel in lines 29–33? Again, refer to the particular word or image that you think creates each of the emotions that you have suggested.

7. Do you think reading this poem would result in the reader developing a positive or a negative attitude towards death? Refer to the poem to support your viewpoint.

8. a   Based on your work for Questions 1 and 7, do you think that 'Deaths and Engines' is a suitable title for the poem or can you suggest another title that you feel would be more suitable? You may like to select a phrase from the poem or to compose a new title.

    b   Whether you decide to keep Eiléan Ní Chuilleanáin's title or to suggest an alternative title, explain why you think your choice of title is appropriate to the poem.

Third reading

9. Write a personal response to this poem. Your answer should make close reference to the text.

STREET 🔊

He fell in love with the butcher's daughter
When he saw her passing by in her white trousers
Dangling a knife on a ring at her belt.
He stared at the dark shining drops on the paving-stones.

One day he followed her   5
Down the slanting lane at the back of the shambles.
A door stood half-open
And the stairs were brushed and clean,
Her shoes paired on the bottom step,
Each tread marked with the red crescent   10
Her bare heels left, fading to faintest at the top.

NOTES

6	shambles:	a sixteenth-century English word for a slaughterhouse where animals are killed for food
10	tread:	the flat, horizontal part of a step
10	crescent:	a curved shape like that of a new moon

EXPLORATIONS

Before reading

1. Many of our television series come from the US, where often a series will be cancelled if it is not successful before it reaches the end of its narratives, or stories.

   a Have you ever watched a series that was cancelled and, as a result, the stories were left unfinished? How did you feel about this situation?

   b Which sort of narrative do you prefer when you are watching television or a film or reading a book – a narrative that has an ending where there are no mysteries or puzzles left or an ending that leaves some mysteries or puzzles unsolved?

   c Do you think that unsolved mysteries and puzzles are part of our experience of living life in the real world? Why?

First reading

2. How do you feel about the way in which this poem finishes in line 11? Explain why you feel this way.

3. a Describe how you imagine 'the butcher's daughter' based on your reading of lines 1–3.

   b What would your reaction be if you saw a woman like this passing you by in the street? Why would you react like this?

4. 'He fell in love with the butcher's daughter', 'One day he followed her'. What impression do these lines give you of the man in this poem? Are you surprised by the way he behaves? Why?

Second reading

5. a   In your own words, describe what the man sees when he looks inside the half-open door in lines 7–11.

    b   How would you feel if you saw this? Why?

6. a   Explain the connection you think the poet is suggesting that we could make between the girl, who is a 'butcher's daughter', her 'knife' in line 3, the 'dark shining drops' in line 4 and the 'red crescent' in line 10.

    b   Can you think of any other ways in which this connection might be explained?

7. In this poem, there are objects, ways of behaving and incidents that are familiar and understandable, but also objects, ways of behaving and incidents that are mysteriously puzzling.

    a   Working in pairs, make a list of the objects, ways of behaving and incidents that you think are familiar and understandable and a second list of the objects, ways of behaving and incidents that you think are mysterious and puzzling.

    b   As a class, share your lists and discuss what you think the poet is trying to suggest about life by featuring this mixture in this poem.

Third reading

8. From the phrases below, choose one which, in your opinion, best describes this poem:

- It is a frightening poem
- It is an annoying poem
- It is a thought-provoking poem
  Explain the reasons for your choice with reference to the poem.

9. In her poetry, Eiléan Ní Chuilleanáin often uses real, concrete images to represent abstract human emotions or qualities. Explain how the concrete images of passing through a doorway, or over a threshold, and climbing up a flight of stairs are used in this poem to suggest the abstract process of change, or transition, from one state to another in a person.

10. 'The traditional roles for men and women are no longer relevant in the Irish society of today.'
    Write out the speech that you would make for or against this proposition. As a class you might like to present your speeches and discuss the various views expressed regarding this topic.

FIREMAN'S LIFT

I was standing beside you looking up
Through the big tree of the cupola
Where the church splits wide open to admit
Celestial choirs, the fall-out of brightness.

The Virgin was spiralling to heaven, 5
Hauled up in stages. Past mist and shining,
Teams of angelic arms were heaving,
Supporting, crowding her, and we stepped

Back, as the painter longed to
While his arm swept in the large strokes. 10
We saw the work entire, and how the light

Melted and faded bodies so that
Loose feet and elbows and staring eyes
Floated in the wide stone petticoat
Clear and free as weeds. 15

This is what love sees, that angle:
The crick in the branch loaded with fruit,
A jaw defining itself, a shoulder yoked,

The back making itself a roof
The legs a bridge, the hands 20
A crane and a cradle.

Their heads bowed over to reflect on her
Fair face and hair so like their own
As she passed through their hands. We saw them
Lifting her, the pillars of their arms 25

(Her face a capital leaning into an arch)
As the muscles clung and shifted
For a final purchase together
Under her weight as she came to the edge of the cloud.

Parma 1963–Dublin 1994

NOTES

Fireman's Lift:		a particular way of lifting an incapable person
2	cupola:	a rounded dome that forms a roof
4	Celestial:	heavenly
5	The Virgin:	Correggio's fresco, in the cathedral of Parma (pictured) depicts the Christian belief that the Virgin, i.e. Mary, Christ's mother, was taken up into heaven when her life on earth was over. This is called the Assumption.
14	petticoat:	an underskirt
17	crick:	a painful cramp in a muscle
26	capital:	the top part of a pillar
28	purchase:	a firm hold

EXPLORATIONS

Before reading

1. **a** Look at the photograph that accompanies this poem of Correggio's 'Assumption of the Virgin' in Parma Cathedral. What three words would you use to describe this fresco? Take it in turns to write one of your words on the board.

    b Based on these words, do you find it surprising that this fresco is located in a cathedral? Why? Share and discuss your thoughts as a class.

First reading

2. **a** In your work on Question 1, did you notice any of the images that Ní Chuilleanáin describes in lines 2–15 of this poem? If so, which ones?

    b Choose one image from the poem that you feel is an effective and vivid description of a part of the fresco that you can see in the photograph.

Explain the reasons for your choice.

3. In lines 2–15, pick out the words or images that are drawn from a religious context and the words or images that are humorous. Are you surprised by this combination? Why?

Second reading

4. What impression do you get of the process of lifting 'the Virgin' up into heaven from lines 2–15? Your answer should make close reference to the words and images in these lines that you feel convey this impression.

5. a In lines 22–25, what words and images does the poet use to convey the effort that the nurses had to put in when they were lifting her dying mother?

   b Using your work for Question 4 and part (a) of this question, discuss the similarities that the poet sees between the situation of 'the Virgin' and her mother's situation. Refer to the poem to support your answer.

6. a 'This is what love sees, that angle'. What part does love play in the two lifting processes involving a person that are described in the poem?

   b Explain how each of the images in lines 17–21 effectively convey this process of lifting by appealing to the senses of sight and touch.

Third reading

7. a 'as she came to the edge of the cloud'.
   From your reading of this poem, what do you think 'the cloud' image represents for the poet's dying mother? Give reasons for your answer.

   b In your own words, explain how this 'cloud' can be seen as another example of Ní Chuilleanáin's use of the image of a threshold to suggest the process of changing from one state to another in a person.

8. Ní Chuilleanáin has described this poem as a 'cheering-up poem'. Based on your work on this poem, do you agree or disagree with her description? Why? Your answer should make close reference to the text of the poem.

9. Discuss how memories drawn from her shared family history help Ní Chuilleanáin to cope with her mother's death in 'Fireman's Lift' and her father's death in 'Deaths and Engines'.

10. Do you find 'Fireman's Lift' an easy or a difficult poem to understand? Why? Support your answer with suitable reference to the poem.

ALL FOR YOU

Once beyond the gate of the strange stableyard, we dismount.
The donkey walks on, straight in at a wide door
And sticks his head in a manger.

The great staircase of the hall slouches back,
Sprawling between warm wings. It is for you.   5
As the steps wind and warp
Among the vaults, their thick ribs part; the doors
Of guardroom, chapel, storeroom
Swing wide and the breath of ovens
Flows out, the rage of brushwood,   10
The roots torn out and butchered.

It is for you, the dry fragrance of tea-chests
The tins shining in ranks, the ten-pound jars
Rich with shrivelled fruit. Where better to lie down
And sleep, along the labelled shelves,   15
With the key still in your pocket?

NOTES		
6	warp:	twist
7	vaults:	arched roofs
7	ribs:	long, curved, narrow strips of stonework that help to support the vaults

EXPLORATIONS

First reading

1. Choose one image from the poem that appealed to you. Explain your choice.

2. **a** Lines 1–3 form the narrative fragment of this poem. In your own words, describe what happens in these lines.

    b Can you clearly imagine this scene based on lines 1–3? Why or why not?

3. **a** What does the donkey do in lines 1–3 that suggests he is familiar with this place? Refer to the poem in your answer.

    b What does the word 'strange' in line 1 indicate to you about the people who have just arrived?

4. The poem moves inside a building in lines 4–11.

    a What type of a building do you think it is? Refer to the text to support your answer.

    b What impression do you get of this building from lines 4–8?

Second reading

5. **a** It is clear from line 1 that at the beginning of the poem, the people are arriving at a place they do not know. What does the phrase 'Where better to lie down/And sleep' suggest to you about how they feel about the place at the end of the poem?

    b What aspects of this place have helped the people to feel at home? Make reference to the poem in your answer.

6. **a** The phrase 'It is for you' is used in lines 5 and 12. What do you think this phrase suggests about why the people who have just arrived are there?

    b How would you feel if someone said this to you about a building?

7. **a** Why do you think it is important that the person has 'the key still in your pocket' when he/she goes asleep?

    b Do you think the people feel completely safe in this place? Why?

Third reading

8. **a** 'Flows out, the rage of brushwood,/The roots torn out and butchered.' Which words in these lines might indicate that violence is a part of this place?

    b Are there any other indications in this poem that power is linked to physical force in this world? Refer to the poem in your answer.

9. What mood or atmosphere is created in this poem? Your answer should make close reference to the text.

10. Do you find this poem fascinating or irritating? Support your answer with suitable reference to the poem.

FOLLOWING

So she follows the trail of her father's coat through the fair
Shouldering past beasts packed solid as books,
And the dealing men nearly as slow to give way –
A block of a belly, a back like a mountain,
A shifting elbow like a plumber's bend –   5
When she catches a glimpse of a shirt-cuff, a handkerchief,
Then the hard brim of his hat, skimming along,

Until she is tracing light footsteps
Across the shivering bog by starlight,
The dead corpse risen from the wakehouse   10
Gliding before her in a white habit.
The ground is forested with gesturing trunks,
Hands of women dragging needles,
Half-choked heads in the water of cuttings,
Mouths that roar like the noise of the fair day.   15

She comes to where he is seated
With whiskey poured out in two glasses
In a library where the light is clean,
His clothes all finely laundered,
Ironed facings and linings.   20
The smooth foxed leaf has been hidden
In a forest of fine shufflings,
The square of white linen
That held three drops
Of her heart's blood is shelved   25
Between the gatherings
That go to make a book –
The crushed flowers among the pages crack
The spine open, push the bindings apart.

NOTES

10	wakehouse:	the house where the dead body was being kept for the wake
12	gesturing:	making expressive movements
14	cuttings:	where parts of the bog have been cut away for use
21	foxed:	discoloured with brownish stains
29	spine:	the part of a book where the pages have been bound together

EXPLORATIONS

Before reading

1. Have you ever become separated from your family or your friends and found yourself on your own in a crowd of strangers? How did it happen? What did you feel? How did your family or friends react when you were reunited with them? As a class, share your stories.

First reading

2. Based on the experiences that you shared before reading this poem, do you think the poet's description of the daughter being separated from her father in lines 1–7 is effective and realistic? Support your view by reference to lines 1–7.

3. a What emotions do you think the poet wants to convey in the nightmarish images in lines 8–15?

   b Can you suggest how these emotions are connected to the daughter's experience of being left behind by her father in lines 1–7?

4. a How do the 'dealing men' in line 3 treat the daughter?

   b How does the father behave towards his daughter at the fair, in lines 1–7, and react when his daughter catches up with him again, as described in lines 16–18?

   c How might these incidents be interpreted as representing the types of roles assigned by society in the past to men and women?

Second reading

5. There is very little information given in the poem about the father, but we do learn about his clothes. What impression do you get of the father from the description of his clothes? Support your points with suitable reference to the poem.

6. In the final section of the poem, lines 16–29, we see the father in his library of books.

   a What do you think the father most enjoys doing: reading the books or organising them in an orderly way? Refer to the poem in your answer.

   b Using your work for Question 5, can you suggest how the father's attitude to his books can be connected to his attitude to his clothes?

7. 'The smooth foxed leaf has been hidden/In a forest of fine shufflings'. Explain how this images can be interpreted in two ways that both suggest that the father represses his

emotions. Refer to the lines quoted above in your answer.

8. 'The square of white linen/That held three drops/Of her heart's blood is shelved'.

   a   How does this image suggest that the daughter wanted to connect emotionally with her father?

   b   How does this image suggest that the father was unable to connect emotionally with his daughter?

Support your answers by reference to the lines quoted above.

Third reading

9. 'The crushed flowers among the pages crack/The spine open, push the bindings apart.'
These lines act as an enigmatic ending to the poem because they can be interpreted in a number of ways.

   a   Examine the different interpretations that could be applied to these lines.

   b   Do you think this enigmatic ending reflects the reality of life? Why?

10. Write a personal response to this poem, highlighting the impact it makes on you. Your answer should make close reference to the text.

KILCASH

from the Irish, c. 1800

What will we do now for timber
With the last of the woods laid low –
No word of Kilcash nor its household,
Their bell is silenced now,
Where the lady lived with such honour,   5
No woman so heaped with praise,
Earls came across oceans to see her
And heard the sweet words of Mass.

It's the cause of my long affliction
To see your neat gates knocked down,   10
The long walks affording no shade now
And the avenue overgrown,
The fine house that kept out the weather,
Its people depressed and tamed;
And their names with the faithful departed,   15
The Bishop and Lady Iveagh!

The geese and the ducks' commotion,
The eagle's shout, are no more,
The roar of the bees gone silent,
Their wax and their honey store   20
Deserted. Now at evening
The musical birds are stilled
And the cuckoo is dumb in the treetops
That sang lullaby to the world.

Even the deer and the hunters   25
That follow the mountain way
Look down upon us with pity,
The house that was famed in its day;
The smooth wide lawn is all broken,
No shelter from wind and rain;   30
The paddock has turned to a dairy
Where the fine creatures grazed.

Mist hangs low on the branches
No sunlight can sweep aside,
Darkness falls among daylight   35
And the streams all run dry;

No hazel, no holly or berry,
Bare naked rocks and cold;
The forest park is leafless
And all the game gone wild.   40

And now the worst of our troubles:
She has followed the prince of the Gaels –
He has borne off the gentle maiden,
Summoned to France and to Spain.
Her company laments her   45
That she fed with silver and gold:
One who never preyed on the people
But was the poor souls' friend.

My prayer to Mary and Jesus
She may come safe home to us here   50
To dancing and rejoicing
To fiddling and bonfire
That our ancestors' house will rise up,
Kilcash built up anew
And from now to the end of the story   55
May it never again be laid low.

NOTES

2	woods laid low:	in the eighteenth and nineteenth centuries, many Irish people blamed the new 'English' landowners who took over from the accepted and integrated Anglo-Norman landowners for the loss of the Irish forests. Thus, the loss of the forests became a metaphor for the loss of the old Anglo-Norman way of life.
3	Kilcash:	now a ruined castle in South Tipperary, but until the end of the eighteenth century it was the main residence of a branch of the Butler family, one of the powerful Anglo- Norman dynasties
16	Lady Iveagh:	the original poem, written in Irish, lamented the death of Margaret Butler, Viscountess Iveagh, who died in 1744

EXPLORATIONS

Before reading

1. Look at the two photographs that accompany this poem. As a class, brainstorm ideas about the ways in which these two photographs could be connected. Write the points on the board as you go along and then note them down.

First reading

2. In stanzas 1–2 (lines 1–16), the bard refers to two people who represent the two key social structures that used to provide his Anglo-Norman society with a sense of order.
   a Explain who these two people were and what social structures they represented in this society.
   b How do lines 1–2 signal that this poem is about a change in Irish society?

3. Although this poem seems to lament the death of Lady Iveagh, the widespread changes that are described by the bard in stanzas 2–5 (lines 9–40) indicate that he is lamenting the breakdown in order caused by the loss of the old Anglo-Norman world and society in Ireland. Explain how this disorder is conveyed in two images connected to (i) the Kilcash house and gardens in stanza 2 (lines 9–16), (ii) the world of nature in stanzas 3–4 (lines 17–32) and (iii) the weather in stanza 5 (lines 33–40).

4. How does the bard convey his longing for the return of the old Anglo-Norman way of life to Irish society in stanza 7 (lines 49–56)? Your answer should make close reference to the images and phrases in stanza 7.

Second reading

5. 'What will we do now for timber' (line 1) 'It's the cause of my long affliction' (line 9) 'And now the worst of our troubles' (line 41) 'My prayer to Mary and Jesus' (line 49)
   a What impression do you get of the bard's emotional and mental state from these lines?
   b Do you think that great changes in society can affect people in these ways? Why?

6. a What is an allegory? In your own words, explain how 'Kilcash' is an allegory for the

great changes that took place in Irish society during the Celtic Tiger years.

b   What effect do you think Eiléan Ní Chuilleanáin wanted this poem to have on Irish people who were living at the time of the Celtic Tiger?

7. a   Following your work on 'Kilcash', would you make any deletions or additions to the notes that the class made for Question 1? Why?

b   Explain how the two photographs that accompany this poem can be seen as representing the Irish society of the late 1700s to early 1800s and as the Irish society of the Celtic Tiger years.

Third reading

8.   It is not surprising that Eiléan Ní Chuilleanáin uses allegory in this poem, as she has already used concrete images to express human emotions in many of her other poems. Choose three examples, from three different poems, of her use of concrete images to express human emotions and qualities that you find particularly effective. Explain the reasons for your choice.

9.   Ní Chuilleanáin believes that the world of nature and the lives of human beings are closely connected. Discuss how this connection is portrayed in 'Kilcash' and in three of her other poems that you have studied. Support your answer with suitable reference to the poems.

10. a   Look at the notes that you made about the two photographs accompanying this poem in Question 1. Were any of the brainstorm ideas similar to the ideas expressed in 'Kilcash'?

b   Write a short paragraph explaining how these two photographs relate to Eiléan Ní Chuilleanáin's poem 'Kilcash'.

TRANSLATION 🔊

for the reburial of the Magdalenes

The soil frayed and sifted evens the score –
There are women here from every county,
Just as there were in the laundry.

White light blinded and bleached out
The high relief of a glance, where steam danced 5
Around stone drains and giggled and slipped across water.

Assist them now, ridges under the veil, shifting,
Searching for their parents, their names,
The edges of words grinding against nature,

As if, when water sank between the rotten teeth 10
Of soap, and every grasp seemed melted, one voice
Had begun, rising above the shuffle and hum

Until every pocket in her skull blared with the note –
Allow us now to hear it, sharp as an infant's cry
While the grass takes root, while the steam rises: 15

    Washed clean of idiom · the baked crust
    Of words that made my temporary name ·
    A parasite that grew in me · that spell
    Lifted · I lie in earth sifted to dust ·
    Let the bunched keys I bore slacken and fall · 20
    I rise and forget · a cloud over my time.

NOTES

Translation:		possibly as when used to describe changing words in one language into another language; possibly as when used to describe being moved from one place to another
Magdalenes:		in 1993, the remains of the bodies of 155 women who had lived and worked in appalling conditions over the previous 100 years were found in unmarked graves during building work on the site of a Magdalene laundry in a convent in Dublin. As most of their names were unknown and with death certificates for only some of them, 154 of the bodies were cremated and reburied in a mass grave in Glasnevin Cemetery in Dublin. Eiléan Ní Chuilleanáin read this poem at the reburial ceremony.
I	frayed:	tattered; torn with ragged edges
5	relief:	possibly as when used to describe the ending of something unpleasant or stressful, such as pain or distress; possibly as in 'high relief', when used to describe a design that stands out from the surface and closely represents the object it depicts
16	idiom:	possibly as when used to describe a specialised vocabulary peculiar to a specific group of people, either in a particular occupation or institution, e.g. the Catholic Church; possibly as when used to describe a phrase with a meaning that is not literal because it does not come from the individual words but from understood usage of the phrase, e.g. 'fallen women' was often used to describe the Magdalene women, indicating that they had been judged to be in some way connected to 'sin'
18	parasite:	an organism that lives on or inside another and thrives at the expense of its host
20	slacken:	loosen

EXPLORATIONS

Before reading

1. a Before you read 'Translations', read the note given for the word 'Magdalenes' in the notes. What is your reaction to this event?

    b How many in the class already knew about this event or about the Magdalene laundries or the women who worked in them? As a class, share and discuss what you know about the women who worked in the Magdalene laundries.

First reading

2. a What impression of the women's working conditions do you get from reading this poem?

    b Choose one image that you feel is particularly effective in conveying these conditions. Explain your choice.

3. a Look at the photograph that accompanies this poem of a Magdalene laundry. What similarities and differences are there between the photograph and the poem?

b   Which of the two has more of an impact on you? Why?

4. a   'Searching for their parents, their names'.
Explain in your own words what this line suggests about the two changes that were made to the women's lives when they were committed to one of these institutions.

b   What effect do you think taking a girl away from her parents, and the rest of her family, would have on the place that she had in her community or society?

c   What effect would changing her name have on her sense of identity?

5. 'White light blinded and bleached out/The high relief of a glance'
A glance can be very expressive, communicating our thoughts and emotions to others. What impression do you get from the lines quoted above of the attitude to self-expression in the Magdalene laundries?

Second reading

6. a   Sound and silence play an important part in this poem. What are the sounds heard in the laundry?

b   Given that this is a group of women working together, what sounds would you expect to hear in the laundry?

c   What does the absence of such sounds tell you about how the women were treated?

7. a   In lines 11–14, the poet imagines one of the women working in the laundry screaming. Explain how the images in these lines suggest the psychological and emotional distress that this scream expresses.

b   Bearing in mind your work for Question 5, do you think any of the women would have actually screamed like this? Why?

c   Which do you find most disturbing, the scream or the silence? Why?

8. a   'Assist them now', 'Allow us now to hear it'
What do these phrases suggest to you about how the poet expects those of us who live in Irish society in the present to react to the way in which the Magdalene women were treated in Irish society in the past?

b   Why do you think the poet feels that it is important for us to react in this way?

Third reading

9. In lines 16–21, the poet creates a persona, one of the Magdalene women reburied in Glasnevin Cemetery, to express the thoughts and emotions of these women after this event.

a   Given the fact that these women were prevented from speaking for much of their lives, how does the poet convey that these words are spoken by someone who is not used to speaking? You might find it helpful to read these lines aloud.

b   Based on your work for Questions 5 and 6, can you suggest why Ní Chuilleanáin decided to end the poem in this way?

10. 'Washed clean of idiom · the baked crust/Of words that made my temporary name ·/A parasite that grew in me'

a   Explain in your own words how these lines could be interpreted as a reference to the Magdalene woman finally being freed from the name that she was given when she entered the laundry.

b   What does her use of the word 'parasite' suggest to you about how she felt about the name that she was given?

11. '· that spell Lifted · I lie in earth sifted to dust · Let the bunched keys I bore slacken and fall · I rise and forget · a cloud over my time.'

a   Discuss how a sense of release could be suggested by three of the images in these lines.

b   Explain what you think these lines mean.

THE BEND IN THE ROAD

This is the place where the child
Felt sick in the car and they pulled over
And waited in the shadow of a house.
A tall tree like a cat's tail waited too.
They opened the windows and breathed   5
Easily, while nothing moved. Then he was better.

Over twelve years it has become the place
Where you were sick one day on the way to the lake.
You are taller now than us.
The tree is taller, the house is quite covered in   10
With green creeper, and the bend
In the road is as silent as ever it was on that day.

Piled high, wrapped lightly, like the one cumulus cloud
In a perfect sky, softly packed like the air,
Is all that went on in those years, the absences,   15
The faces never long absent from thought,
The bodies alive then and the airy space they took up
When we saw them wrapped and sealed by sickness
Guessing the piled weight of sleep
We knew they could not carry for long;   20
This is the place of their presence: in the tree, in the air.

NOTE

13	cumulus:	a type of cloud formation that appears as a mass of rounded clouds, like cotton wool, piled on top of a flat base. This formation is often associated with fine weather.

EXPLORATIONS

Before reading

1. a Family memories play an important part in this poem. Does your family have a particular memory that they always recall when they meet up? If so, perhaps you might like to share it with the class.

    b How do you feel about family memories – do you like hearing about them? Why or why not?

First reading

2. Choose one phrase or image from this poem that you particularly like and explain why you chose it.

3. a Why do the people stop at the bend in the road?

    b From your reading of lines 3–6, describe in your own words how you imagine the bend in the road.

4. 'Over twelve years it has become the place/Where you were sick one day on the way to the lake.'

    a What made this place become somewhere to be remembered for the people? Refer to the lines quoted above in your answer.

    b Based on your reading of lines 9–12, describe the changes that have taken place in this twelve-year period.

Second reading

5. a 'The faces never long absent from thought'.
    This line is taken from the final section of the poem (lines 13–21). In your own words, explain what changes are described in this section.

    b What does this line tell you about the people's reaction to these changes?

6. 'Piled high, wrapped lightly, like the one cumulus cloud/In a perfect sky, softly packed like the air,/Is all that went on in those years'.

    a Discuss how the poet appeals to the senses of sight and touch in these lines in order to create a vivid image of a cloud.

    b Explain how these lines could be a comparative image describing the way in which memories of 'all that went on in those years' are stored by the people.

7. a 'This is the place where the child/Felt sick in the car and they pulled over'.
    Describe the tone (the emotion in the voice) of these lines.

    b 'Where you were sick one day on the way to the lake./You are taller now than us.'
    How is the tone in these lines different to the one that you described in part (a)?

c   Can you suggest why this
     change in tone takes place?
     You might find it helpful
     to refer back to your work for
     Question 4.

Third reading

8. This poem begins with the real and
    concrete image of people travelling
    in a car and then goes on to explore
    the abstract idea of life. Can you
    explain how a family living their life
    together could be compared to
    them taking a car journey? Support
    your answer by reference to the
    poem.

9. 'This is the place of their presence: in
    the tree, in the air.'
    a   What is it about the bend in the
         road that encourages the
         people to think about their
         memories of their loved ones
         who are dead?
    b   What do you think Eiléan Ní
         Chuilleanáin wants to suggest
         to us about the importance to
         family life of having a shared
         family history made up of
         memories?

10. Imagine that you have been asked to
    suggest a poem for a new collection
    entitled *The Importance of Memories*.
    Write a piece explaining why you
    would choose this poem as part of
    the collection.

ON LACKING THE KILLER INSTINCT 🔊

One hare, absorbed, sitting still,
Right in the grassy middle of the track,
I met when I fled up into the hills, that time
My father was dying in a hospital –
I see her suddenly again, borne back   5
By the morning paper's prize photograph:
Two greyhounds tumbling over, absurdly gross,
While the hare shoots off to the left, her bright eye
Full not only of speed and fear
But surely in the moment a glad power,   10

Like my father's, running from a lorry-load of soldiers
In nineteen twenty-one, nineteen years old, never
Such gladness, he said, cornering in the narrow road
Between high hedges, in summer dusk.
                                    The hare   15
Like him should never have been coursed,
But, clever, she gets off; another day
She'll fool the stupid dogs, double back
On her own scent, downhill, and choose her time
To spring away out of the frame, all while   20
The pack is labouring up.
                            The lorry was growling
And he was clever, he saw a house
And risked an open kitchen door. The soldiers
Found six people in a country kitchen, one   25
Drying his face, dazed-looking, the towel
Half covering his face. The lorry left,
The people let him sleep there, he came out
Into a blissful dawn. Should he have chanced that door?
If the sheltering house had been burned down, what good   30
Could all his bright running have done
For those that harboured him?
                                And I should not
Have run away, but I went back to the city
Next morning, washed in brown bog water, and   35
I thought about the hare, in her hour of ease.

NOTES

Killer Instinct:		an instinctive tendency to kill or be ruthless
7	absurdly:	ridiculously
7	gross:	disgusting
16	coursed:	hunted
32	harboured:	sheltered

EXPLORATIONS

Before reading

1. a   As a class, agree on your own definition of the term 'killer instinct' and note it down.

    b   With your agreed definition in mind, discuss the answer to the following question. Who do you think has the most power: those having the killer instinct or those 'lacking the killer instinct'? If possible, see if you can agree as a class on who has the most power. If not, note down the numbers for the two options.

First reading

2. a   The poem opens with a description, in lines 1–4, of a memory from Ní Chuilleanáin's past concerning the time when her father was dying in 1970. In your own words, explain what she recalls in this narrative fragment. Your answer should make close reference to the text.

    b   How is the hare's state different to the poet's state in these lines?

3. a   According to lines 5–10, the poet, in the present, saw a photograph of another hare in the newspaper and this triggered her 1970 memory. How is the hare in the photograph different to the one in 1970?

    b   Explain how the idea of death and the idea of running away on a quest for escape link the newspaper photograph in the present to the poet's memory set in 1970. Refer to the text in your answer.

4. a   In lines 11–14, we are presented with another memory from the past, set in 1921, as the poet remembers her father telling her about an incident from his youth. Summarise in one sentence the incident described in this narrative fragment.

    b   Can you suggest what two ideas connect this memory to the present in lines 5–10 and to the memory set in 1970, in lines 1–4? Support your answer by reference to the text.

Second reading

5. a   'The hare/Like him should never have been coursed'. What impression do you get from these lines of the poet's attitude to those who were

hunted (her father and the hare) and those who were hunting (the greyhounds and the soldiers)?

b What ability do the hare and her father share, in lines 15–29, that enables them to escape from their hunters? Explain in your own words how this ability actually helped the hare and her father to escape.

c How does this ability change the balance of power between the hunted and the hunters?

6. a 'But, clever, she gets off; another day/She'll fool the stupid dogs'.
How does the poet feel about the photographed hare's escape in these lines?

b As well as the fact that she was clever, can you suggest what basic instinct may have also helped the hare to escape?

7. a Along with his cleverness, what basic instinct do you think may have helped the poet's father to escape?

b What decision did he make that enabled him to escape?

c How does the poet feel about this decision? Your answer should make close reference to the text.

Third reading

8. a How is the poet's attitude towards what the hare did to escape different to her attitude towards what her father did to

escape? Support the points you make by reference to the poem.

b Do you think there are different codes of right behaviour for animals and humans? Why?

c Which particular code of right behaviour for human beings do you think the poet feels her father broke by going into the house?

9. In lines 33–5, the poet refers again to her memory, set in 1970, of running away from her dying father's bedside to 'the hills'.

a Based on your reading of lines 1–4 and lines 33–5, explain how the world of nature helped her to return to his bedside in 1970.

b She now recognises that she should have returned to her father because of certain codes of right behaviour. Can you suggest which codes in particular would have made her go back?

10. a Based on your work on this poem: do you feel the need to reconsider the view that you held in the discussion for Question 1? Why?

b There are two groups in this poem: those having the killer instinct (the greyhounds and the soldiers) and those lacking the killer instinct (the hare and the poet's father). Which group would you join? Explain the reasons for your answer by reference to the poem.

TO NIALL WOODS AND XENYA OSTROVSKAIA,

MARRIED IN DUBLIN ON 9 SEPTEMBER 2009 🔊

When you look out across the fields
And you both see the same star
Pitching its tent on the point of the steeple –
That is the time to set out on your journey,
With half a loaf and your mother's blessing.   5

Leave behind the places that you knew:
All that you leave behind you will find once more,
You will find it in the stories;
The sleeping beauty in her high tower
With her talking cat asleep   10
Solid beside her feet – you will see her again.

When the cat wakes up he will speak in Irish and Russian
And every night he will tell you a different tale
About the firebird that stole the golden apples,
Gone every morning out of the emperor's garden,   15
And about the King of Ireland's Son and the Enchanter's Daughter.

The story the cat does not know is the Book of Ruth
And I have no time to tell you how she fared
When she went out at night and she was afraid,
In the beginning of the barley harvest,   20
Or how she trusted to strangers and stood by her word:

You will have to trust me, she lived happily ever after.

NOTES

Niall Woods:		this poem is addressed to Eiléan Ní Chuilleanáin's son, Niall Woods, on the occasion of his marriage
3	Pitching:	setting up
3	steeple:	a tall tower with a tapering roof, usually found on churches
9	sleeping beauty:	a beautiful princess is cursed and sleeps for many years. She is awakened by a kiss from a prince who has been on a long and difficult quest to reach her and they marry.
14	the firebird:	a bird with glowing feathers that steals golden apples from the tsar's garden in a Russian folktale. Prince Ivan, his son, sets out on a long and difficult quest to find the bird. He is successful and he also meets and marries a beautiful princess.

| 16 | the King of Ireland's Son: | a prince of Ireland marries the Enchanter's Daughter, Fedelma, but she is stolen from him. The prince goes on a long and difficult quest and eventually finds her. |
| 17 | the Book of Ruth: | a story from the Old Testament about Ruth, who because of her loyalty to her dead husband's mother leaves her home country and goes to Bethlehem with her. There, Ruth helps to harvest the barley in the fields belonging to a man called Boaz who is impressed by her loyalty and courage. In time, Ruth and Boaz marry. Considered by some to be a type of folktale. |

EXPLORATIONS

Before reading

1. a   Folktales and fairytales have been told since ancient times not only in Ireland, but all over the world. Working in pairs, choose a folktale or a fairytale that you remember and write a short summary (four to seven sentences) outlining the beginning of the narrative or story (the main characters, the incident that triggers the rest of the narrative or story), the middle of the narrative (what happens next to the characters) and the end of the narrative or story (which of the characters are happy, sad, dead, etc.; what future they will have).

    b   Share your summaries, discussing and noting down the features that the folktales and fairytales have in common.

First reading

2. What two words or phrases would you use to describe this poem? Support your two words by reference to the poem.

3. Pick out the phrases and images in lines 1–5 that remind you of a folktale or fairytale. Discuss the reasons for your selection.

4. a   The poet compares her son's marriage to a 'journey' in line 4. In your own words, explain how getting married could be seen as setting out on a journey or a quest.

    b   Can you suggest how the idea of a journey or a quest could be connected to folktales? You should find your work on Question 1 helpful.

Second reading

5. a   'Leave behind the places that you knew'.
    In this line, the poet says that the young couple's lives will change after their marriage. What sort of changes do you think she might be referring to in this line?

    b   How do you think the young couple might be feeling about having to make these changes?

6. a   'All that you leave behind you will find once more,/You will find it in the stories'.
    In your own words, explain how the poet is trying to reassure her son and daughter-in-law in the

lines above about the changes they will have to make.

b   Are you surprised by this advice that she gives to them? Why?

7.   In lines 9–21, Ní Chuilleanáin refers to some folktales and fairytales. Using the brief summaries of the narratives of these folktales (see the notes) and your work for Question 1, as a class discuss what messages you think the young couple might find in these folktales and fairytales about how to live their lives successfully as a married couple.

8.   a   'You will have to trust me, she lived happily ever after.' Explain in your own words what the connection is between the idea of living 'happily ever after' and the messages that you found in the folktales and fairytales during your discussion for Question 7.

b   Suggest how the idea of living 'happily ever after' can be connected to the poet as a mother attending the marriage of her son.

Third reading

9.   a   Examine how the influence of the past on the present, through folktales and fairytales, is explored in this poem.

b   Examine how the influence of the past on the present, in the form of memories that create a shared family history, is explored in 'The Bend in the Road'.

10.   'Folktales and Fairytales in Today's World' is the title of an article you have been asked to write for your school magazine. In your article, discuss your views on whether there is or is not a place for folktales and fairytales in today's world.

EAVAN BOLAND

(1944–)

Prescribed for Higher Level exams in 2020 and 2021

Eavan Boland was born in Dublin in 1944, daughter of the painter Frances Kelly and the diplomat Frederick Boland. She was educated at Holy Child Convent, Killiney, and Trinity College, Dublin. For some years she lectured at Trinity College in the English department before becoming a literary journalist, chiefly with *The Irish Times* but also with RTÉ, where she produced award-winning poetry programmes for radio. She married the novelist Kevin Casey, exchanging the Dublin literary scene for family life in the suburbs, where she wrote prolifically.

New Territory (1967) was her first volume of poetry. Her second volume, *The War Horse* (1975), deals with the Northern Ireland 'Troubles' and with the way violence encroaches on our domestic lives. The poem 'Child of Our Time' is taken from this volume. Her third volume, *In Her Own Image* (1980), explores the darker side of female identity, 'woman's secret history'; it deals with real but taboo issues such as anorexia, infanticide, mastectomy, menstruation and domestic violence. The fourth collection, *Night Feed* (1982), celebrates the ordinary, everyday, domestic aspect of woman's identity. The fifth volume, *The Journey* (1986), and the sixth, *Outside History* (1990), consider the image of women in Irish history as illustrated in painting and in literature – a tale of exploitation and repression, of being marginalised and kept from the centre of influence. The seventh collection, *In a Time of Violence* (1994), deals specifically with Irish national and historical issues such as the Famine, agrarian violence and the Easter Rising. It also focuses on the theme of women as mothers and the relationship between mothers and daughters. The poem 'This Moment' is taken from this volume. Among her notable later volumes are: *The Lost Land* (1998); *Against Love Poetry* (2001); *Domestic Violence* (2007) and *A Woman Without a Country* (2014).

The place of the woman writer in Irish literature, mythology and history is a prominent theme in Boland's poetry and other writings. Her pamphlet *A Kind of Scar* (1989) examines this issue. Her collection of autobiographical prose, published in 1995, is entitled *Object Lessons: The Life of the Woman and the Poet in Our Time*. In 1980 she was joint founder of Arlen House, a feminist publishing company. She has won many awards for her poetry and essays, including a Lannan Award for *In a Time of Violence*. *Against Love Poetry* (2001) was a *New York Times* Notable Book of the Year. In 2012, Eavan Boland won a PEN award for her collection of essays, *A Journey with Two Maps: Becoming a Woman Poet*. Since 1996, she has been a professor of English at Stanford University and she divides her time between California and Dublin.

THE WAR HORSE 🔊

This dry night, nothing unusual
About the clip, clop, casual

Iron of his shoes as he stamps death
Like a mint on the innocent coinage of earth.

I lift the window, watch the ambling feather   5
Of hock and fetlock, loosed from its daily tether

In the tinker camp on the Enniskerry Road,
Pass, his breath hissing, his snuffling head

Down. He is gone. No great harm is done.
Only a leaf of our laurel hedge is torn –   10

Of distant interest like a maimed limb,
Only a rose which now will never climb

The stone of our house, expendable, a mere
Line of defence against him, a volunteer

You might say, only a crocus its bulbous head   15
Blown from growth, one of the screamless dead.

But we, we are safe, our unformed fear
Of fierce commitment gone; why should we care

If a rose, a hedge, a crocus are uprooted
Like corpses, remote, crushed, mutilated?   20

He stumbles on like a rumour of war, huge
Threatening. Neighbours use the subterfuge

Of curtains; he stumbles down our short street
Thankfully passing us. I pause, wait,

Then to breathe relief lean on the sill   25
And for a second only my blood is still

With atavism. That rose he smashed frays
Ribboned across our hedge, recalling days

Of burned countryside, illicit braid:
A cause ruined before, a world betrayed.   30

BACKGROUND NOTE

This poem stems from an incident when the front garden of Boland's new house in the suburbs was invaded a number of times by a stray horse, presumed to belong to local Travellers. Perhaps the horse had lived there when the site was open fields.

NOTES

4	mint:	place where money is coined
6	hock:	joint on a horse's leg corresponding to the human ankle
6	fetlock:	tuft of hair above and behind the horse's hoof
27	atavism:	resemblance to remote ancestors; in this instance the horse's violation of the domestic garden stirs race memories of English colonial violence and the destruction of Irish homesteads
29	braid:	anything plaited or interwoven, such as hair or ribbon, or the gold and silver thread decoration on uniforms; it might refer to rebel uniforms

EXPLORATIONS

First reading

1. On a first reading, what do you see? Visualise the night, the garden, the atmosphere, the animal. What sounds are there in this scene?

2. a At one level, this horse is made real to the reader. How is this realised? What words best convey the shape, size, movement, etc. of the animal to us? Explore sounds of words as well as visual images.

   b What is your first impression of the horse?

3. Do you think this horse carries a sense of menace or threat? Examine the first four couplets in particular. Explore the imagery, the sounds of words and the rhythm of the piece in coming to a conclusion.

4. How is the fragility of the domestic garden conveyed to us? What words or images suggest this?

Second reading

5. What do you notice about the speaker's reactions to this intrusion? Do they change as the poem progresses? Make specific references to the text.

6. a Could this piece be read as a political poem, with the horse as a symbol of violence? What evidence do you find in the poem for this reading?

   b At a symbolic level, what is being suggested here about the nature of violence?

Third reading

7. How do you read the poem? What themes do you find it deals with and what levels of meaning do you notice?

CHILD OF OUR TIME

For Aengus

Yesterday I knew no lullaby
But you have taught me overnight to order
This song, which takes from your final cry
Its tune, from your unreasoned end its reason,
Its rhythm from the discord of your murder   5
Its motive from the fact you cannot listen.

We who should have known how to instruct
With rhymes for your waking, rhythms for your sleep,
Names for the animals you took to bed,
Tales to distract, legends to protect,   10
Later an idiom for you to keep
And living, learn, must learn from you, dead,

To make our broken images rebuild
Themselves around your limbs, your broken
Image, find for your sake whose life our idle   15
Talk has cost, a new language. Child
Of our time, our times have robbed your cradle.
Sleep in a world your final sleep has woken.

BACKGROUND NOTE

This poem was inspired by a press photograph showing a firefighter carrying a dead child out of the wreckage of the Dublin bombings in May 1974.

EXPLORATIONS

First reading

1. If you hadn't read the title or the last three lines, what might suggest to you that the poem was written to a child? Examine stanzas 1–2.

2. The speaker acknowledges that it was the child's death that prompted her to compose this poem ('you have taught me overnight to order/ This song'). How does she feel about the child's death in the first stanza? Examine the words and phrases describing the death: 'your final cry', 'your unreasoned end', 'the discord of your murder'. What do these phrases tell us about the way the poet views the death?

3. In the second stanza, notice that the main clause consists of the first word and the final five words in the stanza: 'We … must learn from you, dead'. The rest of the stanza relates to 'we', presumably adult society.
   a In what way has adult society failed, according to the poet?
   b What particular aspect of childbearing and education does the poet focus on?
   c 'Later an idiom for you to keep/And living, learn'.
      In your own words, what do you think is meant by this? ('Idiom' here means style of expression.)

4. In the third stanza the child's body is described poetically as 'your broken/Image'. What does this picture suggest to you?

5. What do you think she has in mind when she says that we need to (a) rebuild 'our broken images … around your limbs' and (b) 'find … a new language'?

6. Does the speaker find any ray of hope for the society in which this calamity occurred? Refer to the text of the third stanza.

Second reading

7. Consider this poem as an elegy, a meditation on death. What ideas on that subject are explored or suggested?

8. Can this be read as a public or political poem? Explain, with reference to the text.

9. Concerning the poet's feelings, do you find here a sense of personal sorrow or community guilt and sorrow? Explain your thinking.

Third reading

10. The poem might be seen as a mixture of dirge and lullaby. What elements of dirge or of lullaby do you find? Consider the theme, the choice of language, the imagery, the repetitions, etc.

THE FAMINE ROAD 🔊

'Idle as trout in light Colonel Jones,
these Irish, give them no coins at all; their bones
need toil, their characters no less.' Trevelyan's
seal blooded the deal table. The Relief
Committee deliberated: 'Might it be safe,   5
Colonel, to give them roads, roads to force
from nowhere, going nowhere of course?'

>   *'one out of every ten and then*
>   *another third of those again*
>   *women – in a case like yours.'*   10

Sick, directionless they worked; fork, stick
were iron years away; after all could
they not blood their knuckles on rock, suck
April hailstones for water and for food?
Why for that, cunning as housewives, each eyed –   15
as if at a corner butcher – the other's buttock.

>   *'anything may have caused it, spores,*
>   *a childhood accident; one sees*
>   *day after day these mysteries.'*

Dusk: they will work tomorrow without him.   20
They know it and walk clear; he has become
a typhoid pariah, his blood tainted, although
he shares it with some there. No more than snow
attends its own flakes where they settle
and melt, will they pray by his death rattle.   25

>   *'You never will, never you know*
>   *but take it well woman, grow*
>   *your garden, keep house, good-bye.'*

'It has gone better than we expected, Lord
Trevelyan, sedition, idleness, cured   30
in one; from parish to parish, field to field,
the wretches work till they are quite worn,
then fester by their work; we march the corn
to the ships in peace; this Tuesday I saw bones
out of my carriage window, your servant Jones.'   35

>   *'Barren, never to know the load*
>   *of his child in you, what is your body*
>   *now if not a famine road?'*

NOTES

Famine Road:		in the Great Famine of 1845–48, the potato crop failed and the people were left destitute and starving. Among the relief works organised to allow the hungry to earn money was road construction, but these roads were rarely meant to be used and often ended uselessly in a bog or field. Thus, the famine road might be read as a symbol of unfulfilled lives that go nowhere.
1	Colonel Jones:	Lieutenant-Colonel Jones was one of the officers in charge of relief works around Newry. There exists a letter from him to Trevelyan reporting on work carried out during the winter of 1846; this may be the source of the exchange here.
3	Trevelyan:	Charles Trevelyan was a senior British civil servant, Assistant Secretary to the Treasury, in charge of relief works in Ireland at the outbreak of the Great Famine in 1845. At first his approach was dominated by the laissez-faire (non-intervention) policy popular at the time and he was concerned that the Irish might be demoralised by receiving too much government help. Later he came to realise that they would not survive without it, but he never really warmed to the Irish, speaking of 'the selfish, perverse and turbulent character of the people'.
4–5	Relief Committee:	committees that organised local schemes to try to alleviate the starvation
22	pariah:	outcast
30	sedition:	conduct or language directed towards the overthrow of the state
33–4	corn to the ships:	despite the starvation, normal commerce was carried on and corn was exported as usual, though grain carts now needed protection against the local population

EXPLORATIONS

First reading

1. Read aloud Trevelyan's letter in the first three lines of the poem. How do you think it should sound? Consider the tone. What is Trevelyan's attitude? What words or phrases convey his attitude particularly well? What do Trevelyan's gestures add to the tone of this? Read it as you think he would say it.

2. Read aloud the Relief Committee's speech to Colonel Jones as you imagine it said. Pay attention to the tone of 'Might it be safe' and 'going nowhere of course'.

3. Read stanzas 3 and 5 (beginning 'Sick' and 'Dusk', respectively). What do you notice about the relief work and the condition of the people?

4. Consider Colonel Jones's letter to Trevelyan ('It has gone better'). What does it reveal about the writer – his priorities, his attitude to the Irish, his awareness of the famine, etc.? Is there evidence of sympathy or of superiority and indifference? Consider phrases such as 'the wretches', 'fester by their work', 'march … in peace'. What is the effect of the hollow rhyme 'bones'/'Jones'? Read the letter aloud as you think he might say it.

Second reading

5. In the third stanza, how is the desperate bleakness of the people's situation conveyed? What image in particular conveys the depth of their degradation? Explain your thinking.

6. Illness isolates and degrades human beings. How is this portrayed in the fifth stanza? Consider the effect of the imagery and the sounds of words.

Third reading

7. Now explore the woman's story (stanzas 2, 4, 6 and 8).
   a Who is speaking in the first three stanzas? Which words suggest that?
   b Consider the tone and read these three stanzas aloud.
   c Who speaks the last stanza? How does the speaker feel? Which words best convey the feelings?

8. Write an extract from that woman's diary as she might compose it following that meeting. Fill it with the thoughts you imagine going through her head as she listened to the consultant.

Fourth reading

9. What statement do you think this poem makes on the status of women?

10. Explain the comparisons implied in the poem between the experience of women and the treatment of the Famine people. Do you find it enlightening? Explain.

11. In her writings, Boland has often expressed concern that history is sometimes simplified into myth. *'Irish poets of the nineteenth century, and indeed their heirs in this century, coped with their sense of historical injury by writing of Ireland as an abandoned queen or an old mother. My objections to this are ethical. If*

*you consistently simplify women
by making them national icons
in poetry or drama you silence a
great deal of the actual women
in that past, whose sufferings and
complexities are part of that past,
who intimately depend on us, as
writers, not to simplify them in this
present.' (From the interview in
Sleeping with Monsters)*

Do you think 'The Famine Road'
shows an awareness of the real
complexity of actual lives from
history? Explain, with reference to
the text.

12. What sense of national identity or
Irishness comes across from 'The
Famine Road'?

THE SHADOW DOLL

They stitched blooms from the ivory tulle
to hem the oyster gleam of the veil.
They made hoops for the crinoline.

Now, in summary and neatly sewn –
a porcelain bride in an airless glamour –   5
the shadow doll survives its occasion.

Under glass, under wraps, it stays
even now, after all, discreet about
visits, fevers, quickenings and lusts

and just how, when she looked at   10
the shell-tone spray of seed pearls,
the bisque features, she could see herself

inside it all, holding less than real
stephanotis, rose petals, never feeling
satin rise and fall with the vows   15

I kept repeating on the night before –
astray among the cards and wedding gifts –
the coffee pots and the clocks and

the battered tan case full of cotton
lace and tissue-paper, pressing down, then   20
pressing down again. And then, locks.

NOTES

Shadow Doll:		this refers to the porcelain doll modelling the proposed wedding dress, under a dome of glass, sent to the nineteenth-century bride by her dressmaker
I	tulle:	soft, fine silk netting used for dresses and veils
2	oyster:	off-white colour
12	bisque:	unglazed white porcelain used for these models
14	stephanotis:	tropical climbing plant with fragrant white flowers

EXPLORATIONS

First reading

1. The function of the doll is explained above in the notes, but what does the title 'Shadow Doll' suggest to you?

2. What do you notice about the model dress?

3. 'A porcelain bride in an airless glamour' – what does this suggest to you about the poet's view of the doll?

4. Do you think the poet understands the doll's significance in more general terms, as an image of something or a symbol? If so, an image or symbol of what?

Second reading

5. What image of woman is portrayed by the doll? Explore stanza 3 in particular.

6. How does this image contrast with the poet's experience of her own wedding? Explore stanzas 5–7.

7. The speaker's reality is more appealing, despite the clutter, but has she anything in common with the 'shadow doll'?

Third reading

8. What does the poem say to you about the image of woman? Refer to the text to substantiate your ideas.

9. Explore the significance of colour in this poem.

10. 'In the main, symbol and image carry the main themes of this poem.' Comment, with reference to the text.

WHITE HAWTHORN IN THE WEST OF IRELAND

I drove West
in the season between seasons.
I left behind suburban gardens.
Lawnmowers. Small talk.

Under low skies, past splashes of coltsfoot,   5
I assumed
the hard shyness of Atlantic light
and the superstitious aura of hawthorn.

All I wanted then was to fill my arms with
sharp flowers,   10
to seem, from a distance, to be part of
that ivory, downhill rush. But I knew,

I had always known
the custom was
not to touch hawthorn.   15
Not to bring it indoors for the sake of

the luck
such constraint would forfeit –
a child might die, perhaps, or an unexplained
fever speckle heifers. So I left it   20

stirring on those hills
with a fluency
only water has. And, like water, able
to re-define land. And free to seem to be –

for anglers,   25
and for travellers astray in
the unmarked lights of a May dusk –
the only language spoken in those parts.

EXPLORATIONS

First reading

1. **a** In this migration, what is the speaker leaving behind her?
   b From what little is said in the first stanza, what do you understand of her attitude to life in suburbia?

2. **a** How does her state of mind alter as she drives west?
   b Explore stanzas 2–3. How does this experience contrast with life in suburbia?

3. According to the poem, what is the significance of hawthorn in folklore?

4. Water, too, is a deceptive source of hidden energies. What is the poet's thinking on this? Explore stanzas 6–7.

Second reading

5. 'The speaker's attitude to the hawthorn is a combination of passionate, sensuous attraction balanced by a degree of nervous respect.'
   Would you agree? Substantiate your views with reference to the text.

6. What do you think this poem reveals about the speaker?

7. What statement is the poet making about our modern way of life?

Third reading

8. List the themes or issues raised by this poem.

9. What is your personal reaction to this poem?

OUTSIDE HISTORY

There are outsiders, always. These stars –
these iron inklings of an Irish January,
whose light happened

thousands of years before
our pain did: they are, they have always been   5
outside history.

They keep their distance. Under them remains
a place where you found
you were human, and

a landscape in which you know you are mortal.   10
And a time to choose between them.
I have chosen:

out of myth into history I move to be
part of that ordeal
whose darkness is   15

only now reaching me from those fields,
those rivers, those roads clotted as
firmaments with the dead.

How slowly they die
as we kneel beside them, whisper in their ear.   20
And we are too late. We are always too late.

EXPLORATIONS

First reading

1. Boland's argument is that Irish history has been turned into myth and therefore rendered false and remote from real lives. Do you think the image of the stars is an effective metaphor for historical myths? Examine the attributes of the stars as suggested in the first two stanzas.

2. In contrast, what aspects of real, lived history are emphasised in this poem?

Second reading

3. The poet chooses to turn her back on myth and this choice brings her, and the reader, face to face with the unburied dead of history. Does she find this an easy choice? Explore her feelings on this. What words, phrases, gestures, etc. indicate her feelings?

4. What do you think she means by the last line of the poem? Explore possible interpretations.

Third reading

5. On the evidence of this poem as a whole, what is the poet's attitude to the historical past?

6. Comment on the effectiveness of the imagery.

THE BLACK LACE FAN MY MOTHER GAVE ME 🔊

It was the first gift he ever gave her,
buying it for five francs in the Galeries
in pre-war Paris. It was stifling.
A starless drought made the nights stormy.

They stayed in the city for the summer.   5
They met in cafés. She was always early.
He was late. That evening he was later.
They wrapped the fan. He looked at his watch.

She looked down the Boulevard des Capucines.
She ordered more coffee. She stood up.   10
The streets were emptying. The heat was killing.
She thought the distance smelled of rain and lightning.

These are wild roses, appliqued on silk by hand,
darkly picked, stitched boldly, quickly.
The rest is tortoiseshell and has the reticent,   15
clear patience of its element. It is

a worn-out, underwater bullion and it keeps,
even now, an inference of its violation.
The lace is overcast as if the weather
it opened for and offset had entered it.   20

The past is an empty café terrace.
An airless dusk before thunder. A man running.
And no way now to know what happened then –
none at all – unless, of course, you improvise:

The blackbird on this first sultry morning,   25
in summer, finding buds, worms, fruit,
feels the heat. Suddenly she puts out her wing –
the whole, full, flirtatious span of it.

EXPLORATIONS

First reading

1. The black lace fan was a present from the poet's father to her mother and was passed on later to the speaker. How do you visualise the fan? What assistance does the poem give us? Examine the details in stanza 4.

2. How do you visualise the scene, the background, the atmosphere of the evening as the woman waits? Look at the details.

3. What do you notice about the man in the poem? What else would you like to know about him? Why is he always late? Is the gift a peace offering or a genuine love token? What does he really feel for her? Can any of these questions be answered from the poem?

4. What do you notice about the woman? Examine the details. What do they suggest about how she is feeling, etc.? While remaining faithful to the text, jot down what you imagine the thoughts inside her head are as she waits.

5. Do you think this was a perfectly matched and idyllic relationship? What is suggested by the poem? Explain.

Second reading

6. How does the poet think of the fan? Does she see it as more than just the usual love token, a symbol in the sensual ritual? Explore in detail her imaginative apprehension of the fan in stanza 5. For example, what is meant by 'it keeps … an inference of its violation' and 'The lace is overcast as if the weather … had entered it'?

7. How do you think the final stanza relates to the rest of the poem? Does the mating display of the blackbird add anything to the connotations of the keepsake?

8. How do you think you would regard the first present from a lover? Were you at all surprised by the fact that the mother in this poem gave away the fan? Explain your thinking.

9. Do you think the poet views the keepsake solely in a romantic or in an erotic way? How do you think she sees it?

10. Examine what the poet herself says (in *Object Lessons*) about the symbol. What does this add to your own thinking on the subject?
'I make these remarks as a preliminary to a poem I wrote about a black lace fan my mother had given me, which my father had given her in a heat wave in Paris in the thirties. It would be wrong to say I was clear, when I wrote this poem, about disassembling an erotic politic. I was not. But I was aware of my own sense of the traditional erotic object – in this case the black fan – as a sign not for triumph and acquisition but for suffering itself. And without having words for it, I was conscious of trying to divide it from its usual source of generation: the sexualised perspective of the poet. To that extent I was writing a sign which might bring me close to those emblems of the body I had seen in those visionary years, when ordinary objects seemed to warn me that the body might share the world but could not own it. And if

I was not conscious of taking apart something I had been taught to leave well alone, nevertheless, I had a clear sense of – at last – writing the poem away from the traditional erotic object towards something which spoke of the violations of love, while still shadowing the old context of its power. In other words, a back-to-front love poem.'

Third reading

11. What does the poem say to you about love and time?

12. In your own words, outline the themes you find in this poem.

13. What images appeal to you particularly? Explain why you find them effective.

14. Comment on the use of symbolism in this poem.

Fourth reading

15. 'The past is an empty café terrace./ An airless dusk before thunder. A man running./And no way now to know what happened then –/ none at all – unless, of course, you improvise'.
In a brief written description, improvise the sequel to the 'empty café terrace' and 'A man running' as you imagine it. Keep faith with the spirit of the poem.

THIS MOMENT

A neighbourhood.
At dusk.

Things are getting ready
to happen
out of sight.   5

Stars and moths.
And rinds slanting around fruit.

But not yet.

One tree is black.
One window is yellow as butter.   10

A woman leans down to catch a child
who runs into her arms
this moment.

Stars rise.
Moths flutter.   15
Apples sweeten in the dark.

EXPLORATIONS

First reading

1. What do you see in this scene? List the items.

2. What senses, other than sight, are involved or hinted at?

3. Do you think this scene is unusual or very ordinary? Explain. What do you think the poet is celebrating here?

4. There is a hint of the mysterious about the scene. Where and what do you think are suggested?

Second reading

5. What do you think is the most significant image in the poem? How does the poet draw attention to its importance?

6. Do you notice any sense of dramatic build-up in the poem? Examine the sequence of ideas and images.

7. Explore the imagery. What do the images contribute to the atmosphere? What is suggested, for example, by 'One window is yellow as butter' and by 'Apples sweeten in the dark'?

Third reading

8. What is the key moment in this poem all about?

9. What do you think the poem is saying about nature?

10. Do you think it is making a statement about the experience of women? Explain your ideas.

THE POMEGRANATE 🔊

The only legend I have ever loved is
the story of a daughter lost in hell.
And found and rescued there.
Love and blackmail are the gist of it.
Ceres and Persephone the names.   5
And the best thing about the legend is
I can enter it anywhere. And have.
As a child in exile in
a city of fogs and strange consonants,
I read it first and at first I was   10
an exiled child in the crackling dusk of
the underworld, the stars blighted. Later
I walked out in a summer twilight
searching for my daughter at bed-time.
When she came running I was ready   15
to make any bargain to keep her.
I carried her back past whitebeams
and wasps and honey-scented buddleias.
But I was Ceres then and I knew
winter was in store for every leaf   20
on every tree on that road.
Was inescapable for each one we passed.
And for me.
            It is winter
and the stars are hidden.   25
I climb the stairs and stand where I can see
my child asleep beside her teen magazines,
her can of Coke, her plate of uncut fruit.
The pomegranate! How did I forget it?
She could have come home and been safe   30
and ended the story and all
our heart-broken searching but she reached
out a hand and plucked a pomegranate.
She put out her hand and pulled down
the French sound for apple and   35
the noise of stone and the proof
that even in the place of death,
at the heart of legend, in the midst
of rocks full of unshed tears
ready to be diamonds by the time   40
the story was told, a child can be
hungry. I could warn her. There is still a chance.

The rain is cold. The road is flint-coloured.
The suburb has cars and cable television.
The veiled stars are above ground.   45
It is another world. But what else
can a mother give her daughter but such
beautiful rifts in time?
If I defer the grief I will diminish the gift.
The legend will be hers as well as mine.   50
She will enter it. As I have.
She will wake up. She will hold
the papery flushed skin in her hand.
And to her lips. I will say nothing.

NOTES

Pomegranate:		the fruit of a North African tree, the size and colour of an orange. In classical mythology it was associated with the underworld.
5	Ceres and Persephone:	Ceres in Roman mythology (identified with Demeter in Greek mythology) was the goddess of corn and growing vegetation, an earth goddess. Her daughter by Zeus, Persephone, was carried off to the underworld by Hades. Ceres wandered over the earth in mourning, vainly searching. In grief she made the earth barren for a year. She resisted all entreaties by the gods to allow the earth back to fertility. Eventually Zeus sent his messenger to persuade Hades to release Persephone, which he did, but not before he had given her a pomegranate seed to eat. This fruit was sacred to the underworld, and so Persephone was condemned to spend one-third of each year there with Hades, only appearing back on earth each spring, with the first fertility.

EXPLORATIONS

First reading

1. The poet says, 'the best thing about the legend is/I can enter it anywhere'. When did she first encounter it and why did she find it relevant to her life?

2. At what other times and in what ways did the legend run parallel to her own situation?

3. How closely do you think the poet identifies with the myth? What evidence is there for this?

Second reading

4. What does the poem tell us about the poet's relationship with her daughter?

5. What does the legend contribute to that relationship?

6. What do you think the poet has in common with Ceres?

Third reading

7. Where and how do the time zones of past and present fuse and mingle? What does this suggest about the importance of myth in our lives?

8. What statement do you think this poem is making about the significance of legend to ordinary lives? Refer to the text.

9. What truths about human relationships are discovered in this poem?

Fourth reading

10. Examine the different motifs in the imagery – fruit, darkness, stars, stone, etc. What do these strands of imagery contribute to the atmosphere and the themes?

11. What effect did reading this poem have on you?

LOVE 🔊

Dark falls on this mid-western town
where we once lived when myths collided.
Dusk has hidden the bridge in the river
which slides and deepens
to become the water   5
the hero crossed on his way to hell.

Not far from here is our old apartment.
We had a kitchen and an Amish table.
We had a view. And we discovered there
love had the feather and muscle of wings   10
and had come to live with us,
a brother of fire and air.

We had two infant children one of whom

was touched by death in this town
and spared: and when the hero   15
was hailed by his comrades in hell
their mouths opened and their voices failed and
there is no knowing what they would have asked
about a life they had shared and lost.

I am your wife.   20
It was years ago.
Our child is healed. We love each other still.
Across our day-to-day and ordinary distances
we speak plainly. We hear each other clearly.

And yet I want to return to you   25
on the bridge of the Iowa river as you were,
with snow on the shoulders of your coat
and a car passing with its headlights on:

I see you as a hero in a text –
the image blazing and the edges gilded –   30
and I long to cry out the epic question
my dear companion:

Will we ever live so intensely again?

Will love come to us again and be
so formidable at rest it offered us ascension   35
even to look at him?

But the words are shadows and you cannot hear me.
You walk away and I cannot follow.

EXPLORATIONS

First reading

1. The poem is occasioned by a return visit to 'this mid-western town' in America where they had once lived. Which lines refer to present time and which refer to that earlier stay?

2. 'When myths collided' – what do you think this might refer to?

3. Explore the mood of the opening stanza. How is it created and does it fit in with the mythical allusions? Explain.

4. On a first reading, what issues do you notice that preoccupy the poet?

Second reading

5. The second stanza contains some memories of the speaker's previous visit. What was important to her?

6. a What insights about love are communicated in the second stanza?

   b What is your opinion of the effectiveness of the imagery used?

7. a The poet uses allusions from myth to create an awareness of death in the third stanza.

What insights on death are communicated to you by this very visual presentation?

   b Do you think this is an effective way of recording the speaker's feelings? Explain your view.

8. Explore the speaker's feelings for her husband at the present time and contrast them with past emotions. Is she content? What does she yearn for?

Third reading

9. Overall, what does this poem have to say about love? What does she think is important?

10. What other themes do you find are dealt with?

11. What does the poem say about women's experience?

12. What do the mythical allusions contribute to the poem?

13. Comment on the effectiveness of the imagery.

Fourth reading

14. What did you discover from reading this poem?

PAUL
DURCAN

(1944–)

Prescribed for Higher Level exams in 2020 and 2021

Paul Durcan was born in Dublin to parents from County Mayo: John Durcan, a barrister and judge, and Sheila MacBride Durcan, a solicitor. He was raised between Dublin and Turlough, County Mayo, where his aunt ran a pub. He began to study law and economics in UCD but left in 1964. For a number of years he lived between London, Barcelona and Dublin. When he worked for the North Thames Gas Board in London he used to visit the Tate Gallery at lunchtime to view the paintings of Francis Bacon in particular.

He married Nessa O'Neill. They settled in Cork in 1970 and have two daughters. She worked as a teacher in a prison and he completed a degree in archaeology and medieval history at UCC. The marriage ended in 1984.

Durcan has travelled widely, as the titles of his volumes demonstrate.

He has been writer in residence in universities, including the University of Ulster and Trinity College Dublin. He has collaborated with artists and musicians. He was commissioned to write poetry in response to paintings by the National Gallery of Ireland (*Crazy about Women*, 1991) and by the National Gallery, London (*Give Me Your Hand*, 1994). He held the Irish Chair of Poetry from 2004 to 2007. As a performing poet, he is known for the mesmeric quality of his readings.

Among his many volumes of poetry are the following: *O Westport in the Light of Asia Minor* (1975), *The Berlin Wall Café* (1985), *Going Home to Russia* (1987), *Daddy, Daddy* (1990), *Greetings to Our Friends in Brazil* (1999), *The Laughter of Mothers* (2007) and *Praise in Which I Live and Move and Have My Being* (2012). A selection of his work, *Life Is a Dream: 40 Years Reading Poems 1967–2007*, was published in 2009. His most recent work *The Days of Surprise* (2015) contains poems on the weather forecast, the war in Syria, retail therapy, and Seamus Heaney, among other topics.

Paul Durcan has won many awards for his poetry, including the Patrick Kavanagh Award, the Irish American Cultural Institute Poetry Award, the Heinemann Award and the Whitbread Poetry Award for *Daddy, Daddy*. In 2014 he won a Lifetime Achievement Irish Book Award.

NESSA

I met her on the first of August
In the Shangri-La Hotel,
She took me by the index finger
And dropped me in her well.
And that was a whirlpool, that was a whirlpool,   5
And I very nearly drowned.

Take off your pants, she said to me,
And I very nearly didn't;
Would you care to swim, she said to me,
And I hopped into the Irish Sea.   10
And that was a whirlpool, that was a whirlpool,
And I very nearly drowned.

On the way back I fell in the field
And she fell down beside me,
I'd have lain in the grass with her all my life   15
With Nessa:
She was a whirlpool, she was a whirlpool,
And I very nearly drowned.

O Nessa my dear, Nessa my dear,
Will you stay with me on the rocks?   20
Will you come for me into the Irish Sea
And for me let your red hair down?
And then we will ride into Dublin City
In a taxi-cab wrapped up in dust.
Oh you are a whirlpool, you are a whirlpool,   25
And I am very nearly drowned.

BACKGROUND NOTE

This is an autobiographical poem about Durcan's first meeting with Nessa O'Neill, whom he later married. He met her on 1 August 1967, sitting at the bar in the Shangri-La Hotel, in the aftermath of a wedding to which he was not invited.

NOTE

2	Shangri-La Hotel:	a well-known hotel, since demolished, that was situated by the seashore in Dalkey, County Dublin

EXPLORATIONS

Before reading

1. Why do you think we use the expression 'falling in love'? What does it suggest?

First reading

2. Has the speaker here fallen in love? Discuss.

3. Think of the poem as a succession of still images, as from a film (ignore the refrain for the moment). What do you see? What story do the images tell as you follow the sequence?

4. a   What suggestions does the whirlpool image bring to the relationship?

   b   How does the whirlpool image change as the story develops?

5. Do you find this account of a first date unusual? Discuss in groups.

Second reading

6. What do we learn about the personality of the girl as she is portrayed in this poem?

7. The poem begins with a succession of images that could be read as humorous, zany or even mocking the usual conventions of love poetry, but do you think this gives way to serious honest emotion at a particular point? Think about this and share ideas in a group discussion.

8. a   Read the final stanza carefully. What has changed about the tone of the speaker?

   b   Has anything altered in the relationship between himself and Nessa?

   c   What does the last line communicate about the speaker's emotional state?

9. 'And then we will ride into Dublin City/In a taxi-cab wrapped up in dust.' This is the equivalent of riding off into the sunset, happily ever after. Where do you think he gets the image from? Do you think it works well here?

Third reading

10. Who do you think has the most power and influence in this relationship? Why do you think this?

11. What might we understand about Durcan's view of women from this poem?

12. 'This is a most unusual love poem.' Discuss.

13. 'Yet it is a very honest and effective love poem.' Discuss.

14. Do you think this poem could be made into a short film quite easily? Explain your thinking.

THE GIRL WITH THE KEYS TO PEARSE'S COTTAGE

to John and Judith Meagher

When I was sixteen I met a dark girl;
Her dark hair was darker because her smile was so bright;
She was the girl with the keys to Pearse's Cottage;
And her name was Cáit Killann.

The cottage was built into the side of a hill;   5
I recall two windows and cosmic peace
Of bare brown rooms and on whitewashed walls
Photographs of the passionate and pale Pearse.

I recall wet thatch and peeling jambs
And how all was best seen from below in the field;   10
I used to sit in the rushes with ledger-book and pencil
Compiling poems of passion for Cáit Killann.

Often she used linger on the sill of a window;
Hands by her side and brown legs akimbo;
In sun-red skirt and moon-black blazer;   15
Looking toward our strange world wide-eyed.

Our world was strange because it had no future;
She was America-bound at summer's end.
She had no choice but to leave her home –
The girl with the keys to Pearse's Cottage.   20

O Cáit Killann, O Cáit Killann,
You have gone with your keys from your own native place.
Yet here in this dark – El Greco eyes blaze back
From your Connemara postman's daughter's proudly mortal face.

NOTES

Pearse:		Padraig Pearse (1879–1916), schoolteacher, writer and iconic leader of the 1916 Rising, for which he was executed
Pearse's Cottage:		a traditional Irish cottage in Connemara now restored and a tourist venue. It was used by Padraig Pearse as a summer residence and summer school venue for his pupils from St Enda's, the school he ran in Dublin.
Girl with the Keys:		the girl who unlocked the cottage for visitors
8	passionate and pale Pearse:	'passionate' presumably refers to his ardent commitment to Irish independence and in particular his view that the activists needed to sacrifice their lives so that the population at large would be aroused to support the cause of independence
23	El Greco:	Domenikos Theotokopoulos (1541–1614) was a major painter of the Spanish Renaissance, who was born in Crete, hence the name El Greco ('the Greek'). He is known for his elongated, tortured-looking figures. Among the many distinctive elements of his figures are large, dark, expressive eyes that seem to communicate the thoughts and feelings of the figures.

EXPLORATIONS

First reading

1. a   At one level, this is a poem about a teenager's passionate infatuation with a girl. Who is the girl, Cáit Killann?

    b   If you were going to draw a sketch of her or make a painting, what details would you include in order to create a true likeness? Search the poem for all details: what does she look like; does she have a very busy day; is she happy, content or something else; what is she thinking as she is 'Looking towards our strange world wide-eyed', etc.

    c   Discuss in groups the aspects that should feature in a true likeness and make a list.

2. Do you think she is aware of the young poet's feelings towards her? Are there any indications of this in the poem?

3. This poem is about the relationship from the writer's perspective. What are his feelings on this? Chart the range of emotions he expresses as the poem develops.

4. Do you think this is a sad love poem? Explain your thinking.

Second reading

5. At another level, this is a poem about political ideals and society. Pearse was an iconic figure who gave his life for Irish independence. The cottage was regarded as a sort of shrine to his memory, a political holy place. Read stanzas 2 and 3 carefully. What is the writer's experience of the place? Explore the complexity of his thoughts here, in a group discussion.

6. Though the terms 'passionate' and 'passion' are used in connection both with Pearse and the young Durcan, it serves to emphasise the differences between their preoccupations and

attitudes to life. Would you agree?
Discuss their differences.

7. The Proclamation of the Provisional
   Government of the Irish Republic
   to the People of Ireland, signed
   by Pearse and the other leaders in
   1916, contains the following political
   promises:
   'The Republic guarantees religious
   and civil liberty, equal rights and
   equal opportunities for all its
   citizens, and declares its resolve to
   pursue the happiness and prosperity
   of the whole nation, cherishing all
   the children of the nation equally...'
   On the evidence of this poem, do
   you think these ambitions for the
   citizens have been achieved?

8. What political point is Durcan
   making in this poem? Do you think
   he is making it in anger or in sadness?
   Explain your thinking.

9. Is it not highly ironic that Cáit Killann
   has the keys to Pearse's cottage?

10. Who is Cáit Killann? Do you think
    she may represent more than just
    the girl Durcan met when he was
    sixteen? Discuss.

Third reading

11. What do you like about this poem?

12. Does this poem reflect the thinking,
    attitudes, values and fears of young
    people in Ireland in present times?
    Discuss this and then write a review
    of the poem under this heading.

THE DIFFICULTY THAT IS MARRIAGE

We disagree to disagree, we divide, we differ;
Yet each night as I lie in bed beside you
And you are faraway curled up in sleep
I array the moonlit ceiling with a mosaic of question marks;
How was it I was so lucky to have ever met you?   5
I am no brave pagan proud of my mortality
Yet gladly on this changeling earth I should live for ever
If it were with you, my sleeping friend.
I have my troubles and I shall always have them
But I should rather live with you for ever   10
Than exchange my troubles for a changeless kingdom.
But I do not put you on a pedestal or throne;
You must have your faults but I do not see them.
If it were with you, I should live for ever.

NOTES

4	array:	here it can mean to cover with or adorn; or to set in order, in lines or ranks
7	changeling earth:	a changeling is a person or thing put in place of another. For example, there are references to changeling children in Irish fairytales. The phrase 'changeling earth' embodies a religious philosophy of life, i.e. that our life on earth is a temporary substitute for authentic eternal life.
9	my troubles:	may refer to depression, which the poet has experienced and has written about elsewhere
12	pedestal:	the base for a statue or sculpture

EXPLORATIONS

Before reading

1. Read only the title. What thoughts, feelings and images would you expect to find in a poem of this title?

First reading

2. **a** Focus on lines 1–4. These first four lines set the scene and outline the problem. What do you notice in these lines? Make a list.

   b What questions are raised in your mind by these lines? List them.

   c Now share your observations and questions in a group discussion.

3. Trace the speaker's line of thinking through the rest of the poem. In your own words, note down the main thoughts.

4. In the first line, the speaker outlines the issue in a precise, motionless, almost mathematical-sounding expression. Now, read through the rest of the poem as a neutral observer. What are the differences between husband and wife that you notice?

5. What are the speaker's feelings towards his wife? Carefully consider each reference to her and examine what it suggests.

Second reading

6. You have been inside the speaker's head for some time now. What kind of person is he? What would you like to ask him?

7. Durcan is writing personally and quite openly about his marriage, yet he is also articulating a dilemma about marriage in general. After careful consideration of the poem, what do you think is the difficulty about marriage, according to the speaker? Read the critical notes on this poem. Do you think the opinion expressed in these notes is justified?

8. Is this a poem about the difficulty of marriage or is it a love poem? Or is it both?

Third reading

9. Read 'Nessa' in conjunction with this poem. What are the differences and similarities in terms of themes and issues raised, mood and atmosphere, and styles of writing?

10. Could you see the two poems as marking different stages of a relationship? What do they say about each stage?

11. Durcan has been praised by critics for 'his emotional directness when dealing with family relations'. What was your reaction to his emotional directness in this poem?

12. Do you think the conversational style of this poem works well? Explain your views on this.

WIFE WHO SMASHED TELEVISION GETS JAIL

'She came home, my Lord, and smashed in the television;
Me and the kids were peaceably watching *Kojak*
When she marched into the living room and declared
That if I didn't turn off the television immediately
She'd put her boot through the screen;   5
I didn't turn it off, so instead she turned it off –
I remember the moment exactly because *Kojak*
After shooting a dame with the same name as my wife
Snarled at the corpse – Goodnight, Queen Maeve –
And then she took off her boots and smashed in the television;   10
I had to bring the kids round to my mother's place;
We got there just before the finish of *Kojak*;
(My mother has a fondness for *Kojak*, my Lord);
When I returned home my wife had deposited
What was left of the television into the dustbin,   15
Saying – I didn't get married to a television
And I don't see why my kids or anybody else's kids
Should have a television for a father or mother,
We'd be much better off all down in the pub talking
Or playing bar-billiards –   20
Whereupon she disappeared off back down again to the pub.'
Justice O'Brádaigh said wives who preferred bar-billiards to family television
Were a threat to the family which was the basic unit of society
As indeed the television itself could be said to be a basic unit of the family
And when as in this case wives expressed their preference in forms of violence   25
Jail was the only place for them. Leave to appeal was refused.

NOTES		
2	*Kojak:*	an American detective series that ran from 1973 to 1978, starring the famous US film and TV actor Telly Savalas. It became hugely popular around the world and had significant cultural influence. People in Ireland used American phrases from it in daily speech.
9	Queen Maeve:	from the old Irish Medb (Anglicised Maeve). She was Queen of Connaught in the Ulster cycle of Irish mythology, when she embarked on the Cattle Raid of Cooley (Táin Bó Cuailinge) to steal the prize bull from Conchobar Mac Neasa, King of Ulster and a former husband. She was also famous for the number of her husbands and lovers.

EXPLORATIONS

Before reading

1. You might like to conduct an anonymous survey of your class members about their TV viewing and internet usage. Here are a few suggestions, but you can construct your own questions.

   a How many hours per evening (on average) do you spend
   (i) watching TV
   (ii) using the internet?

   b For the most part, do family members
   (i) watch the TV as they eat
   (ii) turn off the TV and talk at meals?

   c Do you watch mostly
   (i) American
   (ii) British
   (iii) Irish TV programmes?
   Rate 1, 2, 3 according to frequency. Discuss the findings of the survey.

2. a Where would you expect to read this title: 'Wife Who Smashed Television Gets Jail'?

   b If this was a headline, what might you expect to find in the rest of the article?

First reading

3. Carefully examine the language of the husband's speech, down to line 15.

   a What clues us in to the fact that he is a witness, giving evidence? Look beyond the obvious.

   b Do you think that he deliberately attempts to show himself in a good light and ingratiate himself with the judge? Where? Explain your view with reference to the language used.

   c How would you describe the tone of his speech – is he justifiably angry, rational and reasonable, self-righteous, etc.? Justify your opinion with references to the phrases used.

4. How does the husband attempt to portray his wife?

5. Examine the wife's speech, as quoted by the husband (lines 16–20). What point is she making? What is your opinion on it?

6. Would you agree that the judge is made to sound delightfully ridiculous by the great disconnection between the type of language he uses (serious-sounding social and moral clichés) and the actual content of what he says? Explore how this is achieved.

Second reading

7. Effective comic writing often uses some of the following techniques: exaggeration, inversion of the usual expectations about people's behaviour and values, take-off of accents, take-off of speech patterns and styles of language, etc. What do you find comic about this poem? Is it a light-hearted comedy or does it have a serious point?

8. Satire can be described as the use of ridicule, irony, etc. to expose folly or vice. What is Durcan actually satirising in this poem? Discuss this and write up your views.

Third reading

9. The literary critic Lucy Collins, in discussing Durcan's use of humour to draw attention to social problems in Ireland, writes that 'many of his poems take an apparently absurd premise and develop it to a telling extreme'. Write a short piece discussing the poem from the perspectives of this statement.

10. Do you think this is poetry? Debate this.

11. What do you like about the poetry by Durcan that you have read so far?

PARENTS

OL 2(

OL 2(

A child's face is a drowned face:
Her parents stare down at her asleep
Estranged from her by a sea:
She is under the sea
And they are above the sea: 5
If she looked up she would see them
As if locked out of their own home,
Their mouths open,
Their foreheads furrowed –
Pursed-up orifices of fearful fish –   10
Their big ears are fins behind glass
And in her sleep she is calling out to them
Father, Father
Mother, Mother
But they cannot hear her: 15
She is inside the sea
And they are outside the sea.
Through the night, stranded, they stare
At the drowned, drowned face of their child.

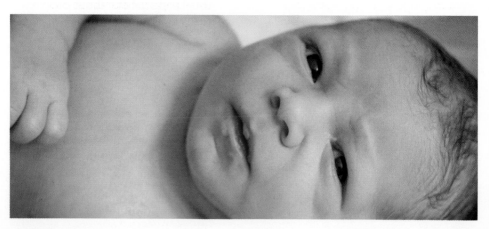

EXPLORATIONS

Before reading

1. Did you ever look up through the sea and experience how distorted everything appears from that perspective? What did you notice?

2. Have you ever held a newborn baby? What thoughts were going through your head? What did you feel? Talk about this in your groups.

3. What do you imagine the baby was experiencing at that moment? Share your thoughts in the group.

4. Do you know how a newborn baby actually sees the world? Find out.

First reading

5. 'A child's face is a drowned face'. This opening line is dramatic, even shocking, but is there any sense in which the image is not totally unreal?

6. The poem is entitled 'Parents'. Consider the references to the perspectives of parents in the poem. What does each image suggest about how they are feeling as they 'stare down at her asleep', 'Estranged', 'As if locked out of their own home', 'mouths open', 'foreheads furrowed', etc.?

7. Now examine the scene from the baby's perspective, as the poet views it. What do you imagine she may be feeling as she looks up from 'under the sea' and sees 'Pursed-up orifices of fearful fish' as 'she is calling out to them ... they cannot hear her'?

Second reading

8. Through the overarching metaphor of the sea, a barrier of silence, carrying its images of distorted fish-like and drowned faces, what insights about the experiences of parents and young children does the poet manage to communicate?

9. Eamon Grennan writes: 'A poetic world of such extremities and such simplicities as those constituted by Durcan's metaphors seems designed to make us see our experiences with new born eyes – new born, that is, in spirit and feeling.'
Did Durcan's metaphors enable you to experience the poem in this way? Discuss the quotation and the question and then write about how you experienced the images in the poem.

10. 'While the image of the sea in this poem has some similarities with the sea in "Nessa", there are significant differences.'
Talk about this in your discussion groups.

Third reading

11. Do you think this is too bleak and disturbing a meditation on the subject or do the insights gained make it worthwhile?

12. Do you think you could write with such honesty?

EN FAMILLE, 1979

Bring me back to the dark school – to the dark school of childhood:
To where tiny is tiny, and massive is massive.

NOTE

En Famille:	in or with one's family; at home, informally. It has a suggestion of 'in private'.

EXPLORATIONS

1. What thoughts are stirred up in your imagination by the image 'the dark school' of 'childhood'? Discuss this in your groups.

2. Are there contradictions between this image and what you might have expected from the title of the poem?

3. What is this poem saying about the writer's experience of childhood and family? Consider both lines.

4. Do you think the brevity works well here? Explain your thinking on this.

MADMAN

Every child has a madman on their street:
The only trouble about *our* madman is that he's our father.

EXPLORATIONS

1. Have you ever felt acutely embarrassed by your parents? Write about an incident.

2. As we know from his writing, Durcan had a troubled relationship with his father. Do you think the humour here takes the sting out of the unhappy memory while still making the point?

"WINDFALL", 8 PARNELL HILL, CORK

But, then, at the end of the day I could always say –
Well, now, I am going home.
I felt elected, steeped, sovereign to be able to say –
I am going home.
When I was at home I liked to stay at home;   5
At home I stayed at home for weeks;
At home I used sit in a winged chair by the window
Overlooking the river and the factory chimneys,
The electricity power station and the car assembly works,
The fleets of trawlers and the pilot tugs,   10
Dreaming that life is a dream which is real,
The river a reflection of itself in its own waters,
Goya sketching Goya among the smoky mirrors.
The industrial vista was my Mont Sainte-Victoire.
While my children sat on my knees watching TV   15
Their mother, my wife, reclined on the couch
Knitting a bright-coloured scarf, drinking a cup of black coffee,
Smoking a cigarette – one of her own roll-ups.
I closed my eyes and breathed in and breathed out.
It is ecstasy to breathe if you are at home in the world.   20
What a windfall! A home of our own!
Our neighbours' houses had names like 'Con Amore',
'Sans Souci', 'Pacelli', 'Montini', 'Homesville'.
But we called our home 'Windfall'.
'Windfall', 8 Parnell Hill, Cork.   25
In the gut of my head coursed the leaf of tranquillity
Which I dreamed was known only to Buddhist Monks
In lotus monasteries high up in the Hindu Kush.
Down here in the dark depth of Ireland,
Below sea level in the city of Cork,   30
In a city as intimate and homicidal as a Little Marseilles,
In a country where all the children of the nation
Are not cherished equally
And where the best go homeless, while the worst
Erect block-house palaces – self-regardingly ugly –   35
Having a home of your own can give to a family
A chance in a lifetime to transcend death.

At the high window, shipping from all over the world
Being borne up and down the busy, yet contemplative, river;
Skylines drifting in and out of skylines in the cloudy valley;   40
Firelight at dusk, and city lights;

Beyond them the control tower of the airport on the hill –
A lighthouse in the sky flashing green to white to green;
Our black-and-white cat snoozing in the corner of a chair;
Pastels and etchings on the four walls, and over the mantelpiece   45
'Van Gogh's Grave' and 'Lovers in Water';
A room wallpapered in books and family photograph albums
Chronicling the adventures and metamorphoses of family life:
In swaddling clothes in Mammy's arms on baptism day;
Being a baby of nine months and not remembering it;   50
Face-down in a pram, incarcerated in a high chair;
Everybody, including strangers, wearing shop-window smiles;
With Granny in Felixstowe, with Granny in Ballymaloe;
In a group photo in First Infants, on a bike at thirteen;
In the back garden in London, in the back garden in Cork;   55
Performing a headstand after First Holy Communion;
Getting a kiss from the Bishop on Confirmation Day;
Straw hats in the Bois de Boulougne, wearing wings at the seaside;
Mammy and Daddy holding hands on the Normandy Beaches;
Mammy and Daddy at the wedding of Jeremiah and Margot;   60
Mammy and Daddy queuing up for *Last Tango in Paris*;
Boating on the Shannon, climbing mountains in Kerry;
Building sandcastles in Killala, camping in Barley Cove;
Picnicking in Moone, hide-and-go-seek in Clonmacnoise;
Riding horses, cantering, jumping fences;   65
Pushing out toy yachts in the pond in the Tuileries;
The Irish College revisited in the Rue des Irlandais;
Sipping an *orange pressé* through a straw on the roof of the Beaubourg;
Dancing in Père Lachaise, weeping at Auvers.
Year in, year out, I pored over these albums accumulating,   70
My children looking over my shoulder, exhilarated as I was,
Their mother presiding at our ritual from a distance –
The far side of the hearthrug, diffidently, proudly.
Schoolbooks on the floor and pyjamas on the couch –
Whose turn is it tonight to put the children to bed?   75

Our children swam about our home
As if it was their private sea,
Their own unique, symbiotic fluid
Of which their parents also partook.
Such is home – a sea of your own –   80
In which you hang upside down from the ceiling
With equanimity, while postcards from Thailand on the mantelpiece
Are raising their eyebrow markings benignly:
Your hands dangling their prayers to the floorboards of your home,

Sifting the sands underneath the surfaces of conversations,   85
The marine insect life of the family psyche.
A home of your own – or a sea of your own –
In which climbing the walls is as natural
As making love on the stairs;
In which when the telephone rings   90
Husband and wife are metamorphosed into smiling accomplices,
Both declining to answer it;
Initiating, instead, a yet more subversive kiss –
A kiss they have perhaps never attempted before –
And might never have dreamed of attempting   95
Were it not for the telephone belling.
Through the banisters or along the banister rails
The pyjama-clad children solemnly watching
Their parents at play, jumping up and down in support,
Race back to bed, gesticulating wordlessly;   100
The most subversive unit in society is the human family.

We're almost home, pet, almost home …
Our home is at …
I'll be home …
I have to go home now …   105
I want to go home now …
Are you feeling homesick?
Are you anxious to get home? …
I can't wait to get home …
Let's stay at home tonight and …   110
What time will you be coming home at? …
If I'm not home by six at the latest, I'll phone …
We're nearly home, don't worry, we're nearly home …

But then with good reason
I was put out of my home: 115
By a keen wind felled.
I find myself now without a home
Having to live homeless in the alien, foreign city of Dublin.
It is an eerie enough feeling to be homesick
Yet knowing you will be going home next week;   120
It is an eerie feeling beyond all ornithological analysis
To be homesick knowing that there is no home to go home to:
Day by day, creeping, crawling,
Moonlighting, escaping,
Bed-and-breakfast to bed-and-breakfast;   125
Hostels, centres, one-night hotels.

Homeless in Dublin,
Blown about the suburban streets at evening,
Peering in the windows of other people's homes,
Wondering what it must feel like   130
To be sitting around a fire –
Apache or Cherokee or Bourgeoisie –
Beholding the firelit faces of your family,
Beholding their starry or their TV gaze:
Windfall to Windfall – can you hear me?   135
Windfall to Windfall …
We're almost home, pet, don't worry anymore, we're almost home.

NOTES

13	Goya sketching Goya:	Francisco José de Goya y Lucientes (1746–1828) was a Spanish Romantic painter and royal painter at the Spanish court in Madrid. Perhaps the reference is to a 'Portrait of Francisco Goya' by Vincente López y Portana (1826) that shows Goya with his palette and brushes looking out from the painting as if he is both painter and sitter.
14	Mont Sainte-Victoire:	the nineteenth century French post-Impressionist painter Paul Cezanne had a home in Provence with a view of the Sainte-Victoire mountains and he often painted them
22–3	'Con Amore' … 'Montini'	'Con Amore' means 'with love' (Italian); 'Sans Souci' means 'without worries' (French); 'Pacelli' and 'Montini' are the surnames of Catholic popes
27	Buddhist Monks:	Buddhism is a spiritual way of life that is 2,500 years old and focuses on personal spiritual development and the attainment of enlightenment into the true nature of life. Buddhists meditate in order to still the mind, be at peace and live each moment.
28	lotus monasteries:	the lotus position is a cross-legged position in meditation
28	Hindu Kush:	a mountain range in Central Asia, running through Afghanistan and Pakistan. Ironically, in the context of the poem, this has been an area of military conflict for over two and a half millennia.
32–3	all the children … equally:	a reference to aspirations in the 1916 Proclamation. Durcan is pointing out the failure to realise these.
34	best go … worst:	these lines echo the social criticism of W. B. Yeats's poem 'The Second Coming': 'The best lack all conviction, while the worst/ Are full of passionate intensity'.
45	Pastels:	drawings or pictures done in a type of crayon etchings; engravings created by using acid on a metal plate; also impressions produced from this etched plate
46	'Van Gogh's Grave':	this is a reference to the grave of Vincent Van Gogh (1853–90), a Dutch post-Impressionist painter who spent much of his life in France and is buried at Auvers-sur-Oise, in a Paris suburb
48	metamorphoses:	changes

49	swaddling clothes:	the bandages that were used to wrap up newborn babies tightly, considered good practice in previous centuries
53	Felixstowe:	a seaside town on the coast of Suffolk in the UK
57	kiss ... Confirmation Day:	a reference to what was formerly a liturgical kiss of peace (like the Continental form of greeting – an 'air kiss' on both cheeks). This had been adapted to a pat on the cheek or handshake for Confirmation
58	Bois de Boulougne:	a famous city park in Paris, also known as one of the city's red light districts
59	Normandy Beaches:	scene of the Normandy landings on 6 June 1944 (D-Day) where the Allies landed on the coast of France in World War II. There are many cemeteries and war memorials in the area, often visited by relatives and other tourists.
61	Last Tango in Paris:	Bertolucci film (1972) starring Marlon Brando and Maria Schneider about the sexual affair between a young Parisian woman and a middle-aged American
63	Killala ... Barley Cove:	seaside villages/townlands in counties Mayo and Cork, respectively
64	Moone ... Clonmacnoise:	historic religious sites, locations of ancient High Cross and monastic ruins in counties Kildare and Offaly, respectively
66	Tuileries:	surviving garden of a destroyed royal palace near the Louvre in Paris
67	The Irish College ... Rue des Irlandais:	founded in the late sixteenth century, it was a Catholic college of education. In the eighteenth century this was extended to a second college, built on the Rue des Irlandais. The college now houses the Centre Culturel Irlandais.
68	orange pressé:	fresh orange squash
68	Beaubourg:	the Pompidou Centre complex in Paris, known locally as the Beaubourg, is a significant centre of culture. It has views across the rooftops of Paris.
69	Père Lachaise:	a cemetery in Paris containing the graves of many famous artists and writers
69	Auvers:	probably Auvers-sur-Oise, a suburb of Paris associated with famous artists. Vincent Van Gogh is buried in the cemetery there.
78	symbiotic:	symbiosis is a mutually advantageous association between organisms or people. There is an echo here too of amniotic fluid, in which a baby is enveloped in the womb.
121	ornithological analysis:	the study of birds
132	Apache:	the term used to describe several related groups of Native Americans in the south-western United States
132	Cherokee:	a Native American people settled in the south-eastern United States
132	Bourgeoisie:	middle class

EXPLORATIONS

First reading

Lines 1–14

1. How does the writer feel about the concept of 'home'? What words, phrases and images communicate this?

2. Describe the view from his window.

3. Is there anything to suggest that he finds this view artistically inspiring? Consult the line notes and then outline your view.

Lines 15–37

4. Would you agree that this section begins with a romanticised view of perfect family life? Explain how you see this.

5. a A 'windfall' can refer to fruit blown down by the wind or unexpected good fortune (such as money). Why do you suppose they named the house 'Windfall'?

   b Personalised house names often reflect the philosophies and ideals of their owners. If so, what do we learn about the writer's neighbours?

   c Do you think the writer fits in well with this community? Discuss.

6. The writer is obviously delighted at their good fortune: 'A home of our own!' But he also feels a deeper spiritual contentment. Explore the references and images here and try to express what he is experiencing in your own words.

7. Ironically, this experience of contentment leads him to think about the less than ideal society all around. Consult the line references and explain what exactly the writer is criticising here.

Lines 38–75

8. You could think of this section as organised along cinematic lines in the following way:

- The opening shot shows the view through the window.

- Then the camera pans to take in the room and shows some details, such as the domestic cat and the pictures.

- It then zooms in to examine the details of the photograph albums 'Chronicling the adventures and metamorphoses of family life'. This is the central section.

- At the end, the camera pulls back a little to show the attitudes of his children and wife to their family reminiscences.

   a Examine the detail of the photographic history. What does this reveal about the writer's family background and personal experience?

   b What does this add to the understanding of family that is being built up in this poem? What are the attitudes of his wife and children to this reminiscence?

Lines 76–101

9. Would you agree that 'home' for them is a very personal, private space in which the adults can be uninhibited? Write about what you discover from the poem about this.

10. How does the metaphor of the home as a sea contribute to Durcan's concept of the ideal home as an uninhibiting place?

11. How do you understand the lines? 'Sifting the sands underneath the surfaces of conversations,/The marine insect life of the family psyche.'

12. Did the children have a happy childhood? Explain your thoughts on this, with reference to the poem.

13. 'The most subversive unit in society is the human family.' Do you think this is actually true or is it an ideal of Durcan's? Debate the issue.

Lines 102–13

14. Durcan is famous for the quality of his poetry reading. In your groups, plan for and perform aloud the litany of words, the type of chant in this section. Each person reads a line in succession. Read as you think it might be said (imagine someone saying it – who, where?), then have a group discussion on the possible ways of saying each line. When ready, perform the section aloud. What does this section convey about the writer's concept of home?

Lines 114–37

15. 'But then with good reason/I was put out of my home:/By a keen wind felled.' What is your reaction to these lines?

16. What pictures and images of homelessness affect you most in this section? Talk about them.

17. The writer gives a new and bitter twist to the idea of homesickness. What is the effect of this?

18. What does he miss most? What image haunts him?

19. 'Windfall to Windfall – can you hear me?/Windfall to Windfall…' What are your thoughts when you read these lines?

20. Do you find the echo of former times in the final line a consolation or desperately sad?

Second reading

21. This poem is both a 'celebration of domesticity' and a record of the poet's feelings after the break-up of his marriage. Critical opinion varies on the appropriateness of writing about this. Some praise his openness and courage in writing about intimate private life; others feel that continuing to revisit it is exploitative. What do you think?

22. 'But then with good reason/I was put out of my home'.
    a   In an online article, critic Alan Dent is trenchant in his criticism: 'Yet this is not an honest appraisal of his shortcomings, it is a self-serving posture. It is a manipulation. The cry of "How unworthy I am!" demands the response "Of course you aren't!"' Is this a fair criticism or is the critic demanding a different type of poem altogether?
    b   Do you think there is a degree of self-pity in this poem?
    c   Read the critical notes to hear what Durcan himself says about the 'good reason'.

23. Collect together all the elements of the ideal home as envisaged by Durcan in this poem. Critique this vision. In what way could it be considered subversive of Irish society?

24. The sea metaphor plays a significant role in imaging the family here. In an interview in *The Irish Times* (10 February 1990), Durcan said, 'To me everything that is good is water-connected or based, even attitudes to life – flowing into things rather than being rigid.'

    a Explore again what Eamon Grennan called 'the extended life of this metaphor' in the third section of this poem (lines 76–86).

    b Explore each of the additions the metaphor gathers as it grows, from 'private sea' → 'symbiotic fluid' → 'home – a sea of your own' → 'hang upside down' → 'hands dangling their prayers to the floorboards' → 'The marine insect life of the family psyche'.

    c What light does this throw on Durcan's concept of the ideal family?

25. 'Even in a poem about private family life, Durcan is aware of wider social issues.'
    Discuss this statement.

SIX NUNS DIE IN CONVENT INFERNO 🔊

*To the
happy memory of six Loreto nuns
who died
between midnight and morning of
2 June 1986*

I

We resided in a Loreto convent in the centre of Dublin city
On the east side of a public gardens, St Stephen's Green.
Grafton Street – the *paseo*
Where everybody *paseo*'d, including even ourselves –
Debouched on the north side, and at the top of Grafton Street,   5
Or round the base of the great patriotic pebble of O'Donovan Rossa,
Knelt tableaus of punk girls and punk boys.
When I used pass them – scurrying as I went –
Often as not to catch a mass in Clarendon Street,
The Carmelite Church in Clarendon Street,   10
(Myself, I never used the Clarendon Street entrance,
I always slipped in by way of Johnson's Court,
Opposite the side entrance to Bewley's Oriental Café),
I could not help but smile, as I sucked on a Fox's mint,
That for all the half-shaven heads and the martial garb   15
And the dyed hair-dos and the nappy pins
They looked so conventional, really, and vulnerable,
Clinging to warpaint and to uniforms and to one another.
I knew it was myself who was the ultimate drop-out,
The delinquent, the recidivist, the vagabond,   20
The wild woman, the subversive, the original punk.
Yet, although I confess I was smiling, I was also afraid,
Appalled by my own nerve, my own fervour,
My apocalyptic enthusiasm, my other-worldly hubris:
To opt out of the world and to   25
Choose such exotic loneliness,
Such terrestrial abandonment,
A lifetime of bicycle lamps and bicycle pumps,
A lifetime of galoshes stowed under the stairs,
A lifetime of umbrellas drying out in the kitchens.   30

I was an old nun – an agèd beadswoman –
But I was no daw.
I knew what a weird bird I was, I knew that when we
Went to bed we were as eerie an aviary as you'd find

In all the blown-off rooftops of the city: 35
Scuttling about our dorm, wheezing, shrieking, croaking,
In our yellowy corsets, wonky suspenders, strung-out garters,
A bony crew in the gods of the sleeping city.
Many's the night I lay awake in bed
Dreaming what would befall us if there were a fire: 40
No fire-escapes outside, no fire-extinguishers inside;
To coin a Dublin saying,
We'd not stand a snowball's chance in hell. Fancy that!
It seemed too good to be true:
Happy death vouchsafed only to the few.   45
Sleeping up there was like sleeping at the top of the mast
Of a nineteenth-century schooner, and in the daytime
We old nuns were the ones who crawled out on the yardarms
To stitch and sew the rigging and the canvas.
To be sure we were weird birds, oddballs, Christniks,   50
For we had done the weirdest thing a woman can do –
Surrendered the marvellous passions of girlhood,
The innocent dreams of childhood,
Not for a night or a weekend or even a Lent or a season,
But for a lifetime.   55
Never to know the love of a man or a woman;
Never to have children of our own;
Never to have a home of our own;
All for why and for what?
To follow a young man – would you believe it –   60
Who lived two thousand years ago in Palestine
And who died a common criminal strung up on a tree.

As we stood there in the disintegrating dormitory
Burning to death in the arms of Christ –
O Christ, Christ, come quickly, quickly –   65
Fluttering about in our tight, gold bodices,
Beating our wings in vain,
It reminded me of the snaps one of the sisters took
When we took a seaside holiday in 1956
(The year Cardinal Mindszenty went into hiding   70
In the US legation in Budapest.
He was a great hero of ours, Cardinal Mindszenty,
Any of us would have given our right arm
To have been his nun – darning his socks, cooking his meals,
Making his bed, doing his washing and ironing.)   75

Somebody – an affluent buddy of the bishop's repenting his affluence –
Loaned Mother Superior a secluded beach in Co. Waterford –
Ardmore, along the coast from Tramore –
A cove with palm trees, no less, well off the main road.
There we were fluttering up and down the beach,   80
Scampering hither and thither in our starched bathing-costumes.
Tonight, expiring in the fire, was quite much like that,
Only instead of scampering into the waves of the sea,
Now we were scampering into the flames of the fire.

That was one of the gayest days of my life,   85
The day the sisters went swimming.
Often in the silent darkness of the chapel after Benediction,
During the Exposition of the Blessed Sacrament,
I glimpsed the sea again as it was that day.
Praying – daydreaming really –   90
I became aware that Christ is the ocean
Forever rising and falling on the world's shore.
Now tonight in the convent Christ is the fire in whose waves
We are doomed but delighted to drown.
And, darting in and out of the flames of the dormitory,   95
Gabriel, with that extraordinary message of his on his boyish lips,
Frenetically pedalling his skybike.
He whispers into my ear what I must do
And I do it – and die.
Each of us in our own tiny, frail, furtive way   100
Was a Mother of God, mothering forth illegitimate Christs
In the street life of Dublin city.
God have mercy on our whirring souls –
Wild women were we all –
And on the misfortunate, poor fire-brigade men   105
Whose task it will be to shovel up our ashes and shovel
What is left of us into black plastic refuse sacks.
Fire-brigade men are the salt of the earth.

Isn't it a marvellous thing how your hour comes
When you least expect it? When you lose a thing,   110
Not to know about it until it actually happens?
How, in so many ways, losing things is such a refreshing experience,
Giving you a sense of freedom you've not often experienced?
How lucky I was to lose – I say, lose – lose my life.
It was a Sunday night, and after vespers   115
I skipped bathroom so that I could hop straight into bed
And get in a bit of a read before lights out:

Conor Cruise O'Brien's new book *The Siege*,
All about Israel and superlatively insightful
For a man who they say is reputedly an agnostic –   120
I got a loan of it from the brother-in-law's married niece –
But I was tired out and I fell asleep with the book open
Face down across my breast and I woke
To the racket of bellowing flame and snarling glass.
The first thing I thought was that the brother-in-law's married niece   125
Would never again get her Conor Cruise O'Brien back
And I had seen on the price-tag that it cost £23.00:
Small wonder that the custom of snipping off the price
As an exercise in social deportment has simply died out;
Indeed a book today is almost worth buying for its price,   130
Its price frequently being more remarkable than its contents.

The strange Eucharist of my death –
To be eaten alive by fire and smoke.
I clasped the dragon to my breast
And stroked his red-hot ears.   135
Strange! There we were, all sleeping molecules,
Suddenly all giving birth to our deaths,
All frantically in labour.
Doctors and midwives weaved in and out
In gowns of smoke and gloves of fire.   140
Christ, like an Orthodox patriarch in his dressing gown,
Flew up and down the dormitory, splashing water on our souls:
Sister Eucharia; Sister Seraphia; Sister Rosario;
Sister Gonzaga; Sister Margaret; Sister Edith.
If you will remember us – six nuns burnt to death –   145
Remember us for the frisky girls that we were,
Now more than ever kittens in the sun.

II

When Jesus heard these words at the top of Grafton Street
Uttered by a small, agèd, emaciated, female punk
Clad all in mourning black, and grieving like an alley cat,   150
He was annulled with astonishment, and turning round
He declared to the gangs of teenagers and dicemen following him:
'I tell you, not even in New York City
Have I found faith like this.'

That night in St Stephen's Green,   155
After the keepers had locked the gates,
And the courting couples had found cinemas themselves to die in,

The six nuns who had died in the convent inferno,
From the bandstand they'd been hiding under, crept out
And knelt together by the Fountain of the Three Fates,   160
Reciting the Agnus Dei: reciting it as if it were the torch song
Of all aid – Live Aid, Self Aid, Aids, and All Aid –
Lord, I am not worthy
That thou should'st enter under my roof;
Say but the word and my soul shall be healed.   165

NOTES

3	Grafton Street:	well-known shopping street off St Stephen's Green in Dublin
3	*paseo:*	a public place designed for walking; a slow, idle walk
5	Debouched:	emerged from a confined space
6	pebble of O'Donovan Rossa:	Jeremiah O'Donovan Rossa (1831–1915) was an important Fenian leader. His monument in St Stephen's Green consists of a bronze plaque fixed into a very large piece of stone that could be seen to resemble an enormous pebble.

7	punk:	a fast, hard-edged style of rock music that originated in the 1970s; punk fashion among followers involved highly distinctive clothes, hairstyles, body piercing, etc.
10	The Carmelite Church in Clarendon Street:	staffed by the Carmelite community, St Teresa's Church, off Grafton Street, is well known for its midnight Mass at Christmas time
13	Bewley's Oriental Café:	also on Grafton Street
14	Fox's mint:	well-known mint sweets, famous for the polar bear icon on the wrapper
20	delinquent:	young offender, hooligan, tearaway
20	recidivist:	person who relapses into crime
20	vagabond:	wanderer, having no settled home
21	subversive:	person trying to overthrow, for instance, the system or the government
24	apocalyptic enthusiasm:	the apocalypse was a revelation about the end of the world; so enthusiasm for the end of the world
24	hubris:	arrogant pride
26	exotic loneliness:	exotic has many shades of meaning, such as foreign, different, unusual
27	terrestrial abandonment:	abandonment of the world, the earth
29	galoshes:	waterproof overshoes
32	no daw:	usually taken to mean 'no fool'
34	as eerie an aviary:	viary is a large cage for keeping birds; eerie, as an adjective, could mean creepy, frightening, ghostly. But it could also be a word play on 'eyrie', which is the nest of a bird of prey, built high up in trees or cliffs.
37	wonky:	slang for unsteady, unreliable
37	suspenders ... garters:	attachments, formerly used to hold up clothes and stockings
38	in the gods:	'the gods' is the term used for the seats at the very top of a steeply raked theatre, giving a bird's eye view of the stage. Here, the dormitory at the top of the house has a similar view of the city.
45	vouchsafed:	conferred as a favour; granted
47	schooner:	a two-masted ship
50	Christniks:	followers of Christ
54	Lent:	religious period (traditionally a time of fasting and penance) between Ash Wednesday and Easter Saturday
61	Palestine:	refers here to what became known as the Holy Land, the region where Christ lived and preached
66	bodices:	the part of women's dresses above the waist

70	Cardinal Mindszenty:	a Catholic bishop in Hungary who opposed both fascists and Nazis in World War II. After torture and imprisonment he managed to take refuge in the United States legation in 1956.
87–8	Benediction ... Exposition:	Benediction is a religious liturgy of prayer where the Blessed Sacrament (Host) is on view (Exposition). It usually ends with a benediction or blessing with the Sacred Host.
95	Gabriel:	a reference to the angel Gabriel in the Bible, who was sent by God to tell Mary that she was to be the mother of the Son of God
117	Conor Cruise O'Brien *The Siege*:	(1917–2008) Irish academic, historian and politician who was a very forthright speaker and writer. One of his most controversial works was *The Siege* (1989), a sympathetic history of Zionism and the state of Israel.
119	agnostic:	a person who believes that the existence of God is not provable
132	Eucharist:	in the Catholic faith, this refers to the celebration of the Mass in which the sacrifice and death of Christ is re-enacted. The poet is making a connection between the nun's death and that of Christ. Her death is another sacrifice.
140	Orthodox patriarch:	a leader of the Eastern European or Orthodox branch of Christianity, usually seen dressed in elaborate priestly robes
143–4	Sister Eucharia etc.:	in former times when a woman became a nun she adopted the name of a saint or holy person as her new religious name. This signified that she had put her former life behind her and was now a member of a new religious family.
148–54	When Jesus heard these words ... faith like this:	in this section an episode from the life of Christ in the Gospels is transposed and applied to modern times, with both humorous and serious effects. The incident is told in St Matthew's Gospel, Chapter 8, among others. Jesus was asked by a centurion (an officer of the conquering Roman army that ruled the Jews) to help his servant who was paralysed. Jesus said that he would come and cure him. But the centurion said, 'Lord, I am not fit that you should come in under my roof. But just say a word and my servant will be healed.... Jesus heard this and was astonished; and he said to the people following, "Amen, I tell you, I have not found such faith from anyone in Israel".'
160	Fountain of the Three Fates:	This fountain in St Stephen's Green, erected in 1956, was a gift from the people of the German Federal Republic to show their gratitude for Ireland's help after the war of 1939–45. It shows the three legendary Fates spinning and measuring the thread of man's destiny.
161	Agnus Dei:	a Latin phrase, translates as 'Lamb of God' and referring to Jesus. It is the opening phrase of a prayer in the Liturgy of the Mass – 'Lamb of God, who takes away the sins of the world, have mercy on us'.

EXPLORATIONS

Note: Part I of this poem is narrated in the voice of one of the Loreto nuns who lost her life in the fire and it is structured as a reminiscence that is at times realistic and at times imagined.

First reading

Lines 1–30

1. In the first thirteen lines the speaker sets the scene, giving us a feeling for the environment around the convent. What details do you notice about the geography of the place, buildings, etc. that she mentions? Use Google Maps to trace her journey from Loreto Convent to the Clarendon Street Church. What do you see?

2. Follow her journey in your mind's eye as you read the poem. Do you see her strolling at leisure, comfortable in her environment, or something else? Examine the detail.

3. She has a particularly good understanding and empathy for the 'tableaus of punk girls and punk boys' she passes on her journey. What particular insights does she articulate about them?

4. In what way might the punks be considered 'conventional'?

5. This leads her to consider her own position. She uses the terms 'delinquent', 'recidivist', 'vagabond', 'wild woman', 'subversive' and 'original punk' and 'ultimate dropout' about herself. Has she lost the plot? Or do you think there is a sense in which these terms could apply to her? How was she more radical than the punks?

6. Did her radical choice lead to an exciting lifestyle?

Lines 31–62

7. 'But I was no daw./I knew what a weird bird I was'.
   a How are these women described as strange or different?
   b What is their attitude to death here?
   c The strangeness is emphasised in the dream metaphor of the schooner. Do you think this is effective?

8. a 'For we had done the weirdest thing a woman can do'. In your own words, explain what this was.
   b Nuns have been described as 'brides of Christ'. Does this concept help you understand the nun's motivation here? Discuss.

Lines 63–84

9. The first five lines of this section describe the fire taking hold in the disintegrating dormitory. What do you notice about the image of the nuns described here?

10. In a somewhat bizarre memory link, their panic-stricken fluttering about in the dormitory reminds her of fluttering up and down the beach on the one memorable holiday of her life. Carefully read the final three lines of this section. What does this communicate about the nuns' attitude to death?

Lines 84–131

11. She refers to that holiday as 'one of the gayest days of my life'. That

seaside experience led her to think of Christ in a new way. Explain this in your own words.

12. 'I became aware that Christ is the ocean/Forever rising and falling on the world's shore./Now tonight in the convent Christ is the fire in whose waves/We are doomed but delighted to drown.'

If you refer back to the concept of nuns as 'brides of Christ', does it help you to understand the attitude to death here? Discuss this.

13. Strange dream-like image connections are made here. The angel Gabriel ('Frenetically pedalling his skybike') whispers in her ear, which reminds her of his message to the mother of God. She thinks: 'Each of us in our own tiny, frail, furtive way/Was a Mother of God, mothering forth illegitimate Christs/ In the street life of Dublin city.'

Though on first reading it may appear shocking, is there a sense in which this explains the religious mission of the nuns? Discuss.

14. Despite the lengthy emphasis on death in the poem, the lively personalities of the nuns and their compassionate understanding for people come across strongly. Do you think this is true of this section? What do you notice about them here?

15. **a** Lines 109–13 give quite a positive, even upbeat view of death. What insights are offered on the subject?

   b What do we learn about the nuns from this?

16. Read lines 114–30. The everyday small talk of the old nun 'wittering on' and the conversational tone of the piece is in stark contrast to the savage, wild animal reality of the fire ('bellowing flame and snarling glass'). What is the resulting effect of this contrast, do you think?

Lines 132–47

17. From the perspective of a religious faith, death is the end of one form of life but the beginning of another. In that sense it is a sort of birth. What are your thoughts on how this is portrayed in the final section of part I?

18. How does the speaker want us to remember them, finally?

Part II (lines 148–165)

19. Though the first section of part II is narrated with visual and verbal humour, a serious point is still being made. Discuss this.

20. What are your thoughts on the final section of the poem? Does it make a good conclusion? Do you think the nun narrator of part I would enjoy it?

Second reading

21. Collect together all the speaker's references to death in the poem. Analyse them and put together a coherent statement on her philosophy of death.

22. Collect together all the references that show the personality of the speaker. Write an obituary for her that does justice to all aspects of her personality.

23. Do you think Durcan understands these women, not only as nuns, but also as human beings? Is he always sympathetic, never critical?

24. Critic Christina Hunt Mahony has written, 'Although Durcan has disdained the term "surreal" as applied to these departures from realism … the point at which the real and the highly imagined collide is a successful and idiosyncratic feature of many of his poems.' Write up your views on this.

25. 'This poem is enhanced by the humour.' Write on this.

OL 20

OL 20

SPORT 🔊

There were not many fields
In which you had hopes for me
But sport was one of them.
On my twenty-first birthday
I was selected to play   5
For Grangegorman Mental Hospital.
In an away game
Against Mullingar Mental Hospital.
I was a patient
In B Wing.   10
You drove all the way down,
Fifty miles,
To Mullingar to stand
On the sidelines and observe me.

I was fearful I would let down   15
Not only my team but you.
It was Gaelic football.
I was selected as goalkeeper.
There were big country men
On the Mullingar Mental Hospital team,   20
Men with gapped teeth, red faces,
Oily, frizzy hair, bushy eyebrows.
Their full forward line
Were over six foot tall
Fifteen stone in weight.   25
All three of them, I was informed,
Cases of schizophrenia.

There was a rumour
That their centre-half forward
Was an alcoholic solicitor   30
Who, in a lounge bar misunderstanding,

Had castrated his best friend
But that he had no memory of it.
He had meant well – it was said.
His best friend had had to emigrate   35
To Nigeria.

To my surprise,
I did not flinch in the goals.
I made three or four spectacular saves,
Diving full stretch to turn   40
A certain goal around the corner,
Leaping high to tip another certain goal
Over the bar for a point.
It was my knowing
That you were standing on the sideline   45
That gave me the necessary motivation –
That will to die
That is as essential to sportsmen as to artists.
More than anybody it was you
I wanted to mesmerise, and after the game –   50
Grangegorman Mental Hospital
Having defeated Mullingar Mental Hospital
By 14 goals and 38 points to 3 goals and 10 points –
Sniffing your approval, you shook hands with me.
'Well played, son.'   55

I may not have been mesmeric
But I had not been mediocre.
In your eyes I had achieved something at last.
On my twenty-first birthday I had played on a winning team
The Grangegorman Mental Hospital team.   60
Seldom if ever again in your eyes
Was I to rise to these heights.

NOTES

6	Grangegorman:	St Brendan's Psychiatric Hospital, Grangegorman, was located in north Dublin
25	schizophrenia:	mental disorder marked by disconnection between thoughts, feelings and actions (dictionary definition)
48	mesmerise:	hypnotise

EXPLORATIONS

First reading

1. 'There were not many fields/In which you had hopes for me But sport was one of them.'
   What do these opening lines hint about the relationship between father and son?

2. According to the speaker, why did his father come 'all the way down' to the match?

3. a Was the match exciting?
   b Did the young man play well?
   c What was his main motivation to play well?

4. a What was the father's reaction?
   b The father doesn't say much, but what thoughts may have been going through his mind at this stage? Write them as a diary entry.

5. a Read the last stanza (lines 56–62). What are your thoughts and feelings on reading this?
   b What would you like to say to the speaker?

Second reading

6. Over half of the poems in the volume *Daddy, Daddy*, from which this poem is taken, are about the troubled relationship with his father. On the evidence of this poem, how would you describe the relationship between father and son?

7. In this poem we mainly get the son's perspective, but could the father have a different view? Discuss this.

8. How is mental illness portrayed in the poem?

9. Do you think the writer deliberately selects details to shock the reader? What may be the purpose of this?

10. Do you think the context in which the game is played is a significant element in the poem?

11. Durcan forces us to look beneath the surface of everyday events to the human unhappiness beneath. Would you agree? Write about this aspect of Durcan's poetry.

FATHER'S DAY, 21 JUNE 1992

Just as I was dashing to catch the Dublin–Cork train,
Dashing up and down the stairs, searching my pockets,
She told me that her sister in Cork wanted a loan of the axe;
It was late June and
The buddleia tree in the backyard   5
Had grown out of control.
The taxi was ticking over outside in the street,
All the neighbours noticing it.
'You mean that you want me to bring her down the axe?'
'Yes, if you wouldn't mind, that is –'   10
'A simple saw would do the job, surely to God
She could borrow a simple saw.'
'She said she'd like the axe.'
'OK. There is a Blue Cabs taxi ticking over outside
And the whole world inspecting it,   15
I'll bring her down the axe.'
The axe – all four-and-a-half feet of it –
Was leaning up against the wall behind the settee –
The fold-up settee that doubles as a bed.
She handed the axe to me just as it was,   20
As neat as a newborn babe,
All in the bare buff.
You'd think she'd have swaddled it up
In something – if not a blanket, an old newspaper,
But no, not even a token hanky   25
Tied in a bow round its head.
I decided not to argue the toss. I kissed her goodbye.

The whole long way down to Cork
I felt uneasy. Guilt feelings.
It's a killer, this guilt.   30
I always feel bad leaving her
But this time it was the worst.
I could see she was glad
To see me go away for a while,
Glad at the prospect of being   35
Two weeks on her own,
Two weeks of having the bed to herself,
Two weeks of not having to be pestered
By my coarse advances,
Two weeks of not having to look up from her plate   40
And behold me eating spaghetti with a knife and fork.

Our daughters are all grown up and gone away.
Once when she was sitting pregnant on the settee
It snapped shut with herself inside it,
But not a bother on her. I nearly died.   45

As the train slowed down approaching Portarlington
I overheard myself say to the passenger sitting opposite me:
'I am feeling guilty because she does not love me
As much as she used to, can you explain that?'
The passenger's eyes were on the axe on the seat beside me.   50
'Her sister wants a loan of the axe …'
As the train threaded itself into Portarlington
I nodded to the passenger 'Cúl an tSúdaire!'
The passenger stood up, lifted down a case from the rack,
Walked out of the coach, but did not get off the train.   55
For the remainder of the journey, we sat alone,
The axe and I,
All the green fields running away from us,
All our daughters grown up and gone away.

NOTES

	Father's Day:	traditionally held in Ireland on the third Sunday in June, it celebrates fatherhood, male parenting and the influence of fathers in society. It complements Mother's Day.
5	buddleia:	a large flowering bush, easy to grow and difficult to kill
23	swaddled:	wrapped up tightly
27	argue the toss:	refuse to accept a decision; quibble over something of little consequence
46	Portarlington:	a town on the borders of counties Laois and Offaly
53	Cúl an tSúdaire:	the Irish for Portarlington, probably visible on the railway station signpost

EXPLORATIONS

First reading

1. a Working in pairs, prepare to read the first section aloud. Choose which part of the dialogue each will read. Think about the frame of mind and mood of each speaker and how each voice should sound. Discuss it and practise before each pair in turn reads aloud for the class.

   b Have a class discussion on the different interpretations and on which interpretation is closest to the text.

2. What did you discover about the two people from this exchange in the poem?

3. Who do you think is the more dominant personality? Explain your views, with reference to the text.

4. a One of the ways in which humour is created is through sudden unexpected shifts in thought and sometimes in tone. Consider the first three lines, for example. Read them aloud dramatically and you will notice the unexpected shift in line 3.

    b Are there other instances of this?

    c In what other ways is the humour created?

5. In the second section there is an unexpected and sudden change in tone from the comic to the contemplative and introspective. What do we learn about the couple from this section?

6. How would you rate the self-esteem of the speaker? Explain your thinking.

7. There is another sudden change in tone at the end of this section, just after the plaintive line 'Our daughters are all grown up and gone away' (line 42). Can you think of any reason for this sudden shift?

8. T. S. Eliot once wrote, 'Human kind/ Cannot bear very much reality'. For best understanding, act out the last section in pairs. You could substitute a sweeping brush for the axe.

9. a Picture yourself on the train as the passenger alone in the carriage with the speaker and his axe. What are your thoughts as he speaks to you?

    b Why do you stand up and leave when he says 'Cúl an tSúdaire'?

10. Would you describe the comedy in this section as more akin to tragi-comedy than the slapstick fun of the first section? Explain your thinking.

Second reading

11. Do you think it ironic that the poem is entitled 'Father's Day'? Write about this.

12. 'Behind the comedy there is always sadness in a Durcan poem.' Is there a balance here or does this poem lean towards one or the other?

13. The critic Maurice Elliott, when discussing Durcan's changes of tone in musical terms, wrote about 'abrupt and rapid tonal changes in a series of surprises … which ultimately leave the reader or hearer on a note of tender and, most often, melancholy compassion'. Do you think this is true of 'Father's Day'? Explain how the shifts in tone work in this poem and describe the ultimate effect on the reader.

14. Do you think Durcan is attempting to question the traditional image of fathers here? If so, what is he saying about fathers?

THE ARNOLFINI MARRIAGE

after Jan Van Eyck

We are the Arnolfinis.
Do not think you may invade
Our privacy because you may not.

We are standing to our portrait,   5
The most erotic portrait ever made,
Because we have faith in the artist

To do justice to the plurality,
Fertility, domesticity, barefootedness
Of a man and a woman saying 'we':

To do justice to our bed   10
As being our most necessary furniture;
To do justice to our life as a reflection.

Our brains spill out upon the floor
And the terrier at our feet sniffs
The minutiae of our magnitude.   15

The most relaxing word in our vocabulary is 'we'.
Imagine being able to say 'we'.
Most people are in no position to say 'we'.

Are you? Who eat alone? Sleep alone?
And at dawn cycle to work   20
With an Alsatian shepherd dog tied to your handlebars?

We will pause now for the Angelus.
Here you have it:
The two halves of the coconut.

NOTES

Jan Van Eyck:

Jan Van Eyck was a Flemish painter (c.1395–c.1441) who worked in Bruges and was considered one of the most significant painters of the fifteenth century

The Arnolfini Marriage:

an oil painting on oak panel, dated 1434, by Jan Van Eyck. It is signed on the back wall of the picture, over the mirror: 'Johannes de eyck, fuit hic 1434' (Jan Van Eyck was here, 1434). And these are the only undisputed facts about the painting! It is also known by other titles: *The Arnolfini Portrait, The Arnolfini Wedding, The Arnolfini Double Portrait* and *Portrait of Giovanni Arnolfini and His Wife.*

The Arnolfinis were a wealthy Italian merchant clan who became merchant bankers in Bruges. There has been debate about which of the Arnolfinis is depicted and which of the wives. It is generally accepted to be a portrait of Giovanni di Nicolao Arnolfini and a wife. The picture has been variously considered to be an official portrait of a marriage, a portrait of a betrothal and even a memorial portrait of a deceased wife. The woman has been described as pregnant or merely holding up her heavy gown. The man's gesture may be a gesture of dismissal or a sign of welcome to the two people coming in, who are reflected in the mirror, one of whom is believed to be the painter.

There are many signs of wealth in the portrait: the expensive clothes, the bed (which was not unusual in the living quarters), the brass chandelier, the mirror (a rare domestic luxury) and even the oranges, which were rare and expensive. From an artistic point of view, it is generally agreed that the painting was remarkable for its time in the realistic depiction of the people and the room, in the use of detail and in the use of light to create a sense of space.

EXPLORATIONS

Before reading

1. First study the painting, discuss it and read the notes and other artistic comment on it. What impression of the Arnolfinis and their lifestyle do you form from viewing this painting? Write about this.

First reading

2. What trait or quality of the Arnolfinis does the poet choose to focus on in the first stanza? What elements in the painting could prompt him to this view?

3. Why do you think this is referred to as 'The most erotic portrait ever made'? Do you think it is?

4. In the poem, the Arnolfinis say they have faith in the artist 'To do justice to the plurality,/Fertility, domesticity, barefootedness/Of a man and a woman saying "we".'
   a What aspect of their lives do they wish recorded?
   b Do you think the painting does this effectively?

5. What other aspects of their lives do the Arnolfinis in the poem wish recorded in order to do them justice?

6. 'The most relaxing word in our vocabulary is "we"./Imagine being able to say "we"./Most people are in no position to say "we".'
   What do you think they may mean by this phenomenon, 'we'?

7. Then the Arnolfinis directly challenge the poet, asking if he has this perfect relationship: 'Are you?', etc. What image of the poet is painted here?

Second reading

8. a In creating this poem, Durcan has selected certain elements of the painting and ignored others. What aspects of the painting has he focused on?
   b Do you think the resulting poem makes a unified, coherent statement? Explain your thinking.
   c What interesting elements of the painting has he ignored?

9. Would you agree with critic Kathleen McCracken that Durcan 'often translates the "story" depicted on the canvas into a contemporary social or personal context'? Write about the poem from the perspective of this statement.

10. Now compose your own poem on the painting.

IRELAND 2002

Do you ever take a holiday abroad?
No, we always go to America.

EXPLORATIONS

1. What does this say to you about Irish people?

2. Can an overheard snatch of conversation be a poem?

3. What constitutes a poem?

4. What are you discovering about poetry from reading Paul Durcan?

ROSIE JOYCE

I

That was that Sunday afternoon in May
When a hot sun pushed through the clouds
And you were born!

I was driving the two hundred miles from west to east,
The sky blue-and-white china in the fields   5
In impromptu picnics of tartan rugs;

When neither words nor I
Could have known that you had been named already
And that your name was Rosie –

Rosie Joyce! May you some day in May   10
Fifty-six years from today be as lucky
As I was when you were born that Sunday:

To drive such side-roads, such main roads, such ramps, such roundabouts,
To cross such bridges, to by-pass such villages, such towns
As I did on your Incarnation Day.   15

By-passing Swinford – Croagh Patrick in my rear-view mirror –
My mobile phone rang and, stopping on the hard edge of P. Flynn's highway,
I heard Mark your father say:

'A baby girl was born at 3.33 p.m.
Weighing 7 and a ½ lbs in Holles Street.   20
Tough work, all well.'

II

That Sunday in May before daybreak
Night had pushed up through the slopes of Achill
Yellow forefingers of Arum Lily – the first of the year;

Down at the Sound the first rhododendrons   25
Purpling the golden camps of whins;
The first hawthorns powdering white the mainland;

The first yellow irises flagging roadside streams;
Quills of bog-cotton skimming the bogs;
Burrishoole cemetery shin-deep in forget-me-nots;   30

The first sea pinks speckling the seashore;
Cliffs of London Pride, groves of bluebell,
First fuchsia, Queen Anne's Lace, primrose.

I drove the Old Turlough Road, past Walter Durcan's Farm,
Umbrella'd in the joined handwriting of its ash trees;   35
I drove Tulsk, Kilmainham, the Grand Canal.

Never before had I felt so fortunate
To be driving back into Dublin City;
Each canal bridge an old pewter brooch.

I rode the waters and the roads of Ireland,   40
Rosie, to be with you, seashell at my ear!
How I laughed when I cradled you in my hand.

Only at Tarmonbarry did I slow down,
As in my father's Ford Anglia half a century ago
He slowed down also, as across the River Shannon   45

We crashed, rattled bounced on a Bailey bridge;
Daddy relishing his role as Moses,
Enunciating the name of the Great Divide

Between the East and the West!
We are the people of the West,   50
Our fate to go East.

No such thing, Rosie, as a Uniform Ireland
And please God there never will be;
There is only the River Shannon and all her sister rivers

And all her brother mountains and their family prospects.   55
There are higher powers than politics
And these we call wildflowers or, geologically, people.

Rosie Joyce – that Sunday in May
Not alone did you make my day, my week, my year
To the prescription of Jonathan Philbin Bowman –   60

Daymaker!
Daymaker!
Daymaker!

Popping out of my daughter, your mother –
Changing the expressions on the faces all around you –   65
All of them looking like blue hills in a heat haze –

But you saved my life. For three years
I had been subsisting in the slums of despair,
Unable to distinguish one day from the next.

                    III
On the return journey from Dublin to Mayo   70
In Charlestown on Main Street
I meet John Normanly, organic farmer from Curry.

He is driving home to his wife Caroline
From a Mountbellew meeting of the western Development Commission
Of Dillon House in Ballaghadereen.   75

He crouches in his car, I waver in the street,
As we exchange lullabies of expectancy;
We wet our foreheads in John Moriarty's autobiography.

The following Sunday is the Feast of the Ascension
Of Our Lord into Heaven: 80
Thank You, O Lord, for the Descent of Rosie onto Earth.

NOTES

15	Incarnation Day:	in the Christian religion, the Incarnation refers to when Jesus, as the Son of God, took human form ('became flesh'). The writer sees Rosie's birth as an incarnation.
16	Swinford:	a town in County Mayo
16	Croagh Patrick:	Cruach Phádraig (in Irish) is a mountain in County Mayo on which St Patrick is reputed to have fasted for forty days. Many pilgrims climb the mountain on the last Sunday of July (Reek Sunday).
17	P. Flynn's highway:	Padraig Flynn, a local politician and former Fianna Fáil Minister for the Environment. Presumably the reference is to a new road built in his constituency.
20	Holles Street:	a well-known maternity hospital in Dublin
23	Achill:	Achill Island, County Mayo
24	Arum Lily:	large, trumpet-shaped flowers
25	the Sound:	Achill Sound, a Gaeltacht village on the east side of Achill Island
25	rhododendrons:	evergreen shrubs with very large, usually pink flowers in May; grows wild in Mayo
26	whins:	a common, thorny, invasive bush that has bright yellow flowers in spring/summer; also called 'gorse' or 'furze'
27	hawthorn:	a thorny hedgerow shrub that produces clusters of white flowers in May and berries in winter
29	bog-cotton:	a plant of the sedge family that grows in wetland and produces white cotton balls on a long stem
30	Burrishoole cemetery:	is in Newport, County Mayo
31	sea pinks:	also known as thrift, an evergreen, grass-like plant that produces globes of pink flowers on long stalks all summer
32	London Pride:	an evergreen plant that bears pale-pink flowers on tall stalks all summer
33	fuchsia:	a shrub with bell-like flowers
33	Queen Anne's Lace:	a tall plant with long fern-like leaves and clusters of tiny white flowers that look like lace
34	Old Turlough Road:	is near Castlebar, County Mayo. Turlough was one of the places in which Durcan grew up.
36	Tulsk:	a village in County Roscommon
36	Kilmainham:	in Dublin 8, where the famous Kilmainham Gaol is located
36	the Grand Canal:	the southernmost of Dublin's two main canals
39	pewter:	a metal alloy of dull silver colour
39	brooch:	an ornamented hinged pin or clasp; formerly could refer to a necklace or bracelet
43	Tarmonbarry:	a village in County Roscommon on the banks of the River Shannon
44	Ford Anglia:	a popular British-made car. Four different models were produced between 1939 and 1967.

46	Bailey bridge:	a temporary, prefabricated bridge
47	Moses:	in the Old Testament story, Moses led the Jews out of slavery in Egypt and to the Holy Land that God had promised them. God parted the Red Sea to help them escape.
60–1	Jonathan Philbin Bowman/ *Daymaker*:	this reference is to the *A Living Word* programme recorded for RTÉ by the late Jonathan Philbin Bowman on 29 February 2000, in which he described how he received two fun, complimentary emails from different friends on a day he was feeling down. He replied as follows: 'You've just made my day. In fact I have a whole new word for you people. You're day makers.'
71	Charlestown:	a small town in County Mayo, which was the focus of a series of articles by the late John Healy. These were highly critical of government policies towards rural areas and were published in *The Irish Times* in the 1960s and 70s. These were later published in book form as *Death of an Irish Town* in 1968.
72	Curry:	a townland near Castlebar, County Mayo
74	Mountbellew:	a small town in County Galway and the site of a famous Agricultural College
75	Ballaghadereen:	a town in County Roscommon
78	we wet our foreheads:	a version of 'wetting the baby's head', i.e. having a drink to celebrate the birth
78	John Moriarty's autobiography:	the autobiography of the late Irish philosopher John Moriarty is entitled *Nostros*. Durcan called it 'one of the most remarkable autobiographies I have ever read in my life'.
79	Feast of the Ascension:	is celebrated on the 40th day after Easter Sunday and commemorates the Ascension of Christ into Heaven

EXPLORATIONS

First reading

Section I

1. Why do you think the speaker was driving 'two hundred miles from west to east' on that Sunday?

2. The speaker is highly energised and excited. How is this excitement conveyed?

3. The poet vividly records all the details of the journey. What is your reaction to this detail?

4. There is a spiritual or religious aspect to the poet's thinking on this journey. Discuss this.

5. a The high point of the drama comes in the final stanza of the section. Listen carefully to the content and the language of the mobile message. Do you think it is an effective piece of communication?

   b How does it contrast with the rest of section I?

Section II

6. The poet records, with a botanist's eye, the flora that signposts his journey. It is as if the entire countryside is giving birth.

a   Search for pictures of these flowers and plants on the internet. Which flowers and plants do you recognise?

b   What is the poet celebrating here?

7.   His reasons for this frantic journey become apparent in stanza 7 of this section.

a   What image of the speaker do you get from this stanza?

b   Do you think that this stanza communicates his love effectively? Write your opinions on this.

8.   This journey reminds him of the many such childhood journeys he made in the company of his father.

a   What was his father's sense of self-identity as an Irish person?

b   What impression of the father's personality do we get from the writer's brief vignette here?

9.   What concept of Irishness does the writer want Rosie to inherit?

10.   Focus on the final stanzas of this section (lines 58–69). The poet has already expressed his great love and affection for his granddaughter. In these stanzas he reveals yet another level of complexity for his joy. Explain this added significance of Rosie for him.

Section III

11.   As with all perfect journeys, this too is a circle. Do you think the writer is calmer on the way back? Explain your thinking.

12.   Consider the detail of the second to last stanza. Describe the atmosphere of the meeting with John Moriarty. Do you think this would be a typical conversation between farmers?

13.   How has the birth of Rosie Joyce affected the writer?

Second reading

14.   'This is a poem of pure joy and celebration.'
Write about everything that is celebrated in the poem.

15.   'The sense of place is important in Durcan's philosophy.'
Discuss this.

16.   Do you think this poem is infused with both the spirituality and ecology of Ireland?

17.   'The poem has all the qualities of a very good diary.'
Write your views on this.

THE MACBRIDE DYNASTY

What young mother is not a vengeful goddess
Spitting dynastic as well as motherly pride?
In 1949 in the black Ford Anglia,
Now that I had become a walking, talking little boy,
Mummy drove me out to visit my grand-aunt Maud Gonne   5
In Roebuck House in the Countryside near Dublin,
To show off to the servant of the Queen
The latest addition to the extended family.
Although the eighty-year-old Cathleen Ni Houlihan had taken to her bed
She was keen as ever to receive admirers,   10
Especially the children of the family.
Only the previous week the actor MacLiammóir
Had been kneeling at her bedside reciting Yeats to her,
His hand on his heart, clutching a red rose.
Cousin Seán and his wife Kid led the way up the stairs,   15
Seán opening the door and announcing my mother.
Mummy lifted me up in her arms as she approached the bed
And Maud leaned forward, sticking out her claws
To embrace me, her lizard eyes darting about
In the rubble of the ruins of her beautiful face.   20
Terrified, I recoiled from her embrace
And, fleeing her bedroom, ran down the stairs
Out onto the wrought-iron balcony
Until Seán caught up with me and quieted me
And took me for a walk in the walled orchard.   25
Mummy was a little but not totally mortified:
She had never liked Maud Gonne because of Maud's
Betrayal of her husband, Mummy's Uncle John,
Major John, most ordinary of men, most
Humorous, courageous of soldiers,   30
The pride of our family,
Whose memory always brought laughter
To my grandmother Eileen's lips. 'John,'
She used to cry, 'John was such a gay man.'
Mummy set great store by loyalty; loyalty   35
In Mummy's eyes was the cardinal virtue.
Maud Gonne was a disloyal wife
And, therefore, not worthy of Mummy's love.
For dynastic reasons we would tolerate Maud,
But we would always see through her.   40

NOTES NOTES

3	Ford Anglia:	a popular British-made car, produced from 1939 to 1967
5	grand-aunt Maud Gonne:	Maud Gonne (1865–1953; pictured) married Major John MacBride (brother of Joseph MacBride, Paul Durcan's maternal grandfather) in Paris in 1903. They had one son, Seán MacBride ('Cousin Seán'), but the marriage was short lived and the separation was acrimonious. MacBride returned to Dublin in 1905. Gonne raised their son in Paris and did not return to Ireland until 1917.
		Maud Gonne had been a famous beauty in her youth and was the inspiration for some of W. B. Yeats's poems. He was in love with her and asked her to marry him many times. She became heavily involved in Irish national and revolutionary politics. In 1902 she played the leading role in *Cathleen Ní Houlihan*, a play written by Yeats and Lady Gregory in which an older woman (an embodiment of Ireland) summons a young man to fight for Irish freedom.
		Gonne's autobiography, published in 1938, was entitled *A Servant of the Queen*, partly a reference to Cathleen Ní Houlihan and partly an ironic title, given her nationalist politics. She is buried in the Republican Plot in Glasnevin Cemetery.
12	MacLiammóir:	Micheál MacLiammóir (1899–1978) was an English-born Irish actor, dramatist, writer, poet and painter. With his partner, Hilton Edwards, he was co-founder, in 1928, of the Gate Theatre, Dublin. He is best remembered for his one-man show *The Importance of Being Oscar*, on the life and work of Oscar Wilde. A man of wit and humour, he was given to melodramatic poses and performances.

15	Cousin Seán:	Seán MacBride (1904–88) was the son of Major John MacBride and Maud Gonne. He was involved in republican politics from an early age, joining the Irish Volunteers in 1919. A member of the IRA, he was at one time Chief of Staff and was imprisoned many times. In 1925 he married Kid Bulfin. He had studied law in UCD and was called to the bar in 1937. He resigned from the IRA when the 1937 Constitution was enacted. He was Minister for External Affairs in the First Inter-Party Government of 1948. He played leading roles in many international organisations, including the Council of Europe, the United Nations and Amnesty International. In 1974 he received the Nobel Peace Prize.
28	Mummy's Uncle John:	Paul Durcan's mother, Sheila MacBride, was a niece of Major John MacBride (1868–1916). From Westport in County Mayo, MacBride became a member of the Irish Republican Brotherhood. He went to South Africa, fought in the second Boer War against the British and was given the rank of major in the Boer Army. As already noted, he married Maud Gonne. He was second in command to Thomas Mac Donagh at Jacob's Factory in the 1916 Rebellion and was executed on 5 May in the aftermath.
33	Eileen:	Paul Durcan's maternal grandmother, Eileen, married Joseph MacBride

EXPLORATIONS

First reading

1. What connotations does the term 'dynasty' have for you?

2. 'What young mother is not a vengeful goddess/Spitting dynastic as well as motherly pride?'
Examine the language carefully. What does it suggest about the tone or atmosphere of the upcoming visit?

3. 'She was keen as ever to receive admirers'.
Comment on the writer's choice of words here. What does it suggest about his attitude to Maud Gonne?

4. 'Only the previous week the actor MacLiammóir/Had been kneeling at her bedside reciting Yeats to her,/His hand on his heart, clutching a red rose.'

a What does this add to the picture of Maud Gonne that is being developed here?

b What poem do you think he may have recited?

5. 'Cousin Seán and his wife Kid led the way up the stairs,/Seán opening the door and announcing my mother.'
How would you describe the atmosphere here? What does it convey about the household of Maud Gonne?

6. The young boy is obviously frightened by the figure of the old woman in the bed. Do you think this is a less than kind description of her? Discuss this.

7. Why was Mummy only 'a little but not totally mortified'?

8. Examine the character portrait of Major John MacBride that

is described here. How is he remembered and whose viewpoint is it?

9. Explain Mummy's attitude to Maud Gonne.

10. 'For dynastic reasons we would tolerate Maud,/But we would always see through her.'
What do you think the writer means by this?

Second reading

11. Consider the title again. Do you think it is an apt one for the poem? Explain your thinking.

12. Consider again the first two lines. From your reading of the poem, describe what these lines mean to you now.

13. How is Maud Gonne portrayed in this poem? Write about this, with reference to the details.

14. a   Would you agree that the portrayal of Maud Gonne is unashamedly biased? Where does this bias show?
    b   How would you describe the tone of the portrayal?

15. What impression of 'Mummy' do you get from the poem?

16. What insight into the nature of clans or dynasties do we get from a reading of this poem?

17. 'One of the most effective technical features of this poem is the realistic, almost photographic detail of some images.'
Write about this.

ROBERT HERRICK

(1591 – 1674)

Robert Herrick was born in London in 1591. His father died when he was only one year old. He was apprenticed to his uncle, a goldsmith, when he was sixteen but he left the apprenticeship when he was twenty-two and matriculated in Cambridge. Herrick turned to the priesthood and was ordained in 1623 and became vicar of Dean Prior in 1629. After the Civil War he was ejected from his vicarage due to his support for the royalists. Following the restoration of the monarchy he was restored to his vicarage where he lived until he died in 1674. He wrote over 2,500 poems in his lifetime. His major publication was *Hesperides or: The Works both Humane and Divine* (1648).

Influenced by the writings of Ben Jonson, Herrick's works use simple language to capture certain truths. Herrick's philosophy was simply that life was short and one should use one's time wisely. This *Carpe Diem* or 'seize the day' attitude can be seen in this poem.

OL 2019

OL 2020

TO DAFFODILS

Fair daffodils, we weep to see
    You haste away so soon;
As yet the early-rising sun
    Has not attain'd his noon.
      Stay, stay,   5
    Until the hasting day
      Has run
    But to the even-song;
And, having pray'd together, we
    Will go with you along.   10

We have short time to stay, as you,
    We have as short a spring;
As quick a growth to meet decay,
    As you, or any thing.
      We die   15
    As your hours do, and dry
      Away,
    Like to the summer's rain;
Or as the pearls of morning's dew,
    Ne'er to be found again.   20

NOTE

| 8 | even-song | evening service of prayers and songs in the Anglican church |

EXPLORATIONS

First reading

1. What words, images or feelings do you associate with daffodils?

2. Does the poet capture anything of the physical aspects of the daffodil in this poem?

3. What aspect of the daffodil does he focus on? Does this make the poem negative or positive in your opinion? What words or phrases support your opinion?

4. What do you think is the central message of the second stanza?

5. What images does the poet use to reinforce this message?

Second reading

6. What do you notice about the length of the lines in the poem? How do they vary? What effect might the poet have been aiming to achieve?

7. How does the rhyming scheme reflect the variation in line length?

8. Write a brief note on the structure of the poem.

9. Identify some contrasting images of growth and death in the poem. What effect do they have in your opinion?

Third reading

10. Write a letter to Robert Herrick outlining your response to his poem.

11. In which of the following collections do you think this poem belongs:

- a collection of poetry about nature
- a collection of poetry about life
- a collection of poetry about death.

   Explain your answer with reference to the poem.

GEORGE HERBERT

(1593–1633)

George Herbert was a Welsh-born poet and orator. Educated at Cambridge, he became a member of parliament in 1624 but turned away from that public life when he took holy orders and became a priest in 1629. He married Jane Danvers and was made rector of a small parish near Salisbury. He died in 1633 of consumption. He is classed as one of the metaphysical poets, a term coined by Samuel Johnson when describing the works of notable poets of this time. The poems of the metaphysical poets had several features in common such as an elaborate use of wit, a questioning of reality, a religious sentimentality and an awareness of poetic form. However, unlike other poetic movements, the metaphysical poets were unaware of the classification, or even each other's writings, during their lifetimes.

This poem is striking in its typographical layout. This style of poetry had been common among the ancient Greek poets but had a brief revival in the early seventeenth century with the renewed interest in ancient writings.

EASTER WINGS

OL 2021

Lord, who createdst man in wealth and store,
    Though foolishly he lost the same,
        Decaying more and more,
           Till he became
              Most poor: 5
              With thee
           O let me rise
        As larks, harmoniously,
    And sing this day thy victories:
Then shall the fall further the flight in me.   10

My tender age in sorrow did begin:
    And still with sicknesses and shame.
        Thou didst so punish sin,
           That I became
              Most thin.   15
              With thee
           Let me combine,
        And feel this day thy victory:
    For, if I imp my wing on thine,
Affliction shall advance the flight in me.   20

NOTES

I	createdst:	archaic form of 'who created'
19	imp my wing:	to mend a broken feather by attaching part of a new feather

EXPLORATIONS

First reading

1. What strikes you about the structure of this poem on the page? What does it look like? How do you think it relates to the title?

2. What does Easter celebrate? What might this mean for Herbert (a priest)?

3. In the first stanza, what do you notice about the first four lines? How do they echo what the poet is writing about?

4. How does the poet use rhyme in the poem?

Second reading

5. How do the words and images in the second stanza echo the first stanza?

6. Does the poem resemble a prayer? In what ways?

7. How does the poet use the images of flight in the poem? What effect do they have? What do you think the poet is trying to capture?

8. 'Though foolishly he lost the same.' What do you think the poet means by this?

Third reading

9. What effect does the poet's use of alliteration have on the poem? Support your answer with examples from the poem.

10. Write a brief note about the poet's religious beliefs as outlined in the poem.

11. Do you like or dislike the poem? In your response identify at least two aspects of the poem that influenced your view.

SAMUEL TAYLOR COLERIDGE

(1772–1834)

Samuel Taylor Coleridge was born in 1772, the youngest of fourteen children. His father was a vicar and master of the local grammar school. After his father's sudden death in 1781, Coleridge went to London to finish his secondary education and went from there to Cambridge. He never finished his degree but instead made plans with another poet in Bristol to start an egalitarian commune in America. He entered into an unhappy marriage with a local girl, Sarah Fricker. He met William Wordsworth and his sister Dorothy and by 1798 they jointly published a collection of poems called *Lyrical Ballads*. These poems formed the basis of the Romantic Movement in poetry.

The Romantic poets turned to nature as the source of all creative spark and praised the pastoral over the urban. They sought to capture great emotional feeling but also to contain it within strict rhyme and metre. They also added supernatural elements and a dash of melancholy to their descriptions of the natural world.

This poem contains many of these Romantic elements. Coleridge wrote the poem in 1797 but it remained unfinished and unpublished until 1816. When he did publish the poem he included a preface that outlined how it had been written. He claimed that he had taken laudanum (an opium substance) for an illness and had dreamed the entire poem. When he awoke he started to write it down but was interrupted by a visitor and by the time he left Coleridge could only remember parts of the poem. The poem retains this fragmentary, dream-like quality.

Suffering from many neuralgic and rheumatic disorders during his life, Coleridge developed an addiction to opium. He continued to write, not only poetry, but also literary criticism and philosophy, until his death in 1834.

KUBLA KHAN

Or, a vision in a dream. A Fragment.

In Xanadu did Kubla Khan
A stately pleasure-dome decree:
Where Alph, the sacred river, ran
Through caverns measureless to man
Down to a sunless sea.   5
So twice five miles of fertile ground
With walls and towers were girdled round;
And there were gardens bright with sinuous rills,
Where blossom'd many an incense-bearing tree;
And here were forests ancient as the hills,   10
Enfolding sunny spots of greenery.

But oh! that deep romantic chasm which slanted
Down the green hill athwart a cedarn cover!
A savage place! as holy and enchanted
As e'er beneath a waning moon was haunted   15
By woman wailing for her demon-lover!
And from this chasm, with ceaseless turmoil seething,
As if this earth in fast thick pants were breathing,
A mighty fountain momently was forced:
Amid whose swift half-intermitted burst   20
Huge fragments vaulted like rebounding hail,
Or chaffy grain beneath the thresher's flail:
And 'mid these dancing rocks at once and ever
It flung up momently the sacred river.
Five miles meandering with a mazy motion   25
Through wood and dale the sacred river ran,
Then reached the caverns measureless to man,
And sank in tumult to a lifeless ocean;
And 'mid this tumult Kubla heard from far
Ancestral voices prophesying war!   30
  The shadow of the dome of pleasure
  Floated midway on the waves;
  Where was heard the mingled measure
  From the fountain and the caves.
It was a miracle of rare device,   35
A sunny pleasure-dome with caves of ice!

  A damsel with a dulcimer
  In a vision once I saw:

It was an Abyssinian maid
And on her dulcimer she play'd,   40
Singing of Mount Abora.
Could I revive within me
Her symphony and song,

To such a deep delight 'twould win me,
That with music loud and long,   45
I would build that dome in air,
That sunny dome! those caves of ice!
And all who heard should see them there,
And all should cry, Beware! Beware!
His flashing eyes, his floating hair!   50
Weave a circle round him thrice,
And close your eyes with holy dread
For he on honey-dew hath fed,
And drunk the milk of Paradise.

Kubla Khan hunting with a falcon, miniature from a fifteenth-century manuscript,
Book of the Wonders of the World

NOTES

1	Xanadu:	otherwise known as Shangdu, the summer palace of Kublai Khan's Yuan dynasty in China
1	Kubla Khan:	Kublai Khan, Mongolian Emperor (1215–1294), grandson of Genghis Khan
3	Alph:	fictional river
7	girdled:	to encircle
8	sinuous:	twisting and turning
12	chasm:	a deep fissure in the earth, gorge, gully
13	athwart:	from side to side, across
22	chaffy:	like husks of corn, worthless things
28	tumult:	loud noisy chaos
37	dulcimer:	musical stringed instrument
39	Abyssinian:	from Abyssinia, ancient name for Ethiopia

EXPLORATIONS

First reading

1. Describe, in your own words, the scene outlined by the poet in the first stanza.

2. How does the poet give the impression of an opulent, extravagant palace?

3. In the second stanza how does the poet capture the power of nature?

4. What elements of the supernatural are included in this stanza? What effect do they have on the poem?

5. In the final stanza the poet talks about himself. What vision does he have?

Second reading

6. Read the first stanza aloud. How does the poet use sound and rhythm in the first stanza?

7. Does the rhythm change? What effect do you think the poet was trying to capture?

8. A fountain was often used a symbol for creativity. How would this interpretation of the fountain and river suit the poem? What might the poet be trying to say?

Third reading

9. The poem is described as a fragment or vision. What elements of the poem make it sound dream-like or fragmentary?

10. What images in the poem stand out to you? Support your explanation with reference to the poem.

11. Identify examples of alliteration and assonance in the poem.

12. Write a paragraph on the poet's use of language in the poem.

13. Imagine that you have been asked to make a short YouTube video to accompany a reading of this poem. Describe some of the images, colours, music, sound effects, etc. that you would use as a background to the reading and explain your choices, based on your knowledge of the poem.

PERCY
BYSSHE SHELLEY

(1792–1822)

The son of an English country gentleman, Shelley was educated at Eton and Oxford, where he spent a rebellious and unhappy youth. Revolutionary in thought, he was anti-religious and anti-monarchy and wrote and spoke publicly on the need for radical social and political reforms. He felt it was the role of the poet to be prophetic and visionary. He lived a fairly unconventional family life, much of it in Italy, where the Shelleys seemed dogged by illness and death. It was here that he wrote some of his best-known poems, such as 'Stanzas Written in Dejection Near Naples', 'Ode to the West Wind', 'Ode to a Skylark' and 'Prometheus Unbound'.

OL 2021

OZYMANDIAS

I met a traveller from an antique land
Who said: Two vast and trunkless legs of stone
Stand in the desert … Near them, on the sand,
Half sunk, a shattered visage lies, whose frown,
And wrinkled lip, and sneer of cold command,   5
Tell that its sculptor well those passions read
Which yet survive, stamped on these lifeless things,
The hand that mocked them, and the heart that fed:
And on the pedestal these words appear:
'My name is Ozymandias, king of kings: 10
Look on my works, ye Mighty, and despair!'
Nothing beside remains. Round the decay
Of that colossal wreck, boundless and bare
The lone and level sands stretch far away.

NOTES

Ozymandias:		another name for Pharaoh Ramses II of Egypt (thirteenth century BC), whose great tomb at Thebes was shaped like a sphinx. It was the historian Diodorus the Sicilian who first referred to it as the tomb of Ozymandias.
1	antique:	ancient
4	visage:	face
8	The hand that mocked:	the hand that imitated, referring to the hand of the sculptor
8	the heart that fed:	the king's heart, which gave life to these qualities and passions that were captured in stone by the sculptor

EXPLORATIONS

First reading

1. The poem is in the form of a narrative or story told by a traveller who had been to 'an antique land'. What suggestions and pictures does this phrase conjure up for you?

2. a What did the traveller actually see, as reported in lines 2–4?
   b What is your first reaction to this scene: interesting, pathetic, grotesque or something else?
   c Why do you think he might consider this worth reporting?

3. Where is this scene? What impressions of the land do we get?

4. Does the poet tell us the name of the place? Why do you think this is?

Second reading

5. What do we learn of the king from this sculpture: his qualities, character traits, etc.?

6. Do you think Shelley appreciates the sculptor's skill? Explain.

7. Relate lines 4–8 in your own words and as simply as possible.

Third reading

The sestet

8. What was your own reflection on reading the words on the pedestal?

9. a Explore the final two and a half lines. What do you see? Really look.
   b What atmosphere is created here?
   c What statement do you think is being made?

10. What do you think this poem is saying about human endeavour and about power? Explain with reference to specific phrases, etc.

11. Consider the imagery. Do you think the imagery is appropriate to the theme? Explain. What pictures do you find most effective?

Fourth reading

12. How does the poet make use of irony to communicate his theme? Do you find this effective?

13. Would you agree that this poem embodies Shelley's view that the poet should really be a kind of prophet or wise person in society? Discuss this with reference to the text.

14. What features of the sonnet do you notice in the poem? Do you think it is a good sonnet?

15. Do you think this poem was worth reading? Why or why not?

ELIZABETH
BARRETT BROWNING

(1806–1861)

lizabeth Barrett Browning was born in County Durham in 1806. She wrote poetry from a very young age, the first at around six years of age. Her mother collected her early works and later published them. Her family had originally become wealthy through their plantations in Jamaica but, during her life Elizabeth wrote repeatedly on the injustice of slavery and campaigned against child labour. By 1844 she had published several volumes of poetry and had been introduced into the London literary scene. She was popular in Britain and the Unites States and captured the attention of a young poet, Robert Browning.

Robert Browning wrote to Elizabeth and they began a secret affair as her father forbade his children from marrying. After her marriage to Robert in 1846, Elizabeth's father disinherited her and she was estranged from her brothers. The couple settled in Italy and had one son. In 1850 she was in contention for the position of Poet Laureate after the death of Wordsworth but the position went to Coleridge. She had suffered from illness throughout her life and took laudanum (an opium substance) for the pain. She died in 1861 in Italy.

OL 2019

OL 2020

HOW DO I LOVE THEE? (SONNET 43)

How do I love thee? Let me count the ways.
I love thee to the depth and breadth and height
My soul can reach, when feeling out of sight
For the ends of Being and ideal Grace.
I love thee to the level of every day's   5
Most quiet need, by sun and candlelight.
I love thee freely, as men strive for Right;
I love thee purely, as they turn from Praise.
I love thee with the passion put to use
In my old griefs, and with my childhood's faith.   10
I love thee with a love I seemed to lose
With my lost saints, – I love thee with the breath,
Smiles, tears, of all my life! – and, if God choose,
I shall but love thee better after death.

NOTES

2	breadth:	width or wide range
4	ideal Grace:	a state of spiritual fulfilment

EXPLORATIONS

First reading

1. Can you measure love? Think of ways you have tried to express how much you love something or someone. Do the words come close to what you are trying to capture?

2. The poet starts with words that are used for measurement. What effect does this have on the poem? Does she find the words satisfactory?

3. Why do you think the poet repeats the phrase 'I love thee' throughout the poem? What effect does this have?

Second reading

4. How does the poet try to capture the timelessness of her love? What words or phrases give you this impression?

5. The poet uses alliterative phrases throughout the poem. Identify some of these phrases and explain what effect they have on the poem.

6. What do you think the poet means by the final line in the poem?

Third reading

7. How does the poet use the sonnet structure in this poem? Compare how the thoughts change from the first and second quatrain (four lines) to the last sestet (six lines).

8. Imagine you are the poet's husband, Robert Browning. How would you feel if you received this poem? Write a letter to Elizabeth in response to her sonnet.

9. This poem has been shortlisted for a book of love poems. Write to the judges outlining why you think this poem should or should not be included in the collection.

ROBERT BROWNING

(1812–1889)

Robert Browning was born in Surrey in 1812. The son of a Bank of England clerk, he wrote his first book of poems, which he later destroyed, by age twelve. He was fluent in French, Greek, Italian and Latin and wrote poems, plays and dramatic dialogues over the course of his career. He wrote to Elizabeth Barrett in 1845 outlining his admiration for her poetry and the pair began a secretive courtship due to the disapproval of Elizabeth's father. They were married in 1846 and lived most of their married lives in Italy. They had one son together, Robert, who was affectionately called 'Pen'.

After her death in 1861, Robert returned to London and continued writing. He was awarded honorary degrees from Oxford and University of Edinburgh. His final book of verse was published on the day of his death in 1889.

OL 2021

MEETING AT NIGHT

I

The grey sea and the long black land;
And the yellow half-moon large and low;
And the startled little waves that leap
In fiery ringlets from their sleep,
As I gain the cove with pushing prow,   5
And quench its speed i' the slushy sand.

II

Then a mile of warm sea-scented beach;
Three fields to cross till a farm appears;
A tap at the pane, the quick sharp scratch
And blue spurt of a lighted match,   10
And a voice less loud, thro' its joys and fears,
Than the two hearts beating each to each!

NOTES

4	ringlets:	a lock of hair in a corkscrew curl
5	prow:	front of a boat

EXPLORATIONS

First reading

1. Describe in your own words the events of the poem.

2. What words or phrases capture the scene at sea?

3. How does the poet capture the movement from the beach to the farmhouse?

4. What words or phrases imply that the visit is a secret?

Second reading

5. What senses does the poet capture in the poem? Identify the words and phrases that capture these senses.

6. 'Than the two hearts beating, each to each!'
   What do you think the poet means in this line?

7. What emotions do you think the speaker in the poem is experiencing? What words or phrases give you this impression?

Third reading

8. What typical romantic imagery is used in this poem? Does the poet use it in a unique way?

9. Imagine you are the person waiting in the farmhouse. Write a diary entry describing the same event from your point of view.

10. Write a brief paragraph on the poet's use of descriptive language in this poem.

WILLIAM CARLOS WILLIAMS

(1883–1963)

The early poetic work of William Carlos Williams shows the influence of two of the major poets of the twentieth century, Ezra Pound and T. S. Eliot. However, he eventually felt limited by this and searched for an authentic American expression in poetry. He found this in writing about commonplace objects and the lives of ordinary people. In this way, he managed to bring out the significance of people and things we might otherwise take for granted. Williams has been an inspiration for some major poets, particularly Allen Ginsberg.

His output includes stories and plays as well as his five well-known books of poetry.

OL 2022

THIS IS JUST TO SAY

I have eaten
the plums
that were in
the icebox

and which   5
you were probably
saving
for breakfast

Forgive me
they were delicious   10
so sweet
and so cold

EXPLORATIONS

Before reading

1. Imagine that you have just eaten a large, and very delicious, bar of chocolate that your best friend had been saving to eat at lunchtime. Write a short note to explain what happened and to apologise for what you have done. You might like to read aloud some of the notes written by the class and discuss the various approaches taken.

First reading

2. a While you were reading 'This is just to say', did you notice any differences between the poem and your piece of writing?

   b Which of the two pieces do you think works better as an explanation and an apology? Give reasons for your answer.

3. a In your own words, summarise the main point that Williams makes in each of the three stanzas of this poem.

   b Do you think he has the points in the best sequence in order to gain forgiveness or would you rearrange the sequence?

4. Williams breaks up his message into very short phrases written on separate lines with no punctuation. Experiment with reading this poem aloud to see what effect this has on the pace, or speed, that should be used when reading this poem and the tone of voice.

Second reading

5. a Williams rarely uses capital letters in his poetry, so there are only two capital letters employed in this poem: 'I' and 'Forgive'. Why do you think he decided to use capital letters for these particular words?

   b Do these words help you to explain what the theme of this poem is? Explain your answer.

6. 'Forgive me/they were delicious/so sweet/and so cold'

   a Alliteration is when two or more words close together begin with the same letter. Can you pick out Williams's use of alliteration in this stanza?

   b In what ways does his use of alliteration help you to imagine how the plums tasted?

   c Why do you think he emphasises how 'delicious' the plums were in his message?

Third reading

7. Which one of the following statements do you think best describes Williams's motivation for writing this poem?

   • He wanted to leave a note reminding the person to buy more plums.

   • He felt guilty about eating the plums but was too embarrassed to speak to the person who had put the plums in the icebox.

   • He wanted to show the person who had put the plums in the icebox that he was genuinely sorry

by leaving the poem as a gift to
make up for the missing plums.

8.   a   If you received this poem,
        would you forgive Williams?
        Why or why not?
    b   Write a short reply to Williams
        explaining how you feel.

9.   Williams said of his poetry, 'I try to
say it straight, whatever is to be said'.
In what ways could this poem be
said to be a 'straight' piece of writing?
You might like to consider (a) the
language he uses; (b) the form of the
poem and (c) the theme.

10. a   This poem, including the title,
       consists of thirty-three words.
       Do you think this piece is too
       short to be a poem?
    b   In your view, what turns a
       piece of writing into a poem?
       Is it the language, the use
       of rhyme, the emotions
       expressed or something else?

FRANCIS
LEDWIDGE

(1887–1917)

rancis Ledwidge was born, the eighth of nine children, in Slane, County Meath. His father died when he was four and Francis had to leave school at the age of fourteen to find work to help to support his family. He played an active part in his local community, both culturally, setting up the Slane Drama Group, and politically, joining the local labour union and the Irish Volunteers

From an early age, Ledwidge enjoyed writing poetry to entertain his friends and he worked hard at developing his poetic skills. Lord Dunsany was so impressed by his work that he introduced Ledwidge to the Dublin literary scene, which included such writers as W. B. Yeats and Thomas MacDonagh. Although Ledwidge was a nationalist, he joined the British army in 1914 shortly after World War I began.

There are some suggestions that he did this because he had been disappointed in love, but Francis himself wrote, 'I joined the British army because she stood between Ireland and an enemy common to our civilization.' However, his attitude changed following the execution of the 1916 leaders, when he declared, 'if someone were to tell me that the Germans were coming over our back wall, I wouldn't lift a finger to stop them'. Nevertheless, he courageously fought on with the British army through the horrors of the war until he was killed by an exploding shell near Ypres, in Belgium.

LAMENT FOR THOMAS MACDONAGH

OL 2
OL 2

He shall not hear the bittern cry
In the wild sky, where he is lain,
Nor voices of the sweeter birds
Above the wailing of the rain.

Nor shall he know when loud March blows   5
Thro' slanting snows her fanfare shrill,
Blowing to flame the golden cup
Of many an upset daffodil.

But when the Dark Cow leaves the moor
And pastures poor with greedy weeds,   10
Perhaps he'll hear her low at morn
Lifting her horn in pleasant meads.

NOTES

	Thomas MacDonagh:	one of the leaders of the 1916 Easter Rising, also a teacher, a poet and a playwright. He was imprisoned and executed in Kilmainham Jail. Because the British authorities were anxious that the funerals and graves of the 1916 leaders might increase anti-British feeling, his body, along with those of the other leaders, was buried in Arbour Hill Cemetery, the cemetery for British soldiers from the nearby Royal Barracks. This is now Collins Barracks where the National Museum is located.
1	bittern:	a type of large brown heron. The males have a loud, booming mating call. Thomas MacDonagh translated an eighteenth-century Irish poem, 'An Bonnán Buí', into English under the title 'The Yellow Bittern'.
6	fanfare:	a sounding of trumpets during a ceremony
9	Dark Cow:	a secret name for Ireland used by Irish people in the eighteenth century when the country was under British rule
10	pastures:	grassy lands used for grazing animals
12	meads:	meadows, an area of grassland often used for hay

EXPLORATIONS

First reading

1. a   Take it in turns to sum up in one sentence how this poem made you feel. Begin with the phrase 'This poem made me feel …'. List each feeling on the board.

   b   What feeling did the majority of the class experience when they read this poem for the first time?

2. a   Choose one phrase or line in the poem that makes you feel the emotion that you named in Question 1.

   b   Explain why the line or phrase makes you feel this way.

3.   From the phrases below, choose two that, in your opinion, best describe the language used in this poem:

   • It is difficult to understand.

   • It is easy to understand.

   • It describes images (word-pictures) that I can imagine easily.

   • It describes images that I find it difficult to imagine.

   Explain your choice of phrases by reference to the poem.

Second reading

4. a   In stanzas 1 and 2 (lines 1–8), the poet describes some of the experiences that Thomas MacDonagh will no longer have because he is dead. In your own words, explain what these experiences are.

   b   What senses does the poet appeal to in his descriptions of these experiences?

5. a   How would you describe the mood (feelings and atmosphere) in lines 1–8? Give reasons for your answer based on your reading of these lines.

   b   Do you think the images the poet uses in lines 1–8 convey the mood in a way that is easy to understand? Why?

6. a   In stanza 3 (lines 9–12), the poet describes the 'Dark Cow', a secret name for Ireland in the eighteenth century. What do you think Ledwidge is hoping will happen to Ireland when he refers to the 'Dark Cow' moving to 'pleasant meads'?

   b   Based on your answer to part (a), can you suggest what Ledwidge hopes that Thomas MacDonagh will know about, even though he is dead, in the final two lines of the poem?

   c   Do you think the mood of lines 9–12 is different to the mood of lines 1–8? Why? Refer to the poem in support of your answer.

7.   Look back at the feeling that the majority of the class experienced when they read this poem for the first time. Based on your work for Questions 5 and 6, do you agree that this majority feeling describes the mood of the whole poem? Or do you think that you need to add in another feeling? Explain your answer with reference to the poem.

Third reading

8. a   Working in pairs with one of you as the reporter and the other as Francis Ledwidge, imagine that you are interviewing Francis Ledwidge. From your reading of the poem, write out the answers that you both think he would give to the following questions:

   •   How do you feel about Thomas MacDonagh's death?

   •   What do you think about where he was buried?

   •   What is your attitude to Ireland becoming an independent country?

   •   Why do you hope that Thomas MacDonagh might somehow know when Irish freedom is achieved?

   b   As a class, listen to some of the interviews and discuss whether you agree or disagree with the answers that are given.

9.   Do you think a reader of this poem needs to know the historical facts that it refers to (for example, what happened to Thomas MacDonagh in 1916 and what the 'Dark Cow' stands for) in order to understand fully what the poet is trying to express? Explain your view and support it by reference to the poem.

10.   This poem was written about 100 years ago. Do you think it should be studied by Irish students in the twenty-first century? Why or why not?

GABRIELA MISTRAL

(1889–1957)

Gabriela Mistral was the pseudonym of the Chilean poet Lucila Godoy y Alcayaga. Born in Chile in 1889, she was of Basque, Spanish and Indian descent. She published some of her early poems in 1904 and won a national literary contest in 1914. Passionate about democratising education, in 1922 Mistral moved to Mexico and worked with the Minister of Education to reform the libraries and set up a national education system. She also worked with the League of Nations in the 1920s and became Chilean consul in Naples, Madrid and Lisbon. She travelled extensively and received honorary degrees from the Universities of Florence and Guatemala. She also lectured in Spanish literature in universities in the United States and Puerto Rico.

Her life was laced with tragedy. Her father, who had been estranged from the family since she was three, died in 1911. Her lover, Romelio Ureta, a railway employee, committed suicide in 1909. Her nephew, whom she regarded as a son, also committed suicide aged 17 in 1943.

Her first collection of poetry, *Sonetos de la Muerte* (love poems for the dead), was published in 1914. 'Let Him Not Grow Up' comes from a collection called *Ternura* (Tenderness) published in 1924.

Mistral was awarded the Nobel Prize in literature in 1945 for 'her lyric poetry which, inspired by powerful emotions, has made her name a symbol of the idealistic aspirations of the entire Latin American world'. She died in 1957 in Hempstead, New York.

Ursula Le Guin, the translator, is an American author known primarily for her science fiction and fantasy novels. She has won numerous awards including the Nebula and Hugo awards. Her most famous work is the *Earthsea* fantasy series of novels.

LET HIM NOT GROW UP

(translated by Ursula Le Guin)

May my little boy
stay just as he is.
He didn't suck my milk
in order to grow up.
A child's not an oak   5
or a ceiba tree.
Poplars, meadow grasses,
things like that grow tall.
My little boy
can stay a mallow-flower.   10

   He has all he needs,
laughter, frowns, skills,
airs and graces.
He doesn't need to grow.

   If he grows they'll all come   15
winking at him,
worthless women
making him shameless,
or all the big boys
that come by the house.   20
Let my little boy see no monsters coming.

   May his five summers
be all he knows.
Just as he is
he can dance and be happy.   25
May his birthdays fit
in the length of a yardstick,
all his Easters
and his Christmas Eves.

   Silly women,   30
don't cry. Listen:
the Sun and the stones
are born and don't grow,
they never get older,
they last forever.   35
In the sheepfold

kids and lambs
grow up and die:
be damned to them!

  O my Lord, stop him,   40
make him stop growing!
Stop him and save him,
don't let my son die!

NOTES

6	ceiba tree:	species of large tree common in tropical countries such as central and south America
10	mallow-flower:	small plant used a lot in traditional medicines, only grows to less than three feet tall
27	yardstick:	stick used for measuring lengths up to a yard (three feet) or 0.9 metres

EXPLORATIONS

First reading

1. What does the poet wish for her son?

2. What reasons does she give for this?

3. What does she compare him to? Why do you think she uses these comparisons?

4. In the third stanza, what is she afraid will happen if he grows up?

5. In the fourth stanza, what aspects of childhood does she focus on? In your opinion, why do you think she chooses these moments?

6. In the fifth stanza, what point does she make about the sun and stones? Do you think this is relevant for a child?

Second reading

7. What is revealed as her main concern in the last stanza?

8. Does this contradict what she has said so far in the poem?

9. 'Let my little boy see no monsters coming.'
   What do you think the poet means by this line?

10. What, do you think, is the symbolic importance of 'the kids and lambs'?

Third reading

11. Imagine you are the son in the poem. Write a response to Gabriela Mistral's poem from your perspective.

12. The poem is full of emotion and contradictions. Write a brief note on the poet's tone and mood in this poem.

13. Do you like or dislike this poem? Give reasons for your answer using reference to the poem.

W. H. AUDEN

(1907–73)

Wystan Hugh Auden was born in York on 21 February 1907 and educated at Oxford and Berlin. He is considered one of the most important English poets of the 1930s, writing on political and social themes. A prolific poet, he wrote in a variety of verse forms, composing both humorous and serious poetry. 'Funeral Blues', originally a song in one of his plays, is taken from the volume *Another Time* (1940), which contains many of his best-known poems, such as 'September 1939' and 'Lullaby'. Auden spent much of his life in the United States, becoming an American citizen in 1946.

OL 2
OL 2

FUNERAL BLUES

Stop all the clocks, cut off the telephone,
Prevent the dog from barking with a juicy bone,
Silence the pianos and with muffled drum
Bring out the coffin, let the mourners come.

Let aeroplanes circle moaning overhead   5
Scribbling on the sky the message He Is Dead,
Put crêpe bows round the white necks of the public doves,
Let the traffic policemen wear black cotton gloves.

He was my North, my South, my East and West,
My working week and my Sunday rest,   10
My noon, my midnight, my talk, my song;
I thought that love would last for ever: I was wrong.

The stars are not wanted now: put out every one;
Pack up the moon and dismantle the sun;
Pour away the ocean and sweep up the wood.   15
For nothing now can ever come to any good.

EXPLORATIONS

First reading

1. What images grab your attention?

2. What do you think is happening in this poem?

3. Do you find it unusual in any way? Explain.

Second reading

4. The first two stanzas create the atmosphere of a funeral. What sights and sounds of a funeral do you notice?

5. It used to be the custom that clocks were stopped in a house where a death had occurred. As well as marking the time of death, this signified that time stood still for the grieving family. Do you think the signs of mourning have been carried to extremes in the first two stanzas? Examine the actions called for.

6. How do you think the first stanza should be read: in a low, defeated tone, semi-hysterical or something else? Read it aloud.

7. Read the second stanza aloud.

8. Do you think there might be a change of tone from the third stanza on? Read stanzas 3–4 aloud.

9. Are you sympathetic to the speaker in this poem?

Third reading

10. What does the third stanza suggest about the relationship between the speaker and the person mourned? Examine each line in detail for the kernel of truth behind the clichés.

11. How do you understand the speaker's state of mind, particularly in the last verse?

12. a Do you take this poem to be a serious statement about loss and bereavement or do you find it exaggerated and over the top? Explain your opinion.

    b Do you think it could be read as a satire, i.e. a poem ridiculing, in this case, the public outpouring of emotion at the funerals of famous people? Read the poem again.

Fourth reading

13. What do you think the poem is saying?

14. Look at the imagery again. How does it fit in with what the poem is saying?

15. Find out what you can about blues music and lyrics. What elements of a blues song do you find in the poem?

16. What do you like about this poem?

WILLIAM STAFFORD

(1914–93)

Villiam Stafford was born in Kansas in 1914. Although the family suffered financially during the American Depression, Stafford's parents consistently encouraged their three children to develop an independently moral view of life through reading and discussion.

This tendency towards independence led the teenage Stafford to embark on a camping trip, during which he developed a close spiritual connection with the natural world: 'The earth was my home; I would never feel lost while it held me.' Later, as a conscientious objector during the Second World War, he refused to fight but did work in areas such as fire fighting and building roads.

In 1948 he began teaching at Lewis and Clark College, Oregon, a position that he retained until his retirement despite travelling widely to share his work with others. It was not until he was in his forties that his first anthology of poetry, *Traveling through the Dark*, was published, which subsequently won the 1963 National Book Award. Until his death in 1993, Stafford maintained the daily habit of rising at four in the morning to write poetry because he found it 'a confirming, satisfying activity to do'.

OL 2022

TRAVELING THROUGH THE DARK

Traveling through the dark I found a deer
dead on the edge of the Wilson River road.
It is usually best to roll them into the canyon:
that road is narrow; to swerve might make more dead.
By glow of the tail-light I stumbled back of the car   5
and stood by the heap, a doe, a recent killing;
she had stiffened already, almost cold.
I dragged her off; she was large in the belly.

My fingers touching her side brought me the reason –
her side was warm; her fawn lay there waiting,   10
alive, still, never to be born.
Beside that mountain road I hesitated.

The car aimed ahead its lowered parking lights;
under the hood purred the steady engine.
I stood in the glare of the warm exhaust turning red;   15
around our group I could hear the wilderness listen.

I thought hard for us all – my only swerving –,
then pushed her over the edge into the river.

NOTE

3   canyon: a deep and narrow opening running between hills

EXPLORATIONS

First reading

1. a   Based on the clues in the first
        and second stanzas, describe
        in your own words how you
        picture 'the Wilson River road'.
    b   Would you like to drive along
        it in the dark? Why or why
        not? Use references from the
        poem to support your view.

2. a   What reason does the poet give
        for saying about the dead deer,
        'It is usually best to roll them
        into the canyon'?
    b   Do you agree with his attitude?
        Why or why not?

3. a   What does the poet discover
        that causes him to hesitate in
        the third stanza?
    b   Can you understand why he
        pauses?
        Explain your answer.

4. a   Were you shocked when you read the final line of the poem? If so, why?

    b   Would you have preferred the poem to end in another way? Describe the ending that you would prefer.

Second reading

5. a   The poet's emotions change a number of times during his experience on the Wilson River road. Go through the poem and trace the emotions he feels.

    b   Based on what you have learned about his feelings, would you consider the poet to be a kind or unkind person? Give reasons for your answer.

6. How does the poet use the senses of sight, touch and hearing in order to make this scene more vivid and easy to imagine? Use references from the poem in your answer.

7. a   Although this scene takes place at night, Stafford still includes some colours in his poem. What colours appear in the poem?

    b   Why do you think he refers only to these colours in the poem?

Third reading

8. It has been suggested that in this poem, Stafford portrays his view of the relationship between the world of nature, represented by the deer, and the world of technology, represented by the car. What do you think this poem says to us about this relationship?

9. Although this poem is written in everyday, conversational language, Stafford uses words and phrases that have layers of meaning.

    a   Discuss the different meanings the word 'still' can have in the following lines: 'her fawn lay there waiting,/alive, still, never to be born.'

    b   In a similar way, consider how the title of the poem, 'Traveling through the Dark', can be interpreted in a number of ways.

10. Imagine that you live on the Wilson River road and you are very concerned about the dangers posed both to people and to deer by the driving conditions in this area at night. Write a letter to the local newspaper trying to persuade the readers that something has to be done to improve the situation.

PATRICIA
BEER

(1919–99)

Patricia Beer was born in Exmouth, Devon, into a Plymouth Brethren family. Her father was a railway clerk and her mother a teacher; Beer wrote a vivid account of her stern upbringing in *Mrs Beer's House* (1968). She won a scholarship to Exmouth Grammar School and achieved a first-class honours degree at Exeter University. She went on to St Hugh's College, Oxford, and lived in Italy teaching English from 1947 to 1953. After a succession of temporary jobs, Beer was appointed lecturer in English at Goldsmiths' College in London in 1962, where she remained for six years. In 1964 she married an architect, John Damien Parsons, with whom she refurbished a Tudor farmhouse in Up Ottery, Devon, where she lived for the rest of her life.

Patricia Beer left teaching to become a full-time writer in 1968. In all, Beer published nine volumes of poetry, one novel and an academic study, *Reader I Married Him*, an analysis of the major nineteenth-century women novelists and their female characters. Patricia Beer made her poems out of the ordinary events of daily life with a wry humour and a sharp eye for detail.

OL 2019

THE VOICE

When God took my aunt's baby boy, a merciful neighbour
Gave her a parrot. She could not have afforded one
But now bought a new cage as brilliant as the bird,
And turned her back on the idea of other babies.

He looked unlikely. In her house his scarlet feathers   5
Stuck out like a jungle, though his blue ones blended
With the local pottery which carried messages
Like 'Du ee help yerself to crame, me handsome.'

He said nothing when he arrived, not a quotation
From pet-shop gossip or a sailor's oath, no sound   10
From someone's home: the telephone or car-door slamming,
And none from his: tom-tom, war-cry or wild beast roaring.

He came from silence but was ready to become noise.
My aunt taught him nursery rhymes morning after morning.
He learnt Miss Muffett, Jack and Jill, Little Jack Horner,   15
Including her jokes; she used to say turds and whey.

A genuine Devon accent is not easy. Actors
Cannot do it. He could though. In his court clothes
He sounded like a farmer, as her son might have.
He sounded like our family. He fitted in.   20

Years went by. We came and went. A day or two
Before he died, he got confused, and muddled up
His rhymes. Jack Horner ate his pail of water.
The spider said what a good boy he was. I wept.

He had never seemed puzzled by the bizarre events   25
He spoke of. But that last day he turned his head towards us
With the bewilderment of death upon him. Said
'Broke his crown' and 'Christmas pie'. And tumbled after.

My aunt died the next winter, widowed, childless, pitied
And patronised. I cannot summon up her voice at all.   30
She would not have expected it to be remembered
After so long. But I can still hear his.

EXPLORATIONS

First reading

1. What impression of the aunt do you get from the first stanza? How do you visualise her?

2. 'He looked unlikely.'
   What do you think the author means by this?

3. How do you imagine the aunt's home looked? Examine the detail in the two opening stanzas.

4. Why do you think the aunt taught the parrot nursery rhymes? Is there a connection with the loss of her baby son?

5. 'He fitted in.'
   How did the parrot fit in?

6. Why do you think the author 'wept'? How does she feel about the parrot?

7. What do you think the poet means by 'pitied/And patronised'? What does this tell us about how people perceived the aunt?

Second reading

8. Read the poem aloud. Jot down what you notice about its sounds and rhythms.

9. How do you react to the first sentence? Is it an effective opening?

10. Comment on the 'jungle' simile in the second stanza.

11. Do you get a sense of place from the references to Devon and the local pottery? Does this enrich the poem?

12. a 'With the bewilderment of death upon him. Said/"Broke his crown" and "Christmas pie". And tumbled after.'
   Comment on these lines. Do you think the lines work well?

   b Can you detect some humour in the clever phrasing?

13. What evidence is there in the poem that the parrot was regarded more as a family member than a mere household pet?

14. How do you feel about the aunt's life? Can you suggest why we are not told her name?

Third reading

15. Briefly state what the theme of the poem is.

16. Would you agree that there is genuine warmth of feeling in this poem?

17. How do you react to the style in which the poem is written? Comment on any three features. You might consider the poet's conversational language, her wry humour, her eye for detail and her use of imagery.

18. What is the mood of this poem? What choice of words and images suggest the mood? Look closely at the final stanza.

19. What have you learned about the character of the author from reading the poem?

Fourth reading

20. Write a paragraph giving your personal reaction to 'The Voice'. Would you recommend it?

DENISE LEVERTOV

(1923–1997)

Denise Levertov was born in Essex in England. Her father had converted from Judaism to become an Anglican parson. She was educated completely at home and at five years old decided that she would become a writer. At the age of twelve she sent her poetry to T. S. Eliot, who responded very positively to her work. She published her first poem at seventeen and her first collection in 1946. During the Second World War she worked as a civilian nurse during the bombing of London.

In 1947 she married an American and soon after moved to the USA with him. By 1956 she had become an American citizen. Her poetry became much less formal and she was heavily influenced by poets such as William Carlos Williams. Her second American volume, *With Eyes at the Back of Our Heads* (1959), established her as one of the great American poets, and her British roots were by now a thing of the past. During the 1960s she became very involved in activism and feminism. She was strongly opposed to the Vietnam War. *The Sorrow Dance*, which expresses her feelings about the Vietnam War and the death of her sister, is a passionate, angry collection. In all, she published more than twenty volumes of poetry. She died in December 1997.

OL 2

AN ARRIVAL (NORTH WALES, 1897)

The orphan arrived in outlandish hat,
proud pain of new button boots.
Her moss-agate eyes
photographed views of the noonday sleepy town
no one had noticed. Nostrils flaring,   5
she sniffed odors of hay and stone,
       absence of Glamorgan coaldust,
and pasted her observations quickly
into the huge album of her mind.
Cousins, ready to back off like heifers   10
were staring:
       amazed they received
the gold funeral sovereigns she dispensed

along with talk strange to them as a sailor's parrot.
Auntie confiscated the gold;   15
the mourning finery, agleam with jet,
was put by to be altered. It had been chosen
by the child herself and was thought unsuitable. She was to be
the minister's niece, now,   20
not her father's daughter.
           Alone,
she would cut her way through a new world's
graystone chapels, the steep and sideways
rockface cottages climbing   25
mountain streets,

enquiring, turning things over
in her heart,
         weeping only in rage or when
the choirs in their great and dark and   30
golden glory broke forth and the hills
skipped like lambs.

NOTES

1	outlandish:	unfamiliar, strange
3	moss-agate:	the colour of a semi-precious green gemstone
7	Glamorgan:	one of the most industrialised counties in Wales due to the rich coal deposits in the area
13	sovereigns:	a British gold coin
16	jet:	a black or dark-brown stone associated with funeral dress in the 19th century
20	minister	member of the clergy

EXPLORATIONS

Before reading

1. a Moving or travelling to different places can be interesting but also challenging because of different customs and attitudes about dress, ways of living and language. Have you ever arrived in a place and noticed how different it was to your home? What were the differences that you experienced?

    b Did you find it easy or difficult to cope with these differences?

    As a class, share and discuss your experiences.

First reading

2. a 'she sniffed odors of hay and stone,/absence of Glamorgan coaldust'.
    What do the smells that the girl notices on her arrival suggest to you about the location of her new hometown?

    b What does the smell that she misses tell you about the locality of the town she has had to leave?

    c Do you think the girl might find it difficult to make such a change? Why?

3. a 'The orphan', 'the mourning finery', 'not her father's daughter'. Based on your reading of these three phrases, can you suggest why the girl has had to move to a new town to live with unfamiliar relatives?

    b In your opinion, does this fact make the girl's situation more difficult for her to cope with? Why?

Second reading

4. a Lines 1–2 and line 16 make it clear that the 'orphan' tries to make a good impression on her unfamiliar relatives by wearing expensive mourning clothes. Based on these lines and the picture that accompanies this poem, describe the mourning outfit that the girl is wearing.

    b How does the 'Auntie' react to the girl's clothes in lines 16–17?

    c Do you think a difference in customs and attitudes has anything to do with her aunt's reaction? Why?

5. a The 'orphan' also tries to make a good impression on her relatives by giving them gifts of money ('gold funeral sovereigns'). In your own words, explain how her cousins react to her gift in lines 12–13.

    b How does the 'Auntie' react in line 15?

    c Again, do you think a difference in customs and attitudes caused these reactions? Why?

6. a 'along with talk strange to them as a sailor's parrot'.
    The third way that the 'orphan' tries to make a good impression on her unfamiliar relatives is by speaking to them. What does

the line quoted above suggest to you about her relatives' reaction to the way that she spoke?

b   Can you suggest what causes them to react in this way?

7.   What impression do you get from lines 22–32 of the type of relationship that the girl develops with her relatives? Explain your answer with reference to this passage of the poem.

Third reading

8.   a   Differences in customs and attitudes can be caused not only by changes in geographical location, but also by historical time. This poem is set in the nineteenth century, when people lived in very different ways to those of the twenty-first century. What do lines 17–19 tell you about the nineteenth century attitude to the amount of independence that young people ought to have?

b   What do you learn about the nineteenth-century custom regarding the social importance of men and women in lines 19–21?

c   Would you find it difficult to cope with this nineteenth-century attitude and custom? Why?

9.   The difficulties that can be caused by differences in customs and attitudes are a theme (an important idea) in this poem. Working in pairs, can you suggest what (a) the orphaned girl,

(b) the 'Auntie' and (c) the cousins could have said or done to reduce their difficulties and to develop a happier relationship?

10.   a   In your opinion, is this a happy or a sad poem? Refer to the poem to support your view.

b   What do you think the poet is trying to tell us about how we should treat people who have different attitudes and customs to ours?

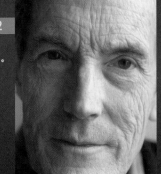

RICHARD MURPHY

(1927–)

R ichard Murphy was born in County Mayo in 1927. He has published numerous collections of poetry, which have won many awards in Ireland, Britain and the US. His collected poems, *In the Heart of the Country*, was published by Gallery Press in 2000. He is a member of Aosdána.

OL 2

MOONSHINE

To think
I must be alone:
To love
We must be together.

To think I love you   5
When I'm alone
More than I think of you
When we're together.

I cannot think
Without loving   10
Or love
Without thinking.

Alone I love
To think of us together:
Together I think   15
I'd love to be alone.

NOTE

Moonshine: either illicit whiskey or foolish ideas or plans, visionary
                                    talk

EXPLORATIONS

Before reading

1. What sort of ideas, feelings and
    images do you usually find in a love
    poem?

First reading

2. What do you notice on first reading
    this?

3. What kind of person do you think
    the speaker is here?

4. The speaker is expressing a dilemma
    or conflict. Describe the dilemma in
    your own words.

Second reading

5. What do you find unusual about this
    love poem?

6. Which of the possible meanings of
    the title do you think best suits the
    poem or could they both apply?
    Explain your opinions.

7. Do you think the poet is taking this
    love stuff seriously? Explain.

THOM
GUNN

(1929–2004)

Thomson William Gunn was born in Gravesend, England in 1929. His parents divorced and his mother committed suicide when Thom was only fifteen. After spending two years in the British national service he studied English literature in Cambridge and graduated in 1953. His first book of poetry, *Fighting Terms*, published in 1954, played with traditional verse forms and rhyme. Gunn emigrated to the United States in 1954 and lectured in Stanford and Berkeley. He lived in San Francisco and embraced the alternative lifestyle emerging in the early sixties. His poetry written in the United States explored themes such as drugs, homosexuality and poetic form. His later collection, *The Man with the Night Sweats* (1992), was dominated by AIDS-related elegies. His final collection *Boss Cupid* was published in 2000. He died in San Francisco in 2004.

OL 202

CONSIDERING THE SNAIL

The snail pushes through a green
night, for the grass is heavy
with water and meets over
the bright path he makes, where rain
has darkened the earth's dark. He   5
moves in a wood of desire,

pale antlers barely stirring
as he hunts. I cannot tell
what power is at work, drenched there
with purpose, knowing nothing.   10
What is a snail's fury? All
I think is that if later

I parted the blades above
the tunnel and saw the thin
trail of broken white across   15
litter, I would never have
imagined the slow passion
to that deliberate progress.

EXPLORATIONS

First reading

1. What words would you associate with a snail?

2. Why do you think the poet describes him as pushing 'through a green/night'?

3. What contrasts are noted in the first stanza? What might they symbolise?

4. What is the primary characteristic of the snail that the poet admires?

5. What images from the poem do you find striking? Explain your answer.

Second reading

6. How does the poet capture the snail's perspective in the poem? Support your answer using reference to the poem.

7. What do you notice about the structure of the poem? How many syllables per line? What does this reveal about the poet's intention?

8. How might the progress of the snail be similar to the creative process?

Third reading

9. Write a note on Gunn's use of language in this poem.

10. Do you think this poem should be included in:

- a collection of poetry about nature

- a collection of poetry about creativity

- a collection of poetry about changing your perspective?

    Explain your answer.

11. Write a descriptive paragraph where you try to make the reader see another creature differently.

12. Do you like or dislike this poem? Explain your answer.

TED
HUGHES

(1930 – 1998)

T ed Hughes is well known as a poet and as the husband of Sylvia Plath. His
work deals not just with nature, where he shows insight into the hidden
cruelty of its existence, but he has also reworked a considerable number of
writings from Greek and Latin writers. Chief among these are the *Metamorphoses*
of Ovid and Seneca's *Oedipus* as well as some Greek plays. His range of poetry
is impressive and its uncompromising depiction of the less pleasant aspects
of creation remains in stark contrast to the more urbane poetry of many of his
contemporaries.

OL 2C
OL 20

HAWK ROOSTING

I sit in the top of the wood, my eyes closed.
Inaction, no falsifying dream
Between my hooked head and hooked feet:
Or in sleep rehearse perfect kills and eat.

The convenience of the high trees!   5
The air's buoyancy and the sun's ray
Are of advantage to me;
And the earth's face upward for my inspection.

My feet are locked upon the rough bark.
It took the whole of Creation   10
To produce my foot, my each feather:
Now I hold Creation in my foot

Or fly up, and revolve it all slowly –
I kill where I please because it is all mine.
There is no sophistry in my body: 15
My manners are tearing off heads –

The allotment of death.
For the one path of my flight is direct
Through the bones of the living.
No arguments assert my right: 20
The sun is behind me.
Nothing has changed since I began.
My eye has permitted no change.
I am going to keep things like this.

NOTES

2	falsifying:	giving a false idea of something
6	buoyancy:	capacity to keep things afloat
10	Creation:	the universe, all that is created
15	sophistry:	using an argument that is false or meant to deceive
17	allotment:	distribution or dealing out
20	assert:	declare or justify

EXPLORATIONS

First reading

1. a   Take a moment after reading this poem for the first time to think about it. Then, within a time limit of 60 seconds, quickly write down a list of words that you would use to describe the hawk in this poem.

    b   Take it in turns to write one of your words on the board. Some words may be repeated – if so, just write the word once. Write down all the words on the board.

2. a   'I sit in the top of the wood, my eyes closed.'
        What does the fact that the hawk has its 'eyes closed' tell you about its attitude to the other creatures in the wood?

    b   'Between my hooked head and hooked feet'.
        Can you suggest how a 'hooked head and hooked feet' might help the hawk to feel that it can safely close its eyes?

3. a   In stanza 2 (lines 5–8), the hawk tells us that it finds 'the high trees', the 'air's buoyancy' and 'the earth's face upward' convenient and an 'advantage'. Explain in your own words why the hawk, a hunting bird, would find each of these convenient and advantageous.

    b   Does the hawk regard these elements as being important in themselves or as being important only because they are helpful to it? Explain your choice.

4. a   In lines 9–11, the hawk says that it took 'the whole of Creation' to 'produce' its 'foot' and 'each feather'. If someone said to you that it had taken 'the whole of Creation' to make him or her, what would your reaction be?

    b   Based on your work for Questions 2, 3 and 4 (a), sum up in two sentences the hawk's attitude to itself and to the world around it.

Second reading

5. a   In lines 14–19, the hawk describes its attitude to killing other creatures. Do you think the hawk feels guilty about doing this? Refer to lines 14–19 to support your view.

    b   Do you think it should feel guilty? Why?

6. a   In line 21, the hawk says, 'The sun is behind me.' It also mentions 'the sun's ray' in line 6, so the sun and the direction of its light are obviously important to the hawk. Bearing in mind that the hawk is a hunting bird, can you suggest why these factors are important to him?

    b   'The sun is behind me' could also be interpreted as suggesting that the sun supports the hawk in its killing. Do you think the hawk feels that this is true? Why? Refer to the poem in your answer.

7. a   'I am going to keep things like this.'
        Are you surprised by this last statement from the hawk or

do you think it matches its attitude in the rest of the poem? Explain your answer with reference to the poem.

b Some critics have suggested that this poem explores the world of the dictator (person who is in complete control in an area). Do you think the hawk is a dictator or is it just following its instincts? Explain your answer.

Third reading

8. Look at the words that were written on the board for Question I. Following your work on this poem, do you feel that any of the words should be crossed out or any new words added to the list? Give reasons for your suggestions.

9. Choose two images from the poem that you found to be striking and explain why you found them to be so.

10. Did the language used by the poet in this poem appeal to you? Explain your answer with reference to the poem.

ALDEN
NOWLAN

(1933–1983)

Alden Nowlan is a Canadian poet, playwright and novelist. He was born in Stanley, Nova Scotia to a life of poverty where education was not valued. His mother, who was only fifteen when he was born, left Alden and his younger sister in the care of his paternal grandmother. He left school after fourth grade and was working in a saw-mill by the time he was fourteen. He manufactured his resumé and at age nineteen managed to get a job in a newspaper in New Brunswick. He published small books of poetry and after he published *Bread, Wine and Salt* (1967) became writer in residence at the University of New Brunswick where he stayed until he died of respiratory failure aged 50 in 1983.

OL 202

IN PRAISE OF THE GREAT BULL WALRUS

I wouldn't like to be one
of the walrus people
for the rest of my life
but I wish I could spend
one sunny afternoon   5
lying on the rocks with them.
I suspect it would be similar
to drinking beer in a tavern
that caters to longshoremen
and won't admit women.   10
We'd exchange no
cosmic secrets. I'd merely say,
"How yuh doin' you big old walrus?"
and the nearest of
the walrus people   15
would answer,
"Me? I'm doin' great.
How yuh doin' yourself,
you big old human being, you?"
How good it is to share   20
the earth with such creatures
and how unthinkable it would have been

to have missed all this
by not being born:
a happy thought, that,   25
for not being born is
the only tragedy
that we can imagine
but need never fear.

NOTE

9   longshoremen: person whose job it was to load and unload ships at port

EXPLORATIONS

Before reading

1. If you could be an animal for a day, what animal would you choose? Why?

First reading

2. What comes to mind when you imagine a bull walrus?

3. What characteristics would you associate with the animal?

4. Why do you think Nowlan calls them the 'walrus people'?

5. What do you think he means when he says 'We'd exchange no cosmic secrets'?

6. What do you notice about the dialogue in the poem? Why do you think the poet writes like this?

Second reading

7. What impression of the poet do you form from reading the poem? Explain your answer.

8. What do you think the poet means by the lines 'how unthinkable it would have been/to have missed all this/by not being born'?

9. How does the poet create a conversational tone throughout the poem?

Third reading

10. Write a letter to the poet outlining your response to the poem.

11. The language used in the poem is deceptively simple. Write a brief note on Nowlan's use of language in this poem.

12. Would you include this poem in:

- A collection of poems about nature
- A collection of poems about growing old
- A collection of poems about regrets?
  Explain your answer.

MARGE
PIERCY

(1936–)

M arge Piercy was born on 31 March 1936 in a Detroit shattered by the economic hardships caused by the American Depression. Her father Robert, like many men at the time, had struggled to find work until he finally got a job installing and repairing machinery. Piercy credits her mother and grandmother as major influences in her life, both in stimulating her imagination and love of reading and in encouraging her to develop a strong sense of her Jewish heritage. Piercy began to write at the age of fifteen. She has always written both poetry and fiction and frequently writes both at the same time. Often she finds herself developing themes from a novel that she is working on in her poetry: an approach that she claims, with some humour, helps her to avoid the dreaded writer's block. Piercy was very much a part of the feminist movement of the 1960s and still works to improve the position of women as well as that of society itself in her wider political activism. She lives and works with her husband, the writer Ira Wood, and a number of her beloved cats in Cape Cod. For Piercy, poetry is essential to the human condition because, as she explains, 'you have to know why, you have to know who you are, you have to know what you're doing and why you're doing it. You have to know what you believe in … That's mostly poetry.'

OL 20

WILL WE WORK TOGETHER?

You wake in the early grey
morning in bed alone and curse
me, that I am only
sometimes there. But when
I am with you, I light   5
up the corners, I am bright
as a fireplace roaring
with love, every bone in my back
and my fingers is singing
like a tea kettle on the boil.   10
My heart wags me, a big dog
with a bigger tail. I am
a new coin printed with

your face. My body wears
sore before I can express   15
on yours the smallest part
of what moves me. Words
shred and splinter.
I want to make with you
some bold new thing   20
to stand in the marketplace,
the statue of a goddess
laughing, armed and wearing
flowers and feathers. Like sheep
of whose hair is made   25
blankets and coats, I want
to force from this fierce sturdy
rampant love some useful thing.

NOTES

20	bold:	brave, daring, courageous
23	armed:	bearing weapons
27	sturdy:	strong, powerful
28	rampant:	occurring in an unrestrained way, growing wildly, out of control

EXPLORATIONS

First reading

1. a How does the poet imagine her lover reacting to her not being beside him when he wakes up?

   b Does she seem to be offended by the fact that he curses her?

   c Why do you think she feels this way about his cursing?

2. a How do you feel when you wake up to a 'grey' morning?

   b Can you suggest why Piercy decided to open this poem with the image of her lover waking in the 'grey' morning?

3. Much of the poem (lines 4–18) is given over to the poet reminding her lover of how it is when she is there. Choose one image from this section that you feel really suggests the strength of her feelings and explain the reasons for your choice.

4. Examine how the poet creates a strong sense of the physicality of her feelings in lines 4–18 by (a) references to parts of the body and (b) references to the senses of sight and touch.

5. 'I am bright/as a fireplace' (a simile), 'like a tea kettle on the boil' (a simile), 'My heart wags me, a big dog/with

a bigger tail' (a metaphor), 'I am/a new coin printed with/your face' (a metaphor).

Take each of the similes and metaphors quoted above and explain in your own words what she is trying to tell her lover about her feelings by using that simile or metaphor.

Second reading

6. **a** 'I want to make with you/some bold new thing'.
   What do these lines tell you about what the poet wants to happen with their love?

   b Are you surprised that she feels this way given what she has said in lines 4–18 or can you understand her feelings?

7. **a** 'the statue of a goddess/ laughing, armed and wearing/flowers and feathers.' In ancient times a statue of a goddess was treated with great respect by the crowds in the marketplace and it would often survive for centuries, so the poet wants their relationship to involve respect and to be long term. Can you suggest what characteristics the other elements in the goddess's appearance stand for?

   b Do you think they are good characteristics to have in a relationship? Why?

8. **a** 'I want/to force from this fierce sturdy/rampant love some useful thing.'
   How do these lines suggest the energy of their love?

   b Can you explain in your own words what the poet wants to do with this energy?

   c Do you think she has been brave to tell him all this? Why?

Third reading

9. Do you see this as a poem about love or passion or commitment, or perhaps all three? Use references from the poem to support your view.

10. Imagine that you want to persuade Marge Piercy to come to your school to talk about this poem. Write a letter to her explaining why you particularly like this poem and why you think it is relevant to you and your fellow pupils.

ELIZABETH SMITHER

(1941 –)

orn in New Plymouth, New Zealand, Elizabeth Smither has produced over thirteen collections of poetry, as well as novels, short stories and children's literature. Among her published volumes of poetry are: *Here Come the Clouds* (1975); *A Pattern of Marching* (1989); *The Lark Quartet* (from which this poem is taken, 1999); *Red Shoes* (2003); *The Year of Adverbs* (2007) and *Horse Playing the Accordion* (2007). In 2002 Elizabeth Smither was named New Zealand Poet Laureate.

OL 2019

OL 2020

ON THE EUTHANASIA OF A PET DOG

Lightly she fell where the vets' hands held her
the two vets who came with shaver and syringe
two young blonde girls just out of vet school
and she died between them, surrounded by petting.

It was three o'clock. All day we sat with her   5
singly or together, making our farewells
while she sniffed the bright day, heart heaving
and lifted her muzzle to the faint breeze.

And when it was over we each wept copiously
the vets departed, we gave in to grief   10
as though we were rushing to basins to bend over
hands held to faces, we stumbled and stooped.

She lay on the carpet so soft and plumped-out
all dehydration gone, all clenching of sinews
she stayed there for hours so we could caress her   15
and talk to her finally, and bless her.

NOTES

2	shaver and syringe:	they needed to shave the dog's leg to find a vein, through which they could administer the drug from the syringe
8	muzzle:	front part of an animal's face, including nose and mouth
9	copiously:	plentifully
13	plumped-out:	a full, rounded shape
14	dehydration:	the loss of fluids
14	clenching of sinews:	the tightening of the tissues that join muscle to bone (could be as a response to pain)
15	caress:	to hug, embrace, touch lovingly
16	bless:	to ask for God's blessing on her; a prayer to guard and protect

EXPLORATIONS

First reading

1. Read the poem silently a number of times and then do a class 'round' of 'I noticed that…' (i.e. every person, in turn, gets to express one sentence beginning with the words 'I noticed that…'). There are no correct answers. All honest responses are equally valuable and should be respected.

2. Collate (collect and put in order), in written form, all the information gathered about the poem, from the 'round'. You could begin by writing it up under the following headings and then add other headings suggested during the class contribution:

a   What did the class notice about the vets? Do you now want to add anything to the list?

b   What did the class notice about the dog? Anything to add?

c   What did the class notice about the people who owned the dog? Anything to add?

d   Other headings?

3. Read the first stanza again. What are your thoughts? Jot them down, briefly.

4. 'It was three o'clock'.
Do you think this half line helps us to understand something of the speaker's feelings? Talk about this in your group. Note the points made.

5. a Using the evidence in the poem, what can you imagine may have been going through the owners' minds before they phoned the vet?

    b Working in pairs, take on the roles of two people in the poem. Imagine who they might be – think about their age; gender; financial status; how long each one has each known the dog; their attitude to euthanasia, etc.

    c Script a possible conversation between these two people that might have happened before the vets were called. Volunteer to read your script aloud or listen to others read theirs.

    d What insights into the poem did you get from this exercise? Discuss these.

Second reading

6. 'While she sniffed the bright day, heart heaving/ and lifted her muzzle to the faint breeze'.
What are your thoughts, on reading these lines? Jot them down.

7. In the third stanza they 'gave in to grief'.
    a Describe the images in the poem through which grief is shown.

    b Do you think these images work well? Explain your thinking.

8. In the fourth stanza:
    a What changes to the dog and to the people do you notice?
    b The atmosphere is different to that in stanza three. How would you describe it?
    c 'She stayed there for hours'. What are your thoughts on this phrase? Talk about it in groups or in the full class.

Third reading

9. What images made the most impression on you? Choose two or three and describe their impact on you. (100–200 words)

10. What did you learn about dealing with death from reading this poem? (200 words)

11. What did you discover about the relationship between humans and their pets? (200 words)

Fourth reading

12. If you have had a pet that needed to be 'put to sleep', write about the experience, in the form of a story, a poem, or a blog.

13. Do you admire the honesty in this poem or do you find it too revealing? Write about your opinion in 100–200 words.

14. Do you think this poem should have an age warning on it or could it usefully enlighten all young people to the realities of life and death? Debate this.

TESS
GALLAGHER

(1943–)

Tess Gallagher was born in 1943 in Port Angeles, Washington, the eldest of five children. Her father Leslie worked as a logger, a dockhand and on the small ranch owned by the family. Writing was very much a part of her life from an early age and she wrote both poetry and fiction; her first published work was a short story. It was when she joined a creative writing class conducted by the eminent poet Theodore Roethke at the University of Washington that, as Gallagher put it, 'poetry did rather kidnap me'. Her first, award-winning, book of poetry was published in 1976 and reflected Gallagher's roots 'in that generation of women writers who stepped forth out of the feminist revolution'. In later years, Gallagher has returned to short story writing, encouraged by her late husband, the writer Raymond Carver. In poetry, her exploration of what it is to be a woman has become an honest inquiry into the nature of being human. Since the late 1960s, in between writing, teaching and working on films, Gallagher has visited Ireland regularly and has embraced Irish culture, delighting in singing 'traditional Irish dirge', counting many Northern poets as her friends and collecting stories from the Irish storytelling tradition.

OL 2

THE HUG

A woman is reading a poem on the street
and another woman stops to listen. We stop too,
with our arms around each other. The poem
is being read and listened to out here
in the open. Behind us   5
no one is entering or leaving the houses.

Suddenly a hug comes over me and I'm
giving it to you, like a variable star shooting light
off to make itself comfortable, then
subsiding. I finish but keep on holding   10
you. A man walks up to us and we know he hasn't
come out of nowhere, but if he could, he
would have. He looks homeless because of how
he needs. 'Can I have one of those?' he asks you,
and I feel you nod. I'm surprised,   15

surprised you didn't tell him how
it is — that I'm yours, only
yours, etc., exclusive as a nose to
its face. Love — that's what we're talking about, love
that nabs you with 'for me   20
only' and holds on.

So I walk over to him and put my
arms around him and try to
hug him like I mean it. He's got an overcoat on
so thick I can't feel   25
him past it. I'm starting the hug
and thinking, 'How big a hug is this supposed to be?
How long shall I hold this hug?' Already
we could be eternal, his arms falling over my
shoulders, my hands not   30
meeting behind his back, he is so big!

I put my head into his chest and snuggle
in. I lean into him. I lean my blood and my wishes
into him. He stands for it. This is his
and he's starting to give it back so well I know he's   35
getting it. This hug. So truly, so tenderly,
we stop having arms and I don't know if
my lover has walked away or what, or
if the woman is still reading the poem, or the houses —
what about them? — the houses.   40

Clearly, a little permission is a dangerous thing.
But when you hug someone you want it
to be a masterpiece of connection, the way the button
on his coat will leave the imprint of
a planet in my cheek   45
when I walk away. When I try to find some place
to go back to.

NOTE

| 8 | a variable star: | a star that has fluctuations in its levels of brightness |

EXPLORATIONS

First reading

1. For Gallagher, 'the image is still the important element' in her poetry. Choose one image from 'The Hug' that you find particularly striking and explain the reasons for your choice.

2. a Describe in your own words the events that lead up to the poet giving her partner a hug in line 7.
   b Can you suggest why these events made her feel like hugging?

3. a What is her partner's reaction when the man asks, 'Can I have one of those?'
   b How does the poet feel about this reaction?
   c How would you feel if your partner said it was fine for you to hug a stranger?

4. a Why do you think she decides to 'walk over' and hug the stranger?
   b Which one of the following words best describes how she feels as she begins to hug the stranger: happy, shy, uncomfortable? Explain your answer.
   c Would you feel the same if you were in her position? Why?

Second reading

5. a 'Suddenly a hug comes over me and I'm/giving it to you',

'I finish but keep on holding/you'.
Based on these lines, would you say that this is a one-person or a two-person hug?
What clues lead you to this conclusion?

   b 'I lean my blood and my wishes/into him. He stands for it. This is his/and he's starting to give it back'.
   From your reading of these lines, would you say that this is a one-person or a two-person hug?
   Explain your answer.

6. 'He's got an overcoat on/so thick I can't feel/him past it', 'This hug. So truly, so tenderly,/we stop having arms'.
   a How do these lines show that her hug with the stranger changes from a physical action to an emotional one?
   b Is there any sense of this change in the description of her first hug with her partner in lines 7–11? Support your answer by reference to the poem.
   c Which of the two hugs do you think is closest to being 'a masterpiece of connection'? Give reasons for your answer.

Third reading

7. a 'He looks homeless because of how/he needs'.

Can you suggest why the poet makes this link between being 'homeless' and having 'needs'?

b   Is the stranger the only person who 'needs' in this poem? Give reasons for your answer.

8. a   'When I try to find some place/ to go back to.'
    Do you think the poet is referring to a real physical place, an emotional place or both in these lines?

b   What 'place' was the poet in before she hugged the stranger?

c   How does her sense of this 'place' change as she hugs the stranger in lines 36–40?

d   Discuss whether the poet could also be seen as being 'homeless' at the end of the poem.

9. a   Gallagher has related how some 'hardcore poetry people' wanted her to take 'The Hug' out of her book of poems because, as she explains, 'In the United States, if you have any jollity in a poem, it can't be a poem with a capital P.' Can you suggest what the differences might be between a poem with a capital P and a poem with a small p?

b   Where do you think the 'jollity', or fun, lies in this poem?

c   Do you think a poem can be fun and still be a poem with a capital P?

10. Imagine you have decided to read 'a poem on the street'. What poem from those that you have studied on the Leaving Certificate course would you choose to read? Explain the reasons for your choice.

LIZ
LOCHHEAD

(1947–)

Liz Lochhead was born in Scotland, in a Lanarkshire mining village, on 26 December 1947. As a child, she spent much of her time drawing and painting. She attended Glasgow School of Art from 1965 to 1970 and then taught art until 1979, when she became a full-time writer.

Although her early writing was mainly poetry, in the 1980s Lochhead also began to write for the stage. Much of her poetry explores what it is to be Scottish and what it is to be a woman, often in a humorous way, while her work as a playwright, featuring a number of adaptations of ancient Greek plays, explores what it is to be human.

Liz Lochhead has won many prizes for her work and in 1998 was listed among Scotland's 'Fifty Most Influential Women' in a Scottish Sunday newspaper. She now lives in Glasgow with her architect husband.

REVELATION

I remember once being shown the black bull
when a child at the farm for eggs and milk.
They called him Bob – as though perhaps
you could reduce a monster
with the charm of a friendly name.   5
At the threshold of his outhouse, someone
held my hand and let me peer inside.
At first, only black
and the hot reek of him. Then he was immense,
his edges merging with the darkness, just   10
a big bulk and a roar to be really scared of,
a trampling, and a clanking tense with the chain's jerk.
His eyes swivelled in the great wedge of his tossed head.
He roared his rage. His nostrils gaped like wounds.

And in the yard outside,   15
oblivious hens picked their way about.
The faint and rather festive tinkling

behind the mellow stone and hasp was all they knew
of that Black Mass, straining at his chains.
I had always half-known he existed –   20
this antidote and Anti-Christ his anarchy
threatened the eggs, well rounded, self-contained –
and the placidity of milk.

I ran, my pigtails thumping on my back in fear,
past the big boys in the farm lane   25
who pulled the wings from butterflies and
blew up frogs with straws.
Past thorned hedge and harried nest,
scared of the eggs shattering –
only my small and shaking hand on the jug's rim   30
in case the milk should spill.

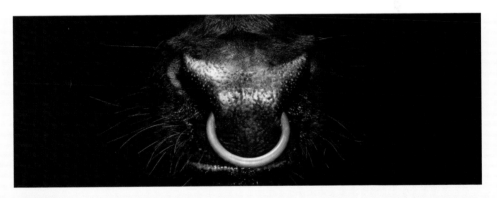

NOTES

	Revelation:	to reveal or disclose information that was not known previously in a dramatic way. Often used about the revealing of knowledge to human beings by God or gods.
1	bull:	in mythology the bull is a symbol for masculinity and a brute strength that can slide over into violence. It can also represent the more primitive desires of human beings that civilisation does not always successfully control.
6	threshold:	a wooden or stone strip forming the bottom part of a doorway
9	reek:	a strong, unpleasant smell
16	oblivious:	unaware of something or someone
19	Black Mass:	a large black physical body; a quasi-religious ceremony that worships the devil
21	Anti-Christ:	the arch-enemy of Jesus Christ
21	anarchy:	disorder
23	placidity:	calmness
28	harried nest:	a nest from which the eggs have been stolen

EXPLORATIONS

Before reading

1. **a** The title of this poem is 'Revelation'. Revelation can mean to reveal or disclose information that was not known previously in a dramatic way. Can you recall a television series, such as *Fair City*, or a film, such as one from *The Lord of the Rings* trilogy, or a book, such as one from the *Twilight* series, where there was a memorable and dramatic revelation of some important information? As a class, share the revelations that you remember.

   b Based on these revelations, discuss the reactions of the people who experienced the revelation – did they feel shock, anger, fear or another similarly strong emotion? Do you think that experiencing a revelation is an easy or a difficult process to go through? Why?

First reading

2. From reading this poem, which one of the poet's memories did you find the most striking? Explain your answer with reference to the poem.

3. **a** Lines 1–7 describe what life was like for the poet as a young girl before she saw the bull. Why does she go to the farm?

   b Do you think she feels safe and cared for by the people at the farm? Why?

c What did she know about 'the black bull' before she is brought to see him?

4. **a** In lines 8–14, the poet uses images (word-pictures) that appeal to the senses of smell, sight and hearing to convey just how dramatic it was for the girl to experience the size and strength of 'the black bull'. Discuss which sense is appealed to in each of the images in lines 8–14.

   b Pick out two images from these lines that you feel vividly convey her impression of the bull's size and strength and explain why you chose them.

Second reading

5. **a** 'He roared his rage. His nostrils gaped like wounds'. What words in this line suggest that the girl understands that the bull's size and strength could easily turn to violent anger and the desire to injure? Give reasons for your choice of words.

   b In lines 19–21, the girl refers to the bull as 'that Black Mass' and the 'Anti-Christ his anarchy'. Explain how both of these references show that she also realises that the bull's violent anger and desire to injure are driven by evil.

   c The girl comments that she 'had always half-known he existed'. What do you think she means by this?

6. **a** Back outside the bull's 'outhouse', the girl realises that because of her revelation about the presence of evil in the world, her feelings and attitudes towards the bull have changed so that they are now very different to those of the hens. What do the hens know about the bull? How is this different to the girl's knowledge of the bull?

b What is the hens' attitude to the bull? How is this different to the girl's feelings and attitude to the bull?

c Do you think she might envy the hens' unchanged state? Why?

7. **a** Lines 24–31 describe how, because of her revelation about the presence of evil in the world, she no longer feels safe and cared for. What emotion drives her to run away from the farm?

b How do the 'big boys' in lines 25–7 also make her feel afraid of her world? Explain how her fear is increased by nature in line 28.

8. Think back to your work for Question 1. Do you think the girl finds her revelation an easy or a difficult process to go through? Explain your answer with reference to the poem.

Third reading

9. **a** As a young girl, the poet went to the farm to collect 'eggs and milk'. Following her revelation, examine how her fear is suggested by her worries about the 'eggs and milk' in lines 22–3 and lines 29–31.

b The eggs and milk are vulnerable because they can be easily broken and spilled. Do you think the girl now feels that she, too, is vulnerable in the world? Why?

10. Would you include this poem in a collection of poetry for young people? Give reasons for your answer based on your reading of the poem.

PENELOPE
SHUTTLE

(1947–)

Penelope Shuttle was born in Middlesex, England, in 1947. From an early age Shuttle was very aware of the natural world, feeling that she was 'part of a continuum with nature and weather'. As a teenager, she read, and was excited by, a wide range of poetry. In 1969 she met the poet and teacher Peter Redgrove, and in spite of a 16-year age difference, the two were drawn together by their 'affinity as poets'. Their marriage was immensely successful both personally and creatively, with Shuttle and Redgrove continuing to write poetry and prose as individuals and as a collaborative pair until Redgrove's death in 2003. Their move to Cornwall in 1970 was equally successful and Shuttle continues to live there today, because for her 'Cornwall is an artist itself … with its glittering light and its granite shadows'.

Shuttle received the first of her many awards for writing in 1974 and she continues to participate actively in all aspects of the world of poetry, ranging from judging poetry competitions to giving readings of her work.

OL 2C

JUNGIAN COWS

In Switzerland, the people call their cows
Venus, Eve, Salome, or Fraulein Alberta,
beautiful names
to yodel across the pasture at Bollingen.

If the woman is busy with child or book,   5
the farmer wears his wife's skirt
to milk the most sensitive cows.

When the electric milking-machine arrives,
the stalled cows rebel and sulk
for the woman's impatient skilful fingers   10
on their blowzy tough rosy udders,
will not give their milk;

so the man who works the machine
dons cotton skirt, all floral delicate flounces
to hide his denim overalls and big old muddy boots,   15

he fastens the cool soft folds carefully,
wraps his head in his sweetheart's sunday-best fringed scarf,
and walks smelling feminine and shy among the cows,

till the milk spurts, hot, slippery and steamy
into the churns,
Venus, Salome, Eve, and Fraulein Alberta,   20
lowing, half-asleep,
accepting the disguised man as an echo of the woman,
their breath smelling of green, of milk's sweet traditional climax.

NOTES

	Jungian:	Carl Jung (1875–1961) was a Swiss psychiatrist whose work in psychology is still influential today. His ideas have also influenced a number of poets, including Penelope Shuttle and her husband, Peter Redgrove.
	Cows:	one of Jung's theories concerns the 'collective unconscious' (the feelings and thoughts about universal themes, or archetypes, that humans as a group inherit from earlier groups). Jung identified several key archetypes that recur, e.g. the mother. One of the symbols used to represent the mother archetype is the cow. For example, the ancient Egyptian goddess Hathor was often shown as a cow to emphasise her 'motherly' qualities. The cow has also been used to symbolise qualities traditionally held to be feminine, e.g. concern for the community or group or being instinctive. Jung believed that men have some feminine elements within them.
4	Bollingen:	a small village located on the north bank of Lake Zurich, Switzerland. Jung built a holiday home there and lived in it for several months each year.
9	stalled:	to stop; to be put in a compartment in a cowshed
11	blowzy:	rough looking
14	flounces:	a frill

EXPLORATIONS

First reading

1. Do you find this an amusing poem? Pick out the parts of the poem that amused you.

2. Using the clues in stanza 2, who do you think usually milks 'the most sensitive cows'? Can you suggest a reason why this is?

3. a What does stanza 3 tell you about how the cows reacted to the 'electric milking-machine'?

   b Are you surprised by their reaction? Why?

4. a What did 'the farmer' and 'the man who works the machine' do to persuade the cows to give the milk?

   b   From your reading of the poem, would you say that the men were comfortable or uncomfortable about what they had to do?

5. a   Do you think the cows were really fooled by what the men did? Refer to the poem to support your view.

   b   Can you suggest why the cows decided to co-operate?

Second reading

6. a   Divide a page into two columns. Put the heading 'Female' over one column and 'Male' over the other. Go through the poem and pick out all the words and phrases that are connected to females and write them in the Female column, then do the same for males in the Male column.

   b   Using your lists, write a description in your own words of how being female is portrayed in the poem, then do the same with male.

   c   Do you agree with the two portrayals? Explain your answer.

7. a   Who would you say holds the most power in this poem, the male figures or the female figures? Support your view with quotations from the poem.

   b   Given the lists that you made for Question 6, are you surprised by this distribution of power? Why?

8. a   'till the milk spurts, hot, slippery and steamy', 'their breath smelling of green, of milk's sweet traditional climax'. How does the poet suggest in these lines that milk is a comforting and nourishing food that promotes life?

   b   'Venus, Eve, Salome, or Fraulein Alberta', 'accepting the disguised man as an echo of the woman'. What do you think the poet is suggesting here about the connection between female figures and the production and collection of milk, the promoter of life?

Third reading

9. a   The poet uses the word 'traditional' in the final line of the poem. A tradition is a custom passed down through the generations. What traditions can you find in this poem?

   b   Do you think we should always keep to the traditional way of doing things? Why?

10. Tell the story of this situation from the point of view of either 'the man who works the machine' or one of 'the stalled cows'.

ZOO MORNING

Elephants prepare to look solemn and move slowly
though all night they drank and danced, partied
and gambled, didn't act their age.

Night-scholar monkeys take off their glasses,
pack away their tomes and theses,   5
sighing as they get ready for yet another long day
of gibbering and gesticulating, shocking
and scandalising the punters.

Bears stop shouting their political slogans
and adopt their cute-but-not-really teddies' stance   10
in the concrete bear-pit.

Big cats hide their flower presses, embroidery-frames and watercolours;
grumbling, they try a few practice roars.
Their job is to rend the air, to devour carcasses,
to sleep-lounge at their vicious carnivorous ease.   15

What a life.
But none of them would give up show-business.

The snakes who are always changing,
skin after skin,
open their aged eyes and hinged jaws in welcome.   20

Between paddock and enclosure
we drag our unfurred young.
Our speech is over-complex, deceitful.
Our day is not all it should be.
The kids howl, baffled.   25

All the animals are very good at being animals.
As usual, we are not up to being us.
Our human smells prison us.

In the insect house
the red-kneed spider dances on her eight light fantastics;   30
on her shelf of silence she waltzes and twirls;
joy in her hairy joints, her ruby-red eyes.

EXPLORATIONS

Before reading

1. Think back to a visit you made to the zoo or to nature programmes you watched on television. How would you describe each of the following animals to a young child: elephants, monkeys, bears, big cats, snakes, spiders? Jot down words and phrases that capture how they move and behave.

First reading

2. On first reading this poem, what do you notice?

3. Did you enjoy the descriptions of the dual life of elephants? Explain your reaction.

4. a   What do the monkeys in their night life personas remind you of?

   b   Do you think the poet describes the day life of the monkeys well? Explain.

5. a   How does she imagine the hidden life of bears?

   b   How does she feel about everyday bears?

   c   Do you think her description has caught an essential truth about the animals?

6. In pairs, explore:

   a   the contrast between the daytime and nighttime lives of big cats. What do you notice?

   b   What words or phrases best catch their frightening fierceness?

   c   What patterns are emerging in this poem?

d   Can you suggest what the poet might be up to?

Second reading

7. a   When you saw the snakes opening their hinged jaws, did you feel welcomed?

   b   Does this description fit in with the tone of the poem?

8. a   'Between paddock and enclosure'.
       Do you think this section accurately describes the experience of some family outings to the zoo? Develop your ideas.

   b   'our unfurred young'.
       What do you think the poet is suggesting here?

   c   'Our speech is over-complex, deceitful'.
       Discuss what this might mean and how it links to the rest of the poem.
       Do you agree with what the poet is suggesting about human beings here?

9. a   Do you think the poet admires the spider? Explain your thinking.

   b   How does this stanza link with the previous one?

Third reading

10. The poet is turning the world as we see it on its head to make us view it afresh and really think about it. What does this poem make you think about? These are the themes.

11. Will your next visit to the zoo provoke new thoughts? Explain.

RACHEL LODEN

(1948–)

Rachel Loden was born in 1948 in Washington DC. Her father, an actor and radio announcer, was blacklisted by the House of UnAmerican Activities Committee (HUAC) and his career was shortened as a result. Her parents divorced and her mother was frequently hospitalised for bouts of schizophrenia. Consequently, Rachel and her brother were cared for in a series of foster homes. The family moved around and lived in Brooklyn, Berkeley, Los Angeles and Westport, Connecticut.

Richard Nixon (former US president and member of the HUAC) has been the inspiration for a lot of her satirical poems about life in the United States in the twentieth century.

This poem comes from her first published collection of poetry *Hotel Imperion* (1999). Her darkly satirical look at the cold objectivity of the benefits department is humorous but also unsettling.

OL 2019

MEMO FROM THE BENEFITS DEPARTMENT

For an eye, not an eye.
For a tooth, forget it.
No benefit if you cut off
your own hand or your own foot:
ditto for war,   5
suicide or riot.

For extremities,
"loss" means severance
at the wrist or ankle joint.
For eyes,   10
the slow or sudden
disappearance of the light.

For life, "loss" means
black limousines,
a brief orbit.   15

If you suffer,
see the Schedule of Sorrows.

Benefits may be paid out
as a lump sum: small
heap of coal, gray-dimpled
gruel, charred box of soot.

20

NOTES

5	ditto:	the same again
21	gruel:	a thin, watery, oat-based meal

EXPLORATIONS

First reading

1. What does the title make you think of?

2. What type of language would you associate with this type of official document?

3. Does the language in the first stanza conform to this expectation? Explain your answer.

4. Do you think the poet is entirely serious in the poem? What gives you this impression?

Second reading

5. What impression do you form of the poet from reading this poem? Explain your answer with reference to the poem.

6. a What does the term 'a lump sum' usually mean?
   b How does the poem change the meaning? Why do you think the poet does this?

Third reading

7. Write a letter to the poet responding to her poem. Outline your thoughts and responses to her writing.

8. What does this poem say about life in the modern age? Explain your answer.

9. The poet has said 'Poetry was a way to make music without making noise… Each line break is a crucial musical decision'.
   How do you think this statement applies to this poem?

KERRY HARDIE

(1951–)

Kerry Hardie was born in Singapore in 1951, grew up in County Down, studied English at York University and now lives in County Kilkenny. She has won many prizes for her poetry. Among her collections are *In Sickness* (1995), *A Furious Place* (1996), *Cry for the Hot Belly* (2000), *The Sky Didn't Fall* (2003), from which 'Daniel's Duck' is taken, and *The Silence Came Close* (2006).

OL 2019

DANIEL'S DUCK

I held out the shot mallard, she took it from me,
looped its neck-string over a drawer of the dresser.
The children were looking on, half-caught.
Then the kitchen life – warm, lit, glowing –
moved forward, taking in the dead bird, 5
and its coldness, its wildness, were leaching away.

The children were sitting to their dinners.
Us too – drinking tea, hardly noticing
the child's quiet slide from his chair,
his small absorbed body before the duck's body, 10
the duck changing – feral, live –
arrowing up out of black sloblands
with the gleam of a river
falling away below.

Then the duck – dead again – hanging from the drawer-knob, 15
the green head, brown neck running into the breast,
the intricate silvery-greyness of the back;
the wings, their white bars and blue flashes,
the feet, their snakey, orange scaliness, small claws, piteous webbing,
the yellow beak, blooded, 20
the whole like a weighted sack –
all that downward-dragginess of death.

He hovered, took a step forward, a step back,
something appeared in his face, some knowledge

of a place where he stood, the world stilled,   25
the lit streaks of sunrise running off red
into the high bowl of morning.

She watched him, moving to touch, his hand out:
What is it Daniel, do you like the duck?
He turned as though caught in the act,   30
saw the gentleness in her face and his body loosened.
I thought there was water on it –
he was finding the words, one by one,
holding them out, to see would they do us –
but there isn't.   35
He added this on, going small with relief
that his wing-drag of sounds was enough.

NOTES

1	mallard:	a type of wild duck
6	leaching:	being drained away or sucked out
11	feral:	wild
12	sloblands:	muddy ground or land
19	piteous:	pitiful

EXPLORATIONS

First reading

1. Focus on the first two stanzas.
   a Describe in sequence what happens.
   b What do you notice about the kitchen, the reaction of the children and the reaction of the adults?

2. Focus on the description of the duck in the third stanza. Read it a number of times, then close your eyes and imagine it in detail. Now write a brief but detailed description of it.

3. What are your feelings on reading the description of the dead duck? Discuss them in groups.

4. Read the fourth stanza.
   a Imagine you are Daniel. What do you see? What thoughts are going through your head?
   b What thoughts might be going through the mother's head?

Second reading

5. This incident provokes a moment of insight or new understanding (an epiphany) for each of the participants – the writer, the mother and Daniel. Describe each of these, using evidence from the text to support your ideas.

6. What do you think are the main issues or themes this poem deals with? Develop your ideas on this.

7. Do you think the poet has a good eye for observation? Support your ideas with evidence from the poem.

Third reading

8. Imagine that you meet Daniel as an adult in later years and he remembers the incident. Write the dialogue as you think it might occur.

9. Write three paragraphs on what you liked about this poem and why.

10. How different from your own world is the world of this poem?

11. Do you think the mother should have brought the duck into the kitchen?

ANDREW
HUDGINS

(1951 –)

B orn in Killeen, Texas in 1951, Andrew Hudgins is the son of a military
family. As a consequence much of his childhood was spent moving from
military base to military base across the American south. He attended the
Huntington College and University of Alabama. His first collection of poetry,
Saints and Strangers, was published in 1986 and was nominated for a Pulitzer Prize.
His poetry is known for its dark humour and narrative voice. His collection *The
Glass Hammer: A Southern Childhood* (1994) is an autobiographical account of
his childhood in poetry form. The collection owes a lot to the southern gothic
tradition of writers such as Tennessee Williams and William Faulkner. Macabre or
violent events are used to explore social issues or childhood memories. While
the collection is autobiographical, Hudgins admits the necessary lies of the
autobiographer. Events are made coherent, characters are added or omitted in
order to enhance the storytelling and the poet is always aware of the presentation
of self to the audience. He currently teaches in Ohio State University.

THE GLASS HAMMER

My mother's knickknack crystal hammer
shone on the shelf. "Put that thing down.
It's not a play-pretty." *Tap, tap,*
against my wooden blocks. "I said,
PUT THAT THING DOWN!"   5

But when she wasn't looking– ha –!
I'd sneak back to the hammer, and heft it.
Enchanted, I held it to my eyes
and watched, through it, the living room
shift, waver, and go shimmery – haloed   10

with hidden fire. Our worn green sofa glowed
and lost its shape, as if some deeper shape
were trying to break loose. The chairs,
the walls, the cross-stitched pictures all
let go, smeared into one another.   15

I scrounged a rust-flecked nail, and hit it.
The hammer shattered in my hand.
Blood spattered on my shorts. I screamed,
was snatched off my fat bloody feet,
rushed to the doctor, stitched, cooed at, spanked,   20

embraced, told *never, never, never*
do that again, and pondered how
I could, the hammer having burst,
and not, therefore, a proper hammer
despite the gorgeous world it held.   25

NOTES

1	knickknack	small worthless household ornament
14	cross-stitched pictures	a popular style of embroidery where a picture, pattern or motto is created using crossed stitches on a plain fabric and framed

EXPLORATIONS

First reading

1. Describe the events of the poem in your own words.

2. What is your impression of the child from the poem? Support your answer with words or phrases from the poem.

3. What impression of the boy's mother do you get from the poem? Support your answer with evidence from the poem.

4. a What aspects of childhood fairytales can you find in the poem?

b   Why do you think the poet uses these aspects?

5.   What difficulty does the child have with the adult warning at the end of the poem?

Second reading

6.   Does the poet capture a child's perspective on the event? What elements of the poem help to capture that perspective?

7.   What images from the poem do you find striking or unusual? Explain your answer.

8.   What effect does using the direct speech of the adult have on the poem?

9.   How does the poet capture the atmosphere of panic in the fourth stanza? Support your answer with reference to the poem.

Third reading

10. Imagine you are the boy's mother. Write your account of the event detailed in the poem, from your point of view.

11. Imagine that you have been asked to make a short YouTube video to accompany a reading of this poem. Describe some of the images, colours, music, sound effects, etc. that you would use as a background to the reading and explain your choices, based on your knowledge of the poem.

12. Do you like or dislike this poem? Give reasons for your answer.

OL 202

OL 20

THE CADILLAC IN THE ATTIC

After the tenant moved out, died, disappeared
– the stories vary – the landlord
walked downstairs, bemused, and told his wife,
"There's a Cadillac in the attic,"

and there was. An old one, sure, and one   5
with sloppy paint, bald tires,
and orange rust chewing at the rocker panels,
but still and all, a Cadillac in the attic.

He'd battled transmission, chassis, engine block,
even the huge bench seats,   10
up the folding stairs, heaved them through the trapdoor,
and rebuilt a Cadillac in the attic.

Why'd he do it? we asked. But we know why.
For the reasons we would do it: for the looks
of astonishment he'd never see but could imagine.   15
For the joke. A Cadillac in the attic!

And for the meaning, though we aren't sure what it means.
And of course he did it for pleasure,
the pleasure on his lips of all those short vowels
and three hard clicks: the Cadillac in the attic.   20

NOTES

| 4 | Cadillac | brand of American car |
| 9 | chassis | underpart of the frame of a motor car |

EXPLORATIONS

Before reading

1. Listen to the Johnny Cash song 'One Piece at a Time'. The poet has said that this song was part of the inspiration for this poem. What strikes you about this song?

First reading

2. Describe, in your own words, the events described in this poem.

3. Why do you think the phrase 'a Cadillac in the attic' is repeated at the end of every stanza?

4. What do you think of when you imagine a Cadillac? What is associated with this type of car?

Second reading

5. Do you think the poet admires the man who did this? What words or phrases in the poem give you this impression?

6. How do you think the landlord felt when he found the Cadillac?

7. What impression of the car do you form from reading the details in the poem?

8. Why do you think someone would undertake such a task?

Third reading

9. How do the actions of the tenant relate to the work of a poet? Explain your answer.

10. Imagine you are the landlord who discovered the car. Write the letter you would send to the tenant who moved out about your discovery.

11. Write a brief note about the language used in this poem.

GARY
SOTO

(1952–)

Gary Soto was born in Fresno, California, to poor working-class Mexican-American (Chicano) parents. As a young man he worked in the fields and the factories of San Joaquin and Fresno. He was educated at California State University, Fresno, and at the University of California, Irvine, where he earned a Masters in Fine Art. He taught at the University of California, Berkeley, for many years.

A prolific writer of novels, short stories, plays, memoirs, poetry and fiction for young people, much of his work deals with the experience of growing up and living in Mexican-American communities.

Among his collections of poetry are *The Elements of San Joaquin* (1997), *The Tale of Sunlight* (1978), *Black Hair* (1985), *Neighborhood Odes* (1992) and *Canto Familiar/Familiar Song* (1994). 'Oranges' is taken from *New and Selected Poems* (1995).

ORANGES

The first time I walked
With a girl, I was twelve,
Cold, and weighted down
With two oranges in my jacket.
December. Frost cracking   5
Beneath my steps, my breath
Before me, then gone,
As I walked toward
Her house, the one whose
Porch light burned yellow   10
Night and day, in any weather.
A dog barked at me, until
She came out pulling
At her gloves, face bright
With rouge. I smiled,   15
Touched her shoulder, and led

Her down the street, across
A used car lot and a line
Of newly planted trees,
Until we were breathing   20
Before a drugstore. We
Entered, the tiny bell
Bringing a saleslady
Down a narrow aisle of goods.
I turned to the candies   25
Tiered like bleachers,
And asked what she wanted –
Light in her eyes, a smile
Starting at the corners
Of her mouth. I fingered   30
A nickel in my pocket,
And when she lifted a chocolate
That cost a dime,
I didn't say anything.
I took the nickel from   35
My pocket, then an orange,
And set them quietly on
The counter. When I looked up,
The lady's eyes met mine,
And held them, knowing   40
Very well what it was all
About.

          Outside,
A few cars hissing past,
Fog hanging like old   45
Coats between the trees.
I took my girl's hand
In mine for two blocks,
Then released it to let
Her unwrap the chocolate.   50
I peeled my orange
That was so bright against
The gray of December
That, from some distance,
Someone might have thought   55
I was making a fire in my hands.

NOTES

15	rouge:	a blusher powder used to give colour to the cheeks
18	used car lot:	an American term for the business where used cars are stored and sold
21	drugstore:	the American equivalent of a cornershop
25	candies:	American term used to refer to all kinds of sweets and chocolate
26	bleachers:	American term used to describe the raised, tiered rows of open-plank seating at sports fields
31	a nickel:	a 5 cent coin in American money
33	a dime:	a 10 cent coin, one-tenth of a dollar

EXPLORATIONS

First reading

For this first reading, think of the poem in four sections:

- Section 1 (lines 1–11): The journey to her house.
- Section 2 (lines 12–21): They greet and walk to the drugstore.
- Section 3 (lines 22–42): At the drugstore.
- Section 4 (lines 43–56): The finale.

Section 1 (lines 1–11)

1. If you filmed the boy's journey to the house, list all the details the film would pick up.

2. What do you think are the thoughts inside his head? Are there any indications as to how he feels?

Section 2 (lines 12–21)

3. If you happened to be passing on the street and you witnessed the girl emerging from her house, the greeting and their departure, what would you think was the relationship between them? Explain your thinking on this.

Section 3 (lines 22–42)

4. In the drugstore scene, what do you think would have been the thoughts inside the heads of (a) the girl (b) the boy and (c) the saleslady? Jot down what you imagine each was thinking and discuss these in groups.

5. In pairs, role play the conversation that might occur if they happened to meet later between (a) the girl and the saleslady and (b) the boy and the saleslady.

6. Role play the conversation about this incident between the boy and the girl one year later.

Section 4 (line 43–56)

7. Try to describe the boy's feelings here.

Second reading

8. What important insights into the lives of young adults does this poem reveal to us? List your thoughts and discuss the question in groups.

9. What do you like about this poem?

10. Do you think the title is a good one? Explain your thinking.

JULIE O'CALLAGHAN

(1954–)

Julie O'Callaghan was born in Chicago in 1954 and moved to Ireland in 1974. Her poetry for children is particularly popular and appears in a number of children's anthologies. Her poetry for adults is highly regarded and in 2001 she won the Michael Hartnett Poetry Award. In April 2003, Julie O'Callaghan was made a member of Aosdána in recognition of the contribution she has made to the arts in Ireland. She was married to the poet Dennis O'Driscoll, who died in 2012.

OL 2

THE NET

I am the Lost Classmate
being hunted down the superhighways
and byways of infinite cyber-space.
How long can I evade the class committee
searching for my lost self?   5

I watch the list
of Found Classmates
grow by the month.
Corralled into a hotel ballroom
Festooned with 70s paraphernalia,   10

bombarded with atmospheric
hit tunes, the Captured Classmates
from Sullivan High School
will celebrate thirty years
of freedom from each other.   15

I peek at the message board:
my locker partner,
out in California, looks forward
to being reunited with
her old school chums.   20

Wearing a disguise, I calculate
the number of months left
for me to do what I do best,
what I've always done:
slip through the net.   25

NOTES

4	evade:	avoid
9	Corralled:	to be put into an enclosure, often used in connection with cattle or other animals
10	paraphernalia:	various objects
11	bombarded:	to attack with objects or to question a person constantly

EXPLORATIONS

Before reading

1. **a** The title of this poem is 'The Net'. How many different types of net can you think of? You might like to collect pictures to show the types of net that you have suggested.

   b Do the different types of net have anything in common?

First reading

2. **a** What type of net is described in the first stanza of the poem? Pick out the words that lead you to this conclusion.

   b From your reading of lines 1–8, can you explain what is being organised using this net?

3. **a** Why do you think the poet describes herself as 'the Lost Classmate' in line 1?

   b Can you explain why she refers to the person that she was when she was at school as 'my lost self'?

   c Do you agree with the poet's view that as a person goes though life, he/she can have different 'selves'? Give reasons for your answer.

4. **a** In your own words, describe how the poet imagines the scene in the 'hotel ballroom' in lines 9–12.

   b Do the images she uses suggest that she considers it a pleasant or an unpleasant experience?

Second reading

5. Using the clues in the first and last stanzas, do you get the impression that the poet does or does not want to be found by 'the class committee'?

6. **a** List all the different words that you would use to describe someone who is your friend.

   b Do the words 'locker partner' in line 17 suggest to you that this person was a friend of the poet's? Explain your answer.

7. From your reading of the poem, what do you think happened during the poet's time at Sullivan High School to make her react in the way that she does to the reunion?

8. Given the poet's reaction to the class reunion, are you surprised that she keeps checking the reunion website? Why?

Third reading

9. **a** 'slip through the net'. How is the net that appears in the final line of the poem different from the net that was described in the first stanza? Explain your answer.

b   As far as the poet is concerned, what are the two nets trying to do to her?

10. Imagine that you are the poet when she was in her teens attending Sullivan High School. Write her diary entry in which she describes her experiences during a day at school.

OL 20

PROBLEMS 🔊

Take weeds for example.
Like how they will overrun
your garden and your life
if you don't obliterate them.
But forget about weeds   5
– what about leaves?
Snails use them as handy
bridges to your flowers
and hordes of thuggish slugs
will invade – ever thought about *that*?   10
We won't even go into
how leaves block up the gutters.
I sure hope you aren't neglecting
any puddles of water in your bathtub
– discoloration will set in.   15
There is the wasp problem,
the storms problem, the grass
growing-between-the-bricks-in-the-driveway problem.
Then there's the remembering to
lock-all-the-windows problem.   20
Hey, knuckleheads!
I guess you just don't appreciate
how many problems there are.

NOTES		
2	obliterate:	destroy completely
9	thuggish:	behaving in violent and lawless ways
21	knuckleheads:	stupid people

EXPLORATIONS

First reading

1. **a** Count the number of problems mentioned in the twenty-three lines of this poem. Would you agree with the poet's decision to give this poem the title 'Problems'? Explain your answer.

   b Some of the problems are vividly described. Choose the two descriptions you like the most and explain why you like them.

2. **a** A lot of the lines in this poem are short, made up of only four or five words. What effect does this have on the pace, or speed, at which this poem is read?

   b Experiment with reading it quickly and slowly and discuss which sounds better. Does the pace that you agreed on suggest anything to you about the speaker's feelings?

Second reading

3. **a** ' – ever thought about that?', 'Hey, knuckleheads!', 'I guess you just don't appreciate/how many problems there are.' How would you describe the speaker's tone of voice in these lines?

   b What does this tone reveal about the speaker's attitude to the way in which other people view the problems that she is worried about?

   c Do you think she is right to worry about these problems? Why?

4. **a** ' – what about leaves? Snails use them as handy bridges to your flowers and hordes of thuggish slugs will invade'. Describe in your own words the picture that you see when you read these lines.

   b How does the poet's use of rhyme in the phrase 'thuggish slugs' help to make the image of the slugs more memorable?

5. The speaker in the poem tends to exaggerate her problems. Do you think she does this because she is trying to be funny or because she is worried? Explain your answer.

6. In one sentence, sum up what you think the theme, or message, of this poem is.

Third reading

7. Examine how the poet creates the impression that the speaker in this poem is in conversation with someone else. You might like to look at the type of language used, the structure of the phrases and the use of questions.

8. A dramatic monologue is where a person speaks and through what is said reveals his/her character. From your readings of this poem, how would you describe the character of the speaker?

9. Imagine that you are a magazine agony aunt/uncle answering problems sent in to you by readers. You have received this poem in the post. Write your reply.

10. The writer of this poem, Julie O'Callaghan, has said, 'I think it [poetry] should be a haven of quietness where you can hear yourself think.' What has this poem made you think about?

MARY
O'MALLEY

(1954–)

Born in Connemara, Mary O'Malley was educated at NUI Galway. She lived in Portugal for eight years and also spent time in France, before returning to Ireland in the late 1980s. She now lives in the Moycullen Gaeltacht, Galway. She has published eight volumes of poetry, which include *Where the Rocks Float* (1993), *The Knife in the Wave* (1997), *The Boning Hall* (2002) and *Playing the Octopus* (2016). Her poetry is rooted in the landscapes, seascapes, history and language of the authentic West of Ireland and she is committed to preserving that culture against the idealised images of the Celtic Revival, the multinationals and holiday home colonisation.

O'Malley has taught on writing courses nationally – NUIG and UL – as well as internationally – in the US, UK, France and Portugal. She facilitated a creative writing group (*as Gaeilge*) in Inis Mór which was filmed for the RTÉ documentary *To the Island* (1993). In 2013 she was Heimbold Professor of Irish Studies at Villanova University. She is a member of Aosdána,

OL 2
OL 2

CAOINEADH MHÁIRE

Why do we love men that are bad for us –
are we that weak? Hardly the kisses,
fruit in the mouth soon melts.
His Spaniard's eyes never settled on me right
but the mouth music lured me.   5

There was something old about his voice
that took the city ground from under me
and brought little yellow shells
scattering up the back streets of Glasgow.
Oh he was handsome, though, like a stag.   10

When I felt the fine sand
between my toes I should have run
to the nearest forgettable city boy
and chanced the ordinary,
but he sang and I was caught.   15

I listened as the hook eased in,
listened for the blas he put on my name
until all I could hear was my own breath
like the tide in a cave, echoing, going out
and the children crying. 20

A grey crow settled on my chest
and took his time.
A high price for a slow song:
"A Pheadair, a Aspail, an bhfaca tú mo ghrá bhán?
Ochon agus ochon o." 25

BACKGROUND NOTE

'Caoineadh Mháire' (Mary's Lament) is one of a set of six poems, entitled 'The Joe Heaney Poems', about the gifted Irish sean-nós singer (old style; plain; unaccompanied). He was married to Mary Connolly, whose family is from Connemara, and they lived in Glasgow for a time. In this poem the poet takes on the imagined persona and voice of Mary, as she tells her story. (For more detail, see the section on Joe Heaney in the critical notes on this poem.

NOTES

4	His Spaniard's eyes:	dark, romantic
5	lured:	enticed, attracted, tempted
6	something old (about his voice):	dating from far back, as 'sean-nós' singing did; also time-honoured, classical
17	blas:	accent; also flavour or taste
21	a grey crow:	also known as the hooded crow, it has a grey body with black head and wings. It eats everything, including carrion. In Celtic mythology, the bird appeared on the shoulder of the dying Cúchulainn. It could be associated with the Morrigan, a phantom queen that foretold death in battle or with the Bean Sí, a female spirit that signals a coming death. With all these associations, it is a sign of approaching death in this poem.

21–22	on my chest/ and took his time:	a reference to Mary's slow death from tuberculosis
24	"A Pheadair, a Aspail, an bhfaca tú mo ghrá bhán?":	'Oh Peter, Apostle, have you seen my fair love?'
25	"Ochon agus ochon o":	variously translated as 'alas and alack' or 'alas, woe is me' and others. Probably best to think of it as an almost inarticulate cry of grief. This is a refrain from *Caoineadh na dTrí Mhuire* (The Three Marys), a lament about the Crucifixion of Jesus and based on a twelfth-century European song. The three Marys are believed to be Mary the mother of Jesus, Mary Magdalene and Mary of Caiphas. It is structured as a conversation between Peter, Jesus, Mary his mother, the Roman soldiers and others. One of the things communicated in the song is the disbelief and distress of Mary, which is heard in these lines. You can listen to Joe Heaney's version on YouTube.

EXPLORATIONS

First reading

Stanzas 1–3

1. Read and listen to the stanzas being read. In pairs or groups, discuss the following issues and any others that come to mind, concerning this section.

   a Focus on Máire; listen to her voice.

- What is she talking about?
- Why was she attracted to the man in the poem?
- From the evidence of the poem so far, do you think she is finding life simple or complicated? Explain your thinking.
- What do you think was going through her head in stanza 3?

   b Examine the words and phrases she uses to describe her experience of falling in love. What do they suggest to you about the experience? Write your thoughts on this.

Second reading

Stanzas 4–5

2. a What do you think has happened in stanza 4?

   b Do you think this was entirely unexpected? Explain your thinking.

   c What would you say to her? Give this careful thought, then write her a letter.

3. Discuss what may be happening in stanza 5. Consult the notes. Jot down your first thoughts on this stanza.

Third reading

4. Can you sympathise with this woman's story? Outline how you feel about it (200 words).

5. Write about two images that made a strong impression on you, say what they suggest to you and what you think they contribute to the poem.

6. Listen to the way she speaks and the phrases she uses.

   a Are there phrases and expressions you have not heard before, don't usually hear or don't use? List them.

b   In groups, discuss:

- What these phrases might mean
- Where they might be heard spoken or by whom
- If you think this personal, conversational language helps the reader understand and identify with the issues in the poem.

Fourth reading

7. Does the poem set you thinking about life? Write your thoughts on this (200 words).

8. Would you recommend or not recommend this poem to others? Outline the reasons for your view (200 words).

NOTE

You may like to read 'Footsteps', the final poem in this set, written in Joe Heaney's voice. It can be found in *The Knife in the Wave* by Mary O'Malley (Salmon Poetry, 1997).

OL 2020

CEALTRACH

The children were never told
about those places. The unbreachable
silence of women protected us
from terrible things.
We heard the dread whisperings   5
and peopled the swarming places with ghosts.

Yet we never knew. They buried
unnamed innocents by the sea's edge
and in the unchurched graveyards
that straddled boundary walls. Those infants   10
half-human, half-soul were left
to make their own way on the night shore.

Forbidden funerals, where did mothers
do their crying in the two-roomed cottages
so beloved of those Irish times?   15
Never in front of the living children.
Where then? In the haggard, the cowshed,
the shadowed alcoves of their church?

That Christian religion was hard.
It mortified the flesh   20
and left mothers lying empty,
their full breasts aching, forever afraid
of what the winter storms might yield,
their own dreams turning on them like dogs.

NOTES

Cealtrach:		a name for an unconsecrated burial ground for unbaptised or stillborn babies
2	unbreachable:	impossible to break through
6	swarming places:	the places where they gathered or crowded (as a cluster or cloud of swarming bees)
9	unchurched:	unblessed; unconsecrated (i.e. not dedicated for religious purposes)
10	straddled:	situated on both sides
13	Forbidden funerals:	the unbaptised were not given religious funeral services
17	haggard:	a small field beside a farmhouse where hay etc. might be stacked for winter
18	alcoves:	recesses, or spaces set back in a wall
20	mortified the flesh:	brought the physical body under control by self-denial and discipline

EXPLORATIONS

First reading

Read the entire poem a number of times and then focus on each stanza in turn.

1. Put yourself in the place of the poet, as a child in the first stanza, listening to the 'dread whisperings'.
   a What were the whisperings about?
   b How did the children react? Is their reaction understandable?

2. a Describe what is happening in the second stanza.
   b What thoughts went through your mind as you read this? Outline them.

3. a What particular pressures did the mothers face in the third stanza?
   b What were your reactions on reading this stanza?

4. Put yourself inside the mind of one of the bereaved mothers in the fourth stanza. Describe what she is feeling.

Second reading

5. Write your impressions of what you think it would have been like to live there, at that time.

6. What do you think are the poet's feelings about the events and issues in this poem? Choose phrases and images that you think best communicate her views and feelings and give your reasons.

7. Outline, briefly, what you consider to be the main themes or issues dealt with in the poem (100 words).

8. Write a 'thoughts-inside-the-head' piece for one of the bereaved fathers.

CAROL ANN
DUFFY

(1955–)

Carol Ann Duffy was born in Glasgow of Irish parents but grew up in Staffordshire, England. She attended university in Liverpool, where she studied philosophy. Her poetry often gives voice to the powerless or the mentally unstable. She is adept at putting herself in somebody else's head and then writing from their perspective, be they psychopaths, maids or tabloid editors. Her poetry has a wry humour and a lot of people who would not regularly read poetry are comfortable with her style.

She has won many awards for her collections, which include *Standing Female Nude* (1985), *Selling Manhattan* (1987), *The Other Country* (1990), *Mean Time* (1993) and *The World's Wife* (1999). This last collection featured a series of poems written from the perspective of the forgotten female: Mrs Midas, Queen Kong, Mrs Lazarus and others.

Among her more recent collections are *Feminine Gospels* (2002), *Rapture* (2005) and *The Bees* (2011). She is also an accomplished playwright and has written picture books for children. In 2009 Carol Ann Duffy became the United Kingdom's twentieth Poet Laureate.

VALENTINE

OL 2020
OL 2022

Not a red rose or a satin heart.

I give you an onion.
It is a moon wrapped in brown paper.
It promises light
like the careful undressing of love.   5

Here.
It will blind you with tears
like a lover.
It will make your reflection
a wobbling photo of grief.   10

I am trying to be truthful.

Not a cute card or a kissogram.

I give you an onion.
Its fierce kiss will stay on your lips,
possessive and faithful   15
as we are,
for as long as we are.

Take it.
Its platinum loops shrink to a wedding-ring,
if you like.   20
Lethal.
Its scent will cling to your fingers,
cling to your knife.

EXPLORATIONS

Before reading

1. What do you associate with Valentine's Day?

First reading

2. What is your first reaction on reading this poem? Discuss the various reactions of the class.

3. The onion is given four times. What is it associated with each time?

4. Is there anything at all romantic about this poem?

Second reading

5. How long will the taste of onion stay on the lover's lips? How long will the couple last?

6. What type of relationship does the couple have? Have they been in love for long?

7. How does the onion promise light?

Third reading

8. How would you feel if you were given an onion for Valentine's Day?

9. The poet uses very short lines regularly in the poem. What effect do these short lines have?

10. Describe each metaphor that the speaker uses to describe the onion.

Fourth reading

11. Read 'My mistress's eyes' by William Shakespeare and compare it with this poem.

12. This poem manages to be both 'cold and passionate'. How?

13. Do you think this is a good love poem? What makes it good or bad?

14. 'Love is particular to individuals and can't be represented by love hearts and teddy bears.'
Does the poet agree? Do you?

PAULA MEEHAN

(1955–)

Paula Meehan was born in the Gardiner Street area of Dublin. She was thrown out of school yet managed to study and attend Trinity College Dublin and Eastern Washington University. She made a huge impact with the publication of her third volume of poems, *The Man Who Was Marked by Winter*, and then with *Pillow Talk*. Meehan's poetry should be read out loud. She is a mesmerising reader of her own work. Her poetry has harrowing lyrical intensity. She uses regular language confidently yet without making it seem ostentatious or over the top. Many of her poems, such as 'The Pattern' or 'The Ghost of My Mother Comforts Me', celebrate women in adversity and gives them a voice. She has also written a number of successful plays. One of these was *Cell* (1999), which was written after the poet had spent time giving poetry workshops in women's prisons.

OL 2022

THE RUSSIAN DOLL

Her colours caught my eye.
Mixed by the light of a far off sun:
carmine, turmeric, indigo, purple –
they promised to spell us dry weather.

I'd a fiver in my pocket; that's   5
all they asked for. And gift wrapped her.
It had been grey all month and damp.
We felt every year in our bones

and our dead had been too much with us.
January almost over. Bitter.   10
I carried her home like a Holy Fire
 the seven miles from town,

my face to a wind from the north. Saw
the first primroses in the maw of a fallen oak.
There was smoke from the chimney   15
when I came through the woods

and, though I had spent the dinner,
I knew you'd love your gaudy doll,
you'd love what's in her
at the end of your seventh winter.   20

NOTES

Russian Doll:		a hollow wooden figure that can be opened to reveal a series of similar figures, gradually decreasing in size, nesting inside each other
3	carmine:	a bright crimson or rich red colour
3	turmeric:	an Asian plant that can be used as a spice or a yellow dye
3	indigo:	a plant that produces blue dye
14	maw:	mouth or stomach
18	gaudy:	very bright

EXPLORATIONS

1. Write a 140-character (25–30 words) tweet describing the month of January in Ireland. As a group, share your tweets – perhaps you could write some of them on the board and discuss the general feeling of the class about January.

First reading

2. **a** What impression do you get from the poem of the poet's attitude to January? Refer to the text of the poem in your answer.

    b Pick out a line or phrase where you feel the poet expresses a similar view of January to the one that you expressed in your tweet for Question 1.

3. **a** What characteristics of the Russian doll caught the poet's attention in lines 1–4? Refer to the poem to support your answer.

    b Can you explain what the poet means when she says that the colours used to paint the doll are 'Mixed by the light of a far off sun'? You might find it helpful to read the notes following the poem.

    c What type of weather did the poet think of when she was looking at the Russian doll?

4. **a** How did the poet feel about paying a 'fiver' for the doll in lines 5–6? Support your answer by reference to the poem.

    b In line 17, we learn that the poet should have spent this 'fiver' on 'the dinner'. Do you think she made the correct decision? Why?

Second reading

5. How do lines 11–13 suggest that carrying the Russian doll made the poet feel as if she was protected from the harsh January weather as she walked back home? Refer to lines 11–13 to support your answer.

6. 'the first primroses in the maw of a fallen oak', 'There was smoke from the chimney/when I came through the woods'. The poet found that both of these sights make her feel more cheerful. Why do you think these sights affected her in this way?

7. **a** What reaction to the doll did the poet expect to get from her daughter?

    b What do you think the poet wanted to celebrate by giving her daughter this gift? Think about what is suggested by the phrase 'the end of your seventh winter'.

Third reading

8. Does the language used by the poet in this poem appeal to you? Explain your answer with reference to the poem.

9. In your opinion, is this mainly a happy poem or mainly a sad poem? Explain your answer by reference to the poem.

10. In this poem, the Russian doll cheered up the poet in spite of the January weather. Look back at your tweet about January in Ireland from Question 1, then write a piece describing what it would take to cheer you up in January.

MOYA CANNON

(1956–)

M oya Cannon was born in Dunfanaghy, Co. Donegal but has lived most of her life in Galway. She was educated in Donegal, at University College Dublin and at Corpus Christi College in Cambridge. She has taught in the Gaelscoil, Inchicore, Dublin; in a school for young Travellers in Galway; and at NUI Galway.

Moya Cannon's writing celebrates the cultural and spiritual in the natural world around her, whether it relates to the present, ancient history, or prehistoric times. Her affinity with nature is seen in the many landscapes and seascapes in her poems. She has lived, as she said 'between two languages' and regrets the loss of Irish and the richness of its words that occurred through emigration and colonisation.

She has published five collections of poetry: *Oar* (1990); *The Parchment Boat* (1997); *Carrying the Songs* (2007); *Hands* (2011); and *Keats Lives* (2015). A bilingual Spanish/English collection of her poems, *Aves de Invierno*, was published by Editorial Pre-Textos, Valencia, Spain in 2015. She has held many writer in residence posts, including Trent University, Ontario in 1994/95 and Heimbold Professor of Irish Studies at Villanova University in 2011. She is a member of Aosdána.

SHRINES

OL 2019
OL 2022

You will find them easily,
there are so many –
near roundabouts, by canal locks,
by quaysides –
haphazard, passionate, weathered, 5
like something a bird might build,
a demented magpie
bringing blue silk flowers,
real red roses,
an iron sunflower, 10
a Christmas wreath,
wind chimes,
photographs in cellophane,
angels, angels, angels
and hearts, hearts, hearts 15
and we know
that this is the very place
the police fenced off with tape,
that a church was jammed
with black-clad young people, 20
that under the flowers and chimes
is a great boulder of shock
with no-one to shoulder it away
to let grief flow
like dense tresses of water 25
over a weir.

NOTES

Shrines:		the name for a sacred or honoured place in memory of a dead person. The shrines in the poem refer to the impromptu or unplanned tributes of flowers, crosses, etc. that are a common sight on roadways to mark the location of a death.
5	haphazard:	unplanned, casual
5	passionate:	intense, emotional
5	weathered:	discoloured by the weather
7	demented:	mad, insane
9	red roses:	in the language of flowers, they signify love
10	sunflower:	in the language of flowers, it is a symbol of faithful love – from the Greek myth of Clytie who turned herself into a sunflower in grief over the loss of her love Apollo.
12	wind chimes:	suspended bells or tubes of varying lengths that create musical notes when blown together by the wind. In Roman times bronze bells were hung in gardens to ward off evil spirits. Today, wind chimes are commonly used to increase the flow of 'chi', the energy of life.
14	angels:	in religious thinking, they are messengers from God or caring spirits such as 'guardian angels'. The term is often used to describe a good, kind, selfless person or when describing babies and young children.
25	tresses:	locks of hair
26	weir:	a dam across a river to regulate the flow of water

EXPLORATIONS

Before reading

1. a   Have you noticed these roadside shrines of bunches of flowers, little crosses, etc.? Describe one you have seen.

    b   Have you attended the funeral of a young person? Jot down any thoughts and feelings you remember experiencing. If you feel able, share these, in small groups.

First reading

2. Read the poem, then do a class 'round' i.e. each person makes a statement about the poem beginning with 'I noticed that…'.

3. Focus on what you noticed about the shrines described in much detail in lines 8–15.

    a   In small groups, discuss your thoughts on the significance of some of these items. What do you think they represent? What are they expressing?

    b   What is the poet's impression of the overall visual effect of the shrines?

    c   Compare the roadside or quayside tributes with formal headstones and grave memorials. What are the differences? Which do you prefer as a memorial and why? Talk about this in small groups.

4. The poet describes the shrines as 'haphazard, passionate, weathered'. What do these words suggest to you about the shrines?

Second reading

5. The reality of the events that these shrines commemorate is recalled by the poet in a number of crisp, clear images. They leave a lot unsaid; it is left up to the reader to fill out the emotion or meaning.
   'that this is the very place/the police fenced of with tape,/that a church was jammed/with black-clad young people,/that under the flowers and chimes/is a great boulder of shock/with no-one to shoulder it away'
   What thoughts and feelings do each of these images awaken in you? Write diary-type notes on each one.

6. Consider the image of grief in the final three lines.
   a What does it say to you about grief?
   b Do you find this image very sad or is there any sense in which it can be seen as helpful to the mourners? Jot down your thoughts on this.

Third reading

7. Do you think the poem deals with issues that are important to young people? First, discuss this in class, then write your thoughts on it (300–500 words).

8. What do you notice about the language of the poem? Outline your thoughts in 200 words.

9. What do you like about the poem? (200 words).

RANDOLPH HEALY

(1956–)

Randolph Healy was born in Scotland but moved to Ireland as a child. He left school early, due to illness, but returned to education and took a degree in mathematical sciences from Trinity College, Dublin. Currently, he works as a teacher of mathematics and physics and runs the publishing house, Wild Honey Press. His poetry differs from the nationalist tradition that explored Irish identity in colonial and post-colonial situations, focusing more on human identity in the context of the physical world and even the Universe. He draws on logic, mathematics and his knowledge of the sciences to set up situations for the reader to contemplate, mostly without intrusion from the poet. Among his works are: *Arbor Vitae* (1997); *Green 532: Selected Poems 1983–2000* (2002); *Rattling the Bars* (2009); and *Hex* (2012).

PRIMULA VERIS

Clustering atop a leggy stem
ten elf green bodices tapered down
to blown about yellow pinafores.

Near the ground a mob of blotched leaves,
belching and gulping, stiff with liquor,   5
watched constellations kink and bend
and languages drift from grammar to grammar.

Sister Mary's favourite flower
cast a light on all the gougers
that she coaxed, effing and blinding,   10
to various degrees of joined-up writing.

One great arching cadence
glosses the world as a double spiral
speaks to itself with epochs for clauses

root shoot and flower   15
stitching together the heavens and the earth

NOTES

Primula veris:		common name 'cowslip', a native flower of the primrose family. This Latin name translates as 'little first one of the Spring' (even though it is not the earliest flowering!). *Primula veris* has been around for many millennia – there are references to it in Norse and Druidic mythology and from Pliny the Elder, the Roman naturalist and poet who died in 79 AD.
1	atop:	on top of (seventeenth-century usage)
2	elf green:	an elf is a supernatural being, in dwarfish form, with magical powers; a fairy or goblin. See *The Hobbit* and *Lord of the Rings* by J. R. R. Tolkien. Book illustrations frequently show elves and fairies dressed in green.
2	bodices:	above-the-waist, tight fitting section of a woman's dress (in fashion from the sixteenth and seventeenth centuries)
2	tapered:	becoming narrower towards one end
3	pinafores:	a type of apron; a dress-like covering that used to be worn by children and women to protect their clothes from dirt, etc.
4	blotched:	with irregular patches of colour
5	liquor:	probably refers to the sap in the leaves
6	constellations:	a constellation is a group of stars that appear to form a pattern. They are traditionally named after their apparent form or a mythological figure. Among the more familiar are Cancer (the crab); Canis Major (the Great Dog); Gemini (the Twins); Orion (the Hunter) and Taurus (the Bull). Eighty-eight constellations cover the entire northern and southern skies.
7	kink:	a sharp twist or curve
7	languages drift from grammar to grammar:	languages change over a long period of time
9	gougers:	Irish slang word meaning dangerous low-life; gurrier; juvenile delinquent
10	effing and blinding:	swearing and cursing

12	arching cadence:	cadence is the rhythmic flow of a sequence of sounds or words, fall in the pitch of the voice; in music it is a sequence of notes or chords that signals the end of a section or of the piece. This is visualised as a great arch. This may be connected to the ancient philosophical and mathematical theory put forward by Pythagoras (born c.570 BC) called The Harmony of the Spheres (or The Music of the Spheres). At the time, it was believed that the sun, moon and planets revolved around the earth, each emitting their own unique resonance based on their revolving orbit. Together they produced a harmony. This music was not audible to the human ear. Nevertheless, it was believed that it had an influence on the quality of life on earth. Pythagoras taught that one could heal using sounds and harmonic frequencies.
13	glosses:	explains; gives the meaning of; reads the world as a double spiral. This may refer to the symbols of two connected spirals that are found on ancient Celtic stone artwork and interpreted as a symbol of balance, recalling cycles of birth and death, creation and destruction alongside each other. But it is more likely to refer to the double helix, which is the structure of a DNA molecule. This carries the genetic instructions for the growth of each living organism. So the Heavens (The Harmony of the Spheres) first glosses or understands the earth to be capable of supporting living organisms.
14	epochs:	a very long period of time, in which great changes and developments occur
14	clauses	a unit of grammar containing a subject and a predicate (verb), but less than a sentence. So, the timeline involved in this discovery is proportionally so great that human epochs are mere clauses or little bits of a sentence to the Heavens.

EXPLORATIONS

Before reading

1. Lie on your back, in a safe field, in the total dark of the countryside ... and look up, for twenty minutes. What do you see? What surprises you? What are your thoughts? If you live in the countryside, away from street lights, this is easy. If you live in a town or a city, then contact relatives or friends and invite yourself for a clear, cloudless night.

2. Look carefully at the accompanying picture of a cowslip. Write a description of it, as if for a biology class.

First reading

Lines 1–5

3. a List all the elements of this flowering plant mentioned by the poet.

   b Do you think this is an accurate description or a poetic one or a combination of both? Explain your thinking.

   c What image in the description do you find most interesting or unexpected? Jot down your thoughts on any two images.

d In these lines, do you think the poet thinks of this flowering plant as male or female? In pairs, discuss this and give reasons for your conclusion.

Lines 6 and 7

4. **a** What is doing the watching here and what is being watched? (Read the accompanying notes to the poem. The critical notes may also help). In small groups, discuss what people understand by these lines.

b This is the first big image of contrast set up in the poem. Read the first two stanzas again and describe the contrast you see.

c What impression of time and space did you get from these lines?

Second reading

Lines 8–11

5. **a** What is happening in Sister Mary's class? Try to describe it as accurately as the poet described the cowslip. In small groups, swap and discuss your descriptions.

b Do you think Sister Mary is a good teacher? What leads you to say this? Have a class discussion about this issue.

Reread lines 7–11

6. This is the second big contrast made. What thoughts come into your mind when you read these lines? Make a note of them.

Third reading

Lines 12–14

7. **a** To whom or what do you think the voice here belongs? (the

critical notes may help). Discuss this section in class and see if you can reach an agreed understanding.

b This is the third and final image of contrast in the poem. Read stanzas three and four together. What contrast is being made here? Talk about this in groups.

8. **a** In the final two lines the poet suggests that the flowering plant may be a link between the heavens and the earth. What are your thoughts on this idea?

b Notice that there is no full stop at the end. We are invited to continue the thought process. Discuss how you might continue the poem.

Fourth reading

9. Is this poem mainly about a flower? Write about all the themes and issues raised by this poem (200 words).

10. Did you find this poem different from your other experiences of poetry? In what way? Jot down your ideas about this.

11. Randolph Healy has said: 'I began to experiment with what a poetry of ideas might look like'.

a Would you say this poem was a product of that experiment?

b Did this experiment work for you and bring you to new spaces and thoughts?

c Compose a letter or an email to the poet, describing your experience of the poem.

FROGS

On a grassy hill, in a luxury seminary in Glenart,
I found, screened by trees,
a large stone pond.
The waters of solitude.
Friends.   5

Patriarchs,
ten thousand times older than humanity,
the galaxy has rotated almost twice
since they first appeared.

They get two grudging notices in the Bible: 10
Tsephardea in Exodus,
Batrachos in the Apocalypse.
I will smite all thy borders with frogs.
I saw three unclean spirits, like frogs.

Their numbers have been hugely depleted,   15
principally by students.

Sever its brain.
The frog continues to live.
It ceases to breathe, swallow or sit up
and lies quietly if thrown on its back.   20
Locomotion and voice are absent.
Suspend it by the nose,
irritate the breast, elbow and knee with acid.
Sever the foot that wipes the acid away.

It will grasp and hang from your finger.   25

There is evidence that they navigate
by the sun and the stars.

This year, thirty-two, I said
"I'll be damned if Maureen has frogs"
and dug a pond.   30
Over eighty hatched, propped up with cat food.
Until the cats ate them.
It was only weeks later we discovered
six shy survivors.

The hieroglyph   35
for the number one hundred thousand
is a tadpole.

Light ripples down a smooth back.
La grenouille.
Gone.   40

NOTES

1	seminary in Glenart:	For a time, in the twentieth century, Glenart Castle, Co. Wicklow was used as a house of studies by the Vincention Order to prepare students for the priesthood (a seminary). It was then named St Kevin's.
4	solitude:	the state of being alone, remote from where people live
6	Patriarchs:	the title was used for the male head of a family or tribe; in general it is applied to someone entitled to respect because of age
7	older than humanity:	it is estimated that the first primitive humans appeared 2.8–2.5 million years ago
8	the galaxy has rotated:	we live in a huge galaxy, The Milky Way, 100,000 light years in diameter. It takes about 200 million years to complete one rotation
10	grudging:	to bear ill will
11–14	Tsephardea in Exodus:	Tsephardea is a Hebrew word meaning 'marsh-leaper'. The Book of Exodus, in the Bible, tells the story of the enslavement of the Hebrews in Egypt and their eventual freedom due to the effect of the ten plagues sent by God and announced by Moses to the Pharoah. The plague of frogs was the second of these: 'And if thou refuse to let them go, behold, I will smite [strike] all thy borders with frogs' (Exodus 8:12; The King James Bible).
14	unclean spirits:	demons
15	depleted:	reduced in number
26–27	navigate/ by the sun and the starts:	evidence from the International Wildlife Encyclopaedia
35	hieroglyph:	a picture representing words, syllables or numbers in ancient Egypt. Ancient Egyptian mathematics used hieroglyphs.
39	La grenouille:	'the frog' in French

EXPLORATIONS

Before reading

1. In your life to date, what has been your experience of frogs? Briefly, jot down your recollections of any encounter.

First reading

Lines 1–5

2. Read this section a couple of times and try to see it through the poet´s eyes. From the evidence in the poem, how do you think the poet

feels on this grassy hill? Discuss this in pairs or small groups.

Lines 6–9

3. **a** Notice the way he addresses and thinks about the frogs – from 'Friends' to 'Patriarchs'. Discuss what this might suggest.

   b As you read the mathematical calculation and the astronomy image (about the galaxy), what was going through your mind? Jot down your thoughts.

Lines 10–14

4. **a** Have you ever heard people giving strange and weird explanations for seemingly 'unusual' events that later turned out to be ordinary? Talk about this.

   b Do you think the frogs got 'a bad press' in the Bible? Suggest a reason for this.

Second reading

Lines 17–27

5. **a** Focus on the language.

   - Where might you find this type of language used?

   - In your opinion, what effect does the poet want to achieve by using this style of language? Discuss these issues and then write up your notes.

   b Debate the value and ethics (morality) of using animals for experimentation.

   c From the evidence in the poem, how do you think the poet feels on this issue? Discuss this in small groups and then give feedback on your views to the class.

Lines 28–34

6. **a** What were your first thoughts on reading this section? Share your thoughts in the group.

   b What do you think it reveals about the poet? Again, share your thoughts.

Lines 38–40

7. **a** What were your thoughts on reading these lines? Make notes.

   b Do you think these lines fit in with the themes and issues explored in the poem? Jot down your thoughts. Share your views on parts (a) and (b) with your group and then add in any other points that you think are important.

Third reading

8. Focus on the poem as a whole.

   a Trace all the information from science, astronomy and history that we get about frogs in this poem. List them.

   b What is the effect of this information on your image of frogs? Write about this in 100–200 words.

9. What has this poem added to your understanding of nature and people? Write about this in 300 words.

10. Think of your place in the universe. What thoughts go through your mind? Write them (100–200 words).

11. What questions would you like to put to Randolph Healy about his poetry? When you have thought about it, do a class 'round' i.e. one statement from each person beginning with: 'A question I have is …'

LINDA
FRANCE

(1958–)

inda France was born in Newcastle-upon-Tyne and after sojourns in Dorset, Leeds, London and Amsterdam moved back to the North-East, where she now lives near Hadrian's Wall in Northumberland.

Among her many collections of poetry are *Red* (1992) – from which 'If Love Was Jazz' is taken; *Storyville* (1997); *Book of Days* (2009); *You are Her* (2010); and *Reading the Flowers* (2016). She also edited the anthology *Sixty Women Poets* (1993). France's early work reflected her passion for jazz; a third of the volume *Storyville* is devoted to exploring the rhythms of jazz in poetry. She has collaborated across the arts, for example with musicians Keith Morris and Lewis Watson and with artist Birtley Aris. She has contributed to the scheme 'Text in Public Art', writing on stone, bronze and iron, which is displayed in public places.

France has won many awards and fellowships for her work, including the Arts Foundation's first Poetry Fellowship in 1993; the Basil Bunting Awards (1989 and 1990); and fellowship at the Tyrone Gutrie Centre in Ireland (1990). She was also the Leverhulme Artist in Residence at Moorbank, Newcastle University's Botanic Garden (2010).

France has a deep commitment to Buddhism and retreats regularly to the Theravadian Monastery at Harnham, on the border between England and Scotland. She says this practice 'feels like a natural development of what I was doing with my writing all those years – watching my thoughts, trying to understand what made me 'me', and wanting to live a better life'.

IF LOVE WAS JAZZ

If love was jazz,
I'd be dazzled
By its razzmatazz.

If love was a sax
I'd melt in its brassy flame   5
Like wax.

If love was a guitar,
I'd pluck its six strings,
Eight to the bar.

If love was a trombone,   10
I'd feel its slow
Slide, right down my back bone.

If love was a drum,
I'd be caught in its snare,
Kept under its thumb.   15

If love was a trumpet,
I'd blow it.

If love was jazz,
I'd sing its praises,
Like Larkin has.   20

But love isn't jazz.
It's an organ recital.
Eminently worthy,
Not nearly as vital.

If love was jazz,   25
I'd always want more.
I'd be a regular
On that smoky dance-floor.

NOTES

1	jazz:	a style of music that originated in African–American communities in New Orleans, USA, in the nineteenth century. The term covers a wide range of music that is distinctive for its improvisations and conflicting and unexpected rhythms. Listen to some. Go to the critical notes on this poem to read what Linda France has to say about jazz.
3	razzmatazz:	a made-up word (neologism); a type of rhyming slang that can be used to mean 'glamorous excitement' or 'insincere activity'
4	sax:	saxophone – a keyed, brass reed instrument
9	Eight to the bar:	music played in double time – very energetic and difficult to play; usually found in swing or jazz music
10	trombone:	brass wind instrument with a sliding tube
14	snare:	a) a trap with a noose to catch small animals; or any kind of trap or temptation. b) snare drum: often used in jazz bands, marching bands and parades. It produces a distinct sharp sound when struck with a drumstick but a very different sound when a brush or a rute is used. You will find examples of the sound on YouTube.
20	Larkin:	Philip Larkin (1992–1985) was one of the foremost English poets of the twentieth century who, for many years, reviewed jazz records for the *London Daily Telegraph*. France refers to him with irony here as Larkin didn't seem to rate love as highly as he did jazz –he didn't marry any of the six women with whom he had relationships.
23	Eminently worthy:	notably distinguished by good qualities. The term 'worthy' is often used in a patronising sense, when what one actually means is 'adequate'.
24	vital:	can mean 'essential to life' or 'full of life and vitality'

EXPLORATIONS

Before reading

1. Go for a night out at a jazz club, where you can let yourself go and dance to the music. Failing that, listen to some jazz.

First reading

2. **a** After you have read the poem a number of times and listened to it being read, do a class round on the poem, beginning with the words 'I noticed that…'

   b What was noticed about the following:

   • The overall comparison between love and jazz in the poem

   • The many little comparisons

   • The speaker's feelings about jazz

   • The words and images used about jazz

   • The speaker's attitude to love?

   Discuss these and any other questions you may have about the poem.

3. In groups, prepare to read aloud the first stanza by discussing the following:

   • What words are naturally stressed as you read?

   • The atmosphere or mood you think the stanza creates for the opening of the poem.

In turn, read the first stanza aloud so that it brings out the atmosphere you want. Then, talk about the different aspects of the readings that you thought worked best. Make notes on what you learned about the poem from this exercise.

4. Follow a similar procedure for each of the next four stanzas. Prepare to read aloud by first discussing:

• Where you think the stresses fall in each line

• The image in the stanza that you want people to see, when you read

• The atmosphere or mood created in the stanza and how you might read it to bring that out.

Note down any ideas about the poem that occurred to you as you went through the process.

Second reading

Stanzas 1–5

5. In groups, discuss the following issues:

• Which were the most exciting, energetic stanzas and how was this effect created?

• Which were the slow, sexy stanzas and how was that mood created?

• Did any stanzas feel louder than the rest? How was this created?

• Other changes in the speed and tone of the poem.

Write up your own notes on the main points of this discussion.

6. From a reading of these stanzas, how do you think the speaker feels about jazz? (100–200 words)

Stanzas 6–9

7. Read these four stanzas carefully and discuss, in your group, the changes you notice from the first five stanzas. Feed the ideas from the group into a class discussion on stanzas 6–9.

Third reading

8. Though the word 'love' is used in every one of the stanzas, it is not discussed until stanza eight. In the poem, what does the speaker suggest about love and what is your own reaction to this? (200–300 words)

9. On what note do you think the poem ends? Do you think the speaker is content, sad, wistful, regretful, or other? Discuss this. Support your views with evidence from the poem.

10. Write about the features of this poem that you most appreciate. (200–300 words)

11. 'If Love Was a Céilí' … Write a response to this title in the form of a poem, essay, story or blog.

BENJAMIN
ZEPHANIAH

(1958–)

Benjamin Zephaniah was born in Birmingham; his mother was from Jamaica and his father from Barbados. As a young boy, he had a difficult time in education and attended approved schools (a type of boarding school for young offenders or young people judged to be beyond parental control). He was on the streets at age thirteen, unable to read or write. It was discovered later that he was dyslexic. He also spent some time in prison for burglary.

As a teenager in Birmingham he first began to compose poems in his head and learned them 'off by heart'. There were many early fans for his political poems, songs and 'dub poetry' (lines spoken to reggae rhythms, sometimes without the backing music). He moved to London and began to perform his poetry at music venues.

The 1980s in Britain was a period of economic depression and social unrest, with high unemployment and discrimination against the black community. There were riots in many cities. Zephaniah became involved with many protests and causes, such as the Anti-Apartheid Movement and the Campaign for Justice for Stephen Lawrence. Issues like these inspired his music and his poetry.

His early poems were collected in The Dread Affair (1985); followed by City Psalms (1992); Propa Propaganda (1996) and Too Black Too Strong (2001). His poetry for younger readers includes Talking Turkeys (1994) and Wicked World (2000). Among his novels for teenagers are Refugee Boy (2001) and Gangsta Rap (2004). His reggae band recordings include: 'Dub Ranting' (1982); 'Us an Dem' (1990); and 'Naked' (2004).

He is on record as saying that he wanted 'to popularise poetry by reaching people who did not read books.' On his relationship with Britain he has said: 'I gotta say I love this country, though I rail against it all the time'. In 2003, in an open letter to The Guardian, he refused the honour of an OBE (an officer of the Order of the British Empire) as he associates the Empire with slavery.

He is Professor of Poetry and Creative Writing at Brunel University, London.

THE SUN

I believe the Blacks are bad
The Left is loony
God is Mad
This government's the best we've had
So I read The SUN.   5

I believe Britain is great
And other countries imitate
I am friendly with The State,
Daily, I read The SUN.

I am not too keen on foreign ones   10
But I don't mind some foreign bombs
Jungle bunnies play tom-toms,
But, I read The SUN.

Man, I don't like Russian spies
But we don't have none   15
I love lies,
I really do love Princess Di
I bet she reads The SUN.

Black people rob
Women should cook   20
And every poet is a crook,
I am told – so I don't need to look,
It's easy in The SUN.

Every hippie carries nits
And every Englishman love tits   25
I love Page Three and other bits,
I stare into The SUN.

I like playing bingo games
And witch-hunting to shame a name
But aren't newspapers all the same?   30
So why not read The SUN.

Don't give me truth, just give me gossip
And skeletons from people's closets,
I wanna be normal
And millions buy it,   35
I am blinded by The SUN.

NOTES

The Sun:		A daily tabloid, for many years Britain's top-selling newspaper, it is owned and controlled by Australian billionaire Rupert Murdoch's News Corporation. The paper has always been controversial, printing sensational stories. Zephaniah did not escape its notice. In 1987, when he was nominated for a visiting fellowship at Cambridge University, *The Sun* ran the following headline and story:

WOULD YOU LET THIS MAN NEAR YOUR DAUGHTER?
This good-looking chap is Mr Benjamin Obadiah Zephaniah.
On Friday he is expected to become a Cambridge don. Just what are his qualities which have appealed to Trinity College?
He is black. He is Rastafarian. He has tasted approved schools and borstals.
And, oh yes, he is a poet. Here is an example of the standard of his work:
(The day dat I met Lady Di, I,
Whas happy no I tell a lie,
I had a pain in my belly, I
Would not f..t near Royalty.)
Is this really the kind of man parents would wish to have teaching their sons and daughters? Our guess is that they would prefer their offspring to start work in a hairdresser's.
From his picture, Mr Zephaniah himself could do with a good shampoo and set. (The Sun, April 27, 1987)

2	The Left is loony:	(loony means lunatic) 'The loony left' was an insulting label used by the Conservative Party and the newspapers that supported it, including *The Sun*, to belittle the social policies of the Labour Party politicians and Labour controlled councils, in the UK general election of 1987. *The Sun* announced that it was going to give a prize – a two-finger statuette – to the looniest council of them all!
4,8		Newspapers, particularly *The Sun*, had great political influence at the time. They were unashamedly biased and could make or break governments by influencing readers. *The Sun* backed the Conservative Thatcher governments but switched to New Labour under Tony Blair.
12	Jungle bunnies:	a racist slang term for black people. It was used originally to refer to African Americans – the city was called the 'jungle' and black people were said to jump fences when running from the police.
12	tom-toms:	a native East Indian drum but the term was used as an insulting reference to the drums of all foreign people generally, who were presumed uncivilised
21 – 23		presumed reference to *The Sun*'s attack on Zephaniah
24	nits:	headlice

24	hippie:	hippies rejected conventional culture. They began as a sub-culture youth movement in the US and UK in the 1960s. They promoted peace and love as the values most essential to society. They were associated with non-violent, anti-government protests ('flower power'). They formed their own communities and had liberal attitudes to sex and the use of drugs. Many writers, artists and musicians were influenced by the culture.
26	Page Three	In August 2013, The Sun ended its 40-year-old custom of featuring topless models on page 3.
28	bingo games	The Sun sponsors bingo gambling
29	And witch-hunting to shame a name:	organised embarrassment of public figures. In 1987 The Sun ran a campaign of rumours about the sexual orientation of famous people.

EXPLORATIONS

Before reading

1. Buy a copy of The Sun and 'study' it to find out for yourself about the following issues and any others that media studies might prompt:

- What are the main areas the newspaper covers?
- Which areas get the most coverage?
- In your edition what were the main stories covered?
- Examine these stories. Do you think the writer's priority was to grab your attention or to lay out the facts carefully?
- Were the stories covered in great or minimal details?
- What was the ratio of words to pictures?
- Could you detect if the writing was neutral and factual or was it for or against an issue or person? Do you think there was bias? It might help to consider the language used – descriptions, use of adjectives, etc.

- Why do you think people read this newspaper?

Air all these issues in a class discussion.

First reading

2. Focus on The Sun reader who speaks in this poem. What did you discover about him from your reading?

   a Do a class 'round', beginning with 'I noticed that…' Note the main points that come up and discuss them further.

3. In small groups:

   a List all the different areas or targets of prejudice you find in the poem.

   b Which statements do you find most shocking or insulting? Explain why.

   c Which statements do you find to be of lesser insult? Talk about your reasons for making this judgement.

   d What did you learn from this discussion about people's views of prejudice?

4. In small groups:

   a Do you think the speaker is completely 'brain-washed' by the newspaper or does he have moments when he is aware of his own shortcomings?

   b Does he act on these self-insights? If not, what do you think might be the reasons for this? Discuss these issues in your group. Make notes on the general conclusions reached.

5. What kind of person do you think the speaker is? Respond to this in about 200 words.

6. Do you have any sympathy for this reader of *The Sun*? Write your answer in the style of a journalist for *The Sun* (100 words).

Second reading

7. From a reading of the poem, what conclusions can you draw about the attitudes and values of *The Sun* newspaper, as portrayed here? Discuss this.

8. a What do you think was Zephaniah's objective in writing this poem?

   b Do you think he should be content that he has done it well? Outline your view in 100–200 words.

9. What do you consider to be the main themes or issues the poet deals with? Do you think they are important? Write your response to this in 100-200 words.

Third reading

10. Listen to Benjamin Zephaniah performing his poetry on YouTube. You could begin with 'Dis Poetry'. Listen to how the rhymes work; hear how the rhythm or beat works. Now try reading 'The SUN' aloud, with those rhymes and rhythms in mind.

11. If you would like to find out more about the issues that preoccupy Benjamin Zephaniah's poetry, listen to his performance of 'To Do Wid Me' on YouTube.

12. Is this a fit subject for poetry? Can one make poetry out of the mean and nasty side of life? Some people will be of the view that 'Yes', poetry is about getting to the heart of things, cutting to the truth, whether that truth is beautiful and romantic or mean and miserable. What do you think? Talk about this.

13. Do you like this poem? Write your opinions, in 200–300 words.

EILEEN
SHEEHAN

(1963–)

ileen Sheehan is from Scartaglin, Co. Kerry and lives in Killarney. Her first volume of poetry, *Song of the Midnight Fox* (2004) is chiefly an exploration of family, sketched with great insight and emotional control. Most memorable among the poems are those about caring for a mother with Alzheimer's disease and also those about a much-loved father. Her second volume, *Down the Sunlit Hall*, was published in 2008. A third volume, *The Narrow Place of Souls*, from which 'My Father, Long Dead' is taken, is forthcoming. Her work has also been published in many journals and anthologies. In 2006 she won the Brendan Kennelly Poetry Award.

Eileen Sheehan teaches creative writing at Killarney College and visits schools on the Poetry Ireland Writers in Schools scheme.

OL 2
OL 2

MY FATHER, LONG DEAD

My father, long dead
has become air

Become scent
of pipe smoke, of turf smoke, of resin

Become light   5
and shade on the river

Become foxglove
buttercup, tree bark

Become corncrake
lost from the meadow   10

Become silence,
places of calm

Become badger at dusk,
deer in the thicket

Become grass   15
on the road to the castle

Become mist
on the turret

Become dark-haired hero in a story
written by a dark-haired child   20

NOTES

4	resin	sticky secretion of trees and some plants
7	foxglove:	tall plant with white or purple flowers
8	buttercup:	yellow-flowered plant
9	corncrake:	a bird that nests on the ground in cornfields or long-grass meadows; has a harsh, grating call; now almost extinct in Ireland
14	thicket:	a tangle of bushes or small trees where deer can hide
18	turret:	a small tower attached to the castle

EXPLORATIONS

Before reading

I.   If you have lost a grandparent, parent, relative, friend, neighbour or any person with whom you shared time and still miss, think about the following:

   • What sparks off a memory of this person. Is it a particular place or object, a scent or phrase of speech, a piece of music or a song or time of day or year or something else?

   • Does the memory come as an image or picture?

   • Are the feelings of grief still raw or have you got to a stage where you are comfortable thinking about the person?

   • If you have reached this stage, describe a few images of this person that you keep with you as you get on with your life. Describe them in 100–200 words.

   This writing is personal to yourself and not for sharing.

First reading

2.   In small groups:

   a   'My father, long dead,/has become air'.
      What does this image suggest to you? Share your thoughts.

   b   'Become scent/of pipe smoke, of turf smoke, of resin'.
      What does this image suggest to you? Share your thoughts on this also.

   c   Make notes on what the group discovered about (a) and (b)

3.   In your group, explore the other images of nature throughout the poem, that are occasions of remembering for the poet.

   a   What different aspects of nature are involved here?

   b   What qualities of the poet's father do you think are being commemorated? Discuss these issues and feed back ideas to the class.

4.   'Become dark-haired hero in a story/ written by a dark-haired child'. Do you think these lines give a strong assurance that the father will be remembered? If so, how? Will these memories be a life-like portrait of the man? Talk about these issues, note the ideas from the group and share with the class.

5.   'My Father, Long Dead'. Would you suggest that a reader needs to take the full title into account when reading the poem? Jot down your thoughts on this and then share with the group. Add in useful points that you heard from others.

Second reading

6.   Do you like this poem as a way of remembering the dead? Write your thoughts on this (100–200 words).

7.   Do you think this poem was prompted by grief or by acceptance and love? Write your thoughts on this and quote references to support your ideas (100–200 words).

8.   How would you describe the mood or atmosphere in the poem? What lines would you choose to show this? Write your thoughts on this, in about 100 words.

Third reading

9. In groups:
   Prepare a choral reading of the poem i.e. everyone reads the poem aloud, at the same time. First decide the mood or atmosphere the poem wants to create. Discuss where you think the stresses fall in each line. Think about the role of the repeated 'Become', that works as a 'stepping-off' word for the ideas in each stanza. Just go for it. It may take a number of attempts to get it right; fine-tune after each attempt.

   a When read well, do you think it sounds like a chant or a prayer? If so, what elements in the poem do you think caused this effect? Collect opinions from each member of the group and take notes.

   b Do you see this as a spiritual poem? Discuss this. Make notes on the points that emerged.

10. Write a piece on the theme of 'memories', in any format you choose: poem, story, dialogue, lyric, blog or other.

KATE
CLANCHY

(1965–)

Kate Clanchy is an English poet who was born in Glasgow and educated in Edinburgh and at Oxford. She has been a teacher of English in London's East End, written radio plays for the BBC, short stories and a non-fiction account of her friendship with a Kosovan woman, *What Is She Doing Here?: A Refugee's Story* (2008), which won the Scottish Arts Council Book Award 2009. Her first novel, *Meeting the English*, won a Costa Book Award in 2013. Her volumes of poetry, *Slattern* (1995), *Samarkand* (1999) and *Newborn* (2004), have all won or been shortlisted for many awards.

Kate Clanchy writes out of personal experiences – love life, journeys, teaching English, renovating an old house, being a mother – with a wonderful freshness of detail and insight that enable the reader to inhabit her spaces and be enriched by the visit.

DRIVING TO THE HOSPITAL

OL 2

OL 2

We were low on petrol
so I said let's freewheel
when we get to the hill.
It was dawn and the city
was nursing its quiet   5
and I liked the idea
of arriving with barely
a crunch on the gravel.
You smiled kindly and
eased the clutch gently   10
and backed us out of
the driveway and patted
my knee with exactly
the gesture you used
when we were courting,   15
remember, on the way
to your brother's: *I like
driving with my baby*,
that's what you said. And
at the time I wondered   20
why my heart leapt and leapt.

NOTES

2	freewheel:	to take the car out of gear and let it glide downhill, hoping to save on petrol (dangerous and now illegal). In the metaphorical sense it means 'to move or act without restraint'.
5	nursing:	as well as referring to the profession of a nurse, the term is also used for breastfeeding a baby
15	courting:	'going out with'

EXPLORATIONS

First reading

1. When you hear the words 'driving to the hospital' what thoughts come into your mind? Jot these down, for discussion later.

2. Do a class round of 'I noticed that…' after the first reading. List the main points raised.

Lines 1–3

3. Do you think the speaker is in a panic about the shortage of petrol? Listen to the way she speaks.

    a What mood or state of mind would you say she is in and what leads you to say that?

    b Working in small groups, each person reads these lines aloud as the speaker might say them. Discuss what kind of reading seems most authentic.

Lines 4 and 5

4. a What picture do you get in your mind when you read these lines? Write a short description of what you see.

    b In small groups, share these descriptions and say what interests you about each.

Lines 6–8

5. a What do you hear when you read these lines? In your own words, describe the sound you

imagine is 'barely/a crunch on the gravel'. Share and say what interests you about how the others hear that sound.

b How would you describe the atmosphere or mood in these lines?

Second reading

Lines 9–19

6. What can you say about (a) the man and (b) the relationship between the man and the woman, in these lines? Select the words or phrases that influenced your thinking.

7. How would you describe the atmosphere or mood in the car, in this section? Again, select words that support your view.

8. 'And/at the time I wondered/why my heart leapt and leapt.'

   a Is this a bit out of sync with the atmosphere in the rest of the poem? In what way? Explain your thinking.

   b Is it an effective way of describing her emotion? What do you think? And what reasons would you offer in support?

Third reading

9. What is really happening in this poem? Jot down your thoughts on this. Now, go back and reread the poem carefully. Are there any words, phrases or images that now take on another layer of meaning for you? Note these down and say what they suggest to you. Share and discuss the class's responses to questions 9 and 10.

10. Talk to your parents or other parents about any journeys to the hospital in these particular circumstances. Ask if they remember what the journey was like and what their thoughts and feelings were. Write this up as a report (no names mentioned; use pseudonyms) (300 words).

11. Do you like this personal, what is often called 'confessional', poetry? Explain what you like or dislike about this style.

12. Do a class round, each sentence beginning with 'A thought I take away from reading this poem is…' Make a note of the thoughts that interested you. Then, write a few paragraphs on what reading the poem meant for you (300 words).

NOTE

You might also like to read 'Driving from the Hospital' or other poems from the volume, Newborn.

COLETTE BRYCE

(1970–)

olette Bryce comes from Derry, Northern Ireland. She was Fellow in Creative Writing at the University of Dundee from 2003 to 2005 and Literary Fellow at the University of Newcastle upon Tyne from 2005 to 2007. Her first collection of poetry, *The Heel of Bernadette* (2000), won the Strong Award for new Irish poets. Her other collections are *The Full Indian Rope Trick* (2004) and *Self-Portrait in the Dark* (2008). She has won many awards, including the National Poetry Competition in 2003. *Self-Portrait in the Dark* was shortlisted for the Poetry Now Award in 2009.

SELF-PORTRAIT IN THE DARK (WITH CIGARETTE)

OL 2022

To sleep, perchance
to dream? No chance:
it's 4 a.m. and I'm wakeful
as an animal,
caught between your presence and the lack.   5
This is the realm insomniac.
On the street window seat, I light a cigarette
from a slim flame and monitor the street –
a stilled film, bathed in amber,
softened now in the wake of a downpour.   10

Beyond the daffodils
on Magdalen Green, there's one slow vehicle
pushing its beam along Riverside Drive,
a sign of life;
and two months on   15
from 'moving on'
your car, that you haven't yet picked up,
waits, spattered in raindrops like bubble wrap.
Here, I could easily go off
on a riff   20

on how cars, like pets, look a little like their owners
but I won't 'go there',
as they say in America,

given it's a clapped-out Nissan Micra ...
And you don't need to know that   25
I've been driving it illegally at night
in the lamp-lit silence of this city
– you'd only worry –
or, worse, that Morrissey
is jammed in the tape deck now and for eternity;   30

no. It's fine, all gleaming hubcaps,
seats like an upright, silhouetted couple;
from the dashboard, the wink
of that small red light I think
is a built-in security system.   35
In a poem
it could represent a heartbeat or a pulse.
Or loneliness: it's vigilance.
Or simply the lighthouse-regular spark
of someone, somewhere, smoking in the dark.   40

EXPLORATIONS

First reading

1. Listen to the first section (lines 1 – 10). What do you see? List everything you notice and share the ideas in a group discussion.

2. How would you describe the mood of the speaker in the first section? What phrases or images suggest this?

3. Is there anything to suggest a reason for her sleeplessness?

Second reading

4. What do we find out about her life circumstances in the second section (lines 11 – 30)?

5. What do we discover about her as a person in this section? Do you like her?

6. In the final section (lines 31 – 40), her mood becomes more downbeat. In your own words, trace her thoughts here.

Third reading

7. Collect all the images of light you find in the poem. What do they suggest to you about the theme being developed in this poem?

8. This poem is described as a self-portrait. If you were actually painting her portrait, what are the characteristics of the speaker you think it should show if it was to represent her accurately?

9. As a love poem, do you find this depressing, hopeful, realistic or something else? Discuss.

10. Read 'Oranges' by Gary Soto (page 510) and discuss the differences between the two poems.

DAVID
WHEATLEY

(1970–)

orn in Dublin in 1970, David Wheatley was educated at the Royal Irish Academy of Music and Trinity College Dublin. He now teaches English literature at the University of Hull. Among his published collections of poetry are *Thirst* (1997), *Misery Hill* (2000) and *Mocker* (2006).

CHRONICLE

My grandfather is chugging along the back roads
between Kilcoole and Newtown in his van,
the first wood-panelled Morris Minor in Wicklow.
Evening is draped lazily over the mountains;
one hapless midnight, mistaking the garage door   5
for open, he drove right through it, waking my father.

The old man never did get to farm like his father,
preferring to trundle his taxi along the back roads.
Visiting, I stand in his workshop door
and try to engage him in small talk, always in vain,   10
then climb the uncarpeted stairs to look at the mountains
hulking over soggy, up-and-down Wicklow.

Cattle, accents and muck: I don't have a clue,
I need everything explained to me by my father.
Clannish great-uncles somewhere nearer the mountains   15
are vaguer still, farming their few poor roods,
encountered at Christmas with wives who serve me oven-
baked bread and come to wave us off at the door.

My grandfather pacing the garden, benignly dour,
a whiskey or a woodbine stuck in his claw,   20
a compost of newsprint in the back of his van.
You're mad to go live in Bray, he told my father,
somewhere he'd visit on rare and timorous raids,
too close to 'town' to be properly *Cill Mhantáin*.

All this coming back to me in the mountains   25
early one morning, crossing the windy corridor
to the Glen of Imaal, where schoolchildren read
acrostics to me of 'wet and wonderful Wicklow',
and driving on down to Hacketstown with my father
we find grandfather's grandfather under an even   30

gravestone gone to his Church of Ireland heaven,
and his grandfather too, my father maintains,
all turned, long since turned to graveyard fodder
just over the county line from their dear old Wicklow,
the dirt tracks, twisting lanes and third-class roads   35
they would have hauled themselves round while they endured,

before my father and I ever followed the roads
or my mountainy cousins first picked up a loy
or my grandfather's van ever hit that garage door.

NOTES

Chronicle:		a detailed record of events in chronological order, i.e. in the order in which they happened
16	roods:	a measure of land, about 400 square metres
19	benignly:	gently or kindly
19	dour:	stern, obstinate; so 'benignly dour' is a contradiction
28	acrostics:	poems in which the first or last letters of lines when read vertically make a word or words
33	fodder:	food, used particularly to refer to food for cattle
38	loy:	a kind of spade

EXPLORATIONS

Before reading

1. Explore your own genealogy. Try to trace your family tree, the record of your father's and your mother's family going back a few generations. Where did they live and what did they do for a living? Do you visit aunts and uncles and meet with cousins?

2. What is your attitude to these older generations? Do you feel proud of them, interested in their lives, sorry for them, couldn't care less? Jot down your thoughts or discuss in groups.

First reading

3. What do you notice about the setting and about the people in this poem?

4. Can you see why the title is appropriate?

5. Do you find the poet's family interesting? Explain your views.

Second reading

6. Focus in particular on stanzas 1 and 4. Would you agree that the grandfather is a larger than life figure? What is the evidence for this?

7. The pace of life is slow. What words, phrases and images suggest this throughout the poem?

8. a   This poem draws heavily on the geography of County Wicklow. Would you agree? Explore the poem in detail for evidence.
    b   All the people mentioned have a particular love of County Wicklow. Write about this, referring to details from the poem to back up your views.

Third reading

9. Write two paragraphs on the main issue or theme dealt with in this poem.

10. Images of roads and of journeys taken or not taken form recurring patterns here. How do these tie in with the meaning?

11. How does the poet feel about his family and relations? Discuss this in pairs or groups and then write up your conclusions, using references to the poem as evidence.

12. Do you think this poem says something important about families and native place or *áit dúchais*? Discuss this and write up the conclusions.

SINÉAD MORRISSEY

(1972–)

Sinéad Morrissey was born in Portadown, County Armagh, educated at Trinity College Dublin and lives in Belfast, where she lectures at Queen's University. She has won many prizes and awards for her poetry. Among her collections are *There Was a Fire in Vancouver* (1996), *Between Here and There* (2001), *The State of the Prisons* (2005), from which 'Genetics' is taken, and *Through a Square Window* (2009).

GENETICS

OL 2020

My father's in my fingers, but my mother's in my palms.
I lift them up and look at them with pleasure –
I know my parents made me by my hands.

They may have been repelled to separate lands,
to separate hemispheres, may sleep with other lovers,   5
but in me they touch where fingers link to palms.

With nothing left of their togetherness but friends
who quarry for their image by a river,
at least I know their marriage by my hands.

I shape a chapel where a steeple stands.   10
And when I turn it over,
my father's by my fingers, my mother's by my palms

demure before a priest reciting psalms.
My body is their marriage register.
I re-enact their wedding with my hands.   15

So take me with you, take up the skin's demands
for mirroring in bodies of the future.
I'll bequeath my fingers, if you bequeath your palms.
We know our parents make us by our hands.

EXPLORATIONS

Before reading

1. What does the word 'genetics' mean? So what might you expect the poem to be about?

2. Have you ever heard expressions such as 'he has his father's hair' or 'she has her mother's eyes'? Do you resemble either of your parents or any other members of your family in any way? Jot down some thoughts on this and what it means to you.

First reading

3. Do you think that the speaker feels happy and secure in her family in stanza 1? What makes you think that?

4. **a** Do you find stanzas 2–3 unexpected coming after the first stanza?

   b What details suggest that this was not an amicable separation?

5. Is there anything you find positive in stanzas 2–3? Explain.

Second reading

6. Replicate the hand shapes the poet makes in stanza 4. Does this remind you of any children's rhyme?

7. Do stanzas 4–5 provide yet another change of mood? Describe this mood and suggest how the poet creates it.

8. 'My body is their marriage register./I re-enact their wedding with my hands.'
   Do you find the thought process here clever and creative, highly original or rather zany and fantastical? What is your reaction to these lines? Jot down your ideas and discuss them in groups.

9. Do you like how the poem ends? What are your thoughts on this?

Third reading

10. Is this poem anything like what you expected on first reading the title? What were you surprised by?

11. Explore the ways in which the images of hands carry a range of ideas throughout the poem. Trace the different ideas carried by the references to hands. Do you think these images tell quite a complex story about family?

12. '"Genetics" provides an unusual and imaginative framework for thinking about the concept of family.' What do you think?

13. Do you find this a positive or a bleak poem? Discuss.

CAITRÍONA O'REILLY

(1973–)

aitríona O'Reilly was born in Dublin in 1973 and grew up in County Wicklow. She attended Trinity College Dublin, where she was awarded a BA, followed by a PhD for her work on American literature. Indeed, the American poet Sylvia Plath has proven to be one of the key influences on O'Reilly's writing. In an article she wrote on Sylvia Plath, O'Reilly noted that 'the connections between a writer's life and her work are numerous, indirect, and mysterious'.

This statement is equally true of O'Reilly's own writing, where she often explores the world of nature and the self. The 'connections' between O'Reilly's life and work are particularly evident in her first anthology, *The Nowhere Birds*, published in 2001, from which the poem 'Interlude 12' is taken.

In this book, her poetry is concerned with childhood, adolescence and her student life, so that, as Jefferson Holdridge commented in his review of it, the anthology offers the opportunity of 'watching the maturation of a poet'.

Although her poetry has been very successfully received, O'Reilly does not limit her work with words to this area alone, as she also works as a freelance writer, critic, teacher and editor.

INTERLUDE 12

OL 2022

With its *gelati* and bougainvillea-draped sculpture,
Italy hovered like a rumour five miles further.
Binn was worthy, litterless, Swiss;

where to breathe was like a sea-plunge, even in June.
Populated by six-foot clean-limbed blondes,
they bled pure gold, if they bled at all. Anaemic Knut   5

('like *Hamsun*') was an exception. He composed
electronically ('like *Kraftwerk*') and afterwards
dropped by for *Kräutertee*. I'd never even heard of *Hunger*.

Hector, who had a scar from nipple to navel, called me 'pure'   10
in nasty English. There was a failed seduction
by a man with a handlebar moustache and gold tooth,

a silly crush on a stout-legged father of five ...
The summer dragged to an end. Where the sun once fell   15
tremendously there was the noise of thunder.

I cracked the ice on the *bier-garten* tables, folded umbrellas,
bid a tender farewell to the urinals. A thousand pounds
in the heel of my shoe might have bought three months

in a Berlin flat. But in the airport a kitten wailed in a basket
dementedly and a jittery pilot sweated over his charts   20
and I was back, convincing them I'd ever been elsewhere.

NOTES

Interlude:		a time, space or event that is very different to what comes before and after it
1	gelati:	the Italian word for ice creams
1	bougainvillea:	a shrub with red or purple flowers that grows in warm climates
3	Binn:	a village in Switzerland that is located in the Swiss Alps
6	Anaemic:	pale and lacking in vitality
7	Hamsun:	Knut Hamsun (1859–1952), a Nobel Prize-winning Norwegian author whose novel *Hunger* describes how a young man is slowly driven mad by hunger and poverty
8	Kraftwerk:	a German group who were electronic music pioneers
9	Kräutertee:	a herbal tea
9	Hunger:	see note for Hamsun above
16	bier-garten:	the German for an open-air bar that serves beer and food

EXPLORATIONS

Before reading

1. Imagine that you have finished your second-level education and you want to take a gap year to go travelling. What reasons would you use to prove to your parents/guardians that you would learn a lot from your travels that would help you (i) as a person and (ii) with your future studies or career, and so persuade them to give you permission and funding?

a   Working in pairs, write out your reasons in 5 minutes.

b   As a class, write each reason that has been suggested once on the board, eliminating any that would not support your case.

c   Referring to the reasons on the board, discuss the main areas of life that can be learned about from travelling.

First reading

2. **a** In lines 1–4, the poet describes her first impressions when she arrived in Binn, having come from the island of Ireland. Can you suggest why the closeness of one country, Italy, to another, Switzerland, made such an impression on her?

   b She was also surprised that despite this closeness, Italy and Switzerland were very different. In your own words, explain how they were different. Refer to the poem in your answer.

3. **a** List the people she remembers from her time in Binn, as described in lines 5–13.

   b Based on your reading of these lines, do you think the poet was travelling with her family, her friends or on her own? Explain the reason for your answer.

4. What signs, described in lines 14–16, warned her that the summer was coming to an end and she would have to leave Binn? Support your answer with reference to these lines.

5. What impression do you get from lines 17–21 of her feelings about returning home? Support your answer by reference to the poem.

Second reading

6. **a** In your own words, describe how you picture each of the four men that she encounters in lines 6–13.

   b What areas of life does she learn about through these experiences?

7. In lines 19–21, the poet is in 'the airport' as she returns to her usual way of life. She seems to notice the kitten and the 'jittery pilot' because she has similar feelings to them. Discuss the feelings that you think she shares with the kitten and the 'jittery pilot'.

8. **a** There are three sections in this poem: the poet's time in Binn (lines 1–13), the ending of summer and her time in Binn (lines 14–19) and the airport (lines 19–21). Read each section, then describe the tone (the emotion in her voice) that is conveyed by her words in that section.

   b From your description of her tone in each section, which experience do you think she found the most difficult to cope with? Refer to the text in your answers.

Third reading

9. **a** Look back at the main areas of life that you decided travelling would help you to learn about for Question 1. Discuss which of these areas the poet learned about in her travels.

   b Do you think that the experiences she had in Binn would have helped her as a person and with her future studies or career? Why?

10. Would you include this poem in a collection of poetry for young people? Give reasons for your answer based on your reading of the poem.

MARTIN DYAR

(1976–)

M artin Dyar was born in Sligo and grew up in Swinford, Co. Mayo. He is a graduate of NUI Galway, Trinity College Dublin (TCD) and Southern Illinois University at Carbondale.

He has taught ethics and literature in the School of Medicine at TCD and been a writer in residence at the International Writing Programme at the University of Iowa, US. 'Death and the Post Office' is from his debut collection of poetry *Maiden Names* (Arlen House, 2013), which was chosen as a book of the year by *The Guardian* and *The Irish Times* and was shortlisted for the 2014 Piggott Prize and the Shine/Strong Award. He was awarded the Strokestown International Poetry Award in 2001 and the Patrick Kavanagh Award in 2009.

OL 201

OL 202

DEATH AND THE POST OFFICE

The job they're given is fairly simple.
Find the place,
go in for half an hour and discuss the settlement.
Consider, if it's appropriate,
the few antiques: the safe,   5
the signs, the switchboard.
Glance at the books, the electrics.
Perhaps fill out some forms.
But these aul' ones, these Cathleens, these Annies,
they can be fierce long-winded.   10
For some of our lads their ways
are just too compelling.

Some accept a drink, some'll have lunch.
We'd a Polish guy who took
a ninety-two-year-old out in the van.   15
She showed him a ball alley.
Fair enough: dozens of ghosts
and no graffiti. But if you're not direct
about the job? You understand,
we've had to weed out the dreamers.   20
Immunity to stories, I find,

is the primary quality.
You don't want to be sitting at an old table,
under a clock that strikes you

as fabulously loud.   25
Or find yourself cradled by the past,
thinking a man need venture
no further west than the brink he meets
in a mouthful of milky tea.
If the archive-harbouring frailty   30
of the postmistress soothes you;
if her wit grants you the lost farm
and maternity of the world;
if her isolated, dwindling village, a place
without a pub or a shop,   35
whose nearest decent

sized town is itself desperately quiet –
if these things move you…
What I mean is, if you can't meet
a forgotten countryside   40
head on, and calmly dismantle her,
fold her up, carry her out,
and ship her back
to Head Office, however ambiguous,
however heavy-handed or fateful,   45
however bloody poignant
the whole affair might seem to you;
if you can't stand your ground

when a steep moment
of hospitable chat and reminiscence   50
might tempt you to put
your mobile phone on silent,
or worse, blinded by plates of fruit cake,
to switch if off completely;
if you cannot accompany   55
an inevitable change, knowing
you did not cause these people, these ways, to vanish,
and if you will not sign off
on expired things for us,
then, I'm sorry, but you are not our man.   60

NOTES

3	settlement:	terms of the financial agreement
7	books:	financial accounts
9	aul':	a pronunciation of 'old'; an insulting term
12	compelling:	creating strong interest; impossible to resist
17	ghosts:	memories about those who played handball there
18	direct:	straightforward; outspoken
20	dreamers:	'dreamer' has many shades of meaning – from the person who dreams while asleep to a daydreamer who fantasises while awake, to someone who has aspirations of what can be achieved
21	immunity:	power of resisting
22	primary:	most important
26	cradled:	comforted, held protectively as you would hold a baby
27	venture:	a risky undertaking
28	brink:	the edge or border (of a steep place for example), beyond which there is danger. (See the 'Drama and the Use of Language' section in the critical notes.)
30	archive-harbouring:	keeping safe the records of the place
30	frailty:	weakness
32	wit:	imaginative and inventive ability
32–33	the lost farm and maternity of the world:	the dream of, one day, returning to the place of origin of the family, to the mother earth that nourished them
44	ambiguous:	having a double meaning
45	heavy-handed:	brutal or harsh
46	poignant:	deeply moving; heart-breaking
50	hospitable:	friendly, welcoming
59	expired:	dead; come to an end

EXPLORATIONS

Before reading

1. What are the values in having a post office in a rural village? Discuss this with friends and relations who live in rural areas.

First reading

2. Read the poem a number of times and listen to it being read on YouTube. What is the poem about? In small groups, talk about what's happening in the poem.

- Who might the speaker be? What role does he play?

- Who might the listener be? What are your first thoughts on this person?

- What other characters do you meet in the poem? What are your first thoughts about them?

- What issues are at stake in this situation?

   Make brief notes on what your group discovered, then exchange ideas with other groups.

3. Focus on the speaker in the poem.

- What are his views on rural post offices?

- What kind of person do you think he is? How would you describe him?

- Do you think he is good at his job?

- Would you like to work for him? Explain your thinking.

   Discuss these issues, in your group. Make notes on any points you want to remember.

4. Focus on the listener. Our only insights on the listener come from what the speaker says.

a What does the speaker imply about the listener? In small groups, discuss this. Note down the points made, together with the phrases or lines used as reference.

b Would you have some sympathy for the (implied) position of the person referred to? Outline your thoughts on this.

5. a Read again what the speaker says and implies about the postmistresses. Make notes on what opinions of them we get from him.

b Behind this one-sided view, other qualities of the postmistresses come to our attention. In small groups, brainstorm these qualities, and list them, with references to the text in each case.

Second reading

6. 'we've had to weed out the dreamers'
   Who or what do you think is being referred to here? Jot down your thoughts on this and then share them with the group. Add to your notes any other good ideas from the group discussion.

7. 'Immunity to stories, I find,/is the primary quality.'
   Have you any suggestions as to why the speaker is so 'down' on stories? In groups, discuss this and then share with the class. Make a note of your findings.

8. Close your eyes and listen to the poem being read again. This time concentrate on the mental images you get.

a Did you find that the imagery helped you to catch the atmosphere and sights of the post office? What in particular? Talk about an image that made an impact on you.

b Now write a detailed description of the post office as you see it, from the poem.

9. What are your feelings for the people involved? What, in the poem, influenced these feelings? Write a letter to one of the people in the poem, outlining how you feel about what's going on.

Third reading

10. Do you read this poem as a warning against applying the business model to community resources or as an attempt to justify the logical basis of business? Debate this in class.

11. This poem raises many big questions that are worth thinking about and talking about, as a class group.

a **Values**
- Why is there so much talk about economic value?
- Make a list of what your class group values in life.
- List these values in order of importance, as the class decides.
- Where on the list did you place economic value?

b **Stories**
- What value do we place on stories – my story, your story, all our stories?

- Count up all the situations where we use stories in everyday life. How many? (Don't forget stand-up comedy.)
- What would a day without stories be like? Imagine such a day – write up your diary.
- What value do stories, novels, plays, films or the odd poem contribute to our lives?

c **The past**
- The speaker in the poem refers to 'archive-harbouring frailty', 'a forgotten countryside' and 'expired things'.
- Does the past have any value for us? List the thoughts of the class on this.

d **Dreamers**

Think, first of all, about who these dreamers are.

- The engineering, architectural, medical, scientific and other inventors/dreamers. Continue the list. What do they bring to our world?
- The political and social dreamers who work for peace in warring communities and try to create fairer societies – what value do they bring to our world?
- The sculptors, painters, musicians, storytellers, poets and artists of all kinds – what value do they bring to our world?
- What other dreamers would the class like to mention? And what do they contribute?

12. Working in pairs, discuss the following:

   a   What you would like to say to the speaker.

   b   What you think the speaker might say in reply. Base this on the poem.

   c   Now, role play a conversation between student and speaker. It works better if, at first, all the conversations run simultaneously, in a type of rehearsal. Then, listen to individual role-playing pairs who volunteer.
   What did you learn about the poem from this exercise? Add to your notes.

Unseen Poetry

Approaching the question

Like any other work of art, such as a painting, sculpture, film or building, a poem needs many viewings or readings before we come to appreciate it fully. All the usual techniques we employ when viewing any new or unusual object can be of use here: first noticing the particularly striking or unusual features; then focusing in on a small area of it; drawing back and trying to see the whole structure; circling around it; finding words to describe it to ourselves; asking ourselves what we like about it; and so on. By circling the object and zooming in and out to examine interesting features, gradually we pick up more and more of the detail until the entire object makes sense for us. Many readings are the key to understanding. Here are some questions you might ask yourself as you read and reread.

What do I notice on a first reading?

List any and everything I notice on first reading the poem. This gives me the confidence to say something about it, even though I don't yet understand the full picture.

What do I see?

- Where is it set? What scene or scenes are featured?
- What pictures strike me as interesting? Focus on a setting or an image. What are my thoughts on it?
- Follow the images through the poem. Is there a sequence or a pattern? Have the images anything in common?
- Do the images or settings suggest anything about the themes or issues the poem might be dealing with?
- What atmosphere or mood is suggested by the visual aspects? Which words or images are most powerful in creating this atmosphere?

What is the poem doing, and how is it structured?

1. Does it tell a story?

- Is there a narrative structure to this poem? If so, what is happening? What is the sequence of events? Am I clear about the storyline?
- What is my reaction to this story?
- Is there a main idea behind the narrative? What is the poet's central concern?
- What do I notice about the shape of the poem?
- If a narrative poem, is it in the genre of a ballad, epic, allegory, etc.?
- Is it serious, humorous, satirical or something else?

2. Is it a descriptive piece, re-creating a scene?

- Is its primary purpose to re-create the atmosphere of an event or the mood of a moment?
- Is it mainly decorative? Or has it a point to make, or a moral to transmit?
- How does the poet want me to feel? What mood is created in this poem? What words or phrases help to create this mood?
- If a lyric poem, is it in the form of a sonnet, ode, villanelle, sestina or something else?
- What is the poet's central concern (theme)?
- Leaving technical terms aside, how would I describe what the poem sets out to do?

The speaker

- Who is the speaker in the poem? What kind of person do I imagine him or her to be? What state of mind is the speaker in? What words or phrases reveal most about the attitude and state of mind of the speaker? Consider the tone of the poem and how it is created.
- What point of view is being put across in the poem? Am I in sympathy with it or not?
- Who is the speaker addressing in the poem?
- What do I notice about the poet's style?
- Does the poet rely heavily on images? If so, what do I notice about them?
- Does the poet use the musical sounds of words to create effects: alliteration, assonance, onomatopoeia, etc.? Does he or she use rhyme? What is the effect? What do the sounds of words contribute to the atmosphere of the poem?

- What do I notice about the type of words (diction) most frequently used – are they ordinary, everyday, learned and scholarly, technical, or something else?

- Does the poet use regular metre (rhythm or regular beat in the lines) or do the lines sound more like ordinary conversation or a piece of prose writing? What is the overall effect? Explore the rhythm of the language.

- Are any of these features particularly noticeable or effective? What do I like? What is my reaction to it?

- Can I identify with the experience in this poem? Has there been any similar experience in my life?

- What are my feelings on reading this poem, and what words, phrases, images or ideas spark off these reactions in me?

- How do I react to it? Do I find it amusing, interesting, exciting, frightening, revolting, thought-provoking, etc.?

- What seems to me most important about the piece?

- At a critical level, do I think it is a well-made poem? What in particular do I think is effective?

Some basic questions

A final line-by-line or stanza-by-stanza exploration should bring the poem into clearer focus and facilitate answers to the basic questions:

1. What is the poem about (theme)?

2: Is it an interesting treatment of this theme?

3. What is important about the poem?

4. How is the poem structured (form and genre: narrative or lyric, ballad, ode, sonnet, etc.)?

5. What are the poet's feelings and attitudes (tone)?

6. How would one describe the atmosphere or mood of the poem, and how is it created?

7. What features of poetic style are noticeable or effective?

8. What are my reactions to the poem?

Comparing a newly read poem with a prescribed poem

- Which ideas are similar?
- Which are different?
- Which poem made the greater impact on you, and why?
- What insights did you get from each poem?
- What is the attitude of the poet in each case?
- Are there similarities or differences in tone?
- How does each poet differ in use of language, imagery, etc.?
- Comment on the form and genre in each case.

Practising your answers

To practise answering similar questions on unseen poems, use any of the poems in this anthology that are not on your prescribed course.

PAST EXAMINATION QUESTIONS

John Keats

'John Keats presents abstract ideas in a style that is clear and direct.'

To what extent do you agree or disagree with this assessment of his poetry? Support your points with reference to the poetry on your course.

(Higher Level 2009)

Often we love a poet because of the feelings his/her poems create in us. Write about the feelings John Keats's poetry creates in you and the aspects of the poems (their content and/or style) that help to create those feelings. Support your points by reference to the poetry by Keats that you have studied.

(Higher Level 2001)

Emily Dickinson

'Dickinson's use of an innovative style to explore intense experiences can both intrigue and confuse.'

Discuss this statement, supporting your answer with reference to the poetry of Emily Dickinson on your course.

(Higher Level 2016)

'The dramatic aspects of Dickinson's poetry can both disturb and delight readers.'

To what extent do you agree or disagree with the above statement? Support your answer with reference to both the themes and language found in the poetry of Emily Dickinson on your course.

(Higher Level 2014)

'Emily Dickinson's original approach to poetry results in startling and thought-provoking moments in her work.'

Give your response to the poetry of Emily Dickinson in the light of this statement. Support your points with suitable reference to the poems on your course.

(Higher Level 2011)

Gerard Manley Hopkins

'Hopkins' innovative style displays his struggle with what he believes to be fundamental truths.'

In your opinion, is this a fair assessment of his poetry? Support your answer with suitable reference to the poetry of Gerard Manley Hopkins on your course.

(Higher Level 2013)

'There are many reasons why the poetry of Gerard Manley Hopkins appeals to his readers.'

In response to the above statement, write an essay on the poetry of Hopkins. Your essay should focus clearly on the reasons why the poetry is appealing and should refer to the poetry on your course.

(Higher Level 2004)

William Butler Yeats

'Yeats uses evocative language to create poetry that includes both personal reflection and public commentary.'

Discuss this statement, supporting your answer with reference to both the themes and language found in the poetry of W. B. Yeats on your course.

(Higher Level 2014)

'Yeats can be a challenging poet to read, both in terms of style and subject matter.'

To what extent do you agree with this statement? Support your answer with suitable reference to the poetry on your course.

(Higher Level 2011)

'Yeats's poetry is driven by a tension between the real world in which he lives and an ideal world that he imagines.'

Write a response to the poetry of W. B. Yeats in the light of this statement, supporting your points with suitable reference to the poems on your course.

(Higher Level 2010)

Robert Frost

'Frost communicates rich insights into human experience using language that is both accessible and appealing.'

Discuss this statement, supporting your answer with reference to the poetry of Robert Frost on your course. (Higher Level 2015)

'Frost's simple style is deceptive and a thoughtful reader will see layers of meaning in his poetry.'

Do you agree with this assessment of his poetry? Write a response, supporting your points with the aid of suitable reference to the poems on your course.

(Higher Level 2011)

'Robert Frost – a poet of sadness?'

Write an introduction to the poetry of Robert Frost using the above title. Your introduction should address his themes and the impact of his poetry on you as a reader. Support your points with reference to the poems you have studied.

(Higher Level 2007)

Elizabeth Bishop

'Bishop uses highly detailed observation, of people, places and events, to explore unique personal experiences in her poetry.'

Discuss this statement, supporting your answer with reference to the poetry of Elizabeth Bishop on your course.

(Higher Level 2016)

'Bishop's carefully judged use of language aids the reader to uncover the intensity of feeling in her poetry.'

To what extent do you agree or disagree with the above statement? Support your answer with reference to the poetry of Elizabeth Bishop on your course.

(Higher Level 2013)

'Elizabeth Bishop poses interesting questions delivered by means of a unique style.'

Do you agree with this assessment of her poetry? Your answer should focus on both themes and stylistic features. Support your points with the aid of suitable reference to the poems you have studied.

(Higher Level 2009)

Adrienne Rich

'Rich's poetry communicates powerful feelings through thought-provoking images and symbols.'

Write your response to this statement with reference to the poems by Adrienne Rich on your course.

(Higher Level 2012)

'Adrienne Rich explores the twin themes of power and powerlessness in a variety of interesting ways.'

Write a response to the poetry of Adrienne Rich in the light of this statement, supporting your points with suitable reference to the poems on your course.

(Higher Level 2010)

'… the desire to be heard, – that is the impulse behind writing poems, for me.' (Adrienne Rich)

Does the poetry of Adrienne Rich speak to you? Write your personal response, referring to the poems of Adrienne Rich that do/do not speak to you.

(Higher Level 2008)

Sylvia Plath

'Plath makes effective use of language to explore her personal experiences of suffering and to provide occasional glimpses of the redemptive power of love.'

Discuss this statement, supporting your answer with reference to both the themes and language found in the poetry of Sylvia Plath on your course.

(Higher Level 2014)

'Plath's provocative imagery serves to highlight the intense emotions expressed in her poetry.'

To what extent do you agree or disagree with this assessment of her poetry? Support your answer with suitable reference to the poetry of Sylvia Plath on your course.

(Higher Level 2013)

'The poetry of Sylvia Plath is intense, deeply personal, and quite disturbing.'

Do you agree with this assessment of her poetry? Write a response, supporting your points with the aid of suitable reference to the poems you have studied.

(Higher Level 2007)

Seamus Heaney

Dear Seamus Heaney …
Write a letter to Seamus Heaney telling him how you responded to some of his poems on your course. Support the points you make by detailed reference to the poems you choose to write about.

(Higher Level 2003)

Eiléan Ní Chuilleanáin

'Ní Chuilleanáin's demanding subject matter and formidable style can prove challenging.'

Discuss this statement, supporting your answer with reference to the poetry of Eiléan Ní Chuilleanáin on your course.

(Higher Level 2015)

Eavan Boland

'Boland's reflective insights are expressed through her precise use of language.'

Write your response to this statement, supporting your answer with suitable reference to the poetry on your course.

(Higher Level 2011)

'The appeal of Eavan Boland's poetry.'
Using the above title, write an essay outlining what you consider to be the appeal of Boland's poetry. Support your points by reference to the poetry of Eavan Boland on your course.

(Higher Level 2005)

Write a personal response to the poetry of Eavan Boland.

Support the points you make by reference to the poetry of Boland that you have studied.

(Higher Level 2002)

Paul Durcan

'Durcan takes a narrative approach to explore a variety of issues in poems of great emotional honesty.'

Discuss this statement, supporting your answer with reference to the poetry of Paul Durcan on your course.

(Higher Level 2016)

PAST EXAMINATION QUESTIONS

William Wordsworth
'It is a Beauteous Evening, Calm and Free'

I.

    a. What words suggest the presence of God in the first eight lines of this sonnet? (10)

    b. 'The poem gives us a sense of a beautiful calm evening' Do you agree? Explain your answer. (10)

    c. How does Wordsworth feel about the child in the poem? Refer to the poem in your answer. (10)

2.   Answer **ONE** of the following: [Each part carries 20 marks]

    i. From your reading of this poem, what things are important to Wordsworth? Support your response with reference to the poem.

OR

    ii. You have been asked to suggest a poem for a collection called 'Peaceful Moments'. Say why you would choose this poem.

OR

    iii. This poem was written around 200 years ago. Do you think it is still worth reading? Explain why or why not.

(Ordinary Level 2004)

Percy Bysshe Shelley
'Ozymandias'

I.

    a. Describe, in your own words, what the traveller reports in stanza one of this poem. (10)

    b. Identify a line or phrase from the poem that made an impact on you and explain why it made an impact on you. (10)

    c. Based on your reading of the poem, do you think the poet conveys a mainly positive or a mainly negative view of Ozymandias? Support your answer with reference to the poem. (10)

2.   Answer **ONE** of the following: [Each part carries 20 marks]

    i. Do you like or dislike this poem? In your response identify at least two aspects of the poem that influence your view. Support your answer with reference to the poem.

OR

ii. Imagine you are the traveller from Shelley's poem. Write a letter to a friend in which you remember your experiences in the desert and explain how you were affected by what you saw. Your letter should demonstrate your knowledge of the poem.

OR

iii. Write a piece about the language in this poem, beginning with one of the following phrases:
   – I find the language in this poem interesting and unusual …
   – I find the language in this poem complicated and challenging …

(Ordinary Level 2016)

Emily Dickinson

'I felt a Funeral, in my Brain'

1.

   a. Describe, in your own words, the funeral scene created by the poet in this poem. (10)
   b. Select a line or phrase from the poem that made an impact on you and explain why it made an impact on you. (10)
   c. In your opinion, is the poet mainly optimistic or mainly pessimistic in this poem? Support your answer with reference to the poem. (10)

2.   Answer **ONE** of the following: [Each part carries 20 marks]
   i. Do you like or dislike this poem? In your response identify at least two aspects of the poem that influence your view. Support your answer with reference to the poem.

OR

   ii. You have been asked to organise a performance of this poem by one or more performers. Describe the set you would create, the costume(s), the make-up, the music you would use and any sound or special effects you think would enhance the performance. Support your response with reference to the poem.

OR

   iii. Write a piece about the language in this poem, beginning with one of the following phrases:
   – I find the language in this poem interesting and unusual …
   – I find the language in this poem challenging and complicated …

(Ordinary Level 2016)

Gerard Manley Hopkins
'Spring'

1.

    a. Choose the image from the first eight lines of the poem that, in your opinion, best captures the beauty of spring. Explain your answer. (10)

    b. Do you think Hopkins creates a sense of prayer in the last six lines of the poem? Refer to the poem in support of your answer. (10)

    c. From the phrases below, choose the one which, in your opinion, best describes this poem.

       • It is a joyful poem

       • It is a seasonal poem

       • It is a spiritual poem

    Explain your answer with reference to the poem. (10)

2.   Answer **ONE** of the following: [Each part carries 20 marks]

  i. Write about **two** differences you notice between the first eight lines (octet) and the final six lines (sestet) of this poem. You should refer to the poem in your answer

OR

  ii. In this poem Hopkins describes the beauty of spring. Write a piece in which you describe the beauty of a different season of the year.

OR

  iii. Write a piece explaining why you did, or did not enjoy studying the poetry of Hopkins on your course. (The other poem by Hopkins on the Ordinary Level course is 'Inversnaid')

(Ordinary Level 2011)

W. B. Yeats
'The Lake Isle of Innisfree'

1.

    a. Write down one thing you learned about the poet W. B. Yeats from reading this poem. (10)

    b. Choose **two** details from the first eight lines of the poem that best capture the peacefulness of the island of Innisfree. Explain your choice. (10)

    c. Do you imagine that you would enjoy living on the Lake Isle of Innisfree? Give reasons for your answer. (10)

2.   Answer **ONE** of the following: [Each part carries 20 marks]

  i. You were asked to write a short piece for a holiday brochure promoting weekend breaks on the Lake Isle of Innisfree. Write the piece making use of some details from the poem.

OR

ii. Compare this poem with any other poem by W. B. Yeats that you have
studied as part of your course.

OR

iii. Imagine you were asked to make a short video to accompany a reading of
this poem. Explain how you would use setting, colour or any other device to
make the reading more interesting.

(Ordinary Level 2006)

'The Wild Swans at Coole'

1.

    a. According to Yeats, what qualities do the swans at Coole Park possess?
Explain your answer. (10)

    b. Which is your favourite stanza in this poem? Explain why you like it. (10)

    c. This poem presents many pictures (images) to the reader. Choose two
which appeal to you and explain why you find them appealing. [You may not
choose images from the same stanza that you wrote about in I (b) above]
(10)

2. Answer **ONE** of the following: [Each part carries 20 marks]

    i. Based on this poem write an article for a travel magazine in which you
encourage tourists to visit Coole Park.

OR

    ii. 'I have looked upon those brilliant creatures, /And now my heart is sore'.
From your reading of the poem, explain why the poet feels like this.

OR

    iii. There are two other poems by W. B.Yeats on your course, 'The Lake Isle
of Innisfree' and 'An Irish Airman Foresees his Death'. Which of these two
poems appeals to you more? Give reasons for your answer.

(Ordinary Level 2010)

'An Irish Airman Foresees his Death'

1.

    a. What, in your view, is the attitude of the airman to the war in which he is
fighting? (10)

    b. Write out the line or phrase from the poem that best shows his attitude. Give
a reason for your choice. (10)

    c. Write a short paragraph in which you outline your feelings towards the
airman. Support your view by quotation from the poem. (10)

2. Answer **ONE** of the following: [Each part carries 20 marks]

    i. 'I balanced all, brought all to mind'
What are the kinds of things the airman is referring to in this line from the
poem?

OR

ii. Imagine the airman has to give a short speech to his fellow pilots as they prepare for battle. Write out the text of the speech he might give.

OR

iii. Suggest a different title for the above poem. Give reasons for your answer, supporting them by quotation from the poem.

(Ordinary Level 2002)

Robert Frost
'Out, Out–'

1.

   a. Which words and phrases in the first twelve lines (ending at '… when saved from work') help to give you a clear picture of the place where the poem is set? Explain your choice. (10)

   b. Describe the boy's reaction when he realised that his hand had been badly damaged by the saw. (10)

   c. Do you think the poet shows sympathy for the boy? Explain your answer. (10)

2.   Answer **ONE** of the following: [Each part carries 20 marks]

   i. Write the diary entry of the boy's sister, in which she records her experiences and feelings on the day the accident happened.

OR

   ii. People have said that this is a very dramatic poem. Do you agree? Explain your answer.

OR

   iii. Which of the following statements best describes your response to the poem?

     – I found the poem cruel because …
     – I found the poem dramatic because …
     – I found the poem sad because …
     Give reasons for your answer.

(Ordinary Level 2007)

W. H. Auden
'Funeral Blues'

1.

   a. How did this poem make you feel? (10)

   b. Do you think that the poet really loves the one who has died? Explain your answer. (10)

   c. Do you like the way the poet expresses sadness at the death of his friend? Give a reason. (10)

2.   Answer **ONE** of the following: [Each part carries 20 marks]

i. Imagine that the poet wanted to choose a line or two from the poem to be written on his lover's tombstone. Which line or lines would you advise him to choose? Write the lines and give reasons for your choice.

OR

ii. Imagine you wanted to perform this poem to music with a group of musical friends. How would you perform it so that people would remember the experience?

OR

iii. What things did you learn about the poet W. H. Auden from reading the poem? Refer to the poem in your answer.

(Ordinary Level 2003)

Elizabeth Bishop

'The Fish'

1.

a. Based on your reading of this extract, which of the following statements do you think best describes the poet's response to the fish?
   - The poet admires the fish.
   - The poet is disgusted by the fish.
   - The poet is fascinated by the fish

   Support your answer with reference to the poem. (10)

b. Based on what you have read in the above extract, what is your own response to the fish? Explain your answer with reference to the poem. (10)

c. Identify one comparison in the poem that you found to be unusual or surprising and explain why you found it to be so. (10)

2.   Answer **ONE** of the following: [Each part carries 20 marks]

i. Do you admire Elizabeth Bishop's use of language in this poem? Explain your answer with reference to the poem, 'The Fish'. In your answer you may choose to refer to the extract provided or to the poem as a whole.

OR

ii. At the end of this poem, Bishop releases the fish, 'And I let the fish go'. Based on your knowledge of the poem, explain why you think she did this. Support your answer with reference to the poem. In your answer you may choose to refer to the extract provided or to the poem as a whole.

OR

iii. You have been asked to make a short video to accompany a reading of this poem on YouTube. Describe the images, colours, music, sound effects, etc. that you would use as a background to the reading and explain your choices based on your knowledge of the poem. In your answer you may choose to refer to the extract provided or to the poem as a whole.

(Ordinary Level 2013)

'Filling Station'

1.

- a. Describe, in your own words, the scene at the filling station created by the poet in this poem. (10)
- b. Identify a line or phrase from this poem that you enjoy and explain why you enjoy it. (10)
- c. In your opinion, is Bishop mainly positive or mainly negative about what she sees at the filling station? Support your answer with reference to the poem. (10)

2.   Answer **ONE** of the following: [Each part carries 20 marks]
   i. Do you like or dislike this poem? In your response identify at least two aspects of the poem that influence your view. Support your answer with reference to the poem.

OR

   ii. Imagine that you are one of the sons in the poem. Write a letter to Elizabeth Bishop in which you respond to what she wrote about your home and your family in the poem, 'Filling Station'. Refer to the poem in your answer.

OR

   iii. Write a piece about the language in this poem, beginning with one of the following phrases:
      – I find the language in this poem interesting and easy to understand ...
      – I find the language in this poem challenging and unusual ...

(Ordinary Level 2016)

Patricia Beer
'The Voice'

1.

- a. What picture of the poet's aunt emerges from this poem? Refer to the poem in your answer. (10)
- b. In your opinion, what part did the parrot play in the aunt's life? Explain your answer by referring to the words and events in the poem. (10)
- c. Which of the following statements best describes your response to the poem? Give a reason for your answer.
   – I found the poem amusing
   – I found the poem sad
   – I found the poem both amusing and sad (10)

2. Answer **ONE** of the following: [Each part carries 20 marks]
   i. Imagine that the poet was asked to make a speech at the 'funeral' of the parrot. Write out the speech that you imagine she might deliver.

   OR

   ii. 'Nature's creatures should not be kept in cages for our amusement.' Write a short piece outlining your views on this topic. You should refer to the poem to support the points you make.

   OR

   iii. Imagine you were asked to make a short film or video using one moment or event from this poem. Describe the moment or event you would choose and explain the kind of film or video you would make.

   (Ordinary Level 2006)

Adrienne Rich
'Aunt Jennifer's Tigers'

I.

   a. Why in your opinion does the poet's aunt choose the theme of tigers for her screen? Give a reason for your answer, based on your understanding of the poem. (10)

   b. 'The massive weight of Uncle's wedding band/Sits heavily upon Aunt Jennifer's hand'. What impression do you get of Aunt Jennifer's marriage from these lines? Explain your answer. (10)

   c. Choose one of the following phrases which in your opinion best reveals the poet's attitude towards her aunt:
   • she admires her
   • she pities her

   Explain your choice. (10)

2. Answer **ONE** of the following: [Each part carries 20 marks]
   i. This poem is full of movement and colour. Choose some words and phrases of both movement and colour which especially appeal to you. Explain your choices.

   OR

   ii. 'Adrienne Rich's poems are very gloomy'.
   Write a piece in which you agree or disagree with this statement. Your response should include some reference to one or both of the other Rich poems on your course – 'Storm Warnings' and 'Power'.

   OR

   iii. In this poem, the poet speaks for her Aunt Jennifer. Write a piece in which Aunt Jennifer tells her own story. You may use the material in the poem to support your response.

   (Ordinary Level 2008)

Sylvia Plath

'Child'

1.
  a. What feelings are expressed by the poet in the first three stanzas of this poem? Support your answer with reference to the poem. (10)
  b. What feelings are expressed by the poet in the last stanza of this poem? Support your answer with reference to the poem. (10)
  c. Choose two lines or phrases from the poem that appeal to you and explain your choice. (10)

2.   Answer **ONE** of the following: [Each part carries 20 marks]
  i. You have been asked to make a short video to accompany a reading of this poem on YouTube. Describe some of the images, colours, music, sound effects, etc. that you would use as a background to the reading and explain your choices based on your knowledge of the poem.

OR

  ii. Which of the following word or words would you choose to describe the language used by the poet in this poem?

  Unusual   Descriptive   Appealing

  Support your answer with reference to the poem.

OR

  iii. There are three poems by Sylvia Plath on your Leaving Certificate English course: 'Poppies in July', 'The Arrival of the Bee Box' and 'Child'. Which of these poems by Sylvia Plath do you most enjoy? Explain your answer by reference to at least one of these poems.

'The Arrival of the Bee Box'

1.
  a. What impression of the poet, Sylvia Plath, do you get from reading this poem? (10)
  b. What words or phrases from the poem especially help to create that impression for you? (10)

2. The following list of phrases suggests some of the poet's attitudes to the bee box:
  • She is fascinated by it
  • She is annoyed by it
  • She feels she has great power over it

  Choose the phrase from the above list that is closest to your own reading of the poem. Explain your choice, supporting your view by reference to the words of the poem. (10)

3. Answer **ONE** of the following: [Each part carries 20 marks]
    i. Imagine you were asked to select music to accompany a public reading of this poem. Describe the kind of music you would choose and explain your choice clearly.

    OR

    ii. 'The box is only temporary.' What do you understand the last line of the poem to mean?

    OR

    iii. Write a paragraph in which you outline the similarities and/or differences between 'The Arrival of the Bee Box' and the other poem on your course by Sylvia Plath, 'Child'.

    (Ordinary Level 2003)

Seamus Heaney

'A Constable Calls'

I.

   a. From your reading of this poem, explain why the constable called to the Heaney home. Support your answer with reference to the poem. (10)
   b. The poet as a young boy observes many details about the constable in the poem. Identify the detail that you find most striking and explain why you find it to be so. (10)
   c. ... I assumed
       Small guilts and sat
       Imagining the black hole in the barracks.

       Explain what you think the poet means by these lines. (10)

2. Answer **ONE** of the following: [Each part carries 20 marks]
    i. What do you learn about the world of Seamus Heaney's childhood by studying this poem? Support your answer with reference to the poem.

    OR

    ii. In which one of the following collections of poetry do you feel this poem best belongs?
        • A collection of poems about rural life
        • A collection of poems about the past
        • A collection of poems about childhood

        Give reasons for your choice with reference to the poem.

    OR

    iii. Imagine you are the young Seamus Heaney. Write a diary entry about the day the constable called. Your diary entry should be based on your reading of the poem.

    (Ordinary Level 2012)

'The Underground'

I.

> **a.** In your opinion, why did the poet choose an underground setting for this poem? Support your answer with reference to the poem. (10)
>
> **b.** Why do you think the poet compares himself to Hansel from the fairytale Hansel and Gretel in the above poem? Support your answer with reference to the poem. (10)
>
> **c.** Choose two lines or phrases from the poem that appeal to you and explain your choice. (10)

2. Answer **ONE** of the following: [Each part carries 20 marks]

> i. Describe the relationship between the poet, Seamus Heaney, and his wife evident in this poem. Support your answer with reference to the poem.
>
> OR
>
> ii. Write a piece about this poem beginning with the following: 'I think "The Underground" is a wonderful love poem because ...'
> Support your answer with reference to the poem.
>
> OR
>
> iii. There are three poems by Seamus Heaney on your Leaving Certificate English course: 'The Underground', 'A Constable Calls' and 'A Call'. Which of these poems by Seamus Heaney do you most enjoy? Explain your answer by reference to at least one of these poems.
>
> (Ordinary Level 2014)

Eavan Boland

'This Moment'

I.

> **a.** Why in your opinion does the poet call the poem 'This Moment'? (10)
>
> **b.** Write out two images from the poem that best help you to picture the neighbourhood at dusk. Give a reason for your choice in each case. (10)
>
> **c.** Taken as a whole, does this poem give you a comforting or a threatening feeling about the neighbourhood? Explain your answer. (10)

2. Answer **ONE** of the following (i) or (ii) or (iii). [Each part carries 20 marks]

> i. Imagine you were asked to make a short film based on the poem, 'This Moment'. Describe the sort of atmosphere you would try to create and say how you would use music, sound effects and images to create it.

OR

ii. Stars rise.
Moths flutter.
Apples sweeten in the dark.

Do you think these lines provide a good ending to the poem? Give reasons for your opinion.

OR

iii. Write a short letter to Eavan Boland in which you tell her what her poems on your course mean to you.

(Ordinary Level 2001)

Liz Lochhead

'Revelation'

1.

    a. What impression of the bull do you get from reading stanza one of this poem? Support your answer with reference to the poem. (10)

    b. Based on your reading of stanza three, what effect does the bull have on the girl in the poem? Support your answer with reference to the poem. (10)

    c. Why do you think the poem is called 'Revelation'? Explain your answer with reference to the poem. (10)

2.   Answer **ONE** of the following: [Each part carries 20 marks]

   i. Using one or more of the following statements, describe your personal response to this poem.

    • I find this poem shocking

    • I find this poem powerful

    • I find this poem thought-provoking

    Support your answer with reference to the poem.

OR

  ii. Use one or more of the following words to write a piece about the poet's use of language in this poem.

Descriptive   Challenging   Dramatic

Support your answer with reference to the poem.

OR

  iii. In which of the following collections of poetry do you think this poem best belongs?

    • A collection of poems about childhood

    • A collection of poems about animals

    • A collection of poems about monsters

Explain your answer with reference to the poem

(Ordinary Level 2015)

Penelope Shuttle

1.

   a. Describe the relationship between the people and the cows in this poem. (10)
   b. Do you think 'Jungian Cows' is a good title for this poem? Explain your answer with reference to the poem. (10)
   c. Which of the following statements best describes your opinion of this poem?
      - I find this poem amusing
      - I find this poem far-fetched

   Explain your answer with reference to the poem. (10)

2.   Answer **ONE** of the following: [Each part carries 20 marks]
   i. Do you enjoy the language used by the poet, Penelope Shuttle, in this poem? Explain your answer with reference to the poem.

OR

   ii. The poet, Penelope Shuttle, sets the poem 'Jungian Cows' in Switzerland. Explain why, in your opinion, the poet could or could not have set this poem in Ireland? Explain your answer with reference to the poem.

OR

   iii. Imagine that you are a journalist sent to report on the unusual farming practices in Bollingen, Switzerland, as mentioned in Penelope Shuttle's poem, 'Jungian Cows'. Write an article for your newspaper based on your knowledge of the poem.

Julie O'Callaghan

'The Net'

1.

   a. Do you think the speaker in this poem is looking forward to her school reunion? Explain your answer with reference to the poem.
   b. In your opinion, what word or phrase best captures the speaker's feelings in this poem? Explain your choice with reference to the poem.
   c. From the three phrases below, choose the one which, in your opinion, best describes this poem.

- This is mostly a humorous poem
- This is mostly an unhappy poem
- This is mostly a serious poem

Explain your choice with reference to the poem.

2.   Answer **ONE** of the following: [Each part carries 20 marks]
  i. Does the language used by the poet in this poem appeal to you. Explain your answer with reference to the poem.

OR

  ii. Think about the title of this poem ('The Net') and answer the following questions.
  - What do you think the title means?
  - Suggest a different title for this poem. Explain your choice.

OR

  iii. Do you think 'The Net' is a poem that appeals to young people? Give reasons for your answer based on your reading of the poem.

(Ordinary Level 2011)

Carol Ann Duffy

'Valentine'

1.

  a. 'I am trying to be truthful.' In your opinion, what is the speaker of the poem trying to tell her lover about her feelings? (10)
  b. Write down one line or phrase from the poem that tells you most about the kind of relationship the lovers have. Say why you think it is an important line. (10)
  c. How do you imagine a lover would feel if he or she received this poem on St Valentine's Day? Explain your answer. (10)

2.   Answer **ONE** of the following: [Each part carries 20 marks]
  i. In what way is this poem different from the normal poems or rhymes that lovers send to each other on Valentine's Day?

OR

  ii. In your opinion, what reply might the lover write to this Valentine? You may, if you wish, write your reply in verse.

OR

  iii. 'Lethal. Its scent will cling to your anger, cling to your knife.'
  Do you think that this is a good ending to the poem? Explain your view.

(Ordinary Level 2003)

Acknowledgements

Higher Level

'"Hope" is the thing with feathers', 'There's a certain Slant of Light', 'I felt a Funeral, in my Brain', 'A Bird came down the Walk', 'I heard a Fly buzz – when I died', 'The Soul has Bandaged moments', 'I could bring You Jewels – ', 'A narrow Fellow in the Grass', 'I taste a liquor never brewed', 'After great pain, a formal feeling comes', by Emily Dickinson from *The Poems Of Emily Dickinson: Reading Edition*, edited by Ralph W. Franklin, Cambridge, Mass.: The Belknap Press of Harvard University Press, Copyright © 1998, 1999 by the President and Fellows of Harvard College. Copyright © 1951, 1955 by the President and Fellows of Harvard College. Copyright © renewed 1979, 1983 by the President and Fellows of Harvard College. Copyright © 1914, 1918, 1919, 1924, 1929, 1930, 1932, 1935, 1937, 1942 by Martha Dickinson Bianchi. Copyright © 1952, 1957, 1958, 1963, 1965 by Mary L. Hampson.

'The Fish', 'The Bight', 'At the Fishhouses', 'The Prodigal', 'Questions of Travel', 'The Armadillo', 'Sestina', 'First Death in Nova Scotia', 'Filling Station', 'In the Waiting Room' From *Complete Poems* by Elizabeth Bishop. Published by Chatto & Windus 2004. Reprinted by permission of The Random House Group Limited.

'Aunt Jennifer's Tigers', 'The Uncle Speaks in the Drawing Room', 'Storm Warnings', 'Living in Sin', 'The Roofwalker', 'Our Whole Life', 'Trying to Talk with a Man', 'Diving Into the Wreck', 'From a Survivor', 'Power', from COLLECTED POEMS: 1950-2012 by Adrienne Rich. Copyright © 2016, 2013 by The Adrienne Rich Literary Trust Copyright © 2011, 2007, 2004, 2001, 1999, 1995, 1991, 1989, 1986, 1984, 1981, 1967, 1963, 1962, 1961, 1960, 1959, 1958, 1957, 1956, 1955, 1954, 1953, 1952, 1951 by Adrienne Rich. Copyright © 1984, 1978, 1975, 1973, 1971, 1969, 1966 by W. W. Norton & Company, Inc. Used by permission of W. W. Norton & Company, Inc.

'Black Rook in Rainy Weather', 'The Times are Tidy', 'Morning Song', 'Finisterre', 'Mirror', 'Pheasant', 'Elm', 'Poppies in July', 'The Arrival of the Bee Box', 'Child' by Sylvia Plath, from *Collected Poems* by Sylvia Plath, published by Faber and Faber Ltd, 2002.

'Begin', 'Bread', 'Dear Autumn Girl', 'Poem from a Three Year Old', 'Oliver to His Brother', 'I See You Dancing, Father', 'A Cry for Art O'Leary', 'Things I Might Do', 'A Great Day', 'Fragments', 'The soul's loneliness', 'Saint Brigid's Prayer' by Brendan Kennelly, from *Familiar Strangers: New & Selected Poems 1960-2004* by Brendan Kennelly (Bloodaxe Books, 2004).

'The Forge', 'Bogland', 'The Tollund Man', 'Sunlight', 'A Constable Calls', 'The Skunk', 'The Harvest Bow', 'The Underground', 'Postscript', 'A Call', 'Tate's Avenue',

'The Pitchfork', 'Lightnings viii' by Seamus Heaney from *Opened Ground* by Seamus Heaney published by Faber and Faber Ltd, 2002.

'Lucina Schynning in Silence of the Nicht', 'The Second Voyage', 'Deaths and Engines', 'Street', 'Fireman's Lift', 'All for You', 'Following', 'Kilcash', 'Translation', 'The Bend in the Road' by Eiléan Ní Chuilleanáin from *Selected Poems*, by Eiléan Ní Chuilleanáin 2008. 'On Lacking the Killer Instinct', 'To Niall Woods and Xenya Ostrovskaia, married in Dublin on 9 September 2009' by Eiléan Ní Chuilleanáin from *The Sun-fish* by Eiléan Ní Chuilleanáin, 2009. All poems reproduced by kind permission of the author and The Gallery Press, Loughcrew, Oldcastle, County Meath, Ireland.

'The War Horse', 'The Famine Road', 'Child of Our Time', 'The Black Lace Fan My Mother Gave Me', 'The Shadow Doll', 'White Hawthorn in the West of Ireland', 'Outside History', 'This Moment', 'Love', 'The Pomegranate', by Eavan Boland from *Collected Poems* by Eavan Boland, Carcanet, 1995.

'If Love Was Jazz', by Linda France, from *Red* by Linda France, Bloodaxe Books, 1992. Copyright © Linda France, 1992, reproduced by kind permission of the author.

'The SUN' by Benjamin Zephaniah from *City Psalms* by Benjamin Zephaniah (Bloodaxe Books, 1992).

'My Father, Long Dead' by Eileen Sheehan, reproduced by kind permission of the author.

'Driving to the Hospital' by Kate Clanchy, from *Newborn*, published by Picador 2004. Copyright © Kate Clanchy 2004. Reproduced with permission of Pan Macmillan via PLSclear.

'Self-Portrait in the Dark (with Cigarette)' by Colette Bryce, from *Self-Portrait in the Dark*, Picador, 2008. Copyright © 2008 Colette Bryce. Reproduced with permission of Pan Macmillan via PLSclear.

'Chronicle' by David Wheatley from *Misery Hill* (2000) reproduced by kind permission of the author and The Gallery Press, Loughcrew, Oldcastle, County Meath, Ireland.

'Genetics' by Sinéad Morrissey, from *The State of Prisons* by Sinéad Morrissey, Carcanet, 2005.

'Interlude 12' by Caitríona O'Reilly, from *The Nowhere Birds* by Caitríona O'Reilly, (Bloodaxe Books, 2001).

'Death and the Post Office' by Martin Dyar reproduced with permission of Arlen House Ltd, Dublin. arlenhouse@gmail.com.

For permission to reproduce photographs, the author and publisher gratefully acknowledge the following:

© Afftomat/Dreamstime.com: 507; © Alamy: 25, 28, 32, 48, 50, 53, 71, 77, 93, 93, 93, 93, 116, 122, 133, 142, 145, 148, 153, 155, 162, 166, 176, 178, 199, 203, 212, 217, 228, 236, 244, 247, 259, 264, 269, 278, 293, 306, 309, 316, 322, 326, 328, 335, 348L, 375, 384, 398, 413, 425, 439, 448, 451, 477, 525, 531, 545, 561, 570, 389; © Birmingham Museum and Art Gallery: 13; © Bridgeman Images: I, II, 16, 44, 75, 102, 139, 209; © Collins: 364, 419; Elizabeth Bishop: 'Brazilian Landscape' and 'Nova Scotia Landscape', undated paintings by Elizabeth Bishop (whereabouts unknown) reproduced from Changing Hats: Elizabeth Bishop Paintings, edited with an introduction by William Benton, published by Farrar, Straus, Giroux (New York 1996)- reproduced with permission of the publishers, copyright © 1996 by Alice Helen Methfessel: 190, 194; © Getty Images: 7, 9, 20, 27, 52, 69, 103, 137, 150, 159, 185, 208, 238, 240, 251, 256, 288, 340, 355, 367, 370, 381, 387, 394, 434, 437, 443,